TWENTY SHILLINGS IN THE POUND

The Diamond Jubilee: summit of The Golden Age. Queen Victoria
returns thanks at St. Paul's Cathedral

TWENTY SHILLINGS
IN THE POUND

by

W. MACQUEEN-POPE

With 42 Illustrations

HUTCHINSON & CO. (Publishers) LTD
London   New York   Melbourne   Sydney   Cape Town

First published December, 1948.
Reprinted - - January, 1949.
Reprinted - - February, 1949.
Reprinted - - - May, 1949.

To
TIMO and BA
so that one day they may know how their
NAN and NANDADDA lived when they,
too, were young

Printed in Great Britain
by The Anchor Press, Ltd.,
Tiptree, Essex

CONTENTS

CONTENTS

LIST OF ILLUSTRATIONS

LIST OF ILLUSTRATIONS

LIST OF ILLUSTRATIONS

FOR THE DEFENCE

(A Word by the Author)

A FEW YEARS AGO, ON ONE OF THE RARE OCCASIONS ON WHICH THE BRITISH Broadcasting Corporation allows me to get near a microphone, I did a talk about the games played by the youth of this country when I was a small boy, over half a century ago, and made the comment that very few of them seemed to have survived.

The result was a positive avalanche of letters from people who had heard me speak. There were thousands of them, and the cost of the replies thereto more than swallowed up the very modest fee which the B.B.C. considered adequate remuneration for my feeble efforts. Not that I cared about that, for all those letters contained heartening words of thanks. They complimented me, they spoke of the joy it had given them to have their youth recalled, they reminded me of other games and customs which had been omitted from my talk—mostly because of the short space allowed me (it was fifteen minutes, I think)—they demanded more (which they have never been allowed to have) and it appeared that 'a good time had been had by all'. Some went even further, bless them, and sent me copies of old papers, actual old toys, and several sent me specimens of those handsome marbles known as 'alleys' which they had treasured— and which I treasure now.

That broadcast and its result set me thinking.

There was also another factor at work. I am a father and a grandfather. My own daughter, when she was young, was always saying, "Tell me what you did when you were a little boy!" Now my grandchildren begin to make the same demand. That request is familiar to all who have dealings with children. Of that I am fully aware.

But the broadcast proved to me that the interest was not confined to children. Grown-ups wanted to know as well. Perhaps they did not want to know what an individual did when he was young, but they wanted to be reminded of what they did themselves and his experiences would awaken their memories and bring to their minds things long tucked away and almost forgotten—little things as well as big things, commonplace then but vanished now, like those men who went about selling flypapers, calling out "Catch-'em alive-oh!" They had pieces of paper to sell, covered with a sticky substance to which flies adhered. They had samples round their top hats, which headgear they purchased from rag and bone shops for

5

twopence each (so plentiful were old toppers in top-hatted times), and they did a roaring trade. Those sheets of paper for fly destruction which they sold were covered with a solution which contained arsenic. It was very unhygienic, but very effective. It killed the flies and as they stuck fast to the scene of their death they were easily disposed of. These men have vanished—and, to a very large extent, so have the flies. Does that awaken a memory of the old-time streets? Of forgotten street characters and cries? If so, this book may recall many memories. For memories are the preservatives of youth. If you can remember, you can be young.

So I made up my mind to write this book. But I decided to attempt more than a mere appeal to nostalgia. I took a look at the life all around me and came to a conclusion. I would try and preserve in memory the Middle Classes of this country, to which I belong, and which seem to me to be in the process of elimination. Also, I have got rather tired of reading description of late Victorian and Edwardian life, written by young people who evidently from their writings knew it not, and I have therefore tried to set down what that strata of society was really like, and how it lived, during that period of its existence.

I had to find a framework, something within which the picture could be focused—and that was easy. I chose the golden sovereign, which was the standard of living in those days. And that sovereign, which was really made of gold, was always worth its quota of twenty silver shillings. Hence the title of this book. It is not about money. It is about Middle Class life when we had golden sovereigns in our pockets, and it ends when the golden sovereign itself ended.

I wish to emphasize very strongly that this book is about the Middle Classes. It is not about the Aristocracy, and it is not about what were then called the Working Classes. So in case anyone feels aggrieved when I speak of the Golden Age, let them realize that I mean the Age of the Golden Sovereign. It will be no use them writing me scathing letters about the misery of certain sections of the community in those days, it will be no use them telling me how their grandfather starved to death, their grandmother went into the workhouse and their fathers and mothers lived under distressing circumstances on less money than would keep a man today in cigarettes for a week. I know all about that. But this book is not about such things, but only about the Middle Classes—and therefore my withers will be unwrung. But one of the reasons why I write this short defence of my action is to save them the expense of wasting pen, ink, paper and stamp in order to denounce me. If they are not interested in the Middle Classes, let them read no further—they have been warned.

6

But there are others, many others. For the Middle Classes are—or were—the majority of this country's inhabitants. And, whatever others may say, they were its backbone too.

So I have tried to draw a picture of a class during a period of its existence, when for by far the greater part of them life was happy, secure and enjoyable, when the days were golden and the nights were gay, when there were smiles on faces and when money went incredibly far in spending power. It is such a short while ago in terms of years, yet it is already remote and has become History. Life has changed completely, so I have tried to give substance to the shadow of what I think were better times—the Age of Plenty, not the Age of Shortage.

I am aware the story is discursive, but then it has no plot. I am aware there are many omissions, but paper is scarce. However, perhaps this picture of an age, which covers one whole reign of a sovereign and portions of the reign of two others, may serve its purpose. For we not only had those human sovereigns but golden ones as well, which were the key to everything which happened.

I have tried to describe babyhood, childhood, schooldays, adolescence and early man- and womanhood during that time when the aged Queen Victoria reigned over us, when King Edward VII kept the Peace of the World, and when his son King George V saw his people go to that War which was indeed to preserve his sovereignty but to take the golden sovereign from us—and all that it stood for.

I shall be accused, by young people, of having drawn too rosy a picture. I can assure them that I have not. At least in my opinion. I have just set down facts as they seemed to me, as they affected me at the time, and I am generally supposed to have a very good memory.

I hasten to assure you the book is not autobiographical, although at times I have used myself as an eye-witness. I have, in my life, done quite a lot in a perfectly humble way, and I have seen quite a lot too. And I have forgotten nothing. My memory is fresh and clear. If it plays me tricks it will be in small details, but even then I may be right as regards my own personal experience of what I set down.

So here is my memory of those times—for your approval, or otherwise. The book is not political, it does not deal with economics or scientific affairs, save in the most casual manner. It tries to be fair and to avoid comparisons, and it also strives to take a detached view. But it may make you think back. It may stir your memory, it may, by so doing, make you young again. And, if you are young now, it may give you an insight into how your parents and your grandparents lived when they were your

7

age—and make you understand them and their point of view a little better.

And if the reading of this book gives one tenth of the pleasure that the writing of it caused, we shall all be happy.

W. MACQUEEN-POPE.

Strand, London. 1948.

A CROSS-SECTION OF A GOLDEN AGE

A MAN OR WOMAN WHO HAS REACHED MIDDLE AGE, OR PASSED IT, HAS more cause for satisfaction than the younger people of today. For they lived in a Golden Age and at least have the memories of it.

Those who live in our land today who did not know it before the year 1914, that fateful year of all years in history, have never known England. That word is used with the full knowledge that it is nowadays customary to say Great Britain. But before 1914, England was the word, and the people who used it knew England—Great Britain— when it was the greatest country in the world and when it was indeed worth while being a son or daughter of that fortunate land. That fast diminishing minority who remember it, and who were of it, have reached the stage in their social history which they used to describe in their economic classification as 'shabby genteel'. For they have known better days.

This is a story of a cross-section of English life. It has nothing to do with the Aristocracy, the upper or ruling classes, the landed gentry, or that strange thing called 'Society'. All those phases have their own chroniclers. Nor does it concern itself with the lives of the poor, or the labouring classes. They also have much literature devoted to them. Historians, novelists and playwrights galore dabbled in both of those records, presenting us with various points of view. The section here illustrated is the Middle Class, in whom writers seldom found inspiration, or, if they did, presented a satiric picture of those people who, during the greatest days of this nation, bore its burden on their back.

The Middle Class has always been inarticulate. It has never been very interested in itself. Its members have been known to disown it. But there it was—a most important section of the community—working, playing, marrying, dying, making love and reproducing itself—paying its rates and taxes and always supplying that great gift of balance, common sense and respectability which kept the prosperity of this country on an even keel. It has been derided, it has been made a figure of fun. But it took no notice and kept on its path. It had the final word in the government of the nation. It always grumbled, it paid its way, but it never gave way.

In these days, when the world is changing with such rapidity, it may be as well to get a picture of it as it really was in its days of happiness, before the barriers burst and landmarks were submerged, before the English became the British and this country began to lose its individuality —an individuality largely given it by the Middle Class.

9

This book is about the English Middle Class—but it was very little different in Scotland and Wales. The inhabitants of those countries were not so vocal then when the word English was used to describe the doings of this race. England was the predominant partner and the common tongue was English—that was good enough for the majority. Indeed, life was so different then as to be almost unbelievable now. It was such a little time ago—but it is being rapidly erased from the memory. The Middle Classes were the heirs of Progress and were coming into their inheritance, in common with their senior and junior relations, the Upper and the Working Classes. The purpose here is to show how little they were aware what that inheritance was to do for them and how they lived whilst it was being thrust upon them. What happened afterwards everybody knows.

The phase which these pages chronicle is the period when the Middle Class flourished and had their best days. This is chosen because the knowledge of it is first hand and not gathered from other books or from other people's information. It starts in 1890 and ends in 1914—when the great days ended also. So it is partly Victorian and partly Edwardian, for although George V sat on the throne in 1914, the times had not altered appreciably.

The days of Queen Victoria and of Edward VII (called 'The Peacemaker') are already history. They are so near in term of time, yet so distant in term of manners and mode of life. Much misconception exists about them. They are described as days of great wealth and abject poverty, days when the rich had much and the poor nothing, days of lavish luxury and oppressed labour. To read about them as seen by some people makes a picture of a pleasure-loving, proud aristocracy and a starving, ragged, ill-clothed and ill-educated mass of human rats who could hardly keep body and soul together.

All those things are true, and all of them existed. They were the extremes of a great era. Those conditions have always existed in the world and it is not a very daring prophecy to say that they always will, in some form or the other.

Events have moved so rapidly, progress—or perhaps this word is preferred with a capital P—has achieved so much, that in the space of little over half a century it has altered the world more completely than the ordinary march of time effected in the previous two centuries.

There was not nearly so much difference between 1714 and 1914 as there is between 1914 and 1947.

It is this breathtaking speed, maybe, which causes so much confusion of ideas amongst those who proclaim their pride in being Victorians or Edwardians and those who, of equal talent and intellect, decry those times as being the very bad old days. To one school of thought they were glorious times, to others despicable. Both are right and, again, both are wrong.

In the Victorian and Edwardian days there was a section of the nation possessed of a tremendous measure of the wealth of the world. They were the few. At the other end of the pole there were people who lived from hand to mouth, who feared unemployment, who existed under shocking conditions and worked under worse, and who found it almost impossible, often quite impossible, to feed and clothe themselves and their children adequately.

But what lay in between? What separated those two extreme points? What made up the rest of our world?

A tremendous community of solid, hard-working, respectable folk, who had, one and all, a stake in the country, called The Middle Class. At times of national crisis, in the speeches of the eminent, or when their votes were solicited by gentlemen desirous of governing them, they were referred to as 'The Backbone of the Nation'. And no more truthful words were ever spoken.

Strangely similar in mode of life, bound by convention, living within their own sphere, which had its grades of social standing, just as marked as in the Aristocracy, who were called The Governing Classes, they had nevertheless an individuality of their own. They had ambitions and desires, and in the main those were of a moderate nature. They wanted security (a thing which is still unattainable), they wanted comfort, happiness, a home of their own, and they wanted to see their children do better than they had done. They made sacrifices for those children which were often successful but seldom appreciated. They had a standard of living which they created for themselves. They did not regard it as luxury, though, if they had only known, it represented something which the world has now lost. They supported one or other of the great political parties—Labour was not then a parliamentary power—but whether Conservative or Liberal in the polling booth, they were all conservative in their method of living and their point of view. The centre of their life was the Home. It was the axis on which their own little world revolved.

They began with the professional classes and they ended with the small shopkeeper and skilled artisan. There was, it is true, a sort of froth on the surface of this great mass of humanity, a foam which lapped against the side of the Upper Classes but never really got beyond the high-water mark of Middle Class—which called itself the Upper Middle Class. But it really only existed in its own imagination. The cleavage between class in those days was most marked. Birth, blood, family and ancestry mattered a very great deal.

There was very little mixing. Marrying above you was just as unpleasant and disastrous as marrying beneath you. And the great majority of the Middle Class knew that. That so-called Upper Middle Class had not the natural attributes of Upper Classdom, and in its heart it knew it. It was snobbery which made it class conscious and desirous of getting above itself. There was a good deal of snobbery about in those days. But snobbery is no crime. It is, perhaps, a realization and an attempt at emulation of something the snob regards as bigger and better. It never gets very far and is usually killed by satire. And although it certainly existed in the Middle Class, it affected the few and not the many. But it was the reason for The Upper Middle Class.

The Middle Class was a world of its own and it had its own strata. It comprised carriage folk and cottagers, people who lived in mansions and people who lived in villas and lodgings. It contained those who pretended they had descended into it from the upper regions, and it contained those who were steadily ascending through its grades on their way to the top. And it was a mass of stability in itself which leavened the nation. It had its own morality—a very high one—and it had its own fixed beliefs. It believed in honouring its father and mother, it believed in honest toil and work well done, it believed in enjoying itself with gusto and, above all, it believed in Quality. It always wanted the best, and what it spent its money on was the best it could get. It did not believe in Change. It was not nomadic. Often families lived in one house—which was their Home—for their entire lives.

There was no question of moving every few years or so, as happened before the Second World War. And when the young people got married, they founded a home as like that of their parents as they could. There might be a different type of furniture, different decoration, different methods of domestic work—but the spirit was the same, the spirit of Home.

All through those Victorian and Edwardian days, at which so much fun is poked, the standard of quality demanded was very high.

The word 'shoddy' was a term of dire reproach. Things were not purchased to wear out and throw away. They were purchased to last a lifetime. That was the spirit of the Middle Class, which represented the solid, sound and tenacious side of our race.

It was the endeavour of the Middle Class to be solvent and to pay its way. By and large, its members were not extravagant. They feared debt, the instalment system was in its infancy and mostly practised by the Working Classes, whom it often led to disaster. The Middle Class preferred to pay its way and to pay Twenty Shillings in the pound. And because of the Middle Class, the country itself paid twenty shillings in the pound and was the richest, most powerful and influential nation the world has ever seen.

Those Victorian and Edwardian days were the Golden Age of the Middle Class. Such times had never been before, such times will never come again. And the standard of the whole thing was that coin of the realm known as the Sovereign. It was the golden token of the golden age.

It has gone now. It was the first casualty of the World Revolution which began in 1914, which carried on through the inter-war period and which flared up with its greatest violence in 1939.

So long as the sovereign was there, the Middle Class was secure. When it vanished, that was the beginning of the end of the class which, more than any other, depended on it. And since its departure and its replacement by paper, that great class of our land has got flimsier and flimsier, until it will shortly, like the sovereign, vanish altogether.

For revolutions fall heaviest upon the Middle Class, as history can prove. The aristocratic heads may fall, but a new ruling class arises to take their places. For the bourgeoisie there is complete elimination.

It has happened in other parts of the world, it is happening now in this country. Abroad it is achieved by violence, as are revolutions. In Great Britain, we do not use violence—we do it all lawfully and by absorption.

In this country today the Middle Class, as it once existed, is being eliminated. Many will prefer to say that it is being reshaped—which is much the same thing. But never again, in living memory, will it know the comfort, the ease of life, the prosperity and—yes—the security which it knew when it took its stand on the golden sovereign, which was worth twenty shillings in the pound.

It may have free education, free medical attention, free legal advice; it may own its own land, its own railways, its own industries, its own transport. It may be happier, it may even have more freedom of a sort— all these things wait to be proved. Already the people who live in our time have luxuries to which their parents were total strangers—luxuries which have ceased to be luxuries and become necessities—which is what is always happening in the world.

But the world has been in the melting-pot, it is a molten chaotic mass, and until it is reforged, and if a new Middle Class arises, there will be discomfort such as the Middle Classes of the Golden Sovereign Days never conceived.

There is Fear in the world today. Fear of a kind those decent Middle-Class people with whom this book is concerned never knew. War is an ever-present dread and too often an ever-present reality. Twice it has seared us since the Golden Days, and Science, of which we know so much (and of which the Golden Age Middle Class knew—and cared—so little) makes it more and more dreadful every year. Twice in under forty years has war stricken the whole of humanity. The First World War (that which killed the sovereign and mortally wounded the Middle Class) was a War to End War. Naturally, it bred the Second World War, which was only a continuance of the first—in a much worse form.

This last was the War for Freedom, for Democracy. That also was a slogan in the first war as well. Well, in company with the other two classes, the Middle Class fought both those wars—and won them. It lost its freedom and it lost itself.

In the days of the golden sovereign there was fear in the Middle Classes, but it was individual and not general fear. It afflicted the few and not the many. Mostly it was the fear of the loss of employment, and it was, even so, much more a fear than a reality. There was fear of disgrace, of loss of prestige, of social standing, of scandal—and this fear formed a shield of morality most beneficial to standards of all kinds. For that Middle Class liked to be respected by its friends and neighbours. It feared divorce, it feared bankruptcy, loss of credit, it feared its dirty linen being washed in public.

It had dirty linen, of course, but it preferred to do its washing at home. One hears all this described as hypocrisy. It may be so according to modern standards, but it may also be that the so-called freedom of thought, speech and action of today is more laxity than freedom. The older Middle Class thought so.

It feared and hated vulgarity—it was vulgar in the proper sense of the word to a great extent in itself—but it disapproved of coarseness, and it did not openly discuss sex. It had a respect for womanhood which has vanished since the days of so-called equality.

Although it was an age of great eating and drinking—of beef and beer —still it respected the ears of its women—whom it referred to as 'Ladies' —and no bad thing either. Young ladies were presumed to be innocent. At any rate, no male with any pretence to the name of 'Gentleman'—a title all liked to claim—would have dreamed of telling even a slightly *risqué* story in front of women who ranked as 'ladies'. Sex discussions between the sexes were unknown. It may have been conventional but it was decent. A girl who lost her character was indeed lost. And she could lose it then for doing things which are now constant daily habit.

Again, it may be that the world is a better place for frankness. That also remains to be proved.

But women in those golden days had not achieved those rights they now possess. They had not achieved what they now call Freedom. A very

14

Field Marshal Earl Roberts, V.C., but everyone called him "Bobs"

"Soldiers of the Queen"

President Kruger—mostly
pronounced "Kroojer"—
also called "Oom Paul"

By permission of Elliott & Fry

Taking the guns into action
in the Boer War—when the
horse mattered a great deal

small proportion of the Middle Classes sent their women to work. The Home was their sphere, and, strangely enough, it was quite usual for the menfolk to be able to provide and maintain that home.

There was men's work and women's work, quite clearly defined. And there was a mystery surrounding woman, which contained the last vestige of real romance the world knew. She was on a pedestal and she was unpredictable. The toast of 'The Ladies' at a public dinner was still coupled with the words 'God Bless 'em'.

And women had their secrets from men. Their legs had not become public property, their clothes were garments of divinity, voluminous, and consequently mysterious, and their underclothing—they would never have dared talk of their 'undies' in mixed company—were not even revealed in advertisements or in the shop windows. Corsets were displayed in such a manner, but the more intimate garments were not for the public eye. Truly life held more thrills for the mere man. Modesty was still a virtue. You could tell a man from a woman at a glance. And parental authority was still a power in the land. The Home was its kingdom.

Life centred about that home. It was a house—for the flat was still regarded as a little unstable, a little foreign—it did not give one a stake in the country—and a stake in the country was what the Middle Class desired and obtained. Life was much simpler, there were no complexes, no inhibitions, no fixations. Maybe they were there, but the Middle Classes, knowing nothing about such things, never suffered in its mind, as do the more enlightened and better informed today—if indeed knowledge which worries is a good thing to have.

Little was known of hygiene. There were fewer medical discoveries, therefore fewer things to die from. There was a high rate of mortality. But it would have been an earth-shattering epidemic which would have caused as many deaths as those which happen annually on the roads today. It was a slow-moving time—although towards the end the tempo quickened considerably, as the age hurried to extinction, gathering impetus as it rolled downhill. Twelve miles an hour was the average traffic speed. You got there just as quickly, for traffic blocks were rare; and if you were a pedestrian—as most of us were—you could cross the road where you liked and reach the other side in safety.

There was leisure, there was time for appreciation of beauty. There was an unspoiled countryside right against London—the internal combustion engine had not wiped it out; there was a sense of adventure which existed because distance had not been eliminated.

The Middle Classes could—and did—have a fine and a gay time at a cost that would stagger the youth of today in the same class.

The pursuit of pleasure was not so intense, there were fewer forms of entertainment—it had not become mechanical. One made one's own fun, one made one's own nights gay—and they were brighter than all the electric lights and neon signs ever made them.

There was, with the sense of standard, a sense of value as well. It had not been swamped by satiety. And Sport was a thing to do—to participate in—rather than to watch. Sport had not become a mere vehicle for gambling—it had not become a highly paid profession either.

The rank of an amateur in sport had a high standing. This may have been snobbery, but it was the last flickering of the Corinthian Age as well. Middle-aged Middle Class men refused to go to professional football matches. Cricket, yes, for there the players were class-conscious. The Gentlemen (you observed the word) entered and left the field by one gate, the 'Players', or professionals, by another. And a great event of the Season was 'Gentlemen v. Players'. Cricket was never so democratic as football—it is not so democratic even today. And in the Middle Class a player of Rugby Football had a higher standing than a player of mere 'Soccer'.

Living was inconceivably cheap, although values were high. A lot of those rich Victorians and Edwardians would be poor folk by modern standards. But it was all a question of the purchasing power of that golden sovereign. Wages were low but so were prices. It did not seem a bad way of life—and to look back upon, it becomes idyllic.

But though those Middle Class people had their fears, there was one great Fear from which they never suffered—the fear of War and Sudden Death.

Those Middle Class people did not know what war meant. And to a very large extent it was the power of the Golden Sovereign which kept them free from it. They knew nothing of war which came home to them. They went to bed every night with the certain faith of waking again in the morning. Fire might destroy their house but it would be from natural causes and not from enemy action against which they had no sure shield. Barring accidents, that house would stand for their time and for the time of their children and their children's children—that was their belief. They had never in their wildest dreams envisaged the horror of an air raid and its bombs. Such things were read of with enjoyment in the tales of Jules Verne, and later in the prophecies of H. G. Wells, but nobody believed them. A few thought it might be possible one of these days—because of Science—to them just a word. War was a distant far-off thing, a matter for professionals, indulged in by foreign nations of less enlightenment than us, and who did not possess the British Navy to keep it secure. We were islanders—we were free—such freedom will never come again—and we were at least the equal of any six foreigners—be they who they may.

A Middle Class individual in those days might expect to live his allotted span and die in bed from natural causes. Parents knew not the tragedy of parting with their children, and seeing their bright young lives extinguished by the thing called War. The Navy and the Army were there for that job. It was the duty of the Middle Class to pay for these Services, but not to man them. We were not a martial or warlike nation. We had lived in Peace at home for almost a century—we had forgotten what a real threat was like, let alone the grim reality. The Middle Class were secure in Peace and in the possession of Empire. They never regarded that Empire as a cause for war. They had done so much to make it and to run it now it was made.

The map of the world had huge splashes of red. That meant it was British—or more commonly English, and it existed because it was right that it should be so. That was their fixed belief. By means of it the Middle Class prospered, for it meant Business and Employment and it was the Middle Class who were the Shopkeepers of our country, in the widest sense.

They not only lived on an island but they were an insular people. And proud of it. London was an English city. It had not become internationalized. Its inhabitants spoke their own language and if they had an accent, at least it was of the soil—or the pavement—and not borrowed from overseas.

And London reflected the times. Here was also a cleavage. The City was the City, the suburbs the suburbs, and the West End very definitely the West End. Commerce had not invaded that portion of the town to the extent it has today. The West End was still Aristocratic, and the eastern part of the West End was the pleasure centre of London. No Middle Class person would have dressed in the West End as at home. To go there was a thrill. The pulses quickened as one went 'up West'. The Strand and Leicester Square, Shaftesbury Avenue (comparatively new then, as London went), the Haymarket and Piccadilly Circus for pleasure, with Oxford Street and Regent Street for shopping—Bond Street was for the affluent.

No self-respecting man would have invaded the West End without gloves on his hands, any more than he would have smoked a pipe in its streets. A topper or a bowler might be worn—in summer a straw hat—and in the laxer Edwardian days a Homburg of green velvet for the more Bohemian—following a Royal fashion. But not a cap and never a soft collar. Those were later innovations. Every man carried a stick or an umbrella. Women, it is true, found it uncomfortable to walk about the West End unescorted. Their isolation was likely to be misconstrued by wicked men. In those days there was little excuse for a mistake. The 'lady of the town' invariably wore make-up, the real lady never. Still woman could not cross Leicester Square at night without fear of being 'accosted'. They knew it, so did not risk it.

There is a general belief that London was a dingy, ill-lit and greyish town then. In winter, it is true, there was much mud and more fog. But in the summer—especially in what was known as 'The Season', then London wore a smile. The great houses which abounded, and had not been demolished to make room for flats, were painted and brightened up. Every house looked fresh, spick and span. Every house had its window-boxes abloom with flowers. London became a hanging garden—a thing of beauty and joy, for money was plentiful and it was spent. A little golden sovereign went a very long way.

What was it like, that golden sovereign? It was a lovely coin, of solid gold—worth its weight in its own metal. It was the handsomest and handiest coin of all time. On one side it bore the head of the monarch—that other sovereign whose symbol it was—and on the reverse it bore St. George himself. A naked St. George, clad only in a waving cloak, which left his arms and body quite free for action, wearing a helmet and mounted on a spirited, rearing steed. He was dealing with a recumbent dragon, prone beneath the horse's feet, with a short and totally inadequate Roman sword.

One might have wondered how he slew that dragon for which task he seemed so ill equipped, but one knew that he had done so and would always do so. He was St. George, his counterfeit presentment on the coin was full of life, vigour and energy, the very counterpart of that England for which he stood, as did the sovereign on which he figured. He was worth every one of those twenty silver shillings into which he could be changed. That figure of St. George, and that sovereign, represented the power of England, for every country in the world welcomed it, would change it freely, and often—more often than not—give considerably more than twenty shillings in exchange, so great was its power.

There were half sovereigns, too, the same in design (although sometimes they carried the Royal Arms on a shield instead of St. George) and a little tricky at night, if you were careless enough to keep all your money in one pocket. For they and a sixpence were much the same size, and it was easy to give one away instead of the nimble silver coin—though why a sixpence should be nimble has never been properly explained.

But only the careless kept their gold, silver and copper mixed up. The two lower orders could jingle in the trouser pocket. The half sovereign lived in the vest or waistcoat pocket or the fob, and the sovereign had a purse of his own. These were round objects of metal, something like a watch and opening the same way. One half had a hole, half surrounded by a metal clip. The hole contained a spring, on which was the representation of a sovereign. On this you slipped your own real sovereigns, one on top of the other, under the clip until the purse was full. You wore it in your waistcoat pocket on one end of your watch-chain—everyone wore watch-chains then—and at the other end was your watch.

The watch-chain, the watch and the sovereign purse were the outward and visible signs of solvency. You pulled out your purse, flicked it open, slipped out your sovereign, and there you were. You could not carry many sovereigns that way, but there was no need, so great was its purchasing power.

To possess several sovereigns gave a sense of well-being and prosperity which no amount of paper money can achieve. They rang, they chinked, they chimed, like a peal of golden bells. What wealth they seemed to represent—and indeed did represent, as compared with today.

What joy to see a bank cashier pour out a heap of sovereigns on the counter. He dug them out of a drawer, filled to the brim, with a scoop. He poured them on to a scale, he weighed them and there you were again, possessed of fifty or a hundred as the case might be, without the trouble of counting. But now he has to count out flimsy, dirty bits of paper, which are not, and never will be, worth twenty shillings in the pound. A pound note is spent very speedily, it was very difficult to spend a sovereign.

When the day dawned—the day when the cashier gave you paper instead of gold—the whole world changed, and it was the beginning of the end of the Middle Class. Their days were numbered, their golden age was past.

It is the purpose of this book to set down what Middle Class life was like in the days of the golden sovereign, and more particularly in the late Victorian and Edwardian days—up to 1914.

There is no desire to be controversial, politically or otherwise. There is no desire to start arguments, to expound on class difference or class warfare. There is simply a desire to inscribe what life was like in the days when the Middle Classes lived in this land and in this City of London, with a golden sovereign or two to jingle in their pockets and to show what effect the spending of those twenty shillings had on their lives. Let the case of the Upper Classes and the Working Classes be set out by experts. Here we have to do with the Middle Class only, to put on record how they lived, how they spent their money, how they dressed, how they travelled about, where they ate and what they ate, what sort of books and papers they read, and what sort of homes they lived in. To show, also, how and where they spent their leisure and took their pleasure, and what manner of entertainment claimed their money, the life of these people—so many of whom still live—set forth as clearly and as truthfully as possible, from actual fact and experience.

Already the period seems far away, already the rush of modern life, with its ever-shifting kaleidoscope, dims those days which are really so near to us and yet so very distant.

Here is an attempt to show the life of the man in the street, his wife and children, from babyhood to manhood, as it was lived when John Bull was the typical figure of our race, and not the shabby little short-sighted man in patched clothes. As it was lived when people walked as often as they rode, when the shops were full of everything and when there was money and to spare. Of days when war had not smitten us and taken its toll of our lives, our health, our possessions, when Quality mattered and when we all had leisure to enjoy that life which seemed to stretch in an illimitable vista of peace before us.

In the days when we had a measure of content and a measure of enjoyment, for all that we worked longer hours for less money. But the times were golden, the standard was golden and the coins we received were golden sovereigns, and were worth, every one of them, Twenty Shillings in the Pound.

CHAPTER I

The Happy Event

IT MUST BE ADMITTED AT THE OUTSET THAT THE LITTLE BOYS AND GIRLS of the Golden Age did not have as good a time as the juvenile products of the paper age. The cult of the child, as it exists today, was unknown. Except when they first appeared on the scene, children were not glorified. Even then they were not looked upon as quite the miracles they are today.

Perhaps that was because it was not considered such a marvellous thing then to produce a child as it appears to be now. Indeed, it was a disgrace not to do so, and that not once but several times. The average family numbered half a dozen. An only child was pitied because it had no little brothers or sisters to play with. The truth was that people could afford children in the days of the sovereign better than they can in the day of the Pound Note. Also, they believed in the home and the family.

Children were more important than motor-cars—there weren't any—and even more important than the pursuit of pleasure. Married people then did not expect to carry on their lives as lived in the days of the single or engagement period. They married—and they settled down. Who settles down nowadays?

Family life was serious then and entailed responsibilities which are not regarded today. There was more discipline, and things were less restless. It was an age of domesticity. The home was a place to live in and not just a species of free hotel, to drop in and out of according to one's convenience. Mealtimes were sacred and adhered to. You had to think of the servants, although the modern idea is that they were mere slaves. In those days the family were expected to obey the rules made by the Father and the Mother. And yet, in the case of child welfare, there was less routine and care than is exercised today—especially as regards health and diet. There were other rules all right and they were strict enough.

Most of the Middle Class babies, in fact the great majority of them, were born at home. They entered the home at once and they drew their first breath and sent up their first wail in their own houses. Very few Middle Class mothers went to hospital or nursing homes for childbirth. The children were born in the best bedroom—that normally occupied by their father and mother—and thus at one fell swoop did the atmosphere of the home and of its own social standing envelop the new-born infant.

In most cases the doctor who presided had known either or both of the parents from infancy too. Young doctors were rather distrusted. The 'family' doctor, maybe without newfangled ideas, but tried and proved in many such cases, was the man in whom reliance was felt. Naturally he was the first to know of the impending 'happy event' and was usually loud in his congratulations. Here was another family on the way—and it was all to the good for his practice.

Strangely enough, although these were the days of family life, when the production and raising of a family was the accepted future of every woman lucky enough to escape what was regarded as the disgrace of spinsterhood—the fact of becoming a mother in the not far distant future was felt by all respectable wives to be a somewhat guilty secret, not to be shared by outsiders until concealment was no longer possible.

For some reason, when a woman achieved the condition of expectant motherhood, she kept it very much to herself. Naturally the 'family' knew, and a few very intimate friends, but such a condition was felt to be slightly indelicate—delicacy was highly esteemed then—and the lady who was to increase the Middle Class very soon became somewhat of a recluse.

Nowadays the news is proclaimed from the housetops. It is shouted out at parties at which cocktails are consumed. The mother-to-be is often commiserated with and asked if she doesn't find it a bore? Friends of both sexes discuss it with her, and point out what she will be missing in the way of social engagements and enjoyment—and sport. That never happened in the days of the sovereign.

Those were days of much more reticence. Despite the fact that an Englishman's home was his castle, where precious little 'dropping in' was allowed, which was practically never 'open house' except for very close friends indeed, and then to nothing like the extent it is today—people still lived much closer to each other. They kept very largely to their own neighbourhood because transport was so different, and they took a much greater interest in the doings of their neighbours than they do now.

Today it is possible to live for years next door to a family, never enter their house, and to know practically nothing about them. Then, everyone in the road knew pretty well all there was to know about everybody else. The bride, on taking up her position in her own home, would be kept under observation by the surrounding matrons. Every time she was seen she was the target for appraising eyes, and the married ladies would nod to each other knowingly.

A birth then was everybody's affair, possibly because of the secrecy.

Nowadays, nobody outside the immediate family cares at all. The bride would be watched and studied on her way to and from church—and practically everyone went to church or chapel then, for these places were the social centres as well as temples of worship—and she would be closely studied during the service. Non-churchgoers watched from their windows, shielded by lace curtains.

Despite the secrecy maintained, keen eyes soon saw what they saw, and the news travelled very fast. Mothers of neighbouring families would discuss it together when they met shopping, or at their 'At Homes', first sending young unmarried girls out of earshot. Sex matters, even if relating to the decently married, were not for the ears of single girls, even though those girls were all destined to go through it themselves and as soon as possible on reaching marriageable age. But the girls did not much mind; they heard the news from the servants, who were, as a rule, the heralds of these and all other local events.

The expectant mother soon went into retirement, long before she became obviously destined for motherhood. She retired from public life and it was stated that 'she is not going about much just now'. This was despite the fact that she could conceal her condition for a much longer period than now, on account of the fashion in clothes and of more ample figures. She would never have dreamed of fulfilling her social engagements up to almost the last moment, as is the custom today. Such a proceeding would have embarrassed her terribly—and also everyone else in company. Her shopping would be done for her—most of it was delivered to the door, anyway. She would, according to her means and social standing, take carriage exercise, or go out after dark, on the arm of her very self-conscious, if somewhat proud, husband.

Of course the arrival of a first child was a tremendous event in the family. Letters were written all round—there was no telephoning because there were very few 'phones outside business places and not so many in them. And the Family would gather.

There was an orgy of needlework and knitting. The expected baby's clothes were home made, as far as possible. Pride was taken in this. The young mother worked herself, so did her mother and the mother-in-law, the grandmothers—all the near female relations. Completed garments were brought out for inspection and greeted with cries of delight. There was the usual doubt as to whether blue or pink ribbon would be wanted—blue for a boy and pink for a girl. And ribbon—bé-bé-ribbon—was used by the mile, there was no lack of it, or any other material in those days of plenty. When a particularly dainty garment was exhibited the ladies nearly swooned with joy. All Middle Class babies of the sovereign age had tremendous wardrobes before they were born.

23

But at the approach of a male, even the father-to-be, these garments were hastily concealed, for it was not delicate to show them in front of gentlemen—obstetric matters were never admitted to be part of the scheme of things at all. If only the wife and her mother or mother-in-law are present, then the little clothes could be shown to the father with propriety. He would handle them gingerly, go all stiff and constrained and get hot under his high stiff-starched collar and feel rather foolish and very guilty. Mostly, however, the garments were only examined as between husband and wife, never when unmarried or unrelated ladies were present.

The expectant mother would receive much advice. She would have to listen to the experiences of the women who had been through it themselves. Things were gone into in great thoroughness of detail, and at even greater length, but nobody was bored—quite the contrary. This—and marriage—were the two all-absorbing female topics. Husbands were well down the course, with the servant problem—there has always been a servant problem—limping in the rear.

The good soul would be entreated not to exert herself, and yet told to take reasonable exercise. She would also be warned that she must 'keep her feet up', which meant lying on the sofa, but that the lighter portions of housework—the genteel dusting of the household treasures and such-like—would do her good. She was warned to avoid shocks—as if any sane person ever wanted to run into them—and almost in the same breath the most awful experiences of such things were poured into her ears. She was told to eat well and to stint herself of nothing—'You have two to look after now, dear'—and her mind was filled with conflicting counsel which, if she was sensible (and she mostly was)—went in by one ear and out of the other.

The doctor would call—although pre-natal treatment was undreamed of—and his carriage at the door was duly noted by all the neighbours within sight who were discreetly screened by their lace curtains. And as the time grew near (it was surprising how many people entirely uncon-nected with the event took it into their calculations with great accuracy) the family excitement grew to a crescendo. And there was a fair state of excitement for some doors on either side as well.

Interest had been fanned by the 'monthly nurse' as soon as engaged. This was the woman who assisted the doctor in bringing young Master or Miss Middle Class into the world. She was, as a rule, quite unqualified, except by great experience. But she was known, trusted and highly recommended from one family to another. She helped whole families into the world. On being 'booked' she would tell all her other clients and the matter would again be discussed in detail.

Sometimes she arrived some days before the happy event, if she could spare the time and if the clients could afford it. Her wages were not high in terms of today, but pretty considerable then. And she cost a lot to keep. She wanted this, she wanted that, she required almost as much attention as the mother herself. Her capacity for the consumption of stout was amazing. Her word was law, and she was autocratic. The servants often detested her, for she made so much 'extra work'. Cold meat she could not endure. But she was necessary, and she knew it.

The Middle Class children of the sovereign age were just as inconsiderate as the children of today regarding the time of their arrival. But sometimes the neighbours would be set into a delightful flutter by seeing the husband dash from the house and set off at a run to fetch the doctor and then the nurse. That meant a long time at the window behind the lace shield—so useful, those lace curtains, they revealed all that was going on and yet concealed the viewer—or so she thought. Good eyes, however, usually detected the onlooker, who in her excitement would frequently fidget the curtains and even pull them slightly aside to see better.

The neighbouring audience would be duly thrilled by seeing the arrival of the doctor's brougham—all good doctors had carriages—and by the sight of him hurrying up the front steps—ninety-nine per cent of the houses had a lot of front steps—with his little black bag in his hand. The front door would open as if by magic, and he would go inside. The vigil would be continued until the return of the husband with the nurse— by cab if such a thing were attainable, or else hurriedly on foot. No taxi-ranks on the 'phone then, and cabs usually only obtainable at the local station.

There was a pleasant sigh as the two entered the house. And even then the spectator would not leave the coign of vantage. For the sight of the husband speeding for help meant that it was happening either quite early in the morning before he left for business, or else on a summer's evening, or Saturday afternoon or Sunday. If early morning, then there was still the smaller thrill of seeing the husband leave for business—he had an importance that day, whereas on ordinary days his passing would have caused no stir at all.

Every husband hoped that he would not have this job to do. He hoped it would occur when he was at the office. There was always his or his wife's mother in the house, or a close relative, to perform this office in his absence—a necessary precaution in pre-'phone days.

So the poor man would go off to the City, or wherever he worked— and would suffer hours of mental agitation. He would be the butt of his fellow workers. The men he met at lunch would 'chip' or chaff him unmercifully. The male is not sympathetic to his brother male in natal

25

circumstances. He is ribald and often bawdy. It is the woman who is sympathetic, but there were few women in offices in those old days. And if there were, nobody would say much about it to her—if she overheard, it could not of course be helped. But strangely enough feminine intuition always told her—that intuition which is so often accompanied by sharp ears, an insatiable curiosity and a power of putting two and two together.

The husband never knew his fate as a father until he reached home. Nobody put his mind at rest by ringing him up—it could not be done. If he were an employer in a fair way of business he might have a 'phone at the office, and in that case he could receive word from one of the family who would go to a shop similarly provided and let him know, for it was long odds against there being a 'phone in the house until far into the nineteen hundreds.

Meanwhile the little affair went on, in that sober-faced, discreetly curtained house, whilst a member of each neighbouring family took turns to keep observation. If by any chance the maid of the momentarily important house came out on an errand, or even to sweep down the front, neighbouring maids were at once sent to gather information. They got it, and reported back. It was a great day for everyone when the Middle Class received a recruit. The movements of the doctor were carefully watched. If he came out and drove away, conclusions were drawn: if he stayed in the house, more conclusions were arrived at. Matrons of neighbouring houses going shopping spread the news to acquaintances until the excitement rippled for quite a distance, like the effect of a stone in a pond.

It might be that the husband returned home before the affair was finished. He was not wanted—any more than he wanted to be there. He would sit in a room, moon about, try and interest himself in the newspaper without success—for he had been gazing at it fruitlessly in the train. He might try and read, but his mind was upstairs and his ears on the alert for every footstep and the voices which sounded as doors opened and shut. He would try and eat, perhaps, but his sense of guilt was upon him. The maid who served him regarded him curiously. His mother or his wife's mother adopted hushed and somewhat formal tones. He was in a state of mortal funk the whole time, and would start up in terror when the doctor came down for a few moments and spoke words of cheer or noncommitment. The poor man soon had recourse to the decanter which stood on the dining-room sideboard.

This decanter, mostly of highly polished oak, had silver mountings and a kind of silver gallows over it—a crossbar of silver or plated metal between two metal uprights. The crossbar had two flaps which closed down mechanically when locked—the key of the decanter was either held by the master of the house or 'kept in a safe place'—and prevented the three heavy cut-glass bottles from being removed.

These bottles, with cut-glass stoppers, held whisky, brandy, sherry or port. Sometimes they carried a little silver label inscribed with their contents, held round their necks by a silver chain, like dumb wine-waiters —sometimes the labels were attached to the front of the decanter. Sometimes there were no such labels at all, and it was necessary to remove the stoppers and smell to detect the contents.

No Middle Class dining-room with any pretence to distinction or style was without its decanter. And it was a point of pride to keep the bottles well filled. If there were no guests then one helped oneself from the spare bottles in the cellarette, a cupboard in the face of the sideboard. But in circumstances such as recorded here, the poor suffering man would judge that only the decanter was suitable. Besides, the doctor might like a drink too.

The husband probably had a study—though what he studied there was never clear—to which lighthearted wives also referred as his 'den'. He might smoke in there. Smoking was not encouraged in the best rooms. It made the curtains smell and also made 'dust'. Women never smoked— only the *demi-monde* or 'fast' women who were not received in Middle Class housholds. Bohemian people such as artists, actors and actressesand writers, who did not regard the conventions, are not included in this chronicle, which is one of respectability. But few men waited to hear that they were fathers anywhere but in the dining-room. Apart from anything else, the social standing of the doctor demanded it. And no man ever chose to sit in the 'drawing-room'.

Middle class husbands of today have a much better time. The anxiety and sense of guilt remain, but they are out of all that proximity which is so devastating to mere men. They can do as they choose in their agony of waiting—and they will hear the 'phone ring in due course. They are out of it all, and that is the best place for them.

The Middle Class husband of the sovereign age had no relief such as this. If agonized sounds from above drove him into the garden—if the season was suitable—he was—and knew he was—the cynosure of curious eyes. If he went for a walk, he knew he was a target of curiosity and ran the risk of being considered 'heartless', too. No, he had to wait head in hands—his only friend the decanter.

But it was all over at last. The doctor would congratulate him on a boy or a girl—mostly the poor man did not care which it was—have a drink to wish the baby and mother luck—and leave things to the women-folk.

And after a sight of his wife and the strange, crumpled and often ugly newcomer, about which he so frequently, in his state of abject panic, said the wrong thing, he would retire to rest in the spare room—often the second best spare room, if the house had one—for a very uncomfortable night before an awakening to a completely strange world in which his own importance had waned considerably.

Next day would be busy. He would have a sheaf of telegrams to dispatch to anxiously waiting relatives—and then would go to the office to undergo more chaff and have the privilege of 'wetting the baby's head' with the office staff, and whenever he met an acquaintance. He also inserted an announcement in a newspaper.

The news spread, maids were sent over to enquire as to health. Closer friends called—always prefacing their remarks by saying, "I'm not coming in but I simply had to enquire . . ." If it were a boy they would smile and say: "Oh, how splendid. How pleased everyone must be." If it were a girl, the smile would be a bit weaker and the congratulations tempered by the opening gambit of, "Oh, well . . ." Useless for the claim to be made that a girl had been wanted. All really good Middle Class people wanted a boy—the first time.

If the poor mother had a bad time and was ill, straw was strewn before the house to deaden the sound of traffic (as traffic was known in those days) and the knocker muffled up. This happened in all cases of bad illness amongst the more genteel of the Middle Class. The straw, if the weather was windy, soon became a public nuisance, but it cast the desired hush on the neighbourhod with great effect.

The little Middle Class baby, wailing in its new home, was the centre of the world. If its tiny mind could receive impressions, it must have thought that attempts were being made to smother it. For that baby soon knew the meaning of clothes.

In the days of the sovereign there were considerably more clothes than there was baby. It had what was known as a 'binder'. This was a length of flannel wound round and round its tiny person and fastened by a safety-pin. Sometimes, despite care, that safety pin entered the baby and it protested with good cause. Then garments were put upon it, many garments, little vests, a curious kind of overall, vest and petticoat in one piece, made of flannel and laced up with tape, then more petticoats. And above all this, the glory of 'long clothes'. Very long clothes indeed, the spotless robes of muslin, *crêpe de Chine*, nainsook and the like, beautifully embroidered or smocked, full of lace and ribbons everywhere—sometimes threaded through the robe itself and with little bunches on the shoulders, bé-bé ribbon, delightful stuff, and always blue for a boy or pink for a girl.

28

Air was excluded. If the baby was moved from room to room, its tiny head was guarded by a shawl—a head shawl, it was called. Its fresh, pink skin and its little pores got no chance to breathe at all, and how it escaped being stifled is a thing we don't know today.

It was never left outside in its pram to get the fresh air. When it went out for an airing that was the least suitable word, for its poor little face was covered by a veil. Bachelor uncles, ignorant men, were known to remove or lift up the veil to give the little creature some air. They would be promptly banished, and the child anxiously watched for possible harm.

The first outing was also a local event. A nurse usually carried the baby, a miracle of finery in its long clothes, its tiny face covered, in her arms. She was dressed up too. She wore a cap with long streamers, a cloak which floated in the breeze and a white dress. It was all very grand. Those neighbours who had not yet inspected the child would come out and beg for a sight. The nurse would gently remove that veil for a few seconds, in case the dangerous oxygen should choke the little thing. But everyone admired the baby, and more especially the clothes and the long, handsome shawl which was swathed round it.

It was inspected by the family. At the christening there was a great gathering. There was usually a good deal of debate beforehand, not so much as to the child's name, as to who were to be its godfathers and godmothers. Most children then were given good old family names, not a bad thing at all.

Sometimes a great event set up a mania in nomenclature. Many women then cursed the Battle of Alma, for it brought forth a spate of Almas, who were thereby dated. The Boer War led to some shocking names being given to children. Some were even christened Mafeking and Kimberley. There was a comic song about it. Many a child got the name of Roberts and Kitchener into a family with no right to them at all. But mostly the family names went on, and the little one had its god-parent's name added.

Although these were the days of sentiment, there was a good business streak. Godparents were selected for their likelihood of benefit to the child, either from legacies or for employment later in life. The more influential you were, the more likely your crop of god-children.

As many of the family as could possibly do so attended the christening, from grandparents down to mere cousins. The little baby received gifts. It had silver mugs, silver spoons, showered upon it. It had silver rattles too, with coral handles, and little bells which rang merrily. They either annoyed the child, or in due course it picked them off and got them into its mouth. But it was all very handsome, stable and good class.

If the Middle Class baby did not derive its sustenance from its mother there were plenty of patent foods, as there are now. But the feeding bottles were very different. They were flat affairs, which slipped easily from the hand, and they had long rubber tubes to them. The baby required considerable power of suction to get the food into its mouth.

The type now in use may be one of the reasons for the more temperate habits which obtain. Those babies of the sovereign age had to fight for it. And they were kept much longer on the bottle. A mother of those days would die of horror at the early date at which the babes now get solid food. They were kept a good nine months on milk. Much later they got beef tea and slops. But it was a long time before their little stomachs and digestions were considered able to tackle 'solids'.

Rickets were an ever-present menace. But babies in those days remained babies. Nowadays they seem to be three years old when born.

As soon as the birth of the baby was announced, samples of all sorts flowed into the house. An economical mother could have fed, washed and powdered her baby for weeks on the samples. No doubt some did.

Enterprising firms had photographs of the newspaper announcement printed on cards, so that these might be sent out broadcast, and did a fine trade. These bore a slight resemblance to memorial cards, but nobody thought of that. It was an age of cards—visiting-cards, cards announcing births, marriages, engagements, deaths, birthdays, Golden and Silver Weddings—memorial cards, so-called because they apprised you of someone's death (you were supposed to treasure them and many did so). But a firm of toy sellers, who started a follow-up system, and sent catalogues with a covering letter near the date of the child's birthday, so that parents could choose presents, were not so lucky. Some of those children were dead and irate letters resulted. Commercial acumen, if carried too far, was vulgar and in bad taste.

Bathing the baby was a more difficult process. This was carried out in the nursery. It was a very poor child which had no nursery—there was plenty of room in those spacious days. In early infancy the child slept, of course, in its cot in its parents' room. That cot was as ornate as the days in which it existed. It was of wickerwork, and loving hands threaded ribbons all over it. It was draped with muslin, yards of it. It had a little canopy, draped from a bent rod overhead. Its tiny bedclothes and its coverlet were works of art. Mothers wept happy tears at the mere sight of it.

But the nursery was the place for ablutions. Nowadays mothers take their children into the bathroom. They bathe them in the wash-basin and, at a surprisingly early age, in the bath itself. Nor does any harm result, though washing a young baby is a tricky matter. But in the sovereign

Field Marshal Lord Kitchener, the victor of Omdurman, who raised the "First Hundred Thousand" in the First World War

By permission of Picture Post Library

The way the Absent-Minded Beggar fought in the Boer War

Actual Sovereigns in the days of the golden sovereign. (*Left to right*): Queen of Spain; King Edward VII; Empress of Germany; Emperor of Germany (the Kaiser); Queen Alexandra; Queen of Portugal; King of Spain; Queen of Norway

Sovereigns-to-be in the time of the golden sovereign. (*Left*): King George VI, (*right*) The Duke of Windsor

days the baby was bathed in its nursery, mostly in a galvanized iron receptacle, such as one steeps clothes in. Later on there were hip baths, a thing never seen today. These were flat affairs some nine or twelve inches deep, with an inclined plane at one end, against which you could lean when bathing. For grown-ups used them too.

The bathrooms of those days were not the bright, efficient places we know now. And the hot-water supply was always temperamental. It depended on the whim of the kitchen range, and kitchen ranges were notoriously difficult. In good moods they were magnificent, in bad ones things of nerve-racking desperation. They consumed much coal, but it was cheap and plentiful—eighteen or twenty shillings a ton gave you magnificent stuff. That hot-water system was not reliable enough for baby's bath.

So the warm water needed was either carted upstairs in kettles from the kitchen (nurseries were always at the top of the house), or else it was boiled on the nursery fire, which was an open one, and for which coal had also to be dragged up the stairs. There were no electric fires or central heating. Gas-fires crept in but were regarded as most unhealthy, especially for babies. And the gas-fires of those days were not very safe or suitable, it must be granted. The ceremony of the bath was rather more prolonged for the little Middle Class child then than now. But then everything was more leisurely. The baby itself was not expected to grow up so quickly.

The bath was the great rite of motherhood—and was revelled in. At length the evening arrived when the husband was allowed to see his offspring in the bath. He had been told of this great treat and had, if truth must prevail, been considerably embarrassed by it. But it was the thing to do and he did it. It was expected of him, and men then had a stern sense of duty. Many of the so-called strict and rigid parents were secretly scared of their children, especially in babyhood. But he duly wondered and admired —and felt rather proud in his inmost heart—and his wife bubbled with joy. Children in scanty attire were never seen in public then, except, strangely enough, at the photographer's, when there was quite a vogue of having them photographed completely nude, a thing never tolerated in the home.

The pictures would be shown round and admired, even if some of the coarser-natured males cracked some jokes (very mild ones), and, strangely enough, it was no shame to have your child's photo displayed in a state of nature in the photographer's window for all to see. But they would never have seen the real baby like that. He or she was always a bundle of clothes. Many a young lady regretted these pictures of herself in the 'altogether' when, as in duty bound, a visitor inspected the 'Family

C

Album', and many a young man ground his teeth at the shame of it when the picture caught the eye of a young lady whom he thought of honouring with his attentions. Who cares today? And what did it matter, anyway? But then the great thing was delicacy, you see.

When children waxed peevish and cried a 'comforter' was pushed into their mouths, a rubber teat which they sucked with the satisfaction of delusion. A most unhygienic arrangement.

The first great step in the baby's career was when it was 'shortened'. That is, when those long clothes ceased to swaddle it, and it got into short skirts and began to resemble a living thing. The mother's heart suffered a pang—only equalled when her son and heir got into his first little breeches. The long clothes were reverently put away—usually a new claimant for them was on its way—and the 'short clothes' went on when the child was three months old. Nowadays the child is practically never in 'long clothes'.

But, except that its feet were freer, and it no longer wore a veil, there was small relief for the youngster. It still had masses of clothes, it now had additional petticoats and it had pinafores, with bunches of ribbon in the shoulders. One of the great features was the sash. This went round the waist of boy and girl alike, with a vast bow at the back, and both boys and girls were petticoated. Little boys then did not achieve the breeches stage for years. They had kilted skirts, like the girls.

The pelisse remained, a fearsome thing. Often it was of velvet, and, very heavy in itself, was also heavily trimmed. Girls wore little bonnets, and looked out charmingly from amidst swansdown. But the lads had strange headgear, often reminiscent of a beefeater's hat in shape if not in stiffness.

Looking back, it is difficult to understand how they managed to play about. They never got into the rompers so popular and useful today. There was always that pinafore to keep them clean—and to be kept clean itself. Petticoats were more numerous in the case of a girl than a boy, and a small boy wore boots sooner, although both sexes had this heavier form of footwear put on them. The child was a species of human clothes-horse. Everything worn was good, but heavy.

The 'prams' were heavy affairs, too, more like a stage-coach than the light, handy vehicles of today. There was room for two, with a little well for the feet, which could be covered over in the case of small tots. The wheels were large, the tyres thin rubber strips. They were difficult to push and unwieldy to turn. But they lasted for years. They were as cumbersome as the old boneshaker as compared with the modern bicycle.

A stranger to our land, taking a quick look at our small children, would have no doubt that we were a maritime nation. Even in infancy we were put into the Navy, so far as our attire went, as soon as possible. It even affected little girls, many of whose blouses had a nautical cut and who wore, as well as boys, the wide sailor straw hat with the upturned brim, a small replica of the headgear which formed the summer wear then of the real Jack Tars. Even before little boys got breeched they had sailor blouses to wear with their navy kilts, and little round sailor caps which usually proclaimed them a member of the crew of either H.M.S. *Victory* or H.M.S. *Excellent*. The baggy sailor blouse, gathered round the waist by elastic, with the correct collar and black silk scarf, was worn by the vast majority, even though beneath it the legs were clothed down to the knees in kilts, and below that again in long black stockings and button boots. Socks were not esteemed and worn only in babyhood.

They looked like a lot of little 'Wrens'. On the arms were stripes and anchors; and anchors, sometimes gold, more often red, adorned the little breast pockets. But there was a lanyard with a whistle attached. That made up for a good deal, although it was soon either broken or confiscated.

Those straw hats referred to had elastic bands which fastened under the chin, to keep the hat on little heads. This elastic had a knack of being pulled at by tiny hands, and of springing back and stinging tiny chins in the vilest fashion. Often, too, it got chewed when nobody was looking. In the winter, little 'reefer' overcoats kept out the cold. Thus early did it dawn on the Middle Class child that Britannia ruled the waves—and sartorially the child as well.

Little girls who were not enrolled in the Senior Service wore little dresses of extreme bunchiness, the stout appearance being enhanced by several petticoats, often starched stiff. The pinafore covered the dress and the inevitable sash went round where the waist was to be later. This was a splash of colour anyhow. It was a long, lavish affair, and often of tartan. Tie-ups graced the shoulders and the skirts always came discreetly below the knees. Best pinafores were lacy affairs, or rich with embroidery. But the load of clothing was always enormous.

Parents of those days knew little of hygiene, of calories, of proteins and the modern food values. There was no immunization except vaccination. Diphtheria, scarlet fever, and other infectious diseases were never guarded against by this means. They ranged the world and took heavy toll. Measles, mumps, whooping-cough and chicken-pox were looked upon as necessary, just as natural as cutting one's teeth. When one of a family got them, it became communal. There was a system known as 'running it through the house'.

The bad after-effects were never realized, nor was any precaution taken against them. As often as not, old-fashioned remedies took pre-

33

cedence over 'doctor's stuff'. A walk round the gasworks was the general cure for whooping-cough. Many people still regarded vaccination with suspicion. The sight of a man or woman with a heavily pitted face was all too common.

Food did not receive the care it does today. Milk came into the house in pewter cans, with a flap to cover it. It was drawn into these and left on the doorstep. Or, when the milkman called later, the milk was drawn straight from a churn in the cart (which resembled a Roman chariot, steed and all), or from a little square push-cart on shorter rounds. There still lingered a few milk-women who carried cans of milk suspended from a yoke across their shoulders. Bread was never packed in cellophane—there was no cellophane either. Butchers' meat was on trays for all the wind and dirt to blow upon. Drains had a pretty habit of smelling, and there was, on account of the macadam roads, plenty of dust.

Children were even allowed to drink milk drawn from the cow—straight from the cow which was milked by an ordinary pair of human hands. One was tethered at the gate of St. James's Park and it was esteemed a treat to have a glass of fresh creamy milk there. It was a penny a glass. It had not been pasteurized, pulverized and gone through all the processes it experiences today before it gets to the human child. According to modern ideas it must have been hopping with germs. Yet little harm came to the drinkers thereof, many of whom are alive today.

Infant mortality was high, very high. Often would you hear a woman claim to 'have had ten and buried eight'. Yet those children died of ordinary complaints and in bed. They did not know the modern improvements of being dashed beneath the wheels of modern juggernauts, or blown into tiny pieces by bombs.

And those who survived provided the generation which was to fight the First World War, in which they suffered hardships and horrors unknown in the last one, and to provide the bulk of the men and women who stood up to the Blitz and fought the menace from the air.

It was the survival of the fittest, and that is not a bad thing for the race in general.

CHAPTER II

Seen But Not Heard

THE FIRST THING EVERY LITTLE MIDDLE CLASS MITE LEARNED WAS THAT 'children are to be seen but not heard'. Thus right away did they become aware of their place in the scheme of things. Good behaviour was esteemed. They were expected to be quiet and to conduct themselves in a manner which was known as 'genteel'. It was pretty hard on them, and for them, but it was excellent discipline, as they were to learn in after life, and it was the reason why people in those days had what were known as 'manners'. Noise was frowned upon. It was considered vulgar. Nobody then conducted a conversation in screams across a crowded room; din was everywhere reduced to a minimum. It was genteel to be quiet, to conduct oneself properly—according to the standards of the day—and people who made a noise were regarded with suspicion and looked upon as outsiders.

The children were not expected to be quiet all the time, of course. They could play in their nursery, in the garden, wherever it was allowed, and make as much noise as they liked—so long as it did not disturb Papa, Mamma—or the neighbours. How much noise the parents could stand was a personal matter, depending on the parents themselves. The time when children had to be seen and not heard was when they were in company with their elders and betters—at meals, walking out in state, or when visitors were present, and they were produced for inspection and compliments.

What the parents meant by being seen and not heard was that there must be no answering back, no arguing, no bad table manners, and that when guests were present, then quietness and good manners must prevail. The youngsters must sit still and speak only when they were spoken to—and then reply nicely and give a proper answer. No child in those days would have dared to butt into the conversation of its elders, or express opinions as they do today. No child in company then would have made demands as to what food it wanted at meal-time. And no child was ever allowed to have cake until it had eaten plenty of bread and butter—white bread and real butter, by the way.

Of course, there were spoilt darlings who transgressed the rules. But these children were justly unpopular, not only amongst grown-up friends and relations but amongst other children as well, who really did behave

35

quite well (under the parental eye) and disliked heartily the little wretches who transgressed—just as much as they did—and do—dislike the little prodigies of behaviour and manners who were held up to them as examples.

Children of the Middle Class were not so close to their parents; they were not a part of the general pattern of the domestic life, but a separate design in that pattern. Where means allowed it, a nanny ruled. Where lesser means obtained, a young girl came in—often little more than a child herself—who took charge of them for the whole or part of the day and who often had considerable influence over them. It all depended on what sort of a nanny or what sort of a nursemaid you got. If good, the children profited. If bad, it was very soon found out and someone else was engaged speedily.

The position between parents and children was one of love and respect. Today it is often camaraderie. That may be better—time will show—but it is certain that the young people of the sovereign days had considerably more respect for their parents than have the children of today and they loved them none the less for that respect. They were nothing like so familiar and they were considerably more obedient.

Children are observant and imitative. They will form their ways upon the example of others. They saw their parents as something above themselves, something of great power and influence—whose word was law. Consequently they imitated their parents' demeanour and did as they were told by these beings whom they felt were not their equals but their superiors.

They were seldom spectators of domestic strife or quarrels between husband and wife—the larger houses gave scope for strife in private—so they maintained their respect for a far longer period and had a better and more lasting discipline.

Children then remained children much longer than they do today, they did not grow up nearly as fast. Consequently they had a longer period of training, and more time for what was considered good or bad behaviour, to take root in their minds and become permanent memories and standards.

Despite all the 'rights' which women are said to have gained, the average Middle Class mother (and it is desirable to stress again that this story is about the Middle Class and no other) had far more freedom. She lived in a bigger space, her house had accommodation for the children, the family was not all mixed up in a small flat—and she could get domestic help with ease. So she could go about, and entertain in the home with considerable comfort and enjoyment.

She was, however, a very good mother, even if her ideas of hygiene would cause a shudder today. She knew all about her children, and she supervised all that happened. And her visit at bedtime was something to which every child looked forward and a memory they carried all their lives. It was a perfect hour.

The father was a bit more remote. A threat to tell the father about a misdeed or fit of naughtiness brought an immediate and sobering response. He worked longer hours than the man of today; often he did not get home until the children were either in bed or just being bedded down.

He would come up to the nursery too, and it was then found that he could unbend. Indeed he often unbent, and would romp with the children when occasion served, without losing dignity or respect. When, however, he said "That is enough" there was no argument, but the children were grateful and pleased with their fun. They discovered that he knew a whole lot of games and how to play them, that he could invent exotic scenes peopled with bears, lions, weird and wonderful animals of his own creation like 'turkey tigers' which thrilled and excited, if they sometimes scared the eager little ones—but there was always safety when Papa was about. He knew stories too—more stories and more exciting ones than Nanny or even Mamma. Also he had pockets from which would emerge delightful things.

He was, to his brood, a beneficent superman—whose word was law, but a law which was just and respected. It was often necessary to be quiet on Sunday afternoons because you must not disturb your father—the children knew he was having a doze (as, nine times out of ten, was Mamma). But there was always some part of the day when he would play with them, which made up for it all. By and large, the Middle Class father was a very good father, who tempered sternness with joy, and had a line which few except very naughty children ever dared to cross. Consequently Papa was believed in and his rulings were not questioned.

The mother was often not able to give very much time to the children because she was busy with her main job and duty—being a mother all over again. But Father had no such close season and filled the breach admirably at those mysterious times which preceded the announcement that a new little brother or sister had arrived. The buffer states between the parents and the children were the nanny or nursemaid, and the servants.

The nanny and the nursemaid could be one and the same thing— she was 'nanny' to the children and 'nursemaid' to the grown-ups. She wore uniform, and thought it no disgrace. If she were a young nanny it often made her very attractive. There was a print dress, or a dress of plain colour, for the mornings, with a white apron, linen cuffs, and a fairly plain cap—often a slim linen collar too, much the same as a hospital nurse wears. But for walks out, the full bloom of the nanny appeared. Then she had a white or a grey dress, a much more ornate and softer apron and (according to her age and general looks or otherwise) an outdoor cap, often with long and waving streamers. Her nurse's cloak was usually grey, but some nannies in the summer—if they were young—burst forth as symphonies in white—a dazzling and attractive sight to behold.

The so-called 'nursemaid' of the lower strata was a young girl who did not wear uniform. She was often barely in her teens and her main job was to take the children for walks. This young person did not wield the power or authority of a uniformed nanny and her age was, from the children's point of view, against her. They knew well enough that she was not really grown-up. Eighteen was, of course, very old to a child then, and twenty an advanced age indeed, with all the adult authority behind it.

But the young things who undertook the exercise of children had rarely reached such maturity and so often met with rebellion. Indeed, she often met with battle. Small use her issuing commands, the children knew she was little more than a child herself and treated her accordingly. It often came to a question of physical strength and trial by combat before she could get obedience. She had a pretty tough time of it. She did not dare administer the rudimentary chastisement such as hand-slapping and minor cuffs which were the prerogative of the nannie proper. She had to achieve her end by argument, pulling, pushing, scuffling and threats.

Those threats—to tell either Mamma or Papa—were her last resource, and usually the effective ones. All children then had an instinctive knowledge—born of generations of domestic discipline—as to how far they could go. It was up to the girl herself. If she had the knack of managing children and of understanding them she got on all right, and as she was usually one of a pretty numerous brood herself, mostly she knew how to handle her young charges.

They might be a little snobbish at first—it was something of a snobbish age, and children are always a strange mixture of snobbery and complete democracy—but stories of her little brothers and sisters—with highlights of their goodness or naughtiness and the rewards or punishments derived from either condition got her a good audition and finally complete understanding. She took them out for walks and she brought them back safely. She did not have to compete with the seething multiple juggernaut which floods the streets today. They went along the quiet suburban roads, or into the park. And there she would romp with them, clinging with delight to this continuation of her own childhood.

Mostly she and the children were firm friends. She did not last if they did not like her—Mamma saw to that, but if she did, there was a

38

close alliance. The children fell down, of course, and bruised or grazed themselves, or cut their knees and suffered all the minor abrasions of extreme youth, but she would deal with them with a rough and ready first aid, and report it all faithfully on her return.

Often she gossiped with others of her kind out with young charges, whilst the two groups of children eyed each other and then, with the mysterious freemasonry of youth, either became friends or desperate enemies. She would perhaps indulge in amatory badinage with passing errand boys or young workmen—but one had to be careful, for children 'notice' such a lot. But by her the children were made a bit class-conscious —for to her they were 'Master Teddy' or 'Miss Grace'.

It was not so with the nannies. These seldom romped or played in public. They were more responsible and more ornate. They had authority and dignity to maintain. But they would gossip too, often to the children's utter boredom. They would go into the park and the children were told to play on the grass, whilst the nannie talked with other nannies —exchanging the family secrets and the news of the children, in being or on the way, their own affairs of the heart or private family matters.

And very often there were long flirtations with dashing soldiers in the glory of scarlet and gold, with sailors—not so often seen, however— policemen or postmen—and any other male who made the right approach. But always there was a watchful eye on the charge, the swift command to look what they were up to—the warning not to run so fast or fall down— —or to 'come away from those dirty little ruffians and play properly'. This was usually in the park, where children of all sorts congregated at the right time and season and where the usual state of the poorer children was much rougher, dirtier and more ragged than today.

Naturally enough, these urchins always had a great attraction for the cleaner and better off Middle Class children, whose one idea was always to break down the antagonism existing between a cleanly, well-dressed child and the greater freedom of shabbiness and dirt. The poorer children would deride the Middle Class children at first. They would display their lack of manners by protrusion of tongues, and other vulgar actions, and utter rude remarks accompanied by loud and shrill whistlings, most attractive to their better-off and more domesticated little auditors, who longed to find out how it was done and who would have given the world to answer in the same coin. This either led to battle and combat and the descent of Nannie with swirling cape and bows to the rescue—with the flight to a short distance of the poorer children, when their defiance was expressed vocally and sometimes by stone-throwing; or to a joining of forces to play.

39

The natural outlaw in every child drew the Middle Class youngsters to the others, first as spectators to a game, which always seemed more desirable than that which they were allowed to play, and then that gradual yet instantaneous fusion of the two groups which took place quite naturally, if hostilities did not break out.

How long that game or fight lasted depended on how engrossed was Nannie in her male or female friend and their conversation. The battle, if battle it were, was by no means always to the rougher children. The Middle Class young were tough and could give a good account of themselves, be they male or female. For class and manners went by the board when physical violence entered.

In the small matter of calling names and manual expressions of contempt the rougher children were easy victors—for the little Middle Class girls and boys had not the knowledge of invective, vocal or physical. Also, in the matter of throwing stones—there were always stones handy in those days—the poorer children scored until Middle Class schooldays taught them how to do it. The uninformed nursemaids, the more juvenile kind, it is to be feared, were not so particular about this fusion of the classes and would often permit—indeed, join in—games with children whom it was not proper for those little ladies and gentlemen to know.

This was sometimes discovered when Mamma took the family for a walk and undesirable acquaintances rolled up and were recognized. Many a young nursemaid, otherwise satisfactory, got 'her notice', her very small remuneration and her immediate marching orders, for reasons of that kind. For there were children with whom it was permitted to play and children who were outside the pale altogether. Class-consciousness was made apparent at a very early age.

But the real nannies were mostly dearly loved by the Middle Class children and there were broken-hearted scenes when age made a parting necessary. Often, indeed usually, the nanny remained a welcome friend— and often a partial dependent for two generations or more.

The small children would go for their outing in a perambulator or a bassinette. When they got older, there was a mailcart.

There are no mailcarts today, but they were delightful vehicles— if at times a little dangerous. They were based upon what their name implied, the light, two-wheeled vehicles which in those days carried Her Majesty's mails—horse-driven—about the country at a spanking twelve or fourteen miles an hour. They were, of course, not quite the same but of similar model and descent, adapted to the purpose of transporting children. They were light and handy. They had two shafts— you could either push or pull—and they were made either of solid wood, or of lattice- or even wickerwork. There was a seat in front and at the back, which could hold two small children, or one larger one, apiece. They sat back to back and there were straps to ensure safety.

Mailcarts were two-wheeled, a metal-spoked wheel on either side, with solid rubber tyres. When pulled or pushed by a grown-up naturally they tilted backwards. This was all right for riders in the front seat, but those at the back had to rely on the strap to hold them in. In front, where the shafts joined the main carriage—the chassis as it would be today—there were two pieces of iron, like big staples, upon which the mailcart, when standing still, kept an even keel. But care had to be exercised when disembarking the little passengers to make those at the back get out first, for otherwise the cart was liable to tip up backwards, with gloomy results—a thing which sometimes happened when hansom cabs met with an accident.

Still, Nannies and Mammas were careful. Accidents only happened as a rule when the children were playing, and the fall was very short. The children loved the mailcarts. The elder or strongest child, girl or boy, would become a prancing steed between the shafts, driven in style by the younger, who sat in state holding the reins, which were either fastened with harness around the child-horse's chest, or else could be made more realistic by means of a bit, which the child playing the horse actually held in its mouth.

All children loved playing horses—they knew nothing of motor-cars —and the mailcart became a very well-known form of vehicle—even Cinderella's coach after a visit to the pantomime. It was anything from a brougham, hansom cab, to a phaeton or dog-cart. It was often a chariot, either Roman or the more vicious kind said to have been used by Boadicea with the scythe-blades on the wheels. Imagination made it what the children desired.

There was the additional delight, after rain, of pulling it through a puddle and making track-marks—a muddy patch had the same result and was more esteemed, because the child passenger could then put his or her little hand on the tyre as it revolved and get really nice and dirty—a persistent ambition of every child, Middle Class or not. This led to trouble, especially in wintertime, with damage to gloves as a further crime—but was usually considered to be worth it.

Mailcarts were well built. They could be of any colour, though with the children red was the favourite, as being the authentic Royal Mail hue. There was general regret when mailcarts were outgrown—and they mostly went to another and younger family just starting to build up. They seldom wore out. The internal combustion engine made them obsolete and their place today is poorly filled, if the children only knew, by the small but more portable push-chair. What romance is there in that

41

compared with a mailcart? But families are smaller now, and the mail-cart held four. . . .

At home, if the weather prevented outdoor exercise, and at all other times, there was the nursery in which to play. There were also the stair-cases—so long as this did not impinge upon the comfort of the parents on the scores of noise. Sliding down the banisters was a common delight which flat inhabitants know nothing about. The landings were large and spacious and made excellent playgrounds as well.

There were lots of cupboards, deep, dark, mysterious, delightful places. And there was the kitchen. The servant, or servants, always welcomed the children, and if there was a cook—as there so often was—and that cook was motherly, as she mostly was—the children got a good many unexpected, surreptitious and therefore delightful tit-bits.

Romance surrounded the kitchen, and the servants were much-desired playmates. Too many kitchen visits were checked by the mamma, but in this she used her own judgment and her knowledge of her domestic staff. Visits to the servants' bedrooms were also delights, their possessions in the way of jewellery and gewgaws always greatly admired—also the odd little boxes—trophies of holidays and such-like seemed always so desirable to the children's minds.

Servants would tell them stories too, and tales of their own adventures. Sometimes, even, children would be allowed to have tea in the kitchen. It always seemed much nicer than tea 'upstairs'—those kitchens were mostly basements—and there were mounds of hot toast swimming in butter, muffins, or crumpets, and very often cakes such as never penetrated to the higher altitudes of the dining- or drawing-room. The little ones listened to the conversation of the servants and picked up all sorts of information.

The house, so large and limitless to those little people, became something which they knew in terms other than those apparent to a grown-up. The pattern of the graining on a skirting-board, to a child playing on the floor, was a veritable picture gallery—it would contain odd grotesque figures, ranges of mountains and delights of which the grown-ups had no idea. Certain corners of the house were friendly too—others seemed sinister places it was best to hurry by.

Those deep cupboards, too, each had their own character and their contents were examined on wet afternoons, providing an Aladdin's cave of wonders to the enquiring childish mind—marvellous, too, for hide-and-seek, especially those filled with clothes. The vast, spacious landings which were then found in almost every house often had the family trunks stored on them, which made grand places for alpine exercise. And the flat 'leads' outside an upstairs window was a place on which to gaze and to desire as a playground. Small children, however, could not be allowed out there—but surreptitious visits came as the years grew. Every nook of the house and all its sounds became familiar to the children.

And there was a multiplicity of sounds unheard today. Water often provided quite an orchestra. There was some wonder known as 'constant supply' in the earlier times of the period under review, but many houses still relied upon a cistern into which water was pumped from the mains at various times of the day, with queer gurglings and rustlings very pleasant to juvenile ears. Patterns of carpets and oilcloth had their own charms too. Little flat dwellers of today, in restricted space, know nothing of the vast range of experiences open to the children of the House age.

Those small people, as to clothes, were, as previously pointed out, in the Navy. When the little boy discarded his blouse and pleated kilt-skirt for the more manly breeches he remained a sailor. His first blouse was nautical, and that persisted when his kilt became a bifurcated garment. This business of going into what were then always called 'knicker-bockers' usually drew a few tears from the sentimental mother, who saw her little one's babyhood slip from him into boyhood, but the father was always very pleased. He felt that another male master had come into his own, for women never dreamed of wearing trousers then.

But the mother's regrets were shortlived; there was usually another baby on the way to replace that budding into boyhood. The little lad, on assuming the true garb of his sex, wore a sailor suit. He usually shed his short socks if he wore such things with his skirts, but not always. He retained the baggy sailor blouse, fastened round the waist by elastic, his knickers reached to the knee and he wore black stockings. Indoors he had shoes but outdoors nearly always boots. He had a sailor collar just like a real Jack Tar, he had a black silk handkerchief round his neck to mark the mourning for Nelson, he had his stripes or badges of rank on his arm, he had his knickers and, best of all, the pockets in them.

Across his chest stretched a flannel singlet, again like a real sailor. This took a good deal of fixing with lengths of tape, which often came undone if not securely tied. Getting into that singlet—or being got into it—was never popular with little boys. He had a breast pocket, in which nestled a wooden whistle strung by a white lanyard round his neck. As pointed out before, it never lasted long without getting broken or lost—if it was not confiscated first on the score of noise. He was also expected to keep his pocket handkerchief, to him a completely useless and inconvenient possession, in that breast pocket too. He usually lost it with all possible speed.

His little knicker pockets were soon crammed with the rubbish of his treasures, but he had an almost inexhaustible storage space in the fullness of his blouse around his waist and mostly became quite portly on account of the possessions stored therein.

When playing about he wore a pinafore, which he detested. His little shirts were cotton (usually a check pattern) or woollen, according to season and state of health. And underneath it all he wore his great abomination—woollen 'combinations'. Every self-respecting boy detested these. They irked him, they were horribly uncomfortable and scratchy when new or freshly washed—for they seemed always to shrink—and they never got in any degree comfortable until they were considered dirty and taken off—when all the agony began again.

Little girls were as feminine as little boys were masculine. No little girls wore shorts—such a thing was undreamed of. They wore little dresses with plenty of ribbons and bows, and little pinafores over them. They had long stockings too, after the sock age, and lots of underclothing, of which numerous petticoats formed a large part, and outdoors they wore hats or poke-bonnets. They had long hair, either quite ornate and bow bedecked or else pulled back from their foreheads and fastened with a semi-circular comb to keep it in place. Their general effect was one of bunchiness. Sashes were a feature. Many of them, too, were nautically clothed, but of course kilted skirts took the place of breeches—they looked like replicas of their little brothers before they were breeched. There were also what were known as pinafore frocks.

The boys wore sailor hats of straw in the summer—real sailors wore them then—and round blue sailor caps as well. Some mothers inclined to fawn coats and jockey caps, but small boys thus adorned were not popular with the seafaring youngsters of the majority, warm and manly in their little blue brass-buttoned reefers. Some children wore what were called 'brewers' caps', knitted, funnel-shaped affairs with a tassel on the end.

There were also 'best' suits, mostly of the sailor kind, although some children with fantastic-minded mothers suffered almost unendurable shame and disgrace by being decked out as Little Lord Fauntleroys, or being garbed in silk blouses and velvet knickers—which, however much the boy thus attired was admired by adults, never failed to get him scorned by other juveniles at parties or elsewhere.

Little girls had little silk party frocks, often high-waisted Kate Greenaway affairs, with little bag-pockets suspended from their waists, white mittens and black ankle shoes—and looked quite charming.

Some boys had the summer spoilt for them by being forced to wear white sailor blouses, or even white suits, on high days and holidays— which got dirty in the twinkling of an eye, and adorned with smears of various hues of green as soon as a garden was reached. Little boys were expected to wear gloves but despised them. They usually solved the problem by losing so many odd gloves that the parents gave up in despair.

You never saw children in jerseys and shorts, or running about in bathing-dresses; the parents would have expired in horror at the very idea.

But there were toys in plenty—and cheap, too. Mostly they were made in Germany and bore that legend upon them. Thus things German became a joke and a standard of cheapness, which led to the Teutonic race being underrated. But there was great variety within reach of all pockets. Strangely enough, most of the toys were not a bit like, except for certain outstanding features, the things they were supposed to represent.

The wooden horses of the period bore the vaguest resemblance to that useful quadruped. It had a round, barrel body, with a blue paper saddle and strips of red paper as harness. It had a flat neck fixed into its rotund body by a slit, but that neck bore a mane and thus it was a horse. Its four legs were round staves fitted into the flat wooden-wheeled platform on which the noble steed stood. But to the children it was a horse, and a horse then was what a motor-car is today.

You could, of course, get horses and carts which were really like what they purported to be, carts of all kinds, with backs which could be removed, and which tilted up to discharge their loads, hay-carts, dust-carts, brewers' drays, trams, buses and coal-carts—all the variety of horsed vehicles of the time. Those horses were nearly always dapple grey.

There were toy fire-engines which pumped real water and model milk-carts complete with practical churns with workable taps. But they were for the older children mostly. Wooden railway engines were equally primitive, resembling puffing billies—they are still about today, only slightly modified in form. Nearly all the toy models were a generation or two behind their time. Toy railway trains resembled Stephenson's earlier efforts.

The little toy guns were muskets with hammer percussion, still bearing a miniature ramrod, the little toy swords (square at the business end instead of pointed) were of the time of Waterloo, and had sabretaches with them like old-time Hussar blades. Pistols were seldom revolvers (although these did come in a bit later), but single-shooters with lions' heads at the breech end of the barrels into which the child put little pink paper 'caps' which (sometimes) went off with a good report, and often spat little sparks into small eyes. But they produced quite a satisfying smell of gunpowder.

The revolvers, when they made their appearance, were just models, although a few could be obtained which actually had a real action of a six-shooter, with revolving drum and all. These were a great prize.

45

Little girls had dolls. The best sort of doll had a waxen head, and was ornately dressed. She had flaxen hair—dark ones were in the minority —and always blue eyes, be she blonde or brunette. Lucky little girls got dolls which could open and shut their eyes and even say 'Mamma'. But casualties were very frequent, for those little waxen heads were very brittle, and many tears were shed. There were dolls with china heads and very set expressions which were also easy to break. Some better dolls had plaster bodies and jointed limbs, but the majority were material filled with sawdust.

Japanese dolls, with papier mâché or plaster heads, were very popular. And so was the Dutch doll, an amazing creation made entirely of wood, with jointed limbs which could be bent about like a lay figure, wooden faces with rather surprised expressions, although quite cheerful, painted features with round blobs of red on the cheeks, and shiny black painted hair. These did not break but were soon disjointed.

Noah's Arks, a popular toy, were made in varying sizes. The animals were wooden and flat, and really quite difficult to distinguish from each other inasmuch as they were all very much alike, and were coloured red, green or yellow, with no regard to nature at all. You knew the camel by his hump, the giraffe by his neck and the elephant by his trunk, but the others were open to dispute. There was a Noah family, sometimes flat but sometimes round to give them the human touch, standing on little circular green bases, all very much alike, and usually some little wooden Christmas trees with bright green wooden foliage, of which no record can be found in the Old Testament but which may have been meant for the trees discovered by the intelligent dove.

Little boys had bows and arrows, too, for Robin Hood was a popular figure and many a little sister was the target for the blunt, brass-tipped shafts, or forced to play the part of the junior Tell if that story had been learnt and was being enacted.

There were, as became a seafaring nation, boats of all varieties, but very seldom steamboats (a few which went by clockwork could be obtained). But just as Waterloo dominated the military manner, so Trafalgar kept the juvenile navies under sail. There were yachts, luggers, fishing-boats, and lifeboats—all kinds of craft. Bricks abounded—wooden bricks, many of which, when placed together in the proper order, made a picture—the forerunner of the jigsaw; and stone bricks in many shapes with which respectable and imposing edifices could be built. There were no Meccano sets but they had an ancestor in cardboard—the Tower Bridge (very modern then) featured in this form as a model to be achieved. It seldom was.

Many children had rocking-horses, which still persist today, noble beasts whether on ordinary rockers or on stands with quite an elaborate system of rollers and pulleys—with open mouths, arched heads, legs stretched at the gallop and glass eyes which almost flashed. They had real horsehair manes and tails, which usually moulted under little fingers.

There were plenty of mechanical toys, little niggers who ran up palm-trees and brought down coconuts on their heads, millers who ascended mills for the purpose of bringing down sacks of flour on trays and such like. There were musical boxes—the advance guards of the gramophone—of many kinds. Mostly they played by turning a handle and always gave their best results when placed on a looking-glass, which seemed to amplify the sound. There were little round shining metal boxes with a lever at the side, through the top of which a rounded steel spike protruded. You placed cut-out cardboard figures on cut-out metal stands, which, when placed against the needle or spike, which was magnetized, circled round and performed evolutions according to the design of the stand when the lever had been pulled.

And there was the cinema in embryo. This was called the Wheel of Life. It was a black metal circular contrivance, like the section of a funnel but open at the top. It had a slot which fitted on a spiked stand. All round the sides of the receptacle were long narrow slits. Inside it you placed strips of illustrated paper, which bore a series of pictures drawn in various stages of action—just as the film of today operates. These pictures faced inwards. Having got the strip into position you gave the metal tube a smart spin and looked through the slits as it revolved. You were rewarded with the sight of two boxers pummelling each other, men running and jumping hurdles, racehorses doing the same thing, all in the most lifelike manner—it was just a primitive cinema, which then was waiting birth in film form.

The golliwog made his appearance in the 'nineties, and was at once popular. The Teddy bear was not long after and swept the board of popularity, ousting the woolly lambs, the odd-looking animals which jumped when you pressed a bulb and the variety of rubber animals which squeaked through a hole in their stomach—but these held their own with small children, being useful for them to chew in the teething stage. There were little Japanese boxes with glass tops in which appeared a small tortoise whose legs and neck shivered and moved when the box was touched. There were countless toys!

And you got marvellous value for the sum of one penny. For that you could purchase monkeys on a stick, or a contraption of wood and wire down which bits of clay with a feather on each side fluttered like the birds they presumably represented.

Small thin canes could be purchased with china heads, gilded over, representing horses or dogs, the canes being highly coloured in red, green, blue or white. Naughty children avoided these when spending their pence, they were handy for parental chastisement. There were little 'swells', frock-coated gentry on cardboard stands with wonderful heads of hair, and when a piece of cotton was pulled they took off their toppers with quite a flourish.

Five shillings would stock a nursery, so vast was the selection. And at Christmastime the gutters of Ludgate Hill and High Holborn were thronged with men, all selling penny toys in bewildering selection.

Other toys belonged to school age, which will be reached soon—but the juveniles of the days of the sovereign had more from which to choose than his descendant of the paper age, and at much less cost.

Very small children then, as now, slept in their parents' room, but the steady flow of new arrivals sent them to the nursery sooner. There, in a kingdom of their own, they did whatever they liked within reason, with their worldly goods, their picture books, their puzzles—glass-topped boxes with printed spider's web, and a piece of quicksilver which they had to manœuvre into the centre of the spider's body (usually they broke the lid to get at the quicksilver which split into a thousand pieces, was lost for ever, and occasioned wails of sorrow), puzzles with little balls to be rolled into slots and scores of other things. There were annuals like *Chatterbox*, *Little Folks*, and scores of other publications, and always a fat volume of *Mother Goose's Nursery Rhymes*.

And there was usually a toy in the house which the children coveted but were only allowed to handle as a treat, for it was really an 'ornament'. This was a crystal globe set in a marble slab. Inside that globe was a village scene with a church, a little man, and sometimes, in a most unlikely manner, a captive balloon as well, all of course in miniature but highly coloured. The crystal was turned upside down, and—wonder of wonders—the scene changed to winter and a blinding snowstorm was in progress which took quite an appreciable while to blow itself out. This was because the crystal was full of water, and at the bottom lay innumerable specks of some white substance which, of course, when the crystal was inverted went to the top and fell again through the water slowly and softly like real snow.

These were fascinating affairs and can be met with occasionally today in curio shops. They cost five pounds now—they cost a shilling to half a crown then. And they were a treasured reward for good behaviour.

The children were mostly bathed in the nursery in a hip bath before a fine roaring coal fire—the coal was carted up flights of stairs by hand, and the fire was safeguarded by a high fender like a row of railings. Mamma

48

superintended the bathing, even if Nanny did the washing, and Papa would drop in too, if at home.

Prayers were said, a serious and regular function, by the little kneeling white-nightgowned figures (no pyjamas then) and the children were tucked into their cribs. These were of iron with railings round them like roofless cages. The children came to know each bar of the cot separately, and every scratch and mark on it, also the little embossed brass embellishments on the bars and the brass knobs on top. These cots gave a feeling of security and children liked to twist their legs in and out of the bars, which sometimes led to them not being able to extricate themselves, which meant yells and a rescue, often to the accompaniment of slaps.

But when the child was in its cot, had had the drinks of water and all the other traditional delays with which every generation tries to cling to the passing of the day, then there would be a little bedtime story, a final tucking up, a long, lingering kiss; the gas would be turned down until just a blue crescent glimmered inside the frosted globe, the inevitable nightlight lit in its saucer of water—or sometimes to extra delight in a little model lighthouse, then Mamma and Nanny would go downstairs, leaving the door open. . . .

Very sleepy, the little boy or girl would lie in that cosy guarded cot, warm, clean and comfortable, would listen to the murmur of grown-up voices which came muffled by doors and distance from below, watch the shadows which the nightlight cast (in winter the fire as well) on the ceiling, until those shadows became the complete oblivion of sleep or formed fantastic figures in the glorious tumbled dreams of a child, sleeping thumb in mouth, secure in a secure age with a tomorrow before it as clear and bright as the day which now slipped from it into peaceful sleep—a sleep which no siren would disturb, no bomb make terrible— but which would be as sound and as solid as the sovereign which typified the age. . . .

CHAPTER III

'For the Sons of Gentlemen'

LIFE CAUGHT THOSE CHILDREN OF THE GOLDEN AGE, AND TOIL BEGAN FOR them a year or two later than the children of today. Few went to school, even kindergarten, until they were six, and there was no compulsory school age. There was, for quite a lot of them, a period under a governess, who came round to the house and attempted to give them lessons. These unfortunate women were almost entirely without any real qualifications for their jobs; they were not very well educated themselves and had no special talent for teaching. But they were of the poorer though genteel strata who had to earn their living, and the methods for women to earn livings then were not very many if they wished to preserve gentility and not sink in the social scale. Not that a governess ranked very high therein, but she was considerably above a 'companion', and miles above a servant or shop-girl.

There were good governesses, mostly snapped up by the wealthier Middle Class, who could command a respectable fee as things went then, but there were a host of unfortunate ladies who led a dog's life trying to teach unwilling children the rudiments of education. They were seldom able to exert any authority. They were outsiders and the child was on his or her home pitch. The servants were offhand with a governess who came daily, or three times a week, and treated her with a mere veneer of respect and consideration. Children are eagle-eyed in this matter and soon would assess the importance of a mentor provided for their good, and would make her life pretty difficult in the cruel way of childhood.

She seldom got the backing she should have done from the lady of the house, who was apt to attribute lack of progress to the method of teaching rather than the application of the little scholar. But eventually, governess or not, the little girls and boys went to school. They started at a kindergarten, kept as a rule by maiden ladies of severe demeanour but of terrific and unimpeachable character and standing.

The gentility of these schoolmistresses was equalled only by their dignity. Not one in a hundred had any qualification for her job, in which she was just like the governess. But her deportment and her manner would impress the Middle Class Mamma, who was usually recommended to the school by a friend, and she would, as a rule, go in awe of the lady whose income she was going to augment by sending her child to the kindergarten.

These kindergarten proprietresses had all the command which the governess lacked, for, unlike her, they operated at home and the children had to go to them, being thus placed at once at a great disadvantage. Also, this was School, a name which begat some terror and misgiving. The children, however rebellious and troublesome at home, were over-awed by the school in the beginning. When they got accustomed to it, and discovered, as children always do, the weak spots in the system and the chink in the teacher's armour, things were different.

Nine children out of every ten went unwillingly—Shakespeare knew all about that. They were told glowing tales by their parents of what a good time they would have, how they would enjoy themselves and what fun Mamma had when she went to school as a little girl, but scarcely one of them believed a word of it.

The inevitable approach of the fatal day, when the limitless leisure of childhood would end, cast a gloom over the final weeks of their freedom, however resolutely they thrust the idea from them and lived for the moment. At last one morning they awoke with the dreadful feeling that this was the Day. Their mothers, with forced gaiety, got them dressed, gave them a special breakfast, which few of them ate—they knew nothing of the occupant of the condemned cell or they might have indulged in analogies—and they were trotted off. Some shed tears and made scenes, but for the most part they went with set faces, rather pale but with stiff upper lips and with an inward determination to be ill if they did not like it.

They soon found out it was not so bad. They were not taught much because the teachers did not know much, but anyway that was not the idea. They acquired discipline without being aware of it, and they learned to sit still and concentrate on their little jobs. They also had good be-haviour drilled into them—the keepers of kindergartens might not have been erudite but they certainly knew how to make children behave like little ladies and gentlemen.

And those children quite enjoyed the organized games, the attempts to make little patterns and to draw little pictures and to master their A B C. They would take some of their artistic efforts home with pride—and receive terrific praise from their fond mammas and from their papas too, after that parent had been duly prompted. Besides, eventually they got slates to draw upon, by means of which they were able to get nice and dirty, and to create exquisite squeaking noises with the pencils without fear of correction. You could spit on slates too, to clean them—enchanting delight.

51

They were taught the rudiments of reading, from mild little books with tepid illustrations and most unexciting stories, but they felt pride as they eventually spelt and stammered out: "Sam and I went for a run hand in hand. We sat by the big pond. My hat fell in. The wind would not let it come to shore," or announce from print the important fact that "Dan has a big dog and six fat pups." The world of literature was opening before them.

Writing was taught them by means of what was known as 'Pothooks and Hangers'. These were curved marks like fishhooks without the barb and in which the curve was at the top or at the bottom according to whether they were hooks or hangers. Judging by the superior penmanship of the period over that of today it was no bad method. After the first stunning plunge they quite enjoyed the kindergarten.

But Papa and Mamma were having discussions at night when the child was asleep on the question of future education. Both knew and agreed upon the importance of this. A good education was essential. The system of education in the age of the sovereign was a good deal different from that of today. It was, for the Middle Class, mostly a matter of private enterprise. The Middle Class child, being a little gentleman, could not, of course, go to a Board School—all the municipal or State schools were then so designated. Elementary and Secondary Schools had not yet evolved. He must go to a proper school and receive a gentleman's education.

Much depended on where the father had received his schooling. Some, of course, had been to good schools like Merchant Taylors, the City of London, other guild schools, grammar schools and the like. Some had been to public schools, though such places as Eton, Harrow, Winchester and the older public schools were not overrun by the Middle Classes.

But the great majority of the Middle Class fathers had received an education at private schools, run independently of any supervision or inspection, but places which put up a terrific veneer of gentility and scholastic excellence. None of them were schools of any tradition or long existence. They were all run on that system of private enterprise which then permeated the entire nation. There still exist such establishments, but they have changed their ways to a very great extent and they are watched and supervised as well, for the most part. Education has now become a real science. In the days of the sovereign it was far from that, it was haphazard and casual.

The father would write for prospectuses to schools which had been recommended to him by business or personal friends. These would point to their own boys as examples of the excellence of the colleges—that was a word of power, for these privately directed establishments all called themselves colleges, without the slightest justification or real knowledge of the meaning of the word.

If the school at which the father himself had been educated was still in being, it was odds on his boy went there too. But if the father had acquired wealth, he would try and do better for the boy, just as a parent does today. It was largely a matter of luck. What is certain is that the great majority of Middle Class lads, between the years 1890 and 1914, went to private schools, such as abounded in the suburbs of every city and town throughout the entire country.

These schools were mostly large private houses which had fallen into a bit of decay through the loss of social standing of the neighbourhood, or because the original owners had moved up the social scale. They were mostly large double-fronted houses, standing in their own grounds—an acre or over—with a carriage drive up to the front door—one of those semi-circular carriage drives where the traffic, horse or foot or wheeled, entered at one gate and left at the other. Those gates had usually got into disrepair and a general seediness pervaded the whole outfit. But just inside the fence fronting the main road, amongst the shrubs, would stand a large board supported by two uprights, which declared the name of the school and of the proprietor, usually in gold paint on a black background. And it was a hundred to one that it would also bear the legend:

'FOR THE SONS OF GENTLEMEN'.

That was the great point—it was for the sons of gentlemen. These were exclusive Middle Class affairs—for the Middle Class. They were exclusively for the sons of the gentry of the Middle Class. Anything in the nature of 'trade'—retail trade—was not accommodated. The Middle Class professional or business man—even though he might be a bank or insurance clerk or a ledger clerk in the very firm which got its living from supplying those Middle Class retailers with the goods they sold—was a gentleman, within the meaning of the school's understanding and social outlook. However prosperous a tradesman might be, if he kept a shop his offspring would not receive their education with the sons of gentlemen.

There were some strange variants in this complex social system. The sons of builders and house decorators got in, but the sons of the grocer could not. The builder did not keep a shop within the meaning of the term. His was a business—commerce. There were lots of funny things like that.

53

However, there were other schools which did not put up the gentle-men's sons legend but stated that they were out to give a good commercial education, and there the sons of shopkeepers mixed with the sons of gentlemen—Middle Class gentlemen—and absorbed the draughts of education from a common fountain—and nobody was any the worse off—indeed, they usually did better in the end than the more Olympian exclusives of the inner social circle. And many of these schools were better planned and were properly built for the purpose of their use—those which catered for budding gentry seldom were.

The exclusive schools, however, were run by men who could boast a degree, and always had it placed clearly after their name. Nearly all these degrees were genuine, and the proprietors of the establishments had been assistant masters after their university careers, often at good schools, but had the ambition to become headmasters instead of assistants. The headmasterships of public schools being few in number and very hard to come by—even housemasterships in fact—they never-theless attained their desire by either saving enough (how they did it on their incomes is a miracle) or by inheriting enough to allow them to open a school of their own.

They were usually very impressive men with beards—always with moustaches—who had impressive leather-scented and book-strewn studies in which they interviewed the parents, sitting behind a large desk on a very large leather upholstered chair much the worse for wear. They wore black morning- or frock-coats, striped trousers, but, what was far more important, college gown and mortar-board hats. That was the livery of a schoolmaster, just as the blue overall and striped apron denoted the butcher or the shirt-sleeves and white apron denoted the grocer. A headmaster interviewing parents of prospective pupils without a gown would have stood a poor chance of success.

Their prospectuses were models of scholastic completeness. They were all-embracing. Everything would be taught the little man which could be of the slightest assistance to him in after life. He could learn it all—French, German, Latin, drawing, reading, writing, English, arith-metic—he could have Greek if he so elected—literature, science, Scrip-ture (there was an insistence that the moral code of the school in this respect was firmly insisted on, though quite unsectarian, of course)—prayers always opened the school day—and also that he would be fitted for the commercial career before him by being taught book-keeping, shorthand and other mysteries which kept the commerce of the country in motion and in the ascendant. He usually found what he had learned of these at school had to be rapidly unlearned in the office.

There were terminal examinations, of course, but these were not all.

The pupils were coached and entered for the public examinations such as the Oxford and Cambridge Locals, the College of Preceptors and even the mighty Matriculation of the University of London. Successes of past scholars were prominently set forth, and as regards the general success attained by pupils of these schools in such scholastic tournaments, that was given in percentage form. Thus you would read—'College of Preceptors—ninety per cent Pass, ten per cent Honours' or something of that kind.

What they did not state was the basic figures on which those percentages were reckoned. A parent assumed that ninety per cent of the scholars succeeded. He found later it only applied to those considered fit to enter—usually a small number. Some schools—mostly those of the purely commercial kind who made no difference between gentlemen's sons and tradesmen's offspring—entered the boys *en bloc* and really reached a very high standard of examination success indeed.

Sport was always an important matter and great attention was devoted to it. The headmaster would dilate on the spirit of sportsmanship—so purely British, of course—the question of health and all the rest. Sometimes there was even a sports master, but mostly one of the form masters did this. Some even had a moderately well-fitted gymnasium and an instructor who attended two or three times a week.

Some also had a room referred to as the science laboratory, which contained a collection of glass jars and test-tubes and retorts in which once a week a man who knew very little about it gave lessons and did experiments which, by their frequent non-success and more infrequent and unexpected success, delighted the students. The parents, however, were much impressed, for the Middle Class man of the period knew nothing of Chemistry, as this branch of science was usually called.

Some schools even had some cases of stuffed birds, curious crustaceans and odd shells which were referred to in passing as the Natural History Museum. The boys could learn music too, for a music master attended. And French was as a rule purveyed by an unfortunate Frenchman who had a dog's life with the extremely British boys brought up on a tradition of Waterloo and Trafalgar. German was, as a rule, not taught so much, and the teacher was usually an Englishman. Very few boys learnt much of modern languages at school.

They were, however, made to learn freehand drawing, for which ninety per cent of them had not the slightest interest or aptitude. History was a matter of dates and battles, geography an affair of rivers, seas, mountains, watersheds, and capital cities, grammar a matter of parsing and analysing sentences. Euclid was mostly learnt parrot fashion, the little wretches who so acquired it being always completely defeated when a nasty cunning master substituted other letters at the apex or bases of the triangles than those shown in the book.

Literature was, according to the scholastic mind, the reading of a few lines of Shakespeare and then parsing them—which is the reason why Shakespeare is so little honoured or understood in this country—or else committing a certain number of lines to the memory and reciting them without any regard to their meaning, or poetry. Arithmetic, algebra and geometry were all taught by the rule-of-thumb method. No imagination went to the teaching of any subject. No effort was ever made to find out the natural bent or interests of a boy. They were all filled up alike, as if they were a succession of little tin cans.

Terminal examinations would show how much of what they had learnt had been retained, but even then the results were never gone into and a boy encouraged to specialize in the subject in which he shone. From the heights of the education to the dregs, the boys learned all in the same way and acquired just enough knowledge to be of the very slightest use to them when they entered the arena of life. They all came out of the same mould. There were honourable exceptions to these schools, of course, but it is true of the great majority.

But then, you see, they were for the sons of gentlemen and the gentlemen's sons met and grew friendly with the sons of other gentlemen. They wore their distinctive school caps—to their parents' pride—their school blazers, their school ties and their school colours around their straw hats in summer. They were the sons of gentlemen. What more was wanted? Little 'swots' were treated with scorn and violence, no gentleman cared a great deal for knowledge—the 18th century was dying hard and overlapped into the 19th.

The parents watched proudly at the annual school sports when their boys contended for a variety of flashy but worthless prizes. They attended the annual Prize Giving—it could not be called a Speech Day—when the school choir sang traditional songs, certain of the boys sang solos, and a scene from Shakespeare was gone through—one cannot say performed.

After an address by the headmaster, which was usually a blatant piece of advertising, an obscure personality would present the prizes to the successful scholars and the certificates won in open examinations. Then would the hearts of the parents of successful boys swell with pride and their demeanour towards the parents of non-prizewinners be patronising and slightly sympathetic.

Boys who had not slunk on to the platform almost dead with self-consciousness and received a book or a certificate from the distributor of such things would have a very unpleasant few minutes with his father the next day—especially when the school report came in—and receive

56

sad and reproachful looks from his mother. The father usually believed that the fault lay with the boy—the mother was not so sure, she considered bad luck and that attack of measles had something to do with it—but neither ever questioned the system of education, or thought that the fact that it cost only four or five guineas a term—although there were always unexpected extras—had anything to do with it.

Fathers fond of sport would go to the playing-field—most schools had one—and watch their son's prowess at cricket or football in matches with other schools of a similar nature. Some of these matches were needle games, for there was always great rivalry between local schools of equal eminence.

The boys themselves ploughed through their school life as something which had to be done. They took very little interest in what they were learning unless they were of the few that liked acquiring education. And those few suffered for their strange perversity. Most of the boys walked to school, often quite a distance. They walked home again for lunch and back for the afternoon, and then again at night laden with a heavy satchel which contained books for the undue amount of homework in which all schools believed.

That homework was the bane of the Middle Class boy. He loathed it but he had to do it. Knotty points would be referred to Father—who often did not know and took refuge in the statement that they taught things another way when he was at school—but some fathers taught their sons a good deal more than the school did. Boys with retentive memories scored heavily in the subjects which could be learned by heart—and most homework was of this nature. Mathematics were seldom taken home, for there cribs could be used with impunity and adult aid evoked. There was a lot of surreptitious cheating at these schools, and cleverer boys helped the less intelligent, either through the goodness of their hearts or by the application of physical force to their persons.

The journey to and from school was often a considerable adventure. It sometimes happened that a Board School was adjacent, and then there was perpetual war between the sons of gentlemen and the lesser breeds without the law known to the Middle Class boys by the generic term of 'blags'—probably a corruption of blackguards.

Stone-throwing, fights and massed pitched battles were frequent. In stone-throwing victory usually lay with the 'blags', for they were unscrupulous and did not mind if an ill-aimed missile went through a house or shop-window, whereas the sons of gentlemen had some scruples on this point, owing to fear of parental action—they being more easily identifiable by means of their school caps. These caps were often regarded as trophies of war—as scalps might be by Red Indians—and 'blags' who could snatch and retain one were heroes amongst their fellows. The becapped boy fought desperately to retain or recapture his endangered or lost head-gear. There was not only the disgrace, there was the expense of replacement which would enrage the father—who would not be placated by the very legitimate excuse.

The 'blags' caps as well were prized by the small 'gentry', who would carry them about as trophies until a mother found them and burned them in disgust. But in personal combat there was little in it, although in pitched battles advantage lay with the privately educated boys. Those heavy book-filled satchels had their real uses then—they were splendid weapons which every boy knew well how to wield.

Most boys joined company with schoolfellows living in the same direction; this convoy system gave additional security against attack, and also it enabled them to play games. These games were of many kinds, varying as to season. But there was a universal one which was a kind of progressive gutter golf. Both boys, with the heels of their boots, would hack a stone out of the macadamized road—which was the reason for the plentiful supply of ammunition for warfare—and then resort to the gutter. The first boy would throw his stone along it. The second boy would then throw his stone in an endeavour to hit the first one. If he succeeded he had another go, if he failed it was the first boy's turn again. Whichever had hit his opponent's stone the greater number of times on the way home was the winner. It made them dirty but they did not mind that—and it certainly got them home without loitering.

There was a small class of these private schools which laid even greater stress on the matter of gentility than others. These were mostly found in the more select or distant suburbs—places which really did not regard themselves as suburbs at all, and in which resided a fair proportion of retired soldiers, sailors, and professional men, and a good proportion of successful business men. There would be found a school, usually run by a father and son, both ex-university men with degrees, and the son usually a 'Blue' as well. Here the small boys would be groomed in good form as well as educated. There was considerably more good form than education. Discipline was strict and personal chastisement part of the scheme of things—very seldom resorted to in the usual private school.

But in these exclusive academies 'lines' were given as punishment —instead of the usual 'keeping in' to relearn the faulty lesson—and the boys had 'six' on either or both hands for the slightest offence. But they were made to understand their position and to realize what good form meant. They were encouraged to be real little snobs. They were made to speak with an Oxford accent. Rows of small boys would stand up and say 'Cow!' 'Bow!' 'Now!' 'How!' 'How now!' like so many incipient little B.B.C. announcers.

These schools had nothing to do with vulgar commercial educati—on boys went from them to the great Public Schools or into crammers for the Services. All forms of business were regarded as low, and on the question of professions there was considerable discrimination. It is doubtful if the son of a chartered accountant would have qualified in these most exclusive educational establishments for the sons of gentlemen. A boy whose parents were of the theatre was placed in one by his misguided mother, who had considerable difficulty in persuading the principal that the theatrical calling was not only a profession but an art. The boy came home from his first morning at school minus his collar and tie, with considerable damage to his clothing and a nice bruise on his cheek. Yes, he had been fighting, he admitted it. It appeared to him, he said, that it was part of the school routine. Perhaps it was a habit of the sons of gentlemen. He didn't know.

The horrified mother, unknown to the boy, called round the same afternoon, whilst her son was at his lessons, to complain to the headmaster. But, whatever his scholastic shortcomings might be, and they were considerable, that headmaster had a sense of humour. He pacified the mother and informed her that her son's opponent was absent from school that afternoon altogether and he considered she might be proud of the fact. . . .

That boy learnt nothing at that school that he ever remembered except that there was a first-class system of bullying, that small boys were matched against each other at fisticuffs by the bigger boys like so many little fighting cocks, and that every other afternoon was devoted to cricket or football, according to the season, at both of which he became pretty proficient. He did not stop there very long, and he lost the Oxford accent which had been drilled into him with all convenient speed at his next school, which was of a commercial nature. He had to lose it!

Girls' schools were very similar. A girl did not have so much trouble taken about her education as a boy. She was not destined for a commercial or professional career—until much later in the period. And then, if she was to go into the City as a shorthand typist, she learnt those arts at a special training school and not at her private school. There were no schools which proclaimed that they were for the 'Daughters of Gentlemen' or even of ladies—the status of women was thus clearly marked, for those boys' schools never said for 'the Sons of Ladies and Gentlemen' —they referred only to the male.

The girls' schools confined themselves almost to elementals. The scholars got a groundwork of reading, writing and arithmetic. There was a smattering of French, drawing, and even painting, for these were desirable 'accomplishments', and to be accomplished was much better for a woman than to be educated.

Education in a woman made men fight shy of her, and marriage was the zenith of her career, so that would never do. The daughters of gentlemen were taught to behave as such, and were given slight nodding acquaintance with literature—much in the same method and by the same means as the boys—and they were taught fancy needlework and music and suchlike things—more accomplishments. Botany was usually in the curriculum—that was ladylike. Of what is now known as domestic science nothing was attempted. Girls were supposed to know these things instinctively. Or it was their mothers' job to teach them.

The private schools for the daughters of ladies and gentlemen did their best to see that the girls ran true to type, and in this they certainly succeeded. Tomboyism and roughness were checked, good deportment, manners, behaviour and speech insisted on—and every unpleasant matter which she was likely to run up against later was rigorously excluded.

Anything relating even indirectly to sex was taboo in both girls' and boys' schools. Special editions of Shakespeare were used, and the more outspoken sections of the Old Testament were never approached in those Bible readings which passed for Scripture lessons. The system was to read chapters of the Bible aloud, each boy or girl reading a verse in turn. It was simple to count ahead and mark your verse, and then to devote your mind to other matters. But one sometimes found that the teachers were 'on to' this little system as well.

But the girls' schools succeeded in making little ladies of their pupils. They had school colours, too, and, like the boys, there was an attempt to infuse them with the school spirit and the honour and glory of their own establishment, which was only partially successful.

The girls had moderate athletic exercises. They had drill as against gymnastics, hockey as against football—though why hockey is or was ever considered a ladylike game is a matter of conjecture—and sometimes netball. The substitute for cricket was lawn tennis, which was then a very ladylike game indeed. There were prize-givings and sports days like the boys' schools, although not so many girls' schools had sports days.

The question of prizes and their acceptability to the lucky winners varied according to the school. Some headmasters and mistresses selected the prize books themselves, and a boy or girl was liable to find himself or herself possessed of *Travels in the Mediterranean* by a clergyman who had once spent a short vacation there, a copy of one of Sir Walter Scott's less exciting works, a travel book which promised well from the illustrations, but was usually extremely dull as to reading matter, or disappointments of that kind.

Some schools, however, showed better sense and allowed the prize-winning boys and girls to select their own prizes from a catalogue of books—with a limit as to price. Then the children were able to get books they wanted and to treasure them doubly because they had won them. The works they chose were not scholastic or elevating, but as they never read the dull or 'pi' prizes, what harm was done?

There was not much difference in the basic cost of a girl's education from that of a boy's—but there always seemed a lot more extras in her case—'accomplishments' came expensive.

There were also boarding-schools for both sexes. These were conducted on much the same principle and in much the same way so far as education went. The children learnt no more away from home than they acquired at a day school. And although holidays were long, those boarded-out children never quite got the same moral code which the home life provided for the others. No doubt it was a natural compensating balance.

Boys—and girls—soon found out that either their parents were not truthful or that times had changed indeed if the statement that their school days were the happiest days of their lives was to be believed. For most Middle Class children of the Golden Age they were periods of tedium and dullness, only relieved by holidays and by the playground.

There was a playground to every school. Sometimes it was simply the back garden of the house in which the school was held. But sometimes it was quite large and wisely asphalted. It would occasionally have a little enclosure in which were parallel or horizontal bars, and in the case of boys' schools it was always walled. On these walls were chalked the goal-posts for unofficial football, and in season cricket was played with chalked wickets too, which did away with the necessity for wicket-keeper or long-stop. Playground football was played with an ordinary indiarubber ball, so was playground cricket, the latter being the more difficult on account of surrounding windows and the ease with which the ball could be hit over the wall and often lost for good.

A Middle Class boy's pockets in those days were caves of mystery, junk-shops in miniature. In them he carried everything he wanted—and the materials for the games he played. There were always several lengths of string, a knife of doubtful sharpness and repair, often a mass of congealed and fluffy sweetmeats, toffee and the like—the stickier and the dirtier the more it was appreciated—odd treasures of no value at all except for swopping and all the paraphernalia for the seasonable sports. Often, too, an object which had had a passing vogue, like a mouth-organ, a Jew's harp or a whistle from a Christmas cracker.

Swopping was a regular business and a boy's capital in this respect was carried in his pocket, which became his bank. Things of no value in themselves could, by good sales talk, be made to acquire something else equally useless, but none the less desirable, because it belonged to somebody else. A boy might gain considerable wealth if he possessed a bullet which had gathered a legend that it had been used at Waterloo and had been actually cut out of a Frenchman's body.

Boys accumulated rubbish like so many little jackdaws, and the litter was always changing hands, acquiring additional value with every swop, until often its original owner would almost beggar himself to get it back again. This method of barter and fluctuation of values might have been part of that sound commercial education of which the prospectus spoke.

Playgrounds, to the eye just arid spaces, were heaven to the Middle Class boys. There they could run, yell, be rough, fight and wrestle in sheer high spirits with their fellows, make friendships and enmities, indulge in feuds and brotherhoods, play their games, and generally make as much noise as they liked and behave as the natural little savages they were, and as all boys should be.

The playground was an inducement to get to school early so as to have a game, a good thing for school discipline; there was a 'break' in the middle of the morning which gave opportunity for noise and exercise to boys who had been sitting at desks and getting bored and inky for quite long enough. There was another welcome break in the afternoon. After school hours the boys mostly scurried home. Tea—and homework—called. And if they were late the parents got annoyed.

Most boys' idea in class-time was to do as little work as was humanly possible and to have as much surreptitious fun as they could manage. Each boy had a separate desk, or sat at a little row of three. But even if the desks were single they were always next to another and sometimes in rows of several at a time. Every boy always wanted to sit next to his particular friend, and masters would often circumvent this for reasons of work and discipline.

Each boy was supplied with pens, which he mostly chewed to pulp, pencils which he whittled away, a piece of indiarubber which he lost or had sneaked by another boy, and his books. Those books he would embellish by drawings and remarks of his own to outdo the efforts with which previous owners had decorated it. He had pen-nibs supplied, too, of a kind which he found quite unsuitable to his own style of penmanship, but which he had to use nevertheless.

All sorts of games were invented to relieve the tedium of class. There was a system of punches, digs, or pinches delivered suddenly and with a whispered injunction to 'pass it on'. He did that and it went the rounds until some boy of a less Spartan disposition, on receiving the painful experience, would cry out—and be promptly punished. An old rubber gym shoe was a fine thing to throw about when a master's back was turned. It was painful to get it flush in the face. It was joy to see it land on another boy.

One lad, smarting from the reception of such a missile, put it in the stove in the schoolroom. He became a hero, for the smell made it necessary for the class to adjourn to the playground. Boys never 'sneaked' —if they did they suffered untold tortures.

Masters at these private schools mostly became pretty good judges of human nature and knew when to press a question and when to let alone. All of them received nicknames—more or less complimentary—from their form, but always pretended to know nothing about it. It was possible for boys to cut curving tracks in a desk lid, if they had a good knife and unlimited patience—such as a prisoner required tunnelling his way out of the Bastille—down which a marble might eventually be rolled. It was also a point of honour to gouge at least one hole through the desk lid per term, and to carve one's name or initials on the inside.

A school nib, with the twin prongs broken off, usually possessed two sharp horns of metal which became compasses and with which one could scratch little circles all over the place—and which could also be stuck into the posterior of the boy in front when he rose to answer a question. Many boys bore this without flinching and only waited for the chance to return the compliment. It was a process of hardening which was to stand many of them in good stead when the days of security went up in the flames of war.

Really organized fights were infrequent, outside of school stories, and there was, except at the ultra-select schools of snobbery, very little bullying. The form masters, hard-worked and underpaid men of considerable patience—and all longing for the chance to become headmasters themselves—never encouraged tale-bearing and managed to keep a pretty good moral tone amongst the boys. They could, and did, impose impositions. They worked overtime with backward boys who failed to pass in their lessons and had to stop in to do them again.

And some schools had a system of weekly reports—which the boys thought unfair—upon which they had to enter their minor misdemeanours, such as 'Inattention', 'Talking', 'Late', 'Disobedience', or any other crime of which their masters might indict them. These had to be shown to the headmaster and finally had to be taken home at the end of the week for parental inspection—and to make sure that they had been shown it was necessary for the parents to sign them. So they were kept informed of their boys' progress.

E

The boys did not like this but it was an inspired measure for keeping them up to the mark. Ordinary boys had a white sheet, boys who repeatedly transgressed got a blue sheet, and very bad boys a pink one. Boys with blue or pink sheets always tried to contrive that their mothers signed them at the end of the week, and never explained the difference in colour. The mothers, good innocents, seldom noticed the difference or attached any importance to it, but a father was more acute. It was possible by good behaviour to turn a pink back into a blue, and eventually to achieve the blameless white sheet once more.

Crazes would run through schools until the masters nipped them in the bud: odd crazes, usually started by one boy, which would spread like wildfire through the whole school. At one school for the sons of gentlemen there was a perfect epidemic of snuff-taking, which did not last long. At another small squares of cardboard, placed under the thumb-nail and flicked through the air, made out-of-season snowstorms until action was taken.

One wild craze occurred when a boy, whose father was a dentist, put a solution on the market, at a penny a time, which had the desirable property of turning any gold or gilt metal dipped into it into silver. Why this inversion of the philosopher's stone should have been popular is hard to tell, but he did a roaring trade until complaints poured in from parents whose property had been spoiled by this solution of mercury, which the lad had purloined from his father's surgery.

The boy was brought to justice by the headmaster, after some intensive detective work, and was ordered to return all the pennies he had acquired. He could not do it, for they were spent, nor would his father disgorge on his account. He went into juvenile bankruptcy (thus was another commercial lesson learned), and his sixpence-a-week pocket-money was estreated for a whole term to satisfy his somewhat unwilling creditors— whose number, however, assumed proportions vaster than his trade when it was found that cash could thus easily be obtained.

Ill-arranged, ill-administered, and formless as the education was that was thus obtained by the sons of young gentlemen, somehow they took their places in due time in the commercial affairs of their nation, and that commerce continued to prosper and increase until war shattered it—a war not of the Middle Class folks' making in any way. They were patriotic lads and lasses, firmly convinced that theirs was the greatest country in the world and that they were the finest people. They were taught so. It is possible that they were quite right.

But their education did nothing to increase their greatness unless, by its mere haphazard scrappiness, it made them the greatest improvisers the world has ever known. For the British were always that and still remain so. It may be the result of the British system of education, specially directed to that end by that Providence which ordained that they should also rule the waves—or so they sang, and so they believed.

But the times of their school-days they remembered best were their playtimes and the games they played therein, and the toys with which they made their youth a thing of joy.

Before them stretched a world of men and of endeavour getting closer and closer every day. They recked little of this in their school-days, except to realize that grown-ups seemed to have a good time and that they wished they were grown up to participate therein. They felt, too, that it was good to be British. They were quite right in that case. They were right in both cases, for those schoolboys and girls of the 1890's and early 1900's were to participate in their youthful adult state in the Golden Age when it was good to be alive and better still to be British. They did not know it, but it was so, and they played their games and enjoyed themselves whilst facing what they thought would be an unclouded future—with the golden sovereign for its glowing sun.

And it cost so few of those sovereigns to pay for their education.

CHAPTER IV

The Games they Played, the Toys they Loved and the Sweets they Ate in School-days

WHEN LITTLE BOYS AND GIRLS LEFT THE KINDERGARTEN FOR A REAL school they also left the Navy. The day of the sailor suit was past and done with, more mature and civilian attire was assumed. The romance of youth was being shed and the garments of everyday life were being assumed.

It did not make so much change for the girls as for the boys. Their dresses were then still essentially feminine but a little more austere, not so many ribbons and sashes—they became more workmanlike. Some girls' schools had almost a uniform—a dark blue overall bodice and skirt which was worn over a white blouse, with straps over the shoulders. The stockings were brown or black and the hats were sometimes school hats with the school badge—they could be any colour but mostly of sober hue, or else a little turban. The older girls had more freedom in this respect, but were not allowed to be too dressy or fluffy—at least during school hours.

The boys went into Norfolk jackets. These were the ancestors of the sports coats of today, but they were worn buttoned up and they buttoned almost to the neck—often with a little waistcoat underneath. They had pleats over each shoulder running the full length of the coat and a belt round the waist. This belt was not fixed on the coat, but was loose, going through pleats to keep it in position. It frequently got lost, to the detriment of the boy's appearance. But then, no self-respecting boy gave two hoots for his appearance. They also wore little lounge suits, very much like their elders but not subject to changes of fashion. The collar was always an Eton collar of starched white linen—it soon lost its whiteness and its starch. This could be worn inside or outside the coat—and if inside it lasted longer, for boys were rough and played rough games with plenty of wrestling and scrambling. The linen Eton collars soon became casualties and suffered grievous harm.

When the boy got into his teens he also wore a dickey—but many boys eschewed these and just let the front of the shirt do, for the openings of the Norfolks or the waistcoats were never extensive. The tie was either a ready-made bow, which clipped over the collar-stud and was always getting pulled off, or an ordinary tie, such as is worn today, with a sailor's knot. Boys took very little heed of what they wore but they were shy of bright colours. Knickerbockers fastened below the knee, either with clasps or straps which usually got broken, but the boys didn't care.

Some boys were made to wear Eton suits. They were unfortunate, for their schoolfellows had a very vulgar name for such attire and a habit of kicking the place left exposed by the short jacket. Also, Eton suits did not go very well with school caps. But the boys did not worry about that. Woe betide the unfortunate lad whose mother made him wear anything conspicuous. He was fair game for the conservative lads, whose one idea was to look as much alike as possible and who had no regard for their clothes at all.

Overcoats were of the ordinary kind, but mackintoshes were heavy and smelt strongly of rubber. Also they always had a cape, with loops inside to support the arms, though why, nobody knew.

Boots—and heavy boots—were the general footwear. Boys were always hard on boots. Economical parents of boys who wore through a new pair of boots in a few days—it could easily be done—were sometimes reduced to having steel plates fixed on the soles—the name of which was 'Blakeys'. The boys did not mind. These curved plates were soon worn thin, because they made sliding possible on pavement or asphalt in mid-summer and the boys enjoyed that. They made every boot so adorned as though it were fitted with a skate.

Scarves or mufflers were regarded as effeminate. If a boy was made to put one on when leaving home it was in his pocket as soon as he was out of parental sight. He might reassume it just before he got home—or he might forget it altogether and suffer reproach. Gloves were absolutely taboo even in the very coldest weather.

In summer most boys wore white flannel cricket shirts, their knicker-bockers—or their trousers when they reached the long-trouser age—being supported by elastic belts of their school colours, which fastened in front by means of a metal catch in the form of a snake.

When a boy passed from knickerbockers into long trousers it took him at least a week to live down the change at school. Shoes were some-times worn in summer—even rubber plimsolls—but always black, except when on the cricket field, when white was considered the right thing. All boys wore flannels for cricket—cricket was a very serious game and the National Game with a vengeance, which demanded proper respect and fitting attire.

Boys had 'best suits' for Sundays and other high days. Some parents insisted on Eton suits for this, and some wicked and thoughtless papas and mammas—mostly mammas—also insisted on their sons wearing a 'mortar-board'. These were the sort of caps worn by schoolmasters and students at universities. The poor little wretches condemned to such headgear were terribly ashamed of it, and dreaded going out in case they met boy friends. Nothing would happen at the moment of meeting, of course, but if the news reached the school—as it was bound to do—revenge would be taken.

Some lads, who sang in church choirs, had to wear them on Sundays as part of a uniform. They escaped disgrace on that account, and also because all choirboys were the toughest possible specimens—it seemed to be a necessary attribute—and well able to look after themselves. But boys who were not in the choir and still condemned to wear such truly diabolical things were little pariahs through no fault of their own. The idea of the parents was that it was genteel. It was just plain rubbish, snobbery and nonsense for which the unlucky boys paid in full.

Some boys, of Scots or partial Scots ancestry, were forced into Scots caps, the ribbon tails of which were always left in the hands of justly affronted Sassenachs, and a boy in a glengarry or tam-o'-shanter was fair game for instant and brutal assault from the all-powerful English.

No boy ever carried a comb in his pocket, or a nail file. He would have been half murdered if discovered using either.

If school was endured by the majority and liked by the few, its rigours were lightened by the games possible to play there, on the way to or from, and on holidays. Those games, and the articles demanded by them, were of great variety, and they were also seasonal.

The year was divided, of course, into two main seasons, those devoted to cricket and football—but those were the organized games. There were other personal pastimes, all of which had their seasons too. These seasons were adhered to strictly, and a boy would no more have played them out of season than his father would have dreamed of shooting partridges in May or pheasants in July. A lot of these games and these playthings seem to have died out, more is the pity.

Today the children of the age of science do not have the same simple wants. They demand mechanical toys—or such as they can get in the days of austerity—and the most popular seem to be models of various methods of transport, with the highlight on motor-cars and aeroplanes. They seem to have abandoned the age-old games of their grandfathers which demanded much physical effort, skill, violent exercise and often a considerable spice of danger. And the children of the sovereign age seemed to play their games more scientifically than the children of the age of science —which is strange.

Games stuck firmly to their seasons. There was (for obvious reasons), a 'Conker' season, a Top season, a Hoop season, and a Marble season.

During each of those periods the particular pastime in vogue held predominant sway. Tops and marbles are seldom in the streets today and hoops are a great rarity. Yet under the sovereign they were everywhere.

Boys still collect 'conkers', but in the older days they did it with a set purpose. They bored a hole in the nuts, through which was inserted a string, heavily knotted at the end to keep the conker in place. Then tournaments resulted. Two boys faced each other. One held his conker suspended, the other smote at it with his. This they did in turn until one of the conkers smashed to pieces. Each of them had declared beforehand how many other conkers his had smashed. The victor then added the score of his victims' victories to his tough nut. The great thing was to own a conker which had won more victories than anybody else's.

Particularly strong conkers, which lasted through a season, were kept carefully to renew their triumphs the following year. They were looked after with loving care. Some boys could boast of chestnuts with Homeric scores of victories—there was a thousand-and-seventy-niner which was never broken, and which its owner treasured until he was middle-aged —when it got lost, to his despair. That was a true 'conqueror'—the real meaning of 'conker'.

Conkers was a boy's game, girls never played it, but in the early autumn every street and almost every corner had its pair of duellists. It may be that children play less in the streets than they did and that the game still survives in its older form in playgrounds, but one seldom sees a boy flourishing a stringed conker nowadays.

Hoops were autumn favourites, too, and were common to both sexes, with a difference. Girls bowled wooden hoops which were driven forward by being repeatedly struck with a short stick, which also guided the hoops when placed against its side to alter its course. Boys disdained wooden hoops. They bowled iron ones by means of a 'skimmer', an iron hook in a wooden handle with which they skimmed the hoop along—not striking it but propelling it forward by continual pressure. Iron hoops made a noble noise as they rushed along, and when they fell down they would vibrate and make a most satisfying din—and all boys delight in noise.

Girls would get inside their wooden hoop, place it against their waists, and by wriggling their bodies make it revolve round and round themselves. Boys did the same with theirs to the detriment of their clothes in muddy weather and often to their toes and insteps if the hoop fell. Iron hoops were very unpopular with old gentlemen, who frequently received them, driven at speed, in their waistcoats when coming round corners, and got winded and covered with mud as a result. They would hurl them away with imprecations, but the boys would recover them when the enemy had passed. Hoops gave splendid exercise.

Marbles belonged to the spring. Nobody bowled hoops then, or played conkers, it just was not done. There were many ways of playing marbles and there were many kinds of marbles too. There were the common shiny earthenware ones, of different colours but somewhat sombre of hue, called 'meggies'. These would be placed in a circle drawn with chalk on the pavement, at wide spacing, and contestants would flick other meggies at them from thumb and forefinger. Those they succeeded in driving out of the circle were their prizes, but the boy who risked his marbles in that circle claimed all ill-aimed meggies as his.

There was another game of incipient gambling called 'The Lucky Board'. This was a small wooden board, or piece of cardboard if stiff enough, of an easily portable size, at the bottom edge of which were cut little arches of varying height and width. Over each arch was written a figure which showed its value. The board was leaned against a wall and the competitors stood at a mark. They rolled their meggies against the board. Those which did not penetrate an arch belonged to the board's proprietor. Those which entered an arch were returned to the marksman, together with the number of meggies over the marked aperture—the value rising as the size got less. It worked out fairly well for everyone, but naturally the odds were on the 'banker'—it was a mild form of roulette.

There were marbles known as 'alleys'. These were of glass with very pretty spiral designs in colour inside them, often intricate and always charming. These were, of course, of special value. Some were the same size as meggies, some as large as a small rubber ball. They also had a gambling or game-of-skill value. The owner of an 'alley' placed it against a wall and ordained a mark—the larger the 'alley' the farther the distance, from which those who wished t compete had to roll their meggies. The first boy to hit it won it. But it was wonderful how rich in meggies the owner of a good alley became, and with what dexterity, speed and skill he picked up the missing meggies in their flight, because more than one boy competed at a time. The boys intent on the prize might—and did—miss the alley, but the owner never lost a single item of his swiftly rolling harvest. A boy who had bankrupted himself in his attempts to hit the alley could claim 'goings back'. The fortunate owner would concede a few meggies to continue the game—and mostly get them back as well.

Plain glass marbles, such as were then found acting as stoppers in bottles of ginger-beer and lemonade, wee called 'glarnies' and eagerly sought for. These glass marbles hermetically sealed the necks of the bottles. They were pushed down the neck by a specially designed wooden instrument until they were held by the grooves at the base of the bottle's neck, when the refreshing liquid could be poured out or, much better, drunk direct from the bottle. There was no way of getting these glarnies unless the bottles were smashed. Despite the fact that small sums of coppers could be collected from returned bottles, very few of them ever found their way back to the makers during the marble season.

Tops were of the springtime too. There was a large variety of 'peg-tops'. Some were of plain wood with a long iron peg, others of lovely shiny boxwood, which cost more money. Boys performed miracles of top-spinning. They would wind the string—cord was better—round the top, which was grooved for the purpose, throw it to the ground with an over-hand jerk, the end of the string remaining between their fingers, and then, not content with making it spin, would entice it on the palm of their hand to continue its revolutions. They would loop the string round the peg and draw it along, still spinning. They would jerk it in the air and catch it on their hand, still revolving merrily, and put it on the ground again to continue its spin there. By giving it a sideways instead of an overhand jerk when releasing the string they would make the top travel quite a distance—and still revolving merrily. It was a real game of skill and science.

There were whip-tops. These were spun by winding the lash of a small whip round the top and then pulling it away smartly, which made the top spin. It was kept spinning by being whipped. The whip-tops were squat affairs with a broad, blunt peg as against the sharp tapering one of a peg-top. They were coloured, mostly green or red, whereas peg-tops were of natural wood.

There were games with tops too, apart from the joy of spinning them. The element of a gamble was never far away in boys' games. A boy would spin his top, his rival would 'peg' his at it. Experts could so throw their top that it would split its rival and continue to spin. The split tops had their uses. They were placed in a circle like the marbles, and boys would spin their tops at them. The broken pieces driven from the encircling chalk line were the spinner's prize. If the challenger failed to remove a certain agreed number by a certain number of throws he forfeited his top.

Girls, as a rule, were unable to spin tops, nor were they encouraged to try. But they had a game of their own called 'Four Stones' which required great skill and dexterity, to say nothing of quickness of eye and fingers, and could be played either with ordinary stones or cubes specially designed and bought for the purpose. You had to pick up a stone, throw it in the air, and whilst it was ascending pick up another and do likewise, until all the stones were in the player's hand and in the air in whirling succession, like the little balls the jugglers use. It demanded very great skill.

Boys had catapults, mostly home-made, and pea-shooters—long tin tubes with a mouthpiece at the end, through which dried peas were shot out of the mouth at passers-by—mostly at people in carts or on bicycles or at a similar disadvantage. Pea-shooters had a high nuisance value and were consequently greatly esteemed. There was Hopscotch, a pavement game, very hard on footwear. Skipping was for girls, in which boys seldom joined. Tipcat and bat, trap and ball seem to have vanished entirely. Both demanded a good eye and much skill.

Many of the communal games remain today, but they seemed a good deal rougher in the days of the sovereign. There was a game called 'Widdy', a kind of combined touch. The boy who was 'He' joined his hands together—and must not unclasp them until he had claimed a victim. Then the two linked hands and pursued the others. Each boy captured joined the human chain, which grew and grew in width, the capturing being done by the two boys on the extreme ends. The pursued would try to break the chain. Getting behind the line of linked boys, they would hammer with their fists on those clenched hands in an endeavour to make them disengage. If this succeeded, those who were still free had won, and the game started all over again. It exists to-day, without its violence as "Chain-He".

There was Jibby-Jibby-Knacker, a most extraordinary game at which you could—and often did—get hurt. That was part of the fun in those days. A boy stood with his back to the wall. Another boy bent down, facing him with hands on either side and made a back, as in leapfrog. The next boy took a flying leap on to that bent back, and if he failed to bring down the bender he joined on to him, bending himself with his arms holding the boy in front. Boy after boy would come thundering on to those backs and, whilst they held, the line lengthened. It held until the weakest link broke and a boy fell. Sometimes it was so strong that a couple of dozen boys would be bending and other boys were seated on their backs, trying to knock them over—for this was permissible when the line got too long. In that case, the boy with his back to the wall shouted 'Jibby-Jibby-Knacker, all fall down', and everyone did so promptly, rain, mud or fine weather. A difficult game to describe but extremely popular. It required considerable physical endurance. No wonder the generation so bred stood up to trench warfare.

Boys played Prisoner's Base, or Chevy Chase, and they played 'Rounders', from which baseball originally sprang. There was a game called 'Policemen and Thieves' which was really an all-in free fight, with nothing barred. There was 'Flying the Garter', an elaborate form of leapfrog. A boy 'made a back' and another boy leapt over him from a mark. The 'back' boy moved to the spot where the leaper had reached the ground. The next boy had to attempt the leap from the original mark. The boy who made the back got further and further away from the leaping-mark until one, two or three hops were allowed until the leap was achieved. The first boy to fail had to make a back in his turn. It was excellent exercise but a bit trying for the boy bending, who was often knocked over.

There was Egg Cap, too. A boy laid his cap, irrespective of the weather, against a wall. Other boys threw a ball at it. If it went in the cap, the owner thereof seized it and hurled it at the boys, who, as soon as the 'egg' (i.e. the ball) was in the cap, flew for their lives. The boy who was hit—and usually it stung him up pretty well—then became the owner of the nest and the hurler of the ball. It could also be played with many caps, in which case the owner of the cap into which the egg fell was the thrower. After a lapse of some fifty years it is difficult to remember exactly how the game ended. It probably went on until everyone was tired—or the bell rang for school. But it was an excellent opportunity for dashing about, yelling, throwing straight and getting a little hurt, all very desirable things to the boys of the Sovereign Age.

Being a boy was quite a strenuous affair in those days. The girls played much gentler games, for they were always expected to be little ladies—that was their main training. Sometimes a girl would attempt to join in with the boys—sometimes a sister was allowed to do so in the garden at home. But girls so doing were at a severe disadvantage. The boys discouraged them—often with physical violence—and always despised them. And the girls regarded the boys as nasty little outsiders.

There were special outdoor joys, too, invented by friendly souls of great understanding who appreciated every boy's desire to be a nuisance and an enemy of society—for there could have been no other reason.

There were things called "Slap-Bangs". These were little twisted packets of pink or blue paper, filled with tiny fragments of flint and some mildly explosive matter. When flung down smartly on the pavement they went off with a most satisfying bang and would startle peaceful pedestrians behind whose backs they went off, for these folk lived a much more serene and quiet life and knew not the sound of motors back-firing or the joys of air-raids.

But the best use for a slap-bang was to throw it just behind the back tyre of a bicycle. It was odds on that the rider would jump off with a curse under the impression that he had a puncture, whilst the boy who was the cause of it, filled with delirious joy at his success, would survey the scene, hands in pockets, with a detached air of innocence. Cyclists were fair game. Any attempt on their part at nonchalance, such as riding with only one hand on the handlebars, or none at all, would be greeted with shouts of 'Any old iron?' or 'Monkey on a grid-iron.'

73

Boys could also obtain little leaden receptacles, in two halves, kept together by a piece of string and elastic. Between the two halves a pink percussion cap was inserted, and these things were let drop on the pavement behind heavy old gentlemen, with eminently satisfactory results to the boy, who had, before the old gent recovered from his shock, plenty of time to conceal the instrument of torture and to assume a wondering air and stare around for the cause of the unwonted sound.

Bits of leather on the end of string, made like suckers, could be made to adhere to wet paving-stones and come off with a grand 'plop'. Sometimes, if the paving-stone was loose, it would come up too! So much the better for the boy. The inventors of these delectable toys were regarded by the boys as angels in disguise—if they ever thought about the matter.

Cricket was played in the street with lamp-posts as wickets—and windows were broken. Football took place all over the road. Traffic in suburban thoroughfares was sparse and slow. Bad boys delighted in fastening the knocker of a front door to a garden gate (if the distance was short), which was productive of much glee and confusion, whilst ringing bells and runaway knocks were splendid adventures.

Boys would pursue horse-driven vehicles with suitable backs and, jumping up, would enjoy a surreptitious ride. Other boys, either not so venturesome, or errand boys with work to do—but in no great hurry to do it—would yell to the driver to 'Whip behind'—which he would do with gusto until the illicit rider was either dislodged or thought he had gone far enough. This cannot be played with motors, and at any rate the state of traffic today would make it sudden death.

The boys of the Sovereign Age had plenty of toys too. The prime favourites were toy soldiers. Some of these were splendid, some not so good, but the boys loved them all. The lead soldiers made in Germany betrayed a lamentable ignorance of the regiments of the British Army and its uniform and accoutrements—strange in such a military nation, given, as was believed, to persistent espionage—or perhaps it was just bluff? These German articles were usually in profile, thin and soft, only recognizable as members of the British Army by reason of their red coats. They wore pickelhaube helmets, but then our own Line Regiments had headgear not unlike it. They stood upon green slabs of lead which usually got broken off.

But the British-made article—manufactured, suitably enough, by a firm called Britain—were as magnificent as our own little—but entirely invincible, so we believed—Army itself. They were proper little models of the men, properly armed and properly uniformed. Almost every regiment was obtainable—horse, foot or artillery, even military bands. The Highlanders were, with their native pugnacity and *élan*, usually depicted in the act of charging the foe—in full regimentals, bearskins and all. The English soldiers were far better disciplined. The cavalry made a brave sight; leaden Household Cavalry usually rode upon prancing steeds. Lancers in their glorious uniforms could move their sword arms and actually point their pennoned lance. The officers' chargers were, as a rule, in a high state of curvetting, to denote who they were. Sometimes, if the officer were Hussar or Lancer, he sat sideways as if turning round, a hand either end of his saddle, watching the behaviour of his men.

There were whole batteries of Artillery—Horse and Field, and a great joy was the Mountain Battery, complete with mules, men, and a little gun which was carried by the mules in sections and which could be put together and actually fired. There was no explosion, but the boys imagined that. The discharge was done by placing a thin strip of lead—like the refill to an 'ever-sharp' pencil—down the muzzle and releasing a kind of upright trigger. The missile travelled quite a distance. Soldiers in encampment could be bought in little boxes, with quite a theatrical back-cloth behind them. Colonial troops, especially the black-faced West Indian Regiment, with their white turbans and red zouave jackets, were very popular, and so were Bengal Lancers.

These British soldiers made by Mr. Britain (who invented the life-like hollowed figure, as against the German flat leaden slab, in 1893, and took most of the trade away from Germany), were sold at the amazing price of 1s. per box—of eight infantrymen or five cavalrymen, an amazingly cheap price for an amazingly good article, which boys justly treasured. They were all hand-finished and coloured. You can still get them today—but the price is more.

Boys amassed quite an army and played splendid games. Forts were obtainable—made of wood—but they always looked more like Rhenish castles than real military fortifications of a modern nature—as modernity went then.

Yet this was not—and is not—a military nation at heart, despite this delight in toy soldiers. There was one other type which must be mentioned. He was a replica of the stolid, splendid Horse or Lifeguards-man who sat—and sits—on guard outside the Horse Guards in Whitehall. But the leaden soldier was, like his human original then, always in full uniform. He even had a model sentry-box complete. He sat on his horse, looking superb. But the great thing was that he could be taken off it! He was affixed by means of a spike of lead which was fastened to his seat and which fitted into a slot in the horse's back. Unmounted, he was not a very gallant figure, with this tail-like appendage to cope with, but he carried out the true cavalry tradition by being extremely bandy.

Boys of a mechanical turn of mind—and there were plenty, because this is a nation of engineers—had plenty of mechanical and clockwork toys. Some were fine accurate models, much as they are today, allowing for differences in design, but cheaper toy trains (again made in Germany) were of a Continental type, and unfamiliar, the engines having extremely long funnels with serrated tops. They were as unlike the splendid British trains and engines as the alien-made troops were to the British-made varieties.

All these toys were cheap—dirt cheap as compared with those of today—and of much finer workmanship and finish. The children of the Golden Age would have thought little of the austerity toys which have had to satisfy children of the Second World War. But neither they nor their parents ever realized their luck. How could they?

Girls had their dolls, their dolls' prams and other feminine toys. They also took much joy in coloured beads, of which one penny bought a tremendous quantity and variety. They would, with needle and thread, make long strings of them—necklaces, bracelets, even rings—and they made a pretty show. Sequins were also in great demand for a similar reason.

Boys were great collectors—it also involved swopping. Stamps were in most demand for collections, although butterflies and birds' eggs were also very popular. Girls collected and pressed flowers and ferns, gold and silver paper and bits of ribbon.

Seashells had a vogue as well, both for girls and boys. And boys liked an aquarium, which started with a couple of goldfish and received additions in the form of newts, tadpoles—which grew into frogs and escaped, to the horror of the household—and even leeches—which killed the rest of the livestock. Many boys kept white mice, and went in for pets like rabbits, pigeons and doves. Girls would delight in a caged canary or budgerigars, which were called love-birds. More households than today boasted a parrot.

All these things were possible because of the larger houses and accommodation. They have little or no place in flats.

In those glorious days of cheapness, when rations and coupons were undreamt of, the children could—and did—let themselves go in the matter of sweets. The purchasing power of a penny was tremendous. A farthing was a common coin and bought quite a lot when sweets—and good sweets—were four ounces a penny. You could get four different lots of sweets, an ounce each, for your penny, and no shop looked askance at a halfpenny or a farthing, either.

There were millions of varieties of sweets. There were even cheap sweets which could be bought at the inconceivable amount of eight ounces for one penny, in small, cheap shops. But there were sweets then, extremely popular with all children, of which their little modern counterparts know nothing. Coconut chips, thin slices of coconut glistening with sugar, coloured pink or white, were very sweet, very satisfying, and took a long time to chew, even if they proved indigestible. But most children were as strong as ostriches in this respect.

'Everlasting sticks', made of some form of pliable toffee and brown in colour, lived up to their name at the rate of four a penny. Toffee in all forms, not broken up and wrapped in paper as is done today, but in big solid slabs, which you broke yourself by means of hammering it on a railing or wall or battering it with a stone; almond rock; Everton toffee, all sorts of toffee—treacle toffee with figs—or at any rate fig-stones—in it; bull's-eyes, humbugs, brandy-balls—very strong, large and hot—and aniseed balls which could be sucked for hours and which yielded a small seed in the middle as a last tit-bit.

Liquorice was made in many ways: in thick sticks, in little twisted ladders, in long strips like ribbons with a pattern on it, which could be torn again into thinner strips, and there was liquorice root which made face, hands and especially mouths most delectably dirty. No good eating that in school, for detection was inevitable—but eating sweets in school was a stolen and therefore double joy. Acid drops and acid tablets of tremendous strength and which really blistered the mouth, boiled sweets of all kinds, some in the shape of gold and silver fish—and fruit-drops, which contained pear-drops, usually red with a most pungent taste and a most penetrating and dreadful stink as well.

There were 'Locusts'—what they were really made of no boy ever knew, but it was firmly believed to be the food eaten by the Israelites during their wanderings (which, it was considered, could not have been so dreadful in consequence)—monkey-nuts (now called peanuts, but always then bought in the shell, which made a fine mess) and some little wrinkled brown nuts called Tiger Nuts, with a very white, very sweet and palatable inside—no nasty shells, you ate the whole thing. Rose fondants for those who were epicurean and cream fondants as well; pralines, known to children in those days as 'satin cushions'; toasted coconut caramels; paregoric lozenges for those who liked a dash of medicinal taste—and some boys bought little tins of Skuse's Herbal Tablets, cocoa nibs, little soft round sweets of coconut paste—white, pink or yellow on one side and chocolate-coloured on the other—delicious little sweets which weighed light and gave plenty for the penny; lime-juice tablets; gelatine lozenges—beautiful and sticky as well as appetizing, which could be used to stick things with when half eaten, and were placed on the forms when boys stood up with excellent results later on, when a sitting posture was assumed and it was time to rise again.

Girls liked 'Cupid's Whispers', round, pink, white or blue sugary sweets with little sentimental mottoes on them. Economical girls and boys who had little to spend and wanted a lot bought 'broken chocolate' —of which a really vast quantity could be obtained for one penny. Its slight staleness and its brokenness did not matter to them at all.

There were all sorts of varieties of chocolate and chocolate cream— not so many perhaps as in later and between war days, but quite enough, and also very cheap. A good solid slab of chocolate, which could be either split into four—grooved for that purpose—or chewed like a sandwich, was the most popular kind. Sherbet was also a favourite—it was more often eaten than drunk, and gave a very pleasant sensation as it fizzed in the mouth. Some children speculated in 'Hundreds of Thous- ands'—and not only ate them but melted them in water and drank the sickly result with pleasure and little harm. There were sugar sticks— which were considered babyish—barley sugar—which was not—and a confection known as sugar candy, which looked like large irregular blocks of crystal in the rough state and was just as hard.

The average amount of pocket money was 6d. per week.

Children were, of course, warned that eating sweets would spoil their teeth. They cared little, nor was there so much care of the teeth then as now. Most boys dodged a toothbrush and only used it on suffer- ance, making a fine mess with the camphorated chalk, or the pink carbolic powder in tins which was not improved by constant dipping of wet brushes—which were the usual form of dentifrice then in use. Boys did not worry about their teeth or, indeed, any form of cleanliness, yet teeth were just as good then and lasted often much better and longer.

Children, too, seemed to have better eyesight—or perhaps not enough care was taken—for a child in spectacles was not a common sight, and children—or at least boys—so adorned had a poor time of it, being called 'Old Four-Eyes'—in that pleasant cruel childish disregard of personal feelings.

Christmas-time was eagerly looked forward to. There was a much more widespread belief in Father Christmas, and children hung up, not only their stockings, but pillow- and bolster-cases, and were, amongst the Middle Classes, delighted and transported with joy at finding that Father Christmas had taken the hint and filled them royally with toys and sweets.

Christmas-time was the great family gathering, a time of goodwill, of the temporary healing of family feuds—soon to break out again— and of tremendous Gargantuan unrestrained eating and drinking. There was no shortage of food in those days: enormous turkeys twirled round before the kitchen range on the clockwork meat-jacks, great joints of beef, geese, pigeon-pies, pheasants, mince-pies—rich soups made out

A Middle Class wedding of the Golden Age. A real Middle Class family poses for a picture of an event which starts another Middle Class home

The City in the days of the sovereign. The children are probably on a sight-seeing trip

Hyde Park Corner in "The Season"—a summer scene in London

of proper stock, and the Christmas puddings! These were made at home, being mixed in a vast earthenware tub, and the children were always allowed to stir it. They were given handfuls of sultanas, raisins, almonds and currants—and helped themselves surreptitiously to more. Christmas-time was gorgeous and has always been the children's time. Crackers—called bon-bons then—were supplied in quantities, with toys, jewellery and paper caps inside and mottoes which delighted the girls. Christmas was a true feast and a wonderful time. And after tea there would be a darkened room and Snapdragon was played.

The children, who had been delighted with the conflagration of the Christmas pudding by means of brandy, now got another thrill. Into the dark room came one of the family draped in a white sheet bearing a large soup plate well filled with brandy which burned with a blue flickering unearthly flame, making the bearer's face ghostly—if not ghastly—and sending a thrill of horrified delight down the little ones' spines. Then, when the burning dish was placed on a table, you picked the sultanas and raisins out of the flames and ate them when cool enough. Scorched fingers were just part of the fun.

There was dressing up and games, and being allowed to stay up late—and finally bed in a condition of exhausted joy of repleted excitement. The powders and doses next day were well worth it—and you started all over again.

Every child tried to keep awake to see Father Christmas, none ever succeeded. But the morning showed that he had called, for there were the toys! Some fathers even had proper costumes for the part in case of detection.

Christmas then was led up to by stages, each increasing the child's excitement; and anticipation rose as November turned into December. The shops broke out in a rash of Christmas—the windows had special displays, festoons of coloured paper, holly and mistletoe were everywhere, Christmas trees, ablaze with little coloured balls and candles, and glittering with frost of ground glass, made the season indeed a festive one. It was worth a pilgrimage to the West End to see the sights. There was always a wonderful show in the window of Fullers' in Regent Street, where a scene, often a landscape, was displayed—it might be a railway station under wintry conditions, or something like that, but very well done and most attractive to children, who had a traditional belief that everything there was made of sweets.

All the big shops ran Christmas bazaars especially for the children. They were most elaborate. It was possible to visit Father Christmas's home at the North Pole, or a diamond or gold-mine, to which and through which you were pushed on little trolleys by men suitably attired and made up, and firmly believed by the children to be genuine natives. You could get a present from Father Christmas himself—on payment of three-pence or sixpence (who sometimes awakened doubts by thus commercial-izing himself), or you could have lucky dips in a vast bran pie for two-pence, threepence or sixpence, according to your wealth and station or those of the accompanying adult escort. Things thus acquired were trashy but were highly valued because of the conditions under which they were obtained. The shopkeepers must have made vast sums.

Christmas Day itself was led up to by a terrific parade of anticipatory glory and never failed to reach the zenith. The festivities lasted all through January by means of parties, visits to the pantomime, the circus, the nigger minstrels and the Egyptian Hall.

There were other joyous events in the child's calendar. Easter was a time of egg harvest—all sorts of Easter eggs, chocolate, sugar, cardboard with gifts inside, chocolate hens on chocolate nests, chocolate cream fish in gold or silver paper, chocolate rabbits and hares, or plaster models of them filled with sweets (the head could be removed)—a perfect cavalcade of confectionery. Nor had St. Valentine's Day become a thing of the past. There were children's valentines—dainty little boxes with layers of lace paper amongst which reclined a present and a highly coloured picture of linked and burning hearts.

Children of Scottish parentage had Hallowe'en to look forward to, with its bobbing for apples, its attempt to get a bite out of a pippin swung on a string and putting a couple of Spanish nuts in the fire, representing a couple supposed to have amatory designs. If the nuts burnt brightly and clearly all would be well, but if they went off pop an ill augury was drawn. You cannot do that with gas or electric fires, nor are they satisfactory for the roasting of chestnuts, either. And very early in the period May-Day still had some slight observance. Children now turned fifty have seen Jacks in the Green.

What the children of the Golden Age lacked in easiness of attire and hygiene they more than made up for in fun, and in plenty.

CHAPTER V

'Chums', 'Chips' and 'Comic Cuts'

BOYS AND GIRLS OF THE MIDDLE CLASS IN THE DAYS OF THE SOVEREIGN
were subject to different influences than the juveniles of today. Things
with them were far less civilized. The age of savagery was still in being,
there were still parts of the globe hardly known at all—and pioneers,
explorers, and suchlike adventurous people were heroes. Distance existed,
the world outside these islands was incredibly remote. There were still
Red Indians likely to go on the warpath, African tribes likely to sweep
down upon settlers in impis of plumed death, trackless forests and arid
deserts 'where no man's foot had ever trodden'—gold rushes in scarlet
shirts, sombrero hats and cracking revolvers, cowboys to combat those
Indians, head-hunters, cannibals, desert islands on which to be cast away—
all sorts of thrilling ideas and possibilities for British boys. Sailing-ships
still rode the waves like great white birds, full of mystery and strange
charm, rounding the Horn in desperate peril; people still talked of
powder-monkeys and cabin boys—and pirates were things of merely
yesterday which probably could and, so far as the Chinese went, did still
exist.

It was possible to believe in hidden treasure. The Spanish Main was an
Ocean of Pure Romance. Aeroplanes had not come to make the world a
restricted particle, nor had the strange exotic lands of storied fame become
commonplace by news-reels, moving pictures and travelogues. A man
who had journeyed there had an income for life as a lecturer, all he wanted
were a few slides and a magic lantern—and what were called 'dissolving
views' were a novelty, one view changing into the other apparently
without the withdrawal of one slide before another filled the glowing
void of light on the white screen.

Buffalo Bill was still alive in the early part of the period—one of the
great boyhood heroes of all time—perhaps even more exciting because
of his proximity than the beloved Robin Hood. Many boys had actually
seen Buffalo Bill when he came to these shores with his show—and
a fortunate few had actually ridden around the arena in the 'original'
Deadwood Coach, whilst real Indians galloped in yelling, fearsome
encircling hordes, in full war-paint, discharging remarkably ill-aimed
arrows, flourishing tomahawks and scalping-knives (the boy's hair stood
on end in sympathy), whilst the guards of the coach replied, it seemed
very ineffectively, with shots from Winchester rifles and six-shooters.

81

Many a boy, taken by his amused elders for that terrific and never-to-be-forgotten ride, clutched his grown-up escort's hand as he thought in his young mind of what might happen if those Indians suddenly decided to take the thing seriously. They *might* be tame, they *might* be harmless, but there was always a tantalizing 'but' at the back of the mind. And then, suddenly, into the ring poured the cowboys, yelling like Indians themselves, firing their guns and revolvers, led by the indomitable, invincible Buffalo Bill himself—Colonel Cody of the shoulder-length hair, the Imperial beard—the true epitome of the spirit of adventure and of American greatness.

It was all right now, the Indians would never dare, and the coach, its part in the act ended, rolled out of the arena, whilst the boy, starry-eyed and silent with excitement, knew that back at school, when he recounted his experiences, he would be a hero—almost a Buffalo Bill himself—at least, an associate. Other less fortunate boys might jeer, but in their hearts they would know him for their superior . . . a great moment in childhood's life indeed.

Buffalo Bill had performed other feats in the show too. He had dashed around the arena on a bronco, whilst another galloping companion threw small glass globes in the air. As fast as he did so, the glorious Bill, his fleet horse's reins loose on its neck, shot the globes out of the air with his rifle with amazing certainty of aim. The boys held their breath in wonder.

Attempts on their part to emulate the feat with their Daisy air-guns, (price 3s. 6d.), with potatoes or anything which came handy for the globes, whilst they ran as fast as they could (horses not being available in back gardens), were always attended by complete failure and practically one hundred per cent of misses. They could not know, of course, that the unerring marksman from the Western Prairies was using a scattergun.

Livingstone's adventures in 'Darkest Africa' and his own discovery by H. M. Stanley were events so recent as to be still discussed and spoken of. Small wonder, then, that boys played at Indians and Cowboys, adored to explore shrubberies, spinneys, woodlands and such places, 'Daisy' air-rifle in hand, and what passed for axe and bowie-knife in belt, ready to encounter savage beasts and equally savage humans at any moment.

Small wonder that they set sail in imaginary boats to find new countries and, upon landing, to run up the Union Jack and claim the land for England, another splash of red on that already heavily besmeared map of the world.

Those boats of fancy were always sailing vessels, and most boys were conversant with the old rig, with capstans, with scuppers, bowsprits, foremasts, mainmasts, mizzens, poops, yards and sheets, ratlines, manning and reefing in tempests, shortening sail, with keel-hauling and walking the plank—for even the Royal Navy had not long taken to ironclads under steam, and in every port and dock one could see barques, brigs, schooners and other delightful craft.

Boys still knew about full raters, two- and three-deckers, a ship of a hundred guns, frigates (they came back again in the last war though scarcely the same as of old), for the spirit of Nelson breathed strongly, and there were shops of the greatest possible fascination where all the gear of the sailing ship could be bought in miniature for use on models of the old wooden walls of England. Little brass cannon on their stepped stands, little riding-lights, green or red, anchors, capstans, windlasses, cutters, admirals' barges, ships' wheels, and even little Jack Tars themselves in their hard, round hats, their blue cutaway coats and white trousers, or coatless in workmanlike striped jerseys, mostly red and white, ready to out grappling-irons and, cutlass in hand, to cut through the landing-nets and board the Frenchman, who would eventually strike her colours to the British hearts of oak and the boys of the bulldog breed.

Those were delectable shops which sold delectable goods and fired the imagination of so many boys with a love of the sea and a knowledge of his country's maritime prowess when she really did rule the waves.

Practically every boy nursed adventure in his heart and was further encouraged in the literature he read. There was a very wide field open to him.

There were many boys' papers. The two most beloved for many years were *Chums* and the *Boy's Own Paper*. Some lucky boys with indulgent parents were able to 'take in', as it was called, both these journals. Those who could have only one championed their choice, and upheld its superiority with argument and, if need be, with blows.

Both papers specialized in adventure, but *Chums* was the more virile of the two. The *Boy's Own Paper* had an educational aspect—it gave instruction whilst it thrilled, and did so of set purpose. Boys learnt as they read, taking this reinforcement to their knowledge as they took a grey powder in a spoonful of jam. It had long interviews with celebrities who had anything to say which might improve the boyish mind or who could impart useful information.

It also had interviews with great sportsmen of the cricket or the football field. It had instructive articles upon how to make things for boys whose taste lay towards carpentering, joinery or other handy hobbies. It showed by description and diagram how to make extremely useful articles at infinitesimal prices. It may be some boys succeeded in so doing, if they had the requisite tools—for possession of these was rather

83

casually assumed—like Mrs. Beeton's cheerful directions to throw in a handful of some article not usually found in Middle Class kitchens—but the majority of boys, even if they started, seldom succeeded in achieving the final creation.

There was also a slant on pets and on being kind to animals and just a suspicion of good healthy piety about the whole thing. But there was also always a good serial—sometimes two—by popular authors and the general make-up and illustration was above reproach.

Chums was far more downright. It did not concern itself with education. It did not worry about instruction—it gave a few hints on hobbies—it gave interviews with the heroes of the bat or the ball, even with wrestlers and athletes of other kinds. It gave, like the *B.O.P.*, a large number of jokes and comic drawings, and they always seemed a good deal more racy in *Chums*, but otherwise it went right out for excitement and adventure. Its serials took away the breath, one could hardly wait for the following week. Here were sea stories, here were tales of men who ran private zoos and traded in wild animals, here were soldier stories of battles with Zulus, Afridi, the Arabs, the wild and wily Eastern corsairs—there was fighting, sudden death, hairbreadth escapes, and blood galore.

And there were genuine pirate stories, too, which had their beginning in Georgian England, in all the glamour of square-cut coats, wigs, rapiers, and pistols (referred to usually as 'barkers'), in which the young hero usually got shipped aboard some vessel to find himself in the South Seas, or in spice-breezed mystic islands, either amongst the pirates themselves or in vengeful search of them. It was all very much like *Treasure Island*, that immortal classic of piracy, with the lid off.

These tales were magnificently told and linger in middle-aged memories. There was one called *The Rogues of the 'Fiery Cross'*. What an entrancing title! The *Fiery Cross* was a pirate ship called after her ensign. It had its beginnings in Devonshire—could any start be more promising? —and there were alluring bits of doggerel to give clues to the search for treasure and the pirates' lair. One recalls:

> He who seeks for fame and land
> First must find the Dead Man's Hand.
> For that symbol is the key,
> Op'ning wealth and mystery.
>
> Copplestones with Grenvilles strive,
> While each fam'ly be alive,
> Each to find the Sapphire Knob,
> 'Ere he lies beneath the sod.
> If their desire is Fortune's smile,
> Come to the West—the Mystic Isle. . . .

Very bad verse, maybe, but what a wealth of thrill it promised—this old, defaced piece of parchment found by the lad who figured as the pivot of the tale. He and his elders undertook the search—they were either Grenvilles or Copplestones—the years stretch between. They found the Dead Man's Hand—a mummified relic—but on it, tattooed in blue—the suggestion being that gunpowder had been used instead of ink—was a map—the Mystic Isle.

But where was this situate?—there was no latitude or longitude shown. But there was a spot marked with a cross—and there, you may be sure, lay the treasure, the gold and jewelled hoard of the old pirate who had buried it. So the search went on for the Sapphire Knob. In a secret passage in an old manor house—a moated grange—the searchers, after many adventures and gropings in the dark, came upon something which shone faintly luminous. What was it? It was shaped like a toad, but it did not move when the most adventurous member of the searchers seized it. It was cold to the touch. It was given a rub and—wonder of wonders—it was a toad cut out of a single immense sapphire—it was the Sapphire Knob. . . .

The tale took one to the Mystic Isle itself—somewhere in the Spanish Main, where such unlikely things as tigers were encountered but were easily explained as being the pets of the pirates and the watchdogs of the treasure. There were dashing heroes named Lally Tollemarch, Admiral Jerry, the Marquise de St. Maur, and sinister people answering to such names as 'Gideon Lickchop'. There were thrilling adventures in every paragraph, gunpowder, the thunder of guns, the crack of 'barkers', and the hiss of crossing rapiers everywhere. It was a magnificent story for boys and its memory lingers on, together with the impression that the author's name was Anstey—but not he of *Vice Versa* fame.

There were school stories and stories of office life. If the schoolboys reading them believed there were such schools they never came across them, and if they expected to find such offices and such doings awaiting their reception when commerce swallowed them up, they were doomed to disappointment bitter and deep. But they made wonderful entertainment and glorious reading. It was to most Middle Class boys of this period Captain Hook, the pirates and Red Indians, rather than Tinkabelle, that made *Peter Pan*.

Having got his copy of *Chums* or the *B.O.P.*, a lad would retire to his room, or one of his secret corners—there was space for such things in those days—and there devour his paper, until he was harried out and driven to bed. Homework suffered the night these periodicals came into the house. Boys took them to bed with them, to read a few lines in the morning as they dressed and made their rather scratchier than usual toilet.

The boys who subscribed to these papers had to face a great problem.

Both published weekly and also monthly numbers. Those monthly numbers carried a coloured plate which every boy desired. They were torn between the desire to read their thrills weekly, or to possess themselves in patience until the end of the month and get that scrumptious coloured picture.

Here, again, the difference between the two papers manifested itself. The *B.O.P.* supplements were often of species of butterflies, birds' eggs, or wild animals. Now nearly every boy worthy of the name had at some time collected birds' eggs and butterflies—often both—and wanted these pictures. The collections frequently languished as other interests grew up—there were stalwarts who carried on into manhood, of course, but with most boys it was a passing phase, and not easy for town dwellers. These would get Cabbage Whites and the commoner kinds: Blues, Coppers, Red Admirals, Tortoise-shells, Magpie moths, Poplar Hawks and the like; or sparrow's, starling's, and an occasional blackbird's or thrush's egg. The desire for these collections soon burned itself out.

But practically every boy collected stamps with keenness and avidity. He swapped, he badgered his elders to bring them home from the office, he purchased cheap packets from small stamp-dealers—to find most of the contents 'duplicates', as he called them.

But here again *Chums* and the *B.O.P.* came in. Artful stamp-dealers advertised. Attractive advertisements ensnared pocket-money or cash begged from fathers or mothers. And these advertisers, knowing the keenness of their young customers, would send whole sheets of stamps by post, 'On approval'. The prices were marked. Few boys could resist them. Reckless expenditure was indulged in, uncles were pestered for cash, fond mothers and aunts harried, and stamps of great magnificence and artistry —all 'unused'—were snapped up eagerly.

Those of Borneo and Labuan, very ornate and given to representation of the flora and fauna of those places—were hot favourites, and Guatemala entered the list with a delightful series portraying trogons, those beautiful birds in all their glory of hue. A set of Sudanese, showing an Arab riding on a camel and thus carrying Her—and later His— Majesty's mails, was also hard to resist. Elders found it difficult to refuse requests to succumb to the lure of the 'Approval Sheets', for stamp-collecting amongst the young was encouraged as having educational value and teaching geography. This it did, undoubtedly, although some ill-informed boys would stick new pages in their stamp albums for the reception of stamps from 'Norge'—a country unaccountably omitted from it by the makers. Young English boys knew little of foreign names or words, and could not have cared less.

But all this additional attraction did not lessen the problem of the weekly or monthly parts, which exercised their minds with a racking problem. It was usually solved by sticking to the weekly parts to lessen the suspense of waiting—for it was mortifying to find that the boys who took them held knowledge of the doings of the current heroes which the subscribers of monthly parts could not achieve until the month's end—and extracting a promise from parents, and seeing that it was kept, that amongst those Christmas presents should be a bound volume of the beloved paper, containing, as it did, all the coloured plates as well. Thus the boy savoured the pleasure of highly coloured art and could read the stories all over again in the fat, handsome, well-bound Christmas Annual form.

There were other journals of an exciting nature as well, but most of these came under the heading of 'penny dreadfuls' and were discouraged by parents or those in charge—it only made them the more attractive. These made no claim to literature—but went all out for blood. The *Magnet*, the *Halfpenny Marvel*, the *Union Jack*, *Deadwood Dick*, *Tales of the Far West*, of all sorts of blood-curdling adventures happening to lads in their teens, whose bravery, coolness and resource were things at which to wonder—either on prairie, in jungle, on African wastes, Siberian steppes, on the boundless ocean or sometimes in much more domestic backgrounds, such as railways or coalmines—boys devoured them all.

Errand boys delighted in them, reading them as they went their basket-laden rounds, usually folded small so as to make them easy to assimilate line by line whilst walking along. But when the tale reached a climax, progress would stop whilst the boy sat either on the handle of his basket on the kerb or the railing or wall of a house until the zenith of excitement had been absorbed. There was not any great hurry in those pleasant days.

These papers and the alleged funny ones which accompanied them were the prized literature of the Middle Class boys—they may have been read by the young sprigs of nobility, but this chronicle takes no record of them, or of the poorer boys whose parents formed the purely Working Classes.

There were other periodicals, too, of a more specialized kind, such as *Hobbies*, which gave away fretwork patterns—most boys dabbled for a while in fretwork and some became proficient. This meant that clock-cases and corner brackets to hold vases would decorate the house—whether the parents appreciated the art or not. But for most boys the desire wore off when the set lost its novelty. It was moderately expensive, too, to boys of limited pocket-money, for one had to buy wood, relays of saws and what-not. There was a paper called *The Regiment*, really intended for soldiers, but the illustrations made it popular with boys of military mind. There were numerous others.

Each boy, too, had his favourite 'comic'. There were a great number of these, but the two outstanding, for purely juvenile readers, were *Chips* and *Comic Cuts*. Of these, *Chips* was the most memorable because it contained each week the adventures of that famous couple 'Weary Willie' and 'Tired Tim', the one tall and thin and wan, the other fat and round, short and cheerful. They were the creation—so far as the drawing went, at any rate—of Tom Browne, a supreme artist in black and white. They have been the progenitors of many another couple since, and perhaps they were in themselves the lineal descendants of Don Quixote and Sancho Panza—their appearance and shape suggested it. There was, however, no pretence of chivalry about them. Their one idea was to live without working, and for years they succeeded.

There have been many other queer couples since, the most famous being Mutt and Jeff. They were Americans, but they sprang from the British stock of *Chips'* great men. 'Weary Willie' and 'Tired Tim' became types, they got into the language, their fame is immortal as are their names. Many people have been knighted for lesser creations than these. And every Middle Class boy adored them. *Comic Cuts* was not so faithful to its leading characters, nor were *Funny Cuts*, the *Big Budget*, *Scraps*, for whom Charles Harrison drew splendidly, and a host of other so-called humorous papers.

But there was another weekly paper given to the cause of hilarity which had a hero even greater than 'Weary Willie' and 'Tired Tim'. This was *Ally Sloper's Half Holiday*. It cannot be said that this was really a paper intended for boys, but they would always get hold of it and enjoy it, even if its main features were a bit over their heads and beyond their comprehension, which was just as well. It was Ally Sloper himself in whom they were interested—and well they might be. For he, the man who had the weekly half holiday which entertained such a vast number of this island's inhabitants, is one of that select band of fictional characters who attained that pinnacle of fame—a firm belief in millions that he really had human existence.

Just as romantic and cultured Americans, bless their hearts, go in pilgrimage to the 'Great White Horse' at Ipswich and the 'Bull' at Rochester to see the places where Mr. Pickwick met so many adventures, just as they go to Baker Street to gaze on the bricks which once contained that wonderful investigator, if annoying man, Sherlock Holmes, just so did many people consider that Ally Sloper actually lived. Once, when there was trouble of some kind on the paper and a report went out that Ally was seriously ill, tens of thousands wrote to ask about him, to pray for his return to health, to make the tenderest enquiries. His features and his dress were familiar in all homes. He was a great man, a true Briton and very largely a perfect representative of his times.

Wilkins Micawber was his father, and Ally (short for Alexander), the spiritual son of that mighty optimist, wore his sire's old clothes, or others made upon that model, even to the hat. His inevitable umbrella, the hall-mark of Middle Class respectability, he had borrowed from Sarah Gamp, who may have been an aunt of his, for he was a character straight from Dickens and therefore British to the backbone. Although in everything he resembled Micawber, one feature differed from that eminenlty genteel personage, and that was his nose. That was large, bulbous and red. Although he was a black-and-white creation, there was no doubt at all as to the colour of his nose. The delicate shading of the artist did that.

He was not so smart in his attire nor so careful of his appearance as was Micawber. His tight-fitting pantaloons, strapped under the boot, were a bit too short in the leg and displayed his elastic-sided footwear too freely. His hat was rather the worse for wear, but in altitude and depth of hatband it was of the Micawber pattern. His cutaway tailed coat, which displayed the portly stomach, was old and not of good fit—evidently one discarded by Wilkins when, for once, something had turned up. But he wore the same tie, he had the shirt front and the eyeglass—and above all, he had the air. Not even the black bottle peeping from the coat-tails nor the enormous patched gamp could detract from that.

Here was Wilkins Micawber alive again—but called Ally Sloper. Always in trouble, always on the brink of disaster, frequently falling in, often being kicked out, but always the master of his fate, the captain of his soul, he and his numerous family filled the front page every week with the vivid picture of their adventurous half holiday. It was one big picture only, but it was enough. He had handsome daughters of comely shape. Tootsie was the best known, who had in turn most attractive girl friends, with such names as Lardy Longsox and similar frivolous nomenclature. He had impish male progeny of the Artful Dodger class, who was Alexander Junior; he had friends like 'The Dook Snook'—a descendant of Montagu Tigg, Esq., also 'The Hon. Billy', and a Scotsman of rather wild appearance whose name was McGooseley. There was also 'Ikey Mo', 'Mrs. Sloper' and 'Tottie Goodenough'. They were all in the paper and in the communal adventure. He was a household word. Children of all ages adored him.

The rest of the paper was not for juvenile consumption. Its jokes were for adult ears and eyes, its drawings of fine young women in tights were intended for adult or at least adolescent eyes. Ally Sloper flourished for a long time. He was called 'The Eminent'—there was an association with the initials 'F.O.S.'—'Friends of Sloper'—with vast membership. He was as English as beef and beer, as Charles Dickens, or the Middle Class. And as timeless and immortal. Indeed, a paper named *Ally Sloper* has been published in Glasgow. Different in form to the original, it gives adventures of 'The Eminent' week by week—a revival for which to be grateful.

He lived, by the way, at 'The Sloperies', and the offices which published the paper were in Shoe Lane, where there was a Sloper museum.

At the turn of the century another boys' magazine made its appearance, a much better type of thing than had been seen before. It was called *The Captain*, and was edited by no less a man than C. B. Fry, that most astonishing combination of brawn and brain that this country—or any other—has ever known. The greatest all-round athlete of his time, an international in almost every game which had an international status, holder of records and the beau ideal of a cricketer—he was also the beau ideal of editorship of a magazine for boys. He is still very much alive, active and flourishing.

Well written, well produced, well bound and well printed, it swept the board. Every boy clamoured for it monthly. Most boys—at least of the Middle Classes—got it too. It was good for them. Once again great people were interviewed, but well interviewed, and well illustrated; men like G. A. Henty, W. G. Grace, told their stories. All the features were good without being ostentatiously informative. The short stories were of the best class and thrilled without blood and thunder; the school stories were, for such things, of super-excellence. They smacked of the Old School Tie and the honour of the School—*Tales of Greyhouse* held boys enthralled, but such things were not regarded as jokes in those days.

There was a character called 'The Long 'Un', who was a very good example of what a gentleman of the times was expected to be. *The Captain* set a standard and kept that standard high. It has not its equivalent today. When it issued badges (in brooch form, for wearing in lapel or preferably cap) in gilt and in silver, it was every boy's pride to be so embellished and decorated.

Old ladies, not in the know, often thought they were, indeed, captains of their school and would tip them handsomely in consequence. This in no way diminished the regard of those boys for *The Captain*. It featured on its cover a long, lean but sturdy athletic figure, very virile, very masculine and also extremely well bred and gentlemanly, who wore sporting attire and a blazer—one imagined him an Oxford or Cambridge Blue, according to your own colour. C. B. Fry was Oxford.

Annuals were always in great demand. There was *Young England*, to be had either once a year in volume form or in monthly parts. That was good, but not nearly so good as *The Captain*, and it died probably before the other arose.

There was a host of juvenile literature. Not the least valuable were little pink paper-covered books profusely illustrated in black-and-white and edited by that great man W. T. Stead, which were called *Books for the Bairns*. They cost one penny, and they dealt with many subjects in a straightforward manner free from all cant or suggestion of 'Pi' style, so suspect of all young people. Many and many a child got his or her first insight into Old and New Testament, Greek and Roman mythology, fables, folk tales, classics, and really good cultural subjects presented in a manner easily understood and digested by means of these little books, and interests were founded which lasted a lifetime. They were amazing productions and amazingly well done.

Little girls had not such an abundance of literature as had little boys, but what they had was good. There was a *Girl's Own Paper*, which was the distaff companion to the B.O.P. and other magazines of a similar kind. Little girls were more given to the fairy tales and such-like things—comics were not intended for them, although they revelled in their brothers' discarded copies. But they never had the equivalent of *Chums*.

Of books for boys and girls there was full measure running over. Boys of the Sovereign Age still read *Robinson Crusoe*, *Gulliver's Travels* (under the impression that it was a tale of adventure—and it says much for that piece of genius that it can be so read and enjoyed), Fenimore Cooper—especially *The Last of the Mohicans* (Uncas, Hawkeys and Chingashgook were popular heroes), and even *The Swiss Family Robinson*, that arch farrago of pious priggishness and pomposity. But for the fact that no right-thinking person could have stood his company for more than a few moments, Robinson Père should have been a world dictator and universal educator, such was his general knowledge and capacity. But he was really the prize bore.

The giants among writers for boys were Henty, Ballantyne, George Manville Fenn and Talbot Baines Reed. G. A. Henty, whose appearance was that of the ideal headmaster, big, burly, keen-eyed and bearded, was the King. His books were a most skilful mixture of excellent adventure stories vividly told, blending history and topography and geography into one interesting whole. Boys read him with avidity, even poring over the maps of the battlefields with which the books were adorned—when occasion demanded—as well as with excellent and lively illustrations. One learnt from Henty without being aware of it. And his titles rang like trumpet calls: *At Agincourt*; *The Bravest of the Brave*; *Through Afghan Passes*; *The Tiger of Mysore*; *Wulf the Saxon*; *One of the Twenty-Eighth*, to name only a few of this prolific author's tremendous output. A 'new Henty' was always demanded as prize, Christmas or birthday present—and always forthcoming.

R. M. Ballantyne covered a somewhat wider field. His two most famous books—he wrote scores—were *Coral Island* and *The Gorilla Hunters*. The last-named was sequel to the first. There were three heroes, named Ralph, Jack and Peterkin. The title of the books fully described their contents. They were well told and eminently readable stories and immensely popular. Ballantyne wrote about all sorts of things, from Vikings to the Fire Brigade, and did it all well. Does anyone read his books nowadays?

George Manville Fenn's long suit was natural history. His books were full of it, and it was woven into the tapestry very cleverly indeed. His stories had plenty of excitement but a noticeable tendency towards drawing a moral. His boys were very manly and very moral, but they were boys. He often had a character inclined to dandyism or sophistication, who always had his life made a burden to him and became an ordinary inconspicuous boy in the end. But good books, all of them.

Talbot Baines Reed was the teller of school tales. His classic was *The Fifth Form at St. Dominic's*. He wrote many others, but that was the great one. Boys adored it, partly because of its well-told tale, and partly because the school it depicted represented their ideal of what a school should be, and partly because it was totally unlike their own—it represented to them a scholastic heaven.

Fred Wishaw, George Macdonald, Ascott R. Hope, Harry Collingwood, Kirk Munro, Robert Leighton, G. Norway, Dr. Gordon Stables, R.N., Hugh St. Leger, Charles W. Whistler, W. H. Kingston, Edgar Pickering, Edward S. Ellis, Herbert Hayens, E. Everitt-Green and R. S. S. Warren Bell (the last had much to do with *The Captain*) were other widely read authors.

When the Boer War broke out books dealing with it and written by Captain F. S. Brereton—*With Rifle and Bayonet*—enjoyed a great vogue.

Treasure Island is a timeless classic. Boys loved *Tom Sawyer* and *Huckleberry Finn*—everyone read *Alice*, and Kipling gave the greatest joy, especially with the magic of *The Jungle Books*.

The old 'Pi' books like *Sandford and Merton*, *Eyes and No Eyes*, and the egregious *Eric, or Little by Little* were already on their way out, though *Tom Brown's Schooldays* had its admirers. Many children lucky enough to meet with *Helen's Babies* formed an acquaintance which endured all their lives, which they pass on to children and grandchildren.

Æsop's Fables were read, not as morals, but as amusing tales, and sometimes Lafontaine got a look in, especially if there was a Doré illustrated edition in the house—which also applied to *Don Quixote*. *Living-*

stone's Travels were scanned—chiefly for the illustrations—and boys made the acquaintance of Dickens and Scott, which they read with much skipping. *Ivanhoe* was the main favourite. Older boys would favour Rider Haggard, Stanley Weyman, Harrison Ainsworth and Bertram Mitford.

Girls adored the books of Rosa Mulholland (Lady Gilbert), Frances Armstrong, Katherine Tynan, Mrs. L. T. Meade, Catherine D. Bell, Annie E. Armstrong, Elinor Davenport Adams, Susan Coolidge and E. Nesbitt. They devoured and wept over *A Peep Behind the Scenes*, *Little Women*, and *Little Wives*, the adventures of Meg, Jo, Beth and Amy.

There was plenty for Middle Class children to read. And on Sundays in the stricter families there was always a copy of the *Pilgrim's Progress* available, often with amazing illustrations, many not a little frightening. But the children read it as an adventure story and missed the religious intent. However, it probably did them good and let them see what real English prose should be like.

There was another great function of youth which cannot be passed over lightly. It still endures today but much of its grandeur has gone, and almost all of its romance. This was the Fifth of November—Guy Fawkes Day.

Little boys—and little girls too—of the Middle Class kept this day in joyous memory. Pennies were saved up and shillings cadged from elders. The object was fireworks, which existed in great variety. The two chief brands were Brocks and Pain's—there were other makers like Wells, but the two giants were best known. Brock had his capital at the Crystal Palace, and the stamping ground of Pain was the rival white elephant—the Alexandra Palace. Across the mighty mass of London these two hurled defiance at each other. Northern Heights sent challenges to the sky and the Southern Hills replied. 'Brock's Benefit' is a household word—Pain never got that fame. But there was little to choose when it came to the domestic fireworks in the back gardens.

Comparatively rich little Middle Class people who had by economy or cajolery—mostly the latter—got together as much as a golden sovereign had a display of amazing magnitude. They had starlights, in their white covers sprinkled with blue stars, Prince of Wales's Feathers, tall, slim pink, yellow, green and blue fireworks, golden rains, squibs, blue devils, Roman candles, devil-amongst-the-tailors, maroons, tourbillions, fiery serpents and catherine wheels. These latter were, in inexpert hands, inclined to strike against revolution, but if they were amenable they were of great esteem. Silver fountains lived up to their name.

Rockets, mostly discharged from empty bottles, soared with a rush and a whistle to the heights, even if they seldom exuded as many coloured balls as hoped for. But there was always the breathless suspense of standing back in the dark, waiting whilst the faint red glow of the ignited dark-blue-twisted paper fuse should send the thing skyward. Often it seemed to go out and a grown-up would approach gingerly to relight it, if possible. Frequently it chose the moment he was bending over it to make its upward rush—and that was an added joy. There were jumping crackers and cannon crackers—the latter giving the most satisfactory results if half buried in the earth or in tin boxes.

There were, too, Chinese crackers, little miniature cannon crackers in appearance, red affairs about one and a half inches long, made of some kind of stuff like blotting paper only thicker, or softish cardboard, with a fairly long fuse. These gave only one explosion. But they were sold in flat paper packets with Chinese characters on them—which added to their enjoyment—and with the fuses all mysteriously knotted together. They could be made to give a splendid series of reports if this main fuse was lit. But boys liked to hold them until the last minute, and then, greatly daring, throw them amongst the girl onlookers, to the accompaniment of squeaks and terror-stricken howls.

There was an even smaller variety, quite tiny affairs, green and red, but very explosive. Again all the fuses were joined together—they could, of course, be unravelled. Bad boys who owed grudges to householders for various reasons, such as reporting broken windows or even personal clouts and chastisements—or sometimes just because they were regarded as obnoxious to self-respecting boys on general principles—liked to get hold of these. They would light the main fuse, creep up to the front door of the obnoxious party, and drop the packet of crackers through the letter-box. Those letter-boxes nearly always had a wire cage or a wooden box to catch the falling mail. Inside that, these little crackers would go on exploding for several minutes on end, filling the house with noise, smoke and a most satisfying stink of gunpowder and sulphur, to the annoyance and often fear of the inmates. You could do nothing about it. You had to let it take its course. And the avenging culprits had vanished in the November darkness.

Bonfires were built with care, rubbish was collected for weeks. A fine night was prayed for: indeed, fine weather around the festival was a matter of necessity if that 'bonnie' was to burn and not become a choking smoulder. Little savage figures danced round it like any Pagan Beltane. And then there were the guys. These were real affairs. Nor did any really self-respecting guys make their appearance before the Fourth of November or at earliest the evening of the third. Seated on old chairs or in mailcarts they were life-sized figures, old suits of clothes or old dresses stuffed out with rags, rubbish and straw, with a real mask for

Church Parade in Hyde Park—the Middle Classes gazed with awe

Royal Ascot—the Middle Classes only looked on at this!

A popular street show, the piano organ, with monkeys

A Water Cart—they laid the dust in summer on the macadam roads

a face and an old hat to top off with—if a tall hat, so much the better.
Little Middle Class boys were not allowed to parade them for pence, much
as they would have liked to do so whilst singing:

> Please to Remember
> The Fifth of November,
> Gunpowder Treason and Plot.
> I see no reason
> Why Gunpowder Treason
> Should ever be forgot,

or the less historical, more vulgar, but eminently satisfying snatch:

> Guy, guy, guy,
> Stick him up on high.
> Chuck him on the bonfire,
> And there let him die.

The guy was never just a boy with a slightly dirtier face than usual,
such as a less ingenious and less painstaking generation tries to pass off,
and with which, in manner most mercenary, it starts operations before
November is even reached. No, the real guys were well made and reaped
a fine copper harvest. Then, perched on the summit of the bonfire,
they were burned with acclamation and ferocity. Fireworks placed in the
pockets added much to the effect.

Guy Fawkes Night was a children's festival eagerly looked forward
to. Despite the gloomiest prognostications of Mamma, there were seldom
any casualties beyond very slight burns to fingers or clothing. And few
children caught the prognosticated cold. They were too excited for that.
It must be admitted that papas also enjoyed the fun—and the letting-off of
the more elaborate pieces. Children could hold starlights, golden rains and
Prince of Wales's Feathers with joy and delight. The event often meant
much family gathering.

But grown-ups had their own Guy Fawkes celebrations too. There
was always a giant bonfire on the summit of Hampstead Heath, and at
other old traditional beacon sites. On these points would converge a
procession of guys of the most elaborate varieties, some requiring horses
and carts to stage their allegorical and topical meaning—like so many
groups of statuary. Political personages were burnt amidst cheers of their
opponents and hoots of their supporters and battle would sometimes be
joined. Hundreds of Krugers went up in flames during the Boer War.
Great crowds looked on. Fireworks were let off and flung about amongst
them, there was considerable horseplay, singing and rough revelry—

and the adjacent public-houses profited very greatly. But the English had celebrated a tradition and that was a most desirable thing in the days of the Golden Sovereign. Even young men of the Middle Class went to those revels, but the young ladies stopped at home. It was not at all genteel, but very English and very enjoyable.

CHAPTER VI

Holiday Joys of the Golden Age

CHRISTMAS MIGHT BE GRAND, EASTER EXCITING, GUY FAWKES DAY A THRILL, but one period of the year shone in brilliant glory for all young Middle Class boys and girls, throwing everything else into the shade, something to anticipate eagerly and to treasure with care—the Summer Holiday.

Children of today love their holidays, but they do not get the same terrific excitement, although they do not miss it because they are unaware. Most of them are used to travelling, to change of scene. Father's car takes them around—often to the coast—almost every week-end. And many of them, before the Second World War made them foot-conscious and railway-conscious again, went away for that summer holiday in the same old car with which they were so familiar.

It was different with little Middle Class children of the 'nineties and early nineteen-hundreds. Their year held remarkably little travel. It was not customary to go away for Easter. Motor-cars, almost unknown in the early period and the prerogative of the rich for almost all of it, were not the vehicles for them. Going for a holiday was not an affair of just getting into the old bus somewhat overloaded with luggage and going to a place. No, indeed! It was the setting out for a journey, almost a pilgrimage for a distant objective.

It was akin to a caravan leaving to cross the Sahara; it was an adventure not to be lightly undertaken, packed full of joy, excitement and not a little pleasurable danger, such as getting lost or suffering some minor injury through slamming of unaccustomed train doors, things in the eye because you *would* hang out of the window—for the major portion of the trek was accomplished by train. That was a delight in itself, because train rides of any length were rarities for children, for the chance came only once a year in all its glory—that departure and journey in the last long days of July or the early free and gorgeous days of August—when school was a thing of the past for six marvellous weeks (an eternity at the beginning) and the sea and the sands were to be childhood's kingdom for a fortnight, or even a month in some cases.

Machine-age children have no idea at all of the turmoil of excitement which seethed in childish breasts when the last few days before the holidays drew near; youngsters to whom jet 'planes and racing cars are commonplaces cannot understand, or even get a glimpse of that world of illimitable distances traversed at what seem today pedestrian rates, when Margate was remote and Bognor a place afar, when Devon and Cornwall were Ultima Thule to the vast majority. They have lost in romance what they have gained in speed.

Nor did the grown-ups spend as much time rushing about the world as they do today. There was the home to look after, and the domestics to consider. The roots of domesticity were deep; they could not be snatched up for week-ends every so often—'week-ends' then were only for the rich and the highly privileged classes—and they were things of some formality even then. There was none of the dashing up by car with a suit-case for two, a couple of tennis rackets and bathing-suits, often uninvited, a request for a shakedown somewhere and a general air of casual noisy enjoyment which is often so very uncomfortable and unsatisfactory in the long run.

Nothing of that kind. If, on a rare occasion, a Middle Class couple went to relations or friends in the country for a week-end, it was by invitation of long standing and it entailed a good deal of preparation, quite a pile of luggage and not a little worry and inconvenience all round. So it was seldom undertaken. Parents had too many responsibilities to rush about in their leisure. The men worked longer hours, if they did not work harder, and very few business men took the Saturday off.

The wives had the young family and their houses to look after, at once their care and their joy. There might be a day's excursion to the country on a Bank Holiday, sometimes by train or sometimes by hired carriage or waggonette—it depended on means and the size of the family. The country could be reached from London by horse-drawn vehicles quite easily, for smiling unspoiled rurality lay within easy reach, although each year the bricks and mortar stretched a little further out, engulfing hamlets and villages, as land was 'ripe for development' (but really for disfigurement and urbanizing). But still, up to 1914, there was plenty of pretty countryside at London's very gates.

Consequently, the Summer Holiday, the yearly trek of the tribe, was a matter of very great importance to young and old alike. It was not a thing to be decided upon lightly. It was a matter to talk over, to discuss *en famille* and with one's friends, all of which gave joyful anticipation (so often the best thing of all), and a delightful unrest spread amongst the hearts of the young, who would go red-faced and starry-eyed as they thought of the pleasures to come.

There were terrific conferences, discipline was slightly relaxed, even the most juvenile members of the family could air their views— "after all, it's for the good of the children, and we must make them happy"—but their wild suggestions, offered at random or as a result of tales told by young school friends of distant places visited or even as a result of their reading, were seldom taken seriously. A memory peeps in of a small boy demanding to be taken to Hispaniola, but who when challenged had only a rudimentary idea as to where this desirable holiday resort might be and sadly admitted it might have been a ship in a pirate book, and even his second choice of Flodden Field—out of his history book—failed to gain parental support. He had been carried away by the magic of place-names—in after life he achieved the second but the first remains unattainable.

Guide-books were bought, letters written, pros and cons weighed, rival resorts contrasted, ways and means gone into, but mostly in those days it came back to the same old place. For Middle Class people (whatever their politics might be), Conservative or Liberal (only two parties then), were all conservative on the subject of holidays, so it was usually the same old place year after year. After all, they mostly had fairly big families, and the primary necessities were good sands and bracing air for the children. So they usually went back, year after year, to the favourite resort, the same places as their descendants visit today, although the places have changed as greatly as have the methods of getting there.

Not only did they go to the same place but nearly always to the same lodgings, the same boarding-houses—referred to in conversation as hotels, with separate tables and other modern ideas casually mentioned—or, if they were affluent, to the same rented house. Sometimes the house would be shared by two friendly families, which saved much expense. But if a house was taken, either jointly or severally, it usually meant that the holiday would be for a month, with the menfolk travelling to town and back by train each day after their fortnight's vacation was over, so it could not be far away.

There was much to be said for this annual visit to the same place. There were favoured spots to be revisited, familiar faces of local celebrities to see, who would welcome the children like old friends, and habit—the stringent thing in childhood—would not be rudely uprooted with new acclimatization. But each family was firmly convinced that the place of its choice was the best place, and that its own quarters therein were the most convenient and desirable it was possible to obtain.

Single people or childless couples could of course wander freely, but the average family just went back to the old place, giving the kiddies great joy by so doing. It may not have enlarged their horizons, but then they knew little about such things, and cared less.

A holiday was a thing to be taken seriously by parents and adults. The preparations began weeks before the event and waves of excitement

99

went through the home, getting larger and larger as the time approached. Wardrobes were overhauled, new clothes were bought, all sorts of things provided which would never enter the heads of people of today. One dressed for a holiday then, one did not undress. One kept up one's station and showed one's position in life just as much by the sea as in Queen's Road, Finsbury Park, London, N., or Thornlaw Road, West Norwood, S.E. (There were not so many Avenues in those days as there were Roads, by the way.)

Your attire could be less formal, slightly more colourful, a little easier, but it could not be slipshod or careless. One was a lady or one was a gentleman, and it was a case of *noblesse oblige*. A man could, and did, wear flannel suits and a blazer, a woman cotton or print frocks or white dresses of piqué, very smart and attractive, of muslin and lace. Hats were less formal too. A man wore his straw boater, but he did that in town; he might, if middle-aged, wear a panama, or sometimes he wore a cricket cap perched rakishly on the back of his head, the small, tight-fitting, authentic cricket cap of club colours, not the big flat cap popularized in the North and seen first in the South at Cup Finals, the headgear of invading hordes.

A man could wear brown boots by the sea, or even shoes, white with brown toecaps and crossovers—and also white cricketing boots or white boating shoes. His trousers were supported by a belt (usually club colours, or plain leather and broad in width), and it was even permissible to wear a coloured cummerbund—usually a deep crimson but sometimes red or blue. Not on Sundays, however; then the holiday attire was shed and men reverted to lounge suits of sober hue, but not to bowlers or toppers. There were some advanced people who still wore flannels on a Sunday, but that was really only permissible on the river—and by the river is meant the Thames.

Women wore their Sunday best as well, and children were not allowed to play on the sands—not the well-brought-up children, anyway. With that skill in improvisation which benighted foreigners called hypocrisy, they were taken for country walks or drives. That was all right, it preserved the conventions. Little Middle Class children of the era did not like Sundays at all.

The ladies all carried parasols, and wore big, floppy hats, to protect their complexions from the sun. There was no lying about in the open to get tanned, no acres of bare flesh looking raw, ugly and painful as the sun burnt it red prior to browning it off. Such a thing was unheard of and also shocking. A woman's complexion was precious—and incidentally was her own. A woman with a fair or delicate skin wore also a veil to fend off the sun's rays. It was nice to be in the sunshine, for it meant fine weather and made the holiday a success, but it never entered their heads that any good came of getting sunburnt and looking like coloured folk.

Nor were they any the worse in health from this abstention. They kept a clear skin and an unwrinkled surface far longer than women do today, even with the aid of face-creams and beauty preparations. So all these clothes and impedimenta meant stacks of luggage. Trunks of enormous size were dragged out of cupboards or off landings, mountains of clothes were selected or discarded, new dresses packed with great care and oceans of tissue paper—no paper shortage then—and children went mad with delight at the domestic upheaval and the comparative untidiness caused thereby.

Mothers also took away enormous supplies of ordinary commodities; soap, tooth powder, all sorts of things like that, for they all seemed firmly convinced that they were going to primitive places where none of the usual requirements could be obtained at all. They must have known, from long usage, that shops abounded, but they always went prepared. 'You never know,' they said. Labels were written and tied on—at least two labels to each bag and trunk and also on the invariable roll of rugs which encircled the parasols, umbrellas and walking-sticks which went too. Sometimes deck-chairs were included.

The children suffered pangs over their toys. They could take only one or two, and there was much heart-searching as to what was to go and what remain behind. Little girls suffered the severest agonies of mind over their dolls, for boys' toys were more portable and less fragile. The favourite doll of final selection usually made the journey clasped in the arms of the owner—and was frequently broken in transit.

The boys stuffed their pockets even fuller than usual, and boys' pockets were small museums in those days. There would be a knife with as many blades as possible—the best kind had also a corkscrew and a weird implement which was said to be what was required for taking the stones out of a horse's hoof.

All boys wanted that in their knife, although the possession of horses was not usual, and they would not have known how to operate anyway. There would be marbles, bits of string, plenty of bits of rubbish for 'swaps', including an odd stamp or two, some pieces of stone which had a value to the owner but to nobody else, possibly a Jew's harp or a catapult, if small enough (if not, it went inside the blouse), a whistle, wheels out of watches, some stubs of pencils, a piece of chalk, some broken crayons and, as a general rule, a glutinous mass of some very fluffy and sticky sweet which was kept in reserve as a tit-bit and always eaten with relish at times when such things were forbidden. Most boys' pockets were rag-bags.

The day would dawn, the last trunk was filled, locked and strapped up (new straps were a last-minute purchase), bags of solid leather (no fibre or zip-fastening then)—everything was dragged or carried downstairs to the hall with great labour and considerable exertion, and then there was the breathless pause of waiting for the cab, carriage or waggonette in which to go to the station.

Travelling-rugs were ready to guard against draughts in trains. Packets of food were prepared to guard against hunger *en route*, and if that last-minute horror of incipient coughs, colds and, worst of all, rashes had been avoided, the family was ready.

The youngsters were by now almost uncontrollable. They could not keep still. It was a waste of breath to tell them not to fidget (usually fidgeting was a serious crime), but Father was there, like a solid, reliable rock, and he would let them dash down the front steps to the gate, to look down the road and report the arrival of the transport. The kiddies were usually on the look-out a good half hour before it could possibly have been expected. This was part of the fun. Up and down the steps they dashed, shouting their news or reporting nothing in sight. Small friends who were not going away—or at least not that day—gathered in an envious little crowd of spectators.

High spirits led to boyish fights and scrambles which broke up the party for the moment, whilst the lads were fetched indoors to be washed and combed again. But the crowd would reassemble and the fortunate children who were going away would 'lord it' (as swank was then called) and patronize the less fortunate until a wild yell—after several false starts—announced that the desired vehicle was at length approaching. A further hauling of luggage, doubts as to whether it would all go on the cab, or whatever it was, a final check over, and at last everyone was inside, and then the holiday began, as the vehicle started away and the domestics or relatives remaining behind stood at the gate waving until it was out of sight, as if the family were either emigrating or going to blaze a trail across a hitherto undiscovered continent.

The holiday began as soon as the driver flicked his horse, or horses, and the wheels began to revolve. For that leisurely drive to the terminus was all part of the adventure, and a grand part of it too. Ahead stretched the illimitable vista of holiday time by the sea and well-beloved surroundings in which to stay.

How splendid to look out of the windows and watch the familiar district and landmarks fall behind, how breathlessly thrilling the approach to the coming train-ride, marked as it was by unfamiliar thoroughfares through which the steady horses drew the holiday-makers,

Sometimes there was not room inside for all the children, and the eldest boy, by right of seniority, would sit on the box beside the driver; what pride and joy this gave, especially if one passed a friend!

High spirits and seething excitement prevailed which the elders found it impossible to check and wisely did not try.

And then the great terminus itself, the scurry and the bustle and the noise of the engines letting off steam. Always in the childish hearts the fear of missing the train and the horror and shame of so doing. But there were numerous and obliging porters who, most amazing of men, seemed to know exactly where the train required would start from. Father had the tickets and would superintend the transport of the luggage—whilst a senior member, ticket in hand, went forward to find a suitable carriage and to hold it against all-comers.

The porters got the mountains of luggage on a trolley at last and the procession moved off towards the barrier—no Middle Class family of the period would let its luggage out of its sight. But the barrier would be reached, the train entered—always a family fight for the corner seats—and the family clambered in; craning necks amongst those of the corner seats watching for Father, who saw the luggage in the van so as to know where to find it at the journey's end, a last pang that he would be left behind, tickets and all, but he never was—the feared loss of the elder boy, who had gone to inspect the engine—the whistle blew, the flag waved, and the Middle Class family were away for their holiday.

Only wealthy members of the Middle Class travelled First Class. Nor did they go Third Class either. They were specially provided for, as if their weight and value to the country was recognized by the railway companies, by the 'Second Class'. These Second Class carriages were not so luxurious as the First Class but were much better and more comfortable than the Third. They were not so expensive as the First but cost a good deal more than the Third.

The Second Class compartment belonged to the Middle Class and they patronized it. It has vanished today and there is every likelihood that the First will follow it. That, we are told, is democracy. The Middle Classes of the Golden Era believed in democracy, but they also believed in individuality—for persons and classes. They knew their place and they kept it, in the Second Class carriages.

The journey was far more comfortable and less crowded than today, even in peak holiday times. There were, it is true, no corridor coaches, or very few on the comparatively short journeys, but, except on excursions trains, there was no overcrowding. The barrier of the Second Class kept the First inviolate, and the Second Class travellers were well able to look after themselves—with the guard as an ally.

Trains were just as quick and far more punctual. Sandwiches and cakes were eaten, sweets were chewed, lemonade was drunk either in fascinating little metal 'tumblers' which folded up like a concertina and sometimes (and best of all) direct from the bottle. Father had a mysterious flask in his hip pocket from the drinking base of which Mamma was sometimes induced to sip—on the score of strain, fatigue, the heat, and worry—and would indeed appear to be considerably refreshed.

And so, still in a state of vast excitement—for the passing panorama of country as the train sped along exceeded anything the modern films could show—the end of the journey was achieved. Here was the well-known station, the family tumbled out—the small fry doing so literally—and the luggage was collected. Again the willing friendly porter was in evidence and the impedimenta was, by a miracle, got on to what was known as a 'fly'—usually an almost worn-out victoria or landau which only the seaside air could have kept in working condition, which was driven by a sunburnt man who wore a fifth-hand coachman's coat with tarnished buttons and a practically napless 'topper'—and they went at a slow jog-trot to their holiday home—which had a welcome for them as well—or they detected one anyway, which was the same thing.

Thereafter it all depended on the weather. There were fewer artificial attractions then than now. Wet days were a horror of frustration, but fine ones were heavenly. The beach was the place. The family did not devote much time to excursions. Mamma sat in a deck-chair, parasolled and maybe veiled against the sun, whilst the children ran wild. Friends and enemies were made and either way it was glorious. An elder sister or brother took charge, and there was usually a nanny. If not, then the general servant was brought along as a help, or a poorer relation gave the housewife-mamma a chance for a holiday in return for one herself, which otherwise could not have been afforded. Papa sat in his deck-chair too, and read his paper.

Bathing was not lightly undertaken, nor was it very popular. The nudity of beach scenes today was quite unknown and would indeed have led to arrests. A dip in the sea was by no means the free-and-easy matter it is today. If it was indulged in at all, it was a matter of considerable organization, hard work and no little discomfort. For many years mixed bathing was not allowed. It was considered shocking—and indeed today, when it is commonplace, the sights provided by the minimum of covering on figures which would be much better clothed supply considerable shocks for the onlooker.

Then, if one wished to bathe, one made considerable sacrifices of time and money too. It was a highly complicated affair, a dip in the briny. Nobody bathed from the beach, a bathe was an affair between the bather and the ocean, not a public spectacle rivalling the Garden of Eden. You went into hiding, you were segregated and you could only bathe at certain hours. You never undressed at home and went to the beach in your bathing-costume. No, you followed Royal precedent and bathed from a machine. This had been started by that decent old family man, King George III, at Weymouth in the 18th century, and the custom endured. True, His Majesty bathed in considerable pomp and a band played the National Anthem and other airs whilst he disported himself in the waves which, as Britannia's chosen, he also ruled. And so the use of bathing-machines continued.

They were a species of caravan on wheels, with shafts, which were dragged into the sea by a horse, although some of them worked with a rope and windlass. Some of them were single, some had two compartments, for married couples or friends of the same sex. They were hot, stuffy and incredibly uncomfortable. There was no ventilation and no light save what came from small apertures high enough up to defeat 'Peeping Toms'. If they had been swept out—and there was a considerable 'if' in it—the first occupant did not fare too badly, but afterwards they got hot, damp, moist and very sandy.

There was a minimum of room, and undressing and dressing were difficult feats. But everyone used them. They formed a long line just in the sea, which was usually up to their axles. There were little ladders from the door down which the bather entered the water. You booked your machine from the proprietor, paying a fee—usually sixpence or a shilling—and you were assigned a number, for all bathing-machines were numbered. Sometimes you got a ticket. The great job was to remember your number when out of the machine, for they all looked exactly alike. The ticket was no good to you then, for you could not take it into the water with you. Forgetful bathers had an embarrassing time —some wicked men were, of course, accused of forgetting on purpose.

You did not undress for bathing in those days—you dressed. You took off your ordinary garments and put on others even less revealing. The men wore a tight-fitting kind of 'combinations', often striped, which covered from the neck to the knee, sometimes with long sleeves like an old-fashioned undervest and sometimes even a little apron.

The women were worse off. They were quite shapeless and terrifically unattractive in their bathing-dresses. They put an unbecoming sort of mob-cap on their heads to cover their hair—and there was a great deal of hair to cover. They wore a loose kind of burnous buttoned up and belted round the waist which reached to the knee, and under that voluminous bloomers. These were supposed to fasten at the knee, but the means to do so were usually missing and they hung forlornly.

Those who could swim did so, but for the most part they just bobbed about, or clung to the rope which hung from the tiny porch which covered the machine door, and shrill feminine screams rent the air as waves soused them. Despite their entirely unprepossessing appearance, wicked men with telescopes or binoculars would watch them, though what thrill they could have derived is problematic today.

There were officials in charge, called bathing women, fat old women of most repellent aspect, who terrified reluctant child bathers not only by their appearance but by their cheerful habit of ducking them, against which indignity and discomfort the small people fought madly.

And when you had finished your bathe you had to climb back into the machine, shed your wet costume and try to get back into your clothes. The women's hair was again the problem, although there was no make-up to bother about. You seldom got properly dry, your clothes never seemed to fit you, you always emerged sticky and uncomfortable with sand in your stockings, your boots and shoes—indeed all over you. And for this you had paid 6d. or 1s. for the machine and a further 1s. for the hire of a costume, if you had not one of your own—a dreadful faded thing dear at any price. Bathing was not very much fun and not nearly so popular or universal as today.

But at the turn of the century, and when Edwardian times swallowed the days of Victoria, more freedom arrived. At some places mixed bathing was allowed. Women adopted a much more attractive bathing attire. It still showed a minimum of flesh, but quite a lot of daring girls walked about the sands in them. It was usually of dark blue cloth, with black stockings and a short skirt, knee-length, with a low-cut blouse and bare neck and arms—almost as *décolleté* as the current evening dress of those days. It had bands of broad ribbon round the edge of the skirt and sometimes a little sailor collar also beribboned. The cap, if worn at all, was much more fetching and sometimes the hair was swathed in a coloured handkerchief.

The men adopted the 'Oxford' bathing-costume. Old-fashioned folk were scandalized. They said the country was going to the dogs and that morals were being undermined by the mixing of the sexes and the shocking display of the human form.

Those feminine bathing-costumes, however, seldom got wet. They were more for show than utility. The joke was that the girl 'wanted to keep her powder dry'. Needless to say, men approved highly.

Even the children wore bathing-dresses like their parents or elders, though 'advanced' parents allowed their little boys to bathe in drawers, and nothing else. These were dark blue or striped and apt to come down and cause much embarrassment. Little girls were muffled up like their mammas. Only bathing fiends, or those ordered by the doctor, took any pleasure in immersion in the ocean—the one because they liked it, the other because they thought it was doing them good. For the rest, the beach, the sea air, were enough. Middle Class ladies did not paddle—a nanny or a servant might do so and not lose caste, but then, she had none to lose. A Middle Class lady—never.

The children felt themselves in paradise, although they did not run about practically naked as they do today. They wore little blouses and little paddling drawers and big straw hats. The first thing on arrival was a visit to the toyshop to buy spades, pails and shrimping-nets and often a little boat to sail. Spades and pails were always taken home, filled with shells, and put away 'for next year'. But they were always unaccountably got rid of by unimaginative adults during the winter and new ones purchased each season. Otherwise children behaved and played much as they do now, and as they will always do at the seaside. They were more frequently told to rest a bit and not get overheated, but they never obeyed, except under duress, and then they were so restless that Papa usually had mercy and let them go, to Mamma's disapproval.

Besides the delight of the shore, free to all, there was quite a lot to do, and a few coppers went far in those days. There were nigger minstrels who became the children's personal friends, but who were soon to be displaced by the less robust if more romantic pierrots. There were donkey-rides on the sands and there were little goat-chaises, tiny governess carts and occasionally miniature hansom cabs, all goat-drawn, which were sheer delight to children firmly convinced that they were the real thing and driving spirited steeds. There was always a Punch and Judy and there was the pier, with the people fishing, and the automatic machines—not so varied then, but always full of chocolate and sweets not met with elsewhere.

A firm called Suchard specialized in this confectionery and it came out of the machine in neat little tin boxes, which could be kept. One slot supplied a nice little flat tin box filled with little sweet balls, somewhat odd in flavour at times, but wholesome and highly esteemed.

There was boating and sailing and the longshoremen to talk to. There was the camera obscura. This was the forerunner of the periscope of the submarine. It was a little circular building, like a Nissen hut, with a circular white-topped table in the middle, which had the effect of a viewfinder. You stood in the dark, exciting in itself, and a beam of brilliant sunshine came through a hole which was in the centre of the roof and fitted with a lens, the position of which could be changed by the attendant by means of a rope. Some of the tables tilted, and according to tilt, and to the changing of the lens, so you saw extensive views of the countryside, the sea and the shore, in natural colours—indeed, rather brighter, it seemed, than Nature. Often quite amazing scenes could be seen in the camera obscura, which certainly did not obscure them, supplied by couples who imagined themselves completely hidden from human observation but who had left that almost god-like eye out of their calculations. A visit to the Camera obscura could be most interesting, and the few pence gave amazing value.

Beach photography played a great part in the holiday. It was of a different kind from that of today, but, strange to say, much quicker. A gentleman with a tripod camera stood in front of his subject, buried his head under a black cloth, came out, removed the shutter or cap, took a tin plate out of the camera, dipped it in a pail of some liquid—and there you were, as large as life and twice as natural. The children were always so photographed, and the complete picture was placed in a black frame, kept in place by reddish gilt filigree at the corners, and a record of a generation was made and treasured! All in a few seconds too.

There were country drives, either by hired carriage, brake or chara-banc—all horse-drawn; one, two, or four horses according to the distance to be travelled. They trotted along the country lanes, giving ample opportunity for seeing the countryside and its beauties. The roads were not tarred, they were of honest macadam and real earth, and the white dust, disturbed by the horses' hooves, powdered the hedgerows, along which finches darted and in which flowers bloomed. A shower restored their vivid greenness and gave that wonderful smell of the earth which was so healthy, so much of the country, but which is so rare today. There was no rush, no hurry, no grinding of machinery, no smell of petrol.

In the fields the men worked in the leisurely fashion of ancient days. There was time to spare, time for pleasurable enjoyment. There were teas in English tea-gardens amidst English flowers and garden scents. Trays heaped with food and teapots of gargantuan size—and two new-laid eggs for everyone. And if Papa and his friends slipped into the village inn—of course the driver must be 'treated'—there were great mugs of English ale, and the inns were open all day. And then the drive back along the lanes again until the smell of the sea overcame the country scents, at a pace which made the holiday seem twice as long as a holiday seems today.

But the centre of all seaside activity and the hub of the seaside universe for the adults was The Bandstand. Military bands, and others wearing what was intended to be some form of military uniform, discoursed the music. They played mostly European music—jazz and its forms were unknown. The conductor was the 'lion' of the week, for bands changed weekly. Girls thrilled at the sight of his moustached manly military splendour, young men secretly envied whilst they openly scoffed—yet were proud if they were allowed to stand him a drink. You could sit in a chair and listen, but the majority and all the younger folk, walked round and round.

It was quite a pretty picture and a very colourful one, for the young men's blazers were striped like the zebra but in all colours, their belts flamed around their waists, their straw hats were new and gleaming, and the club colours blazed in the summer sun. Some few adopted yachting caps, but this rather transparent device was not good form. All carried canes.

Young folk 'got off', 'clicked', gave and received 'the glad eye'—according to the slang of the period. Conversations were notable for more witticism than wit, and the popular catchword of the day—there was one every year, like "My word, if you're not off"—was constantly repeated. The conventions of home were relaxed, and young ladies who would have died in horror at the thought of being 'picked up' at home allowed this to be achieved with perfect ease, for holiday time was a land of pretence—nobody was himself: or herself they were on holiday from that.

They all laid claim to a social status they did not possess, and nobody believed anyone, but it was part of the fun. The men were all in professions, or naval or military officers on leave. If there were a few who were clean-shaven in a moustached age, they said they were actors. The young ladies were all of great wealth and family. That holiday, so rare, so precious, was all the better for change of outlook and identity. It was good for them, there was no harm in it—it helped to blot out the shop, the office, the bank, and the humdrum social round. It brought a real touch of romance . . . many of those bandstand acquaintances endured even when the disguise was off, and led to fellowship for life, and all retained nostalgic, romantic memories of the 'nice boy at Broadstairs', that 'ripping girl at Eastbourne'. . . .

But the holiday time, so limitless in its first few days, drew inexorably to its close. The last few days were packed feverishly with all the things which had been looked forward to and then put off, so that memories might accrue.

And there was the question of the presents. The Middle Class always took presents home to their relatives and friends whenever they went away. There were trinket boxes made of plush—green, red or brown—with a photographic view on the top covered in with glass. There were little workboxes covered with exotic shells, not to be picked up on the local beach but felt to be appropriate and of the right atmosphere all the same, with 'A Present from Margate', or wherever it was, on the lid. There were books of views, little shiny wooden needlecases and what-nots with a transfer view of a local beauty spot—or the Pier—on them—cups, teapots, tumblers, all bearing the legend of their maritime origin, and there were pairs of tiny miniature opera-glasses, made of what was called ivory, but was really just bone, which, when looked through, if the feat should be achieved and the eyes sufficiently screwed, showed also a view of the resort, and numberless other 'novelties'.

Later there came the craze for Goss china, and other less expensive earthenware products, bearing the local coat of arms, made in all sorts of shapes and patterns. Many people formed big collections of this and had cabinets to hold it. They showed it to their friends, as trophies of wide and far-reaching travel. But no Middle Class person ever went home empty-handed or without presents. It was quite unthinkable..

But the last day came, as all last days must, to the depression of the younger adults and the open grief of the children. No use the parents being cheerful and saying 'all good things must come to an end'. That was no comfort at all. To the children it meant the loss of the sands, of their new-made friends and the approaching tyranny of school once more. To the young and single people of the family there was the harrowing thought that, down there, it would be the same tomorrow and the next day, with all the delights happening to others but not to them. The book must close. All of them hoped the last day, the day of their departure, might be wet; that seemed to lessen the pang of parting.

The previous evening the children had gone reluctantly to bed and seen their things packed up. The more adult youngsters had taken their last turn round the bandstand in the evening. Farewells were spoken under the stars, in the flickering light of Chinese lanterns and fairy-lights, to the last strains of the band, to the final songs of the pierrots, with the wash of the waves as a background of sighs. The world would claim them now for another twelve months.

On the last morning of all the children were taken in solemn procession to the sea to say good-bye to it—'next year will soon be here' they were told—and then they went rather silently to the station. That 'fly' had lost its charm, that last glimpse of the ocean as they turned the corner was a heartbreak. Only the train home and its never-failing thrill revived them to any degree—even though every revolution of the wheels took them further and further from holiday land . . . towards home and towards the ordinary world's routine.

It was over for another year. But they soon recovered, and the Middle Classes resumed their work refreshed, invigorated with happy memories and the anticipation of the next summer to come, which would be just like this, only perhaps better, when they would do all the things they meant to this time, but which they had missed doing. They never feared the cloud of war to hide their life's sun—nor was enjoyment killed by satiety. Holidays were good, and cheap; you could get magnificent accommodation for £2 2s. per week—all in. . . .

But as their homeward-bound vehicle rolled out of the town terminus for the last stretch it was usually followed by a ragged, nondescript figure with hardly any boots to his feet, whose appearance was belied by his powers of endurance, for he would run behind a cab for miles, to earn a sixpence at the other end by helping with the luggage. It was his holiday season, too. . . .

CHAPTER VII

Adolescence

BOYS AND GIRLS OF THE GOLDEN SOVEREIGN AGE, OR AT LEAST SO FAR AS the Middle Classes were concerned, did not grow up as fast as they do today. Modern babies seem to be born at about three years old and to have an amazingly quick development. The youth of those days matured more slowly. It was probably because they were not such an intimate part of their parents' lives as they are now, and partly because the families were larger and they were constantly surrounded by young people—environment means so much to a child.

But, of course, infancy slipped into childhood, and then, for boys and girls alike, there was a day when, strangely enough, the old ways seemed to be insufficient, the beloved toys lost their hold, and something which was beyond their comprehension happened to them. The chrysalis of early youth had burst and they were emerging in true form.

A boy would get out his army of toy soldiers ready for a long, delightful and exciting campaign. Somehow the urge had gone. They no longer interested him. Other toys, too, were gradually neglected. The boy had probably long since lost the delight in the various 'sets' which had once given him such joy—those things fastened on a big piece of cardboard: policemen's uniforms—or at least accoutrements—soldiers' uniforms, postmen's outfits—even the glory of a steel helmet with waving plume and a steel breastplate and sword to match which had once given him transcendent joy, or the lancer's hat, plastron and even toy lance, with scarlet and white pennant which had awakened envy in his young companions—the lure was lacking. Drums and trumpets stirred him not.

He would still cling to his air-gun, and the toy revolver, firing caps, had already been replaced by an air pistol, either black or plated, which fired slugs or darts—pretty dangerous—and which had a powerful spring which shot out beyond the end of the barrel and had to be pushed back for reloading.

He cared less now for games with toys than for sport in which he could participate actively. The reason was apparent in the long trousers which now adorned his youthful legs. He was 'getting a big boy now', he was told. Children's parties, even with conjurer or magic lantern, lost their thrill. Custards in glasses, decked with a small ratafia biscuit, did not taste so glorious.

But magic lanterns were part of almost every household, and had sets of slides kept in long, thin, red cardboard boxes. The slides were about nine inches long, and were divided up into a series of small square pictures, which either told a familiar story or were slightly educational as travel views. But children loved the magic lantern, and at Christmas parties or birthdays nothing exceeded the joy of the white sheet hung in the darkened room, whilst a grown-up manipulated the rather powerful oil-lamp in the lantern and did his best to make the slides tell a coherent story. They were, of course, always out of order, and frequently cracked. There were also gaps in the tale or tour because of slides which had become casualties.

Some slides—solo slides, these—actually moved, which was achieved either by turning a small handle—as in the case of a highly coloured and twinkling star, always a great favourite, or by pushing a small lever, which with luck would superimpose another section of slide on the one showing. Thus men rowed in boats or tigers jerked across a jungle. The star was the popular feature, and the children were encouraged to sing 'Twinkle, Twinkle, Little Star' whilst it was being exhibited. Such were the simple joys of those days.

Magic-lantern shows had an atmosphere all their own. It was 'a treat'—children were taught to appreciate a 'treat', which were then rare, but which would be quite usual things in a modern child's daily routine—and they gave themselves up to the enjoyment of the show, heightened by the fact that they were seated in a dark room, which made it unfamiliar, and the scent of hot tin and scorching varnish, which always accompanied such a display as the lantern got hot, was to them what the smell of the gaslight and the oranges had been to their parents in a theatre. Also, there was always the delirious chance of the exhibitor burning himself and cursing loudly before he could remember his youthful audience. That added a sharp tang to the joy.

Some children possessed—usually for a short spell only—a Toy Panorama. This was like a cardboard toy stage with a place for a candle in the middle. A panorama view on rollers ran all round, and showed itself coloured and illuminated in the proscenium arch as you turned the rollers. Children always tried to manipulate this themselves—with or without permission—and the result was usually a good and satisfying conflagration, with the panorama a heap of ashes, a hole burned in the tablecloth, and a general scolding and whacking as an epilogue.

Most children, unless their parents disapproved of the Theatre on principle, had a toy theatre—a Pollock, a Redington or a Skelt. These have now become a fashionable cult, but in the Sovereign Age they were toys. Few children ever succeeded in staging a show—it was a very complicated affair—but the joy of having the sheets, either plain or coloured, of cutting them out, and of fixing them into the little metal slotted stands with their handles—which always got twisted and out of shape owing to inexpert eagerness—occupied many happy hours, as did rolling up and down the 'tumbler' curtain, and setting, or trying to set, the scenes. The mere opening and shutting of the 'grave' trap was a romantic thing; a child felt he was standing on the very verge of the land where dwelt the immortals in his gorgeous Christmas visit to the Pantomime.

Certain go-ahead and advanced children scorned the candles of the footlights and would endeavour to light their little theatre with this new electric light. Perhaps their parents would encourage this exploration into science—which they reported learning at school—and often the mamma was not aware of the process and its attendant dangers—for there was precious little electricity about in the late 'nineties and early 1900s. So the boys—girls never dabbled—would spill sulphuric acid all over the tablecloths, ruin handkerchiefs and inflict torture on themselves in an endeavour to wipe it up, and then, if they did succeed in wiring their playhouse, it would go up in flames in one gigantic fuse.

And another memory creeps in here of two lads, about ten years old, who had seen at a pantomime at the Grand Theatre, Islington, a scene which struck them as being in every way remarkable, desirable, and just the thing for them.

It represented the 'Picture Gallery' in the castle of Baron Stoney-broke. It had curious ancestral portraits, but the one in the middle was what mattered. It was a delineation of a very tough pugilist, of menacing aspect, low of brow, and of ferocious, not to say repellent, demeanour, who was stripped to the buff down to the waist and held his 'mits'—covered with 'skin gloves'—at the ready—in other words he had 'put up his dukes'.

Unsuspecting members of the cast were lured before this picture. "Don't you think it's striking?" they were asked. "Very," they replied, and lo and behold, a real fist shot through the painted glove, smiting them in the eye or on the nose, to the delight of all the audience, but to the especial delight of small boys—and two small boys in particular. They decided they must do this at home. It was not possible on their toy stages—they had two or three apiece, these young-sters, for one of them was of theatrical parentage and descent and had infected the other.

No, it must be life-size, and it must be 'practical'. They set to work. They begged an old kitchen tablecloth from an easy-going aunt—mother to one of them—and they got the servant to wash it for them as white as possible. Then, with infinite pains, charcoal and concentration, they drew a replica of the wonderful scene as well as they could. With truly terrific labour, and to the great detriment of everything else, they painted the whole thing in watercolour, exhausting their paint-boxes at an early stage and spending their pocket-money—and small change cadged from aunts and uncles—on more colour still.

At last it was ready—they had kept it secret (or thought they had, though doubtless the grown-ups of the household knew all about it, for it was in bulk a very big secret indeed). They got it up, they hung it across a window alcove in a sitting-room and they locked the door until the performance should start. They had envisaged a large and delighted audience. But the only visitor to turn up that evening was an uncle of a portly, not to say fat, habit. The boys could not wait. He must see the show—the creative desire could be restrained no longer. They decided it could be a dress rehearsal. They tossed up who should do the talking as the exhibitor of the picture, and who should do the punching through the quite cleverly disguised hole.

The uncle was consequently invited to come upstairs and see a marvel. Being good-natured and fond of children, as most fat men are, he obliged. He stood before the painted scene and admired it. The boy actor said his part—word for word he had memorized it. The uncle made suitable answers, and then they stood before the picture of the pugilist. "Don't you think that's a striking picture?" said the boy exhibitor, trembling with excitement. "Very," replied the uncle, just as if he had learned his lines. It was the cue. The other boy's fist shot through the aperture in the glove. They had made one mistake. In their perspective that hole was built to their own measurements, not to those of an adult. That fist, shot out well and truly with all the weight of a sturdy lad behind it, caught the uncle fair and square in the middle of his protruding stomach and winded him. He gasped and turned purple.

The boy outside the scene turned to fly, but there was no escape for the lad working the effect. As soon as he had breath the indignant uncle tore down the sheet, ripped it across, and clouted both the would-be pantomime producers soundly and well. It was an end of their experiments at that time, although he of the well-aimed fist has partaken in many pantomimes since very actively—but never since has he painted the scenery.

That pantomime scene was used for one performance only, despite its great success *qua scene*. But it lives in a couple of memories still. Would children today take all that trouble? Perhaps it is as well if they do not. They could not get the tablecloth, anyway. But there were no such things as coupons or dockets then, and tablecloths cost a mere song.

This same relinquishment of playthings happened to the girls too. Childish things, dolls' houses and the like, began to languish, but the dolls themselves still kept a hold upon the girl's heart. Indeed, some girls never quite put them away all their lives—still treasuring them as grown women and always willing to play with them. But they began to become less absorbing. This usually happened about the same period in a girl's life as in a boy's. His trousers lengthened, the knickerbockers became real trousers and reached to his feet. The girl's skirt lengthened, but not quite so far. It went about mid-calf, or a trifle lower, and the hair, up to then usually loose about the face, or plaited into pigtails, began to be tied back with a bow at the nape of the neck, or it was coiled in a very neat plait indeed or in ringlets tied behind the head with a bow. Bows and ribbons were universal, even the little girl's pigtails or hair was so adorned. There was plenty of ribbon then.

This alteration of coiffure was unique in the girl, the boy had no counterpart. But he would be conscious of increasing adolescence in other ways. He began to take a slight interest in his appearance and was no longer so grubby and dirty and slovenly as before.

And about now the first little doubt would grow in the minds of the children concerning the omniscience of the parents. It usually occurred over homework—bane of both sexes—when Mamma frankly said that it was so long since she went to school that she had forgotten. Papa usually held out longer, but would grunt and sweat a little and show discomfort over some of the problems and growl that they did things differently to this new-fangled way when he was at school. Belief in Father's superior knowledge, however, endured much longer than in Mamma's.

The change in the girls was always greater than in the boys. Girls then, as now, grew up much more quickly. Boys were rougher then and perhaps a little crueller. They were certainly more destructive. The killer instinct was more fully developed—strange since Peace had reigned so long, but maybe it has found full vent since. The trapping and slaughter of birds was quite customary, and any boy who had a dog trained it at once to pursue cats, which were most boys' enemies. Every dog then went for a cat on sight.

Today they seem to have lost that urge, and a good thing too. A modern dog will not take the slightest notice of a cat it meets in the street nine times out of ten, unless the cat, its old instinct proving too strong, takes to flight. But few cats do that. Some will arch their backs and reverse their ears when a dog comes into view, but mostly they survey them quite calmly and nothing happens. It was not so in the days of the sovereign. Then there was truth in the saying, 'A cat-and-dog life'. Nowadays, boys seem to like cats—good luck to them —but fifty years ago every boy, on sighting a cat, would whoop, throw stones or quickly use his catapult—indeed they believed the 'cat' in that word meant it literally. Cats, on their part, vanished into thin air at the mere sight of a boy—of their own household or not. They are very wise animals.

The boy approaching adolescence was a very uncouth creature. He was still growing rapidly and showed lengths of knobby wrist, red hands and plenty of lank ankle. He was self-conscious to a degree, and clumsy with it. He was frequently referred to as a 'lout'. Girls did not appear so self-conscious, but they let off steam by a tremendous amount of giggling. There was a great deal of suspicion and avoidance between the young people of different sex. Boys always imagined that girls were laughing at them, and they were right. They had been taught, of course, to be little gentlemen and that it was 'ladies first', but there was often a bit of hair-pulling and similar ferocity when occasion offered.

The 'pet' craze began to fade away too. The aquariums were thankfully got rid of, or claimed by the younger children in their turn. The white mice vanished, and the pigeons too, but little girls would cherish the cage-birds and the rabbits, and the tortoise, self-centred and self-supporting, would still loaf about the garden.

The boy, it was decided, had to acquire polish. If he had not been sent there already he had to attend a dancing-class, and to most lads this was plain purgatory, where the young male felt at a severe disadvantage to the young female—as indeed he was. Most young Middle Class boys despised dancing, but were made to learn. A few years after they were glad. But there was a tough strata, a narrow vein of stubborn quartz in the male rock of the time, who definitely rebelled and steadfastly refused to even try to learn dancing, much less attend a class, and who remained non-dancers all their lives, not even falling for the craze of the dance-hall when it came in. These boys could never see the pleasure of violent exercise in a close room, getting hot and tired for no reason at all, to say nothing of consorting closely with the despised girls. If they had to take exercise there was football or cricket for them. Some determined primitive males still remain out of that rebellious boyhood, even though their sporting days are past.

A dancing-class meant your best clothes, clean hands, face and handkerchiefs, and the abomination of patent dancing-pumps—which meant clean stockings too, on account of holes in the ordinary ones. All that was horror to Middle Class boys of the Sovereign Age. It also meant, more often than not, the wearing of gloves—white gloves—always an object of contempt to the lads of the period. Girls, of course, loved the dancing-class and would ostentatiously dance together to show their contempt for the boys, of which there were never enough to go round anyway.

But girls had other hardships. They had to be 'accomplished'. Whether they had any aptitude or not, they had 'accomplishments' thrust upon them. The most general was music—as exemplified by piano-playing. The girl of those times had a music-mistress, and the family endured with resignation the ceaseless hours of note-fumbling which ensued before even a simple tune stumblingly emerged. The practising was even worse. But, then, it was expected of every girl. She simply had to be able to play the piano. No music was obtained then from gramophones or from the radio—the one was only just invented, the other unheard of altogether and a misty idea in Marconi's youthful brain. It was up to the mistress and the daughter of the house to make music—and to sing, for the girls learnt that as well.

The itinerant teachers disguised their pupils' lack of ability as long as they could, for the lives of these poor folk were hard and very precarious. Some families expected the boys to learn the piano too, but their musical education was not persisted in or insisted on to the same degree. Boys who liked it and could do it continued their music, scrappy as it might be, but most boys soon gave it up. It was easy to do so. One only had to shut one's mind to it and simply not learn.

Boys are very dogged, and were even more so then. Their resistance always outlasted the most determined attempts at tuition. And, anyway, it did not matter if a man could play or not. He was not a candidate and competitor in the marriage market. On the other hand, the girl most certainly was. The violin was forced on some children, without their own tastes being consulted, but the excruciating sounds at purposely difficult lessons from boys and girls alike, who could not care less, soon caused these to be dropped. Not so the piano. It was a matter of shame to a girl if she had not a Party Piece which she could play more or less exactly.

Boys scored over girls in another way. The girl was expected to be an expert needlewoman and was kept up to the mark in this respect by the vigilance and persistence of Mamma. The boy was outside such things. But his father expected him to shine at sports, and mostly he did his best in that respect. He was critical about his cricket bats, he wanted the best and usually got them. He kept them with care, he oiled them and he looked after them. No longer were they used for hammering in the stumps. A cricket bat had become something of as much regard to the boy as his sword was to a warrior of old, or a rifle and its cleanliness to a soldier—battles were fought mainly with rifles in those days, and it was not so long since the Martini-Henry breechloader had almost revolutionized warfare.

Boys became bossy now, and were very severe upon the younger members of their family, who, unless within grasp and prepared to undergo 'torture', would deride them and their authority. Girls who had young brothers and sisters assumed airs of age and superiority which were, to the small fry, quite insufferable. Skirmishing went on continually. Boys, too, were ashamed of the young females of their families, and if made to accompany them on outings would, if they met boy friends, almost apologize for their kiddie sisters. Their kiddie brothers were not even referred to, as beings of a lesser breed, not even visible to adolescent eyes at all.

Girls in the lengthening skirt and 'hair back' age were openly contemptuous of boys and spoke of them, when forced to, in most derogatory terms. They had terrific friendships with other girls, which entailed much mutual encircling of waists and almost continued whispering and giggling. Boys were not contemptuous of girls, the word is far too mild. They gave the appearance of having wiped them completely out of their minds and out of existence. Yet both of the sexes, young as they were, were becoming acutely conscious of each other and, despite their façade of indifference, both knew it full well.

A boy at this age would display considerable reluctance to go about with his family, even if the outing were one which had, only a year or so before, been much prized. He was so self-conscious as to be continually embarrassed, and he never knew to what indignity his mother would reduce him—for he felt his manhood already upon him. She might speak of his rough hair or his unclean hands in front of perfect strangers in public places, and such things were not to be endured. Yet he had to go, and when he went he enjoyed himself—the ice once broken. For still those holiday 'treats' kept their attraction when once you were there and they had begun.

Going to church was expected of young people, and this was another ordeal. Mostly they had been to Sunday-school and had endured the boredom of that, except for the precocious little 'pi' ones who liked it, because it took them out of the very dull Sunday at home for a short space. The parents sent them for the good of their moral and religious education, of course, but also in their hearts they knew it was to get an hour or so of peace on a Sunday afternoon when, replete from the extremely heavy and satisfying Sunday midday dinner, they wanted a little repose.

Church- or chapel-going to the majority of boys was boredom *in excelsis*. They took little delight in the hymns—if they could really sing the choir got them. And it would seem that the better a boy sang the tougher he was and the more disreputable, for a greater gang of young desperadoes than the choirboys of those days could not be met with.

119

No self-respecting lad listened to the sermon or made the slightest attempt to understand it, and deep relief was felt when the collection was taken, for that was a sign the end was near. They hated wearing their best clothes, they hated sitting still, they hated keeping quiet, and they had to do all these things, for the eyes of their elders were upon them, and if their father was a dignitary of the church, a churchwarden or a sidesman, any deviation, however slight, from the strictest decorum would entail a very severe penalty, for nearly all fathers believed in corporal punishment and resorted to it as a corrective, adding good advice as well. It is extremely doubtful if either did the slightest good or made the slightest impression on the minds of the boys of the age.

Church or chapel had another horror. You had to walk home with your family quietly and sedately. And you met their friends, who would stand and chat for what seemed years, and who always, out of courtesy at least, took some notice of the youngsters, who did not desire this attention at all. Dear elderly ladies and nice elderly men would ask them awkward questions about their behaviour, their lessons ('Beastly cheek' was the mental comment), and say with much gusto, "He'll soon be taking up some church work now, won't he?"

The parents would agree smilingly, though there might be doubts in their minds, and even in their eyes, and the wretched embarrassed young lad about whom it was said would yearn for the ground to open and swallow him. Sometimes earnest men of religious minds would even lay their hands on the boy's shoulders—and had been known, when caps were respectfully, and as an afterthought, removed, to pat them on the heads. They little knew how near their kindly benevolence had brought them to death.

Girls, however, did not mind going to worship on Sundays. They could show off their new clothes and take note of the wardrobe of other girls, criticize, pull them to pieces and regale their particular friends with gossip afterwards. Boys had not this satisfaction. They never gossiped. And in many a boy's savage little heart—they were more nearly akin to savages then than now—lurked the misty idea that in some way church- or chapel-going was effeminate. They determined to throw it overboard as soon as they could. But often habit engrained in youth was too strong for them.

It was a very definite moment in a boy's approach to maturity when he got his first watch. That was an event of considerable magnitude. It marked a stage of responsibility. It was manhood's first rung, the next being a razor and the last a latch-key. Most boys did not attain to the latch-key until they 'came of age'; then, at a family celebration, at which the young man made his first little speech and usually a complete ass of himself, his father solemnly presented him with this significant badge of manhood and freedom amidst the kindly plaudits of the family and friends assembled to do honour to the day. Not that a latch-key meant much freedom in some families even then. But it was the visible and outward sign that one had reached years of discretion.

The watch, however, was the first stage. It was given either as a birthday or a Christmas present—and it was either of white metal, gun-metal or silver. No boy was trusted with a gold watch, and quite rightly so. That was another twenty-first birthday present, and most men today still use that link with their youth as long as they live.

The first watch was usually a Waterbury. It came from America and had 'Made in U.S.A.' or some similar legend blazoned across the dial. It was a large watch and it was keyless. It cost five shillings, and it went as well as a watch of that price could possibly be expected to. It had a loud tick, so long as it was left unmolested, and it kept pretty good time. Boys displayed it proudly to watchless friends, and mostly wore a silver chain of some thickness across their waistcoats to secure it. Later, the watch-chain would have a sovereign purse and a metal matchbox in the opposite waistcoat pocket as a further anchor, but not yet.

The boys at the watch age did not get hold of many sovereigns, or even half-sovereigns—the usual tip was a large, massive, and opulent-looking five-shilling piece—noble coins now known no more. Their correct denomination was a crown, but nobody called them that. They were 'five-bob bits' or 'cartwheels', and to a boy their purchasing price was illimitable.

In the case of the boy, a silver pencil-case usually decorated the end of the watch-chain. This pencil-case was either a present or had been won at the School Sports as a 'Consolation Prize' for '100 yards, under 14', or perhaps as a member of a victorious tug-of-war team.

There were no eversharp pencils then, the writing part was either an ordinary pencil of small size or a flat one, according to the shape of the case. It was never used much on account of refills being a bother—there was always an ordinary pencil, or stub of one, in another pocket. There were some sort of self-propelling pencils, but they were rather orna-mental and slim. Sometimes they worked on the screw principle, but more often the lead was brought into action by a little knob at the side which was pushed along a slot. They were delicate, fancy affairs, usually in some sort of pattern, made like little guns with agate or cornelian butts to them, and regarded by boys as bothersome and effeminate. They were girls' pencils—because no girl could ever sharpen a pencil properly or had a knife with which to do it. For a short while a pencil made in semblance of a screw obtained a ready sale and boys liked those—but somehow they died out.

A boy's first watch suffered many tortures. It was constantly being wound and adjusted—which usually ended in the top coming off. The boy would excuse himself for this by pointing out to his father that it was owing to his desire to act up to paternal advice, and, now that he had a watch, to be punctual, that had brought about the disaster. But all too often the inner case was removed to have a look at the works and to show to disbelieving friends that the watch was 'jewelled', which it was not.

A boy then got another watch, which was silver and had usually been the property of his mother when she was young. This would be a smaller, slimmer affair altogether, with a chased back and usually some floral emblem enamelled on the dial. They were pretty little affairs, but boys did not show them as freely as the Waterburys, because the taint of the female was on them.

Another drawback was that these watches always required winding by key, and there was nothing so easily lost as a watch-key. But some wise and benevolent firm put little watch-keys on the market fashioned like miniature revolvers. The boys liked those and fastened them to the watch-chain. Men and boys alike wore their watch-chains—which were called alberts out of compliment to the late lamented Prince Consort—across their stomachs in their lower waistcoat pockets.

Later came a vogue when the watch-chain ascended to the top pockets and the chain was worn across the chest. Smart young men had leather watch-chains with a little stirrup on them. It added a touch of sporting horsiness to the appearance. But in the early days the watch-chains went across the stomach and tailors provided a special button-hole for them to pass through. This was supposed to baffle pickpockets, but it never did.

A growing young lady did not get a watch as soon as a boy. But she got her first bit of jewellery. That was her great stage of development. As a child, jewellery was forbidden a girl, except perhaps a coral necklace on state occasions. But now she got her first trinkets. Like the boy's watch, they were silver. She would get a little silver bracelet, either of chain or one which expanded or contracted under finger pressure. She might also have a little silver brooch or two, and a locket suspended from a little chain of pearls, imitation but good, around her neck. She was not allowed to deck herself with the tawdry, gimcrack finery seen today on very young people, which clashes and tinkles as they approach like an old-time carthorse.

Later, when she got a watch too, it was usually a small silver or gunmetal one, of miniature size, which she wore on her breast suspended from a metal true-lovers' knot. The time could only be ascertained by digging in the chin and making faces as one peered down at the small dial so inconveniently placed. But she achieved the watch age very much later than the boy, and never, until quite mature in years, did she get a latch-key. That was a male prerogative entirely. Even the mistress of the house, despot as she was, seldom bothered about one. There was always the maid to answer the door. Wrist-watches were almost unknown, though some ladies wore their watches on their wrists in broad leather straps, which surrounded the watch and held it.

Boys' friendships in external appearance differed from those of the girls. A boy might have a pal to whom he was devoted. The two went about together, shared their property, their sweets, their 'comics', and often their pocket-money, had the same tastes and enjoyed the same things. Or there was a gang which hunted together and carried on warfare with other gangs of boys from different streets. But the boy who had a watch gave up the gang and devoted his thoughts to higher things.

The young adolescents never mixed. Boys did not go about with girls and girls were never allowed to mix with boys. There was far greater discipline and not so much freedom—or looseness, as it would have been called then.

There were no Boy Scouts or Girl Guides during a great part of the time. Ninety-nine per cent of the public had never heard of Baden-Powell until he defended Mafeking in the Boer War and stepped into the top rank of national hero-worship—a niche he never lost, as did so many of his contemporaries and those who went before him. There was no similar movement to the Scout movement. The Boys' Brigade attached to the churches were not for the Middle Class. But what boys and girls learn today from being Scouts and Guides they then learnt at home.

These children, maybe savages at heart, had good table manners. They were not the riotous young things at meals such as are often met with today. They were not allowed to seize and consume what they happened to fancy. It was always a case of bread-and-butter first—then some jam—and then cake. No bread-and-butter, no cake. No leavings were allowed—no crusts were shirked—clean plates were the rigid rule. No child dared speak with its mouth full, or would touch any food without permission. No child would get down from the table without permission having first been obtained.

They had their own diet at lunch and at solid mealtimes, plain food but good, and lots of vegetables. They had to eat it, whether they liked it or not. They survived the ordeal. They got plenty of good plain puddings, too, mostly of the milk variety—there was very often a spot of rebellion when rice puddings were too frequent, but it was soon suppressed—and they had suet puddings with golden syrup, or baked jam roll, or good plum duff, and, of course, stewed fruit. There was never a shortage of any kind of food. Enough was wasted and thrown away in the ordinary Middle Class household to supply rations today for a family of four or five.

When boys got their watches and girls their trinkets there was also an increase in pocket-money. It was not large, but it was more, and it was always accompanied by a little well-meant lecture on taking care of the money and learning its value. They got a good deal more, they were told, than their fathers and mothers at a similar age. They listened, but they were not very impressed. Yet it was in many cases true enough. It is inherent in parents, however strong their sense of discipline, to give their children better than they had themselves.

The young folk began to read more, and to sample more adult books. Boys now took to Rider Haggard, Stanley Weyman and similar books of adventure or romance—but the romance must have a coating of excitement. Girls surreptitiously sampled 'Ouida', or Marie Corelli, and also bought *Smart Novelettes* at twopence a time to devour highly sentimental but very proper love stories of aristocratic personages—all titled—or else of how a highly born young man placed his hand and heart at the disposal of a maid of low degree who, by her sweetness of disposition and her terrific domestic talent, eventually won the parents over to her side, usually after being at death's door. The girls loved it all—for it was a sentimental age, and none the worse for that.

Parents now sometimes took their growing young people to the Theatre, as apart from Pantomime. But only to Shakespeare or classic plays—and as some old English comedies were included in that, the youngsters must have wondered a good deal, except that it was mostly *She Stoops to Conquer*, *The School for Scandal* or *The Rivals*. Congreve and the others were not played at all. It was a circumspect age and very proper.

Some easy-going, advanced people took their children to see musical comedies, then in the first flight of their popularity. They hoped and believed that whilst the youngsters would like the music, the dancing, and the fun, they 'would not understand' the rest of it.

No young people of either sex ever received sex instruction from their parents or at school. Sex was a thing to cover up, as was the human figure. It was something to be ashamed of and never to be mentioned before young people at all. The growing excitement of adolescence needed explanation somehow, and the young people had to find out for themselves. The boys got furtive and congregated around a well-informed lad, who in the younger stages seldom got the facts right. The girls

124

giggled, walked away, or were covered with blushes if one of their number, inclined to be 'fast', talked about such things. But, of course, the knowledge came, just as soon, if not so directly, as it does today. Parents were more restrained before their children, and there were plenty of wives who still addressed their husbands by their surnames.

Anatomical differences were hidden at a very early stage indeed. Nudity was unknown, either in fact or in print, and children taken to a picture gallery were hurried past the Venuses and the nymphs and had their attention directed the other way when undraped statuary had to be passed by. This is now looked upon as hypocrisy—but it worked pretty well, and there was a far higher respect for womanhood as a mysterious thing apart, more delicate and tender than the rough-hewn male, which is entirely lacking in these later days of so-called sex equality. One can visualize the day when 'women first' will only be the rule in shipwrecks—if ships still exist as a means of transport—because of the children. If so, the women have asked for it.

But schooldays were drawing to a close. Public examinations were tackled. The boys would pass the Oxford or Cambridge Senior Locals, the First Class College of Preceptors, and in some cases the Matric.

There was satisfaction if they passed and passed well, and something of disaster if they did not. They had finished their education. They had absorbed the knowledge it was considered essential for them to have. They had all been educated the same way by the same method. There had been little, if any, attention shown to a special bent or a special aptitude. The schools had a curriculum to which they must adhere, indeed they would have found their resources seriously strained had they attempted to go beyond it. It was to a large extent a blind alley education with which the young Middle Class man or boy had to face the world. He had a curious jumble of facts in his head, he knew a little about a lot of things and not much about any special subject. He had no real qualifications whatever. Few Middle Class boys got the benefit of a university career unless they happened to win a scholarship, and then their university life was not a very happy one in those highly class-conscious days. They went out to face the world no better equipped than any of their competitors in the battle, which, at any rate, made it fair.

And it really was when they entered upon their real work that their true education began. Much depended on the nature of their parents and their own standards of culture. Some children, lucky to be born into a family who delighted in Art or Literature, had a better equipment than the rest for social life and perhaps a greater quickness of mind for the points to be picked up in commerce, for many parents also educated their children without seeming so to do, by taking them about and showing them the sights. Bound volumes of *Punch* taught them much contemporary history, but very few children looked at a newspaper.

They were, however, all sure of one thing. They were the heirs to greatness. They were British, with a contempt for all foreigners, and especially the French, who, their history books told them, were their hereditary foes whom they always trounced. They were children of the Empire upon which the sun never set; they could never never never be slaves. Their Navy, and their Army, were both invincible. The Middle Class youth firmly believed all this. And at that time he was right. No threat of compulsory military service hung over his head. That was for benighted foreigners, not for free-born Britons. Less than fifty years changed all that.

CHAPTER VIII

'Something in the City'

IT WAS WHEN THEY LEFT SCHOOL THAT THE FULL IMPACT OF THE WORLD IN which they lived was encountered and understood by the young people of the Golden Age. Up to then their lives and their thoughts, apart from the difference of discipline and upbringing, had been sheltered, as is the case with young folk today. Home is still home to children, even if it is a tiny flat. But the world into which the young 'Sovereign Agers' found themselves plunged was a very different place. They had to find their bearings in it and their true situation in the scheme of things, although that took time. By far the greater portion of them became 'Something in the City'.

Some, of course, went into their father's business, if he were established in his own, although it was the custom then for a youth to serve an apprenticeship, as it were, in the office of a friend of his father's, to get him licked into shape and to ingrain still further discipline before he mixed with his father's own staff. This was wise, for it did away with any feeling of favouritism in the parental office, and when the boy did join it he was experienced and not in the position of having to be taught everything by those who were just employees and liable, very justly, to regard him as a possible menace to their own jobs. 'Something in the City' was the usual thing, for it was respectable, and that was the main thing. The black coat was the badge of Middle Class respectability, even if the black coat was only metaphorical in the case of beginners.

That strata of the Middle Class which kept shops of their own expected their boys to follow them. The eldest son went into his father's business, shop or office, as if it were entailed. He might have views of his own, but he would find it very difficult to escape his destiny. Only if he showed remarkable talents in another direction—such talents as could not be denied—could he make his getaway, and that also took time. Younger sons had a wider choice—or, at any rate, a wider opportunity. For them jobs were either found by their father, or they got them through answering advertisements in the papers.

There were social grades in all this. A boy articled to a solicitor, an architect or a chartered accountant was definitely a slight cut above a mere lad in an office, as was the boy who, by influence, got into a bank or an insurance company. Boys going into the Civil Service—usually the less specialized grades—were in a class by themselves. Civil Servants then, as now, had their own social standing, and were regarded with mixed feelings. Smart business men regarded them as stick-in-the-muds and men of little enterprise, in receipt of small fixed salaries and automatic rises—automatons themselves indeed—but conceded the desirability of a pension.

But despite all this there was the aura of Government around them, which had a social value of its own. Fathers were very active on their sons' behalf, even if they were simple clerks themselves. They would ask people they could trust not to snap their heads off for interest on their sons' behalf, and if they could get them into the firms for which they worked themselves, presuming the firms were big enough, they felt that they had given the boy a real chance in life. Employers were never averse to this, if the father was a good and trusted worker. It gave them a double hold over both father and son.

Choosing a boy's career is always a difficult one, and was so then, for perhaps the scope was more limited, although business was so very much better. Class-consciousness made added mountains to get over, and a boy of humble Middle Class standing had not much choice when it really came to cues. Their own childish ambitions for engine-driving, being explorers, and such-like had long been dissipated. No Middle Class youth entered either of the two Services—or very few indeed, and only if there was considerable wealth behind him. Those professions were closed shops. They were for 'gentlemen', as the word was then most widely understood, for most men by manners were gentlemen. A real 'gentleman' was a man of the leisured or upper classes. Nor did many boys want to be members of the fighting forces, despite the military ardour of their youth and their favourite toys.

The British were not a military nation; they are not today, even after two world wars. No private schools then had cadet corps. That was the perquisite of a few public schools. If a young man had martial yearnings he could join the Volunteers, which later became the Territorials. He could wear his uniform now and again on parade, he could sacrifice his precious summer holiday to going under canvas and training hard. He could endure the sarcasm of being called a 'Saturday-afternoon soldier', although he was really a staunch upholder of the Voluntary system in which the country so firmly believed.

It boasted that its Army was volunteer to a man. So it was. Apart from the real first-class stiffening of youths who were the sons of soldiers brought up in the regiment they afterwards joined, and so predestined, all the members of Her—and His—Majesty's Forces were volunteers. Recruiting-sergeants—large, fine men with waxed moustaches, extra smart uniforms which they wore magnificently, rosettes in their caps, and bemedalled chests—frequented certain spots, notably the region of Trafalgar Square, swaggering up and down, appraising likely young men with their eye, and sometimes asking them outright if they wouldn't like to 'take the shilling'? As a rule the young men fled precipitately.

But still the Army was Volunteer. It got its volunteers from unlucky misfits in life, when their boots began to let water and their stomachs were completely empty, and when they had tried the Embankment as a bedroom and found it cold, draughty and inconvenient. It got them from young men of emotional nature who had been jilted by their girls. It got them from young men who feared that justice was on their track and the arm of the law was stretching out for them, who could enlist under a false name and be hidden safely in quarters. It got them from young men full of temporary martial ardour but more full one fateful evening, of cheap beer.

But it also got them in shoals, full measure and brimming over, when England really went to war. There was not much standing back then from a very great proportion of British youth. They had a patriotism of their own. It was a curiously British form of patriotism. It was not that they wished to die for their country, it was not that they had an overwhelming love for the country of their birth about which, by and large, they knew little.

It was not so much the thought of fighting for, or dying for, the flag which, they were told, had braved a thousand years the battle and the breeze (though in point of fact the Union Jack has not braved the breeze for half a thousand years)—it was none of these things. It was more a determined desire to 'show the foreigner', as we should say today. It was a desire to put him in his place, to demonstrate to him that they themselves (as representative Britons) were not going to have any of his nonsense, be he who he may. It was the feeling then which permeated all classes that 'what we have we hold', and it was 'hands off' to any poor benighted interfering talker of gibberish (any foreign tongue was gibberish and every foreigner was an object of mirth and derision) who dared to think he had the cheek to challenge us—the salt of the earth.

That was the spirit which took England to war—real serious war—and it is much the same today. Only now the Voluntary system is a thing of the past—and had it been so sooner there might not have been such a protracted First World War and the whole course of history might have been changed. Yet in the First World War it raised the 'First Hundred Thousand' in record time, and it brought about the miracle of the Home

Guard in the Second World War—whose true achievement history will assess.

So a Middle Class young man did not go into the Army or the Navy. He was scarcely aware of them, except in the abstract and as a very attractive part of pageantry. Wars such as he knew were little affairs which happened far away, the job of a small but professional army of experts, who always won. He did not feel it to be any affair of his. The word 'conscript' was hardly known. He had been told by his father that he had a much better commercial chance than the young Frenchman or German, because they, poor scum, had to be conscripts, and waste precious years in military training, whereas he could devote his whole energies to the prestige of Britain's commerce, which partly on account of this flying start was the greatest in the world.

The young man was duly grateful for this. He knew it was because we were an island realm that we were so favoured, and he believed hazily that we ruled the waves by Divine Appointment—we might even have been forgiven for boasting about it in our second National Anthem because it seemed so true. The figure of Britannia was for us, as a race, what the exhibition of the Royal Arms over a shop might be—a sign that we were by Providence appointed the most favoured of worldly nations.

But he did not bother his head about things like that, any more than he did about the duties and privileges of citizenship. He knew vaguely as a youth that one day he would have a vote, but he was not at all interested in politics—that was the affair of those of more mature years. Meanwhile he had got to find his feet and enjoy the freedom of the easy and carefree life upon which he was at that moment embarking.

If means did not allow him entering a profession—and public school-boys had by far the better chance therein—if his father had no business or shop of his own, or little influence of any kind, then he had to find a job for himself by answering advertisements in the public prints. The best paper for this was the *Daily Telegraph*, which carried the greater part of the commercial advertising of the day.

The boy would read the 'Situations Vacant' column and, finding some which he thought he might have a shot at, would consult with his father. Then between them they would write the fateful letter. It was written by the son on a sheet of good notepaper, after several rough drafts, beneath which was put another sheet of ruled paper, the rules to show through and keep the lines even, and was dictated by the father, who also kept an eagle eye on the spelling. After several attempts and derogatory remarks on his son's writing, the father would be satisfied. The envelope was carefully addressed to the firm, box number, or the nom-de-plume c/o an advertising office stated in the advertisement, a penny stamp affixed

—it was penny postage then—and the letter dropped in the pillar-box.

As it went in and fell, the heart of the youth dropped with it. There went the end of his bright youth, there went the end of irresponsibility. There went school, which did not seem so bad now he had left. Of course, it might not receive an answer at all. But it might lead to a terrifying interview with a prospective employer, and therefore was a thing to be feared. It might even lead to a job. The youth was filled with misgivings, in any event, and seldom wanted any supper. He would go to bed quite subdued and the parents would sit up and discuss his prospects. The mother always drew a rosy picture, but the father, like all fathers, had a much clearer view of his offspring.

Eventually the lad would get a job in the City. The procedure was much the same as today but the demeanour of the applicant was very different. Today the boy applying for the job is apt to ask the questions and decide whether or no he shall take the position. Then the applicant was suitably humble and was keen to get the job. In his heart he might not want it—he knew that Life had got him now—but it had to be done, so he surrendered and did his best. He stood in awe of his employers in the days of the sovereign. It was he who feared to lose his job, not the employer who feared he might go.

And so, one fateful Monday morning, the Middle Class lad, in his new and manly ready-made suit (costing between 18s. and £1), in his new little ready-made overcoat (costing 12s. 6d. to 15s.), and with his little bowler hat on his head, would get into a third-class railway carriage and start to be 'Something in the City', one of a horde of similar lads, all knowing as much—or as little—as each other, all taking their step over the threshold of their careers. His wages would be anything from 6s. to 12s. 6d. a week. Only youths who had greatly impressed their prospective employers got 12s. 6d.—the average was 7s. 6d. to 10s.

The father, who probably travelled second class, would buy his son his third class 'Season Ticket' and the youth was rather proud of it; it seemed a passport to independent manhood. He would be expected, on principle, to make a small contribution to the family exchequer, and was mostly quite proud to do so. He had not nearly so many ways of spending his money then—no pictures to rush to at least twice a week, and the money went so much farther. Also, many families had a tradition that out of his first week's earnings he should buy a present for his mother. This he was pleased to do.

He would find himself, once in the City, in an almost purely masculine world. In the 'nineties and the very early nineteen hundreds women had a very tiny part in it indeed. A woman in the City streets was stared at.

Some firms were employing women typists, but it was a great innovation, and the typewriter itself was still anything but general. Most firms still wrote their correspondence by hand, using for the purpose what was called 'copying ink'—a thick, purple liquid kept in stone bottles and made by a firm called Antoine.

The copying of these letters was the first hurdle the Middle Class youth had to take. He was, of course, the Office Boy, although at home he was always referred to as a 'Junior Clerk'. He had to copy those letters in the 'Letter Book'. But this did not mean he had to write the letters out by hand in copy form. The letters were actually copied by a somewhat difficult and complicated process which he had to master. The Letter Book was a leather-bound tome with an index and numbered pages. The leaves were of the thinnest tissue paper. These had to be damped with a wide, thin brush, an oilskin sheet (thick) being placed under the page so damped. Then a piece of thick blotting-paper was placed over the damp page, another oiled sheet over that, and the book was closed and committed to the Copying Press, which looked for all the world like Caxton's original printing-press, only it was made of iron, enamelled black. It worked in the same way. The boy seized two brass handles—one at each end of a long arm which worked on a screw which screwed down the upper plate on to the book—and dried the damped page. The book was then removed, the blotting-paper taken out, the letter to be copied put under the damp sheet, the book closed and pressed again—and if luck was in, there was a copy on the page.

Some of these presses linger in old offices and junk-shops. But inexpert hands and judgment did not find this job so easy. The page might be made too dry, in which case the copy was too faint, but had taken off enough of the ink to make a second copy valueless. Most beginners made the page too wet, which produced a grand purple smear, and in either case the letter had to be rewritten. But the beginner soon learned the requisite dampness and pressure required, although he spoilt many letters in the learning and also fell into another trap, that of so overdamping the page that it came out altogether in a spongy, filmy mass. But after a short time copies of six letters were made at once at lightning speed. It was just a matter of experience and knack.

This method of copying had a good deal to recommend it. Today, of course, carbon copies are filed. A copy once taken out of a file seems always most reluctant to go back and seldom in its right order. It also has a knack of getting lost—or going into the wrong file, which is much the same thing when wanted in a hurry. A letter book was never lost. It was impossible.

And the beginner's job was also to index these letter books. He not only entered the letter by page number under the right heading in the general index, but he cross-indexed the pages as well. Thus every letter bore, in blue pencil, the page on which the previous letter could be found and the page on which the next one appeared. A whole correspondence could be easily traced. And these copies could not be altered. A carbon copy can.

But in his very early days the young Something in the City bore a grudge against old-fashioned members of the staff who used quill pens—there were still plenty—for the thickness of the ink on letters so written made it necessary to take great care in copying. Most things in offices then were done by hand. All those mechanical devices and filing systems—which save so much time when they work—were unknown and unwanted. Office hours were nominally from nine to six, but usually nearer 6.45, and sometimes later. There was an hour for lunch but no tea interval.

The second snag the young beginner struck was the telephone. Today children use them with facility. Then practically no Middle Class houses, even wealthy homes, had a telephone. They were things of commerce and trade. And so the new office boy, on being told to ring up 'So-and-So', was in a real dilemma. He was shown how to do it but he was afraid of the machine. It was, most definitely, not the machine age. The usual telephone then was a wall instrument—made in Sweden mostly—and it had a hook bearing the receiver on one side and a handle to turn on the other. You turned the handle a few times, removed the receiver—and waited.

It took a good time to get the Exchange, and then a female voice said "Number, please"—and you gave it in and waited again. Altercations between subscriber and the mysterious operator were constant affairs. The National Telephone Company ran the service—free enterprise. It was a good joke, even in those days, and has been so ever since. There were not many telephones and consequently fewer exchanges—Avenue, Central, London Wall, Gerrard (the West End), Hop, and some geographical ones—few as compared with now. The 'number engaged' signal was a hooting noise, as of tugs befogged in the Thames.

The young Middle Class beginner took quite a time to master the 'phone, but he did so in the end, even to using the spare earphone provided if the line was indistinct, as it mostly was, and to switching the call through to a principal, not by means of a plug but by a little switch with a hand pointing to the necessary extension. That extension was a table instrument on four bent legs with a receiver on it—a straight one with an ebonite handle in the middle of which was a little lever to press down whilst speaking, otherwise you were not heard. That had its points too. You could discuss something without being overheard at the other

133

end. The 'phone, for a beginner, was full of pitfalls, but became familiar in time. And you could give yourself a slight but pleasant electric shock if you held down the receiver hook and turned the handle at the same time.

The City then was a maze of tall hats. The topper was the headgear of commerce. Even if men did not wear it to and from their homes, they had one in the office which they always assumed when making a business call. They wore it even with lounge suits. But men of substance wore the frock-coat and the tall hat at all times, their junior partners or managers compromising with a. morning coat. Members of the Stock Exchange wear tall hats to this day. But other stockbrokers and their clerks went bareheaded, a fashion largely adopted also by junior clerks out on their messages. If people took them for stockbrokers, so much the better. Even bank messengers wore the topper, and debt collectors—who called round for overdue accounts—wore them as well, with most unsuitable suits or overcoats. It did not matter so long as the topper was there.

A Middle Class boy soon adopted an 'office coat', which everyone except the principals wore too. It was an old coat, kept at the office and worn therein to save the ordinary coat getting shiny at the elbows and along the forearms. He soon adopted 'cuff protectors', which he made himself out of pieces of white paper, folded over and slipped on over the cuffs. Those cuffs were of white linen. The men of the period wore white linen shirts with stiff-starched fronts and cuffs, but the lads compromised with 'dickeys' and detachable cuffs which had a habit of slipping down over their knuckles and wanted a lot of keeping clean—protectors or not. They had to last a week.

A lad's lunch-money was reckoned at a shilling. He lunched at an A.B.C.—and a shilling was ample. Indeed, he soon found out how to do it for considerably less, and was, when he had made some friends, often led into little shops kept by Italians where much highly coloured pastry was consumed instead of the more solid food his mother insisted on his having.

The tastes of boyhood died hard and he could get a lot of confectionery for a few pence, with nobody to say 'Enough'. If he wanted a very good square meal at a very small price he could go to Wilkinson's—who had branches—and get a plate of *Beef à la Mode*—a wonderful dish, piled high with carrots, potatoes and other vegetables thrown in, and a solid but well-cooked and well-served sweet for a shilling. You gave the waiter a penny. There were other eating-houses, too, of a lower grade, and shops with sausages sizzling in the windows amongst browned and appetizing-looking sliced onions, whilst constant jets of steam ascended from special pipes for that purpose.

There were also the establishments run by Messrs. Lockhart. But these were beneath the Middle Class dignity—they were 'A Good Pull-up for Carmen', and there were carmen in plenty, for traffic was horse-drawn. Lockhart's provided music-hall comedians with a never-failing joke. References to having taken their best girls to dine at the Café de Lockhart, or that they had been supping at their favourite hotel—Lockhart's—were surefire laughs. The publicity probably did Lockhart's a lot of good. Their fare was plain but excellent; a special dish of theirs was a steak-and-kidney pudding for sixpence—most substantial and filling. It was facetiously referred to by customers as 'a baby's head'.

There was an hour for lunch and plenty of time for a walk round. Men thronged the streets in their toppers and horses thronged the roads. The first motor-propelled vehicles were things of wonder and derision. The young Middle Class boy delighted in crossing the road, even in the very busiest parts, whilst the traffic—to him quite a maelstrom—was in full flood. Country folks wondered at the temerity of Londoners, dodging under horses' heads and edging their way through the traffic. The Mansion House was looked upon as a spot of particular danger, but the boy or man who was 'Something in the City' would rather have died than use the subway which arrived when the Tuppenny Tube came into existence.

The City itself was a very different place. The old churches had not been bombed to nothing, the old streets bore many traces of the past ages, Birch's still stood in Cornhill to show what London was like when men wore square-cut coats and three-cornered hats—also to show you what real turtle soup could taste like and to what heights English cheese-cakes and tarts could ascend. Also you could get the best wines and spirits there. But that was for men of money.

City Fathers dined at Crosby Hall, the Ship and Turtle, Pimm's, Sweetings, The London Tavern, the City Arms and other good rest-aurants which abounded—or at the old chop-houses like the George and Vulture off Lombard Street, which retained its Dickensian atmo-sphere and superb food, and where you got no bills but were informed by the head waiter what there was to pay.

There were amazing nooks and corners where you stepped back into past centuries. That same Crosby Hall had been a residence of Richard III, there were old Queen Anne houses in odd courts—and even older houses too, in all sorts of unlikely places. There was the delightful back-water of St. Helen's Place, there was the mediaeval touch of St. Ethelburga's. St. Paul's Churchyard was a mixture of modern city and old Cathedral Close, with shops jostling quiet old houses, and a provision shop in a corner where there was a display of cheeses and eatables such as you could not see today. There was Cloth Fair to take you right back to mediæval times. There were tailors' shops, jewellers, and men's out-fitters of super excellence. And there was Amen Corner with its book-shops and publishers. London was a far more romantic place. The Guildhall was unscathed, and therein stood London's twin giants Gog and Magog—who in more miniature form beat on bells in Cheapside every hour when a quaint little mechanical pageant took place.

There were other pageants too, quite a lot of them. Foreign royalties were always coming to town. They would be entertained to a civic lunch at the Guildhall and would ride by with a military escort whilst City men and boys looked on and cheered. Famous soldiers, back from one of those triumphant little wars, would be entertained by the Right Honourable the Lord Mayor, and it was another sight to see them.

There was a good deal of colour and excitement in life to be gathered during that lunch hour. But it was only an hour—big magnates did not linger over lunch, but much business was done in the bars and wine-shops in those days—and they abounded in the City. There was far more drinking in all walks of life. And the pubs were open all day.

People definitely worked harder. There were no week-ends and very few bosses took the Saturday morning off. Saturday was a full half-day and offices did not close until two o'clock. It was permissible to relax the formal dress on a Saturday, but not very many did so. Discipline was better maintained. People wanted to work. The supply of labour far exceeded the demand, and that made for service and doing one's best.

Yet employers were on the whole very fair people. But you were not allowed to make many mistakes. Office errors were not tolerated as they are today. Business on the whole was conducted with great integrity. A man's good name—a firm's good name—was of the utmost value. Slipshod methods did not pay, inferior work or service did not pay. Quality was de-manded. A man's word was his bond. Competition was keen, but under-hand methods led to quick disaster. There were the great swindlers of the time—every age has produced them, but the rank and file of commerce believed in honesty. To go bankrupt was complete disgrace. A man very seldom recovered from it. It was something to be avoided at all costs. It carried social as well as commercial outlawry.

That may sound severe, but it was a fine repressive spirit when it came to people inclined to be shady. They did not dare. Whitaker Wright, Hooley, and the others who crashed and figured in courts, were the minority of their time and did not shake the credit of the City of London, which was built on the foundation of sound business principles. Men did not embark on risky ventures or take the gambling risks which became so frequent after the First World War. A man's own character was a great part of his capital and the same was true of a firm. Employees were proud of the firms for which they worked. They took the greatest interest in them. They gave of their best. They had a standard of living which satisfied them, and did not spend most of their time trying to reach a much higher altitude—or putting up a façade of being what they were not. Those that did paid the price.

Yet there was much more individualism and far less centralization. There were many more banking firms then than now. Their cheques of varied colour lent a rainbow tint to the post. Some have gone, some are merged into others, some remain. But they all did big business then.

There were the Capital and Counties, whose black-and-white cheques slightly resembled those of the great Bank of England itself (which had not then grown its extra storey, but which was the greatest bank in the world and held far more gold than any other bank in the world); the London and Provincial (with yellowy-brown cheques); Smith Payn & Smith (pink cheques); the Union Bank, which merged into the Union of London & Smiths Bank; the London & South-Western (green or pink cheques); the City Bank (pink cheques); which became the London City & Midland on merging with the London & Midland, whose cheques were blue on white with black lettering (now the Midland Bank); Parrs (green cheques); and the London & County, which merged with the Westminster Bank into the London County & Westminster, when its previously pink cheques went green. Now it is just the Westminster Bank —with cheques pink again—and many others.

It may be that all these mergers are not quite accurately stated. If so, apologies are offered and no harm is intended. All that is wished to be stressed is the far greater number of banks and varieties of cheques in those days.

And in the provinces there were many old-established, sound and prosperous banks, many of which have been swallowed up. To have a banking account then was a guarantee of character. You were not allowed to be a man of straw by a bank. They kept their customers up to the mark and they did not want doubtful accounts. To have an account at the Bank of England was a perfect guarantee of financial stability.

There were smaller banks, like the Birkbeck, Farrows, and the Penny Bank, which foundered in disaster, but even so did not cause a ripple on the face of London's vast, gigantic credit.

There were a great many more callers at the office, for the telephone was not the sole means of doing business and people liked to meet and do their deals face to face. Office boys were kept busy at the enquiry doors. All sorts of people called in. Men of nautical aspect called with great sacks of various furs to sell. Deaf and dumb men offered terrible

137

poems relating to a soldier's life, with a wood-cut illustration, with pathetic expressions of imploring salesmanship. Men would come round offering theatre tickets, obviously 'Complimentary', for sale at extremely cheap rates and always for West End flops. There was quite a traffic in these, which the introduction of the Entertainment Tax put a stop to.

The streets had far more life and colour, there was a much brisker air, and people smiled as they went about. Even the docks had a bigger touch of romance—for sailing-ships were still quite plentiful. There was, too, the annual pageant of the Lord Mayor's Show. This was more rich and more picturesque than the procession of today.

A youth in the City, out on an errand, could manage to see it twice if he knew his way about. There was a fine excuse for delay all ready made and to hand. This special London show attracted far greater attention then. Men with offices on the route gave parties for young people and their escorts, and supplied first-class lunches. Considerable crowds thronged the streets. Eager, hoarse-voiced men in the gutter vended 'Pammerammer Views of the Lord Mayor's Show—all 'ighly coloured'. They were of paper, folded square, and they opened out like the panorama they called themselves.

There was no doubt about the highly coloured part of it. Great splashes of gaudy colours, without any semblance of probability, and with little regard for the outline of the features it was to decorate, made a garish if bright show. But the artist was too optimistic. He included things which were never seen. It is doubtful if anyone had ever seen them in a Lord Mayor's Show: such as elephants, Indian princes on prancing horses and other objects not commonly viewed in the November streets of London, whether in the Lord Mayor's Show or not. Children, their hopes thus aroused, were apt to be tearfully disappointed when the show failed to realize the pictures.

There was another panorama on sale too. This was 'all made to wind up' and it did. A long paper roll, depicting the Show in much better style and with more regard to actuality, but still a bit too hopeful, was enclosed in a gilt metal cylinder, with a little handle to unwind it. It was kept from vanishing inside by a metal tab. Eager fingers soon pulled this off and the pictorial representation was seen no more. Both cost the sum of one penny each, and both were in great demand. They never varied in design or picture, year after year.

There were more uniforms in the old Shows, and more cavalry. There were allegorical cars with becostumed and professional 'supers' posing thereon, who always looked better on the outward journey than on the return, on account of lavish liquid refreshment. But there was the City

Marshal at the head, looking every inch a soldier, almost a Field Marshal, in fact, and there was the same wonderful coach with the same satisfying and magnificently robed Lord Mayor in it. The coachman was an object of great interest. He was massive and he was gorgeous. He was a well-known and familiar figure, for he had commercialized himself by posing for an advertisement for a certain brand of polish. But it did not in the least detract from his impressiveness.

City merchants who were not on the Common Council, and who could not ride in the Show in carriages wearing tall hats and coats with wonderful fur collars or aldermanic robes, were apt to complain that the Show interrupted business. But if there had been any real talk of stopping it they would have risen in their wrath. For London was an English city, proud of its English ways and jealous of its old traditions. It was modern, it boasted, but it did not destroy the past. What had pleased their fathers pleased these merchants too. They did their business in their own British way. They knew nothing of efficiency experts in office organization, they knew nothing of so-called American hustle—of which they had heard and considered cheap and nasty, not to say inefficient. Yet they prospered, they made money, they had solid investments, and they often retired at forty with a very comfortable fortune.

New lines of trade were always opening, new markets were being discovered. There was a good deal of head-shaking at German competition, of cheap and bad goods which were flooding markets once their own preserves. But they put their faith in the British quality—it was the best. They believed this and there was reason for their belief.

All the same, German competition was growing, and there was a thing beginning to be talked about called 'Protection'—a change from the Free Trade which had lasted so long and so profitably. But there was no fear, no despondency. The country was secure and sound at heart. A European war was unthinkable—who would dare? All the same, this German Kaiser was a bit of a problem—the naughty boy of Europe, in fact. But the British Navy and the might of Britain's wealth could soon deal with him. That was their idea, deep-rooted and sincere.

There were odd characters and odd beggars in the City then. One case in particular. Every day for several years a man progressed along the gutter of Bishopsgate Street up to the junction with Threadneedle Street. He was a pitiful sight. Neatly dressed in an old but well-cut and well-cared-for blue suit, a well-brushed if aged bowler hat on his head, he proceeded along this beat in the most painful manner. He was always clean and closely shaven, but his affliction was great. It was to the observer a dreadful case of paralysis. The poor man moved only a yard or two at a time. One leg was stiff and helpless. He had to drag it after him and bring it round in a semi-circular curve before he could make the next step. His progress was therefore very slow and entailed many rests. One of his arms was curled up to his shoulder, the fingers crooked and helpless. In his other hand he held a small tray, bearing matches and umbrella rings. He never offered them for sale, he just carried them. He never spoke a word, he did not even acknowledge the small silver which compassionate passers-by placed on the tray. They never took a box of matches or a ring. Some men gave him alms every day. It was quite an agonizing spectacle.

One day he was missing. The regular patrons saw him no more. The Law had got him. How he was detected, or whether somebody gave him away, was never known. The police did not have to watch parked motor-cars then. But it appeared that each evening he crawled into a tobacconist's, shop where he changed his small money for larger coins. He often took three or four pounds a day, big money then. Still, with his dreadful crawl, his pain-racked and twitching face, he would get as far as London Bridge. There, quite worn out, he would lean against the parapet.

When the crowd going home was at its height, and when after some three quarters of an hour he was sure that there were no observers about who had seen him come to rest, he joined that homegoing crowd with brisk step, his paralysis gone, his two arms swinging gaily. He would board his train to his suburban station. There was evidence given to the effect that in the oyster season he was a regular customer at the little shop near his home station for a dozen of the best. And then he would go to his neat and well-kept prosperous suburban home.

When he was arrested and imprisoned his wife declared she never knew how her husband earned his money, and there was every reason to believe her. She said she thought he was 'Something in the City'. Undoubtedly he was. Those who had given him alms took it well. They decided that his supremely good and well-sustained performance was worth it. But nobody else tried it on.

It did not take the young Middle Class boy long to become a real little City clerk and commercial man. His career had started. His parents had high hopes. They did not have to worry about their daughters. Their future was marriage. A Middle Class father desired to keep his daughters at home until they married and to have them brought up like ladies. This was his wife's job and she did it well.

But already there was a shudder of female unrest in the land. It grew and grew as the days of the life of the sovereign shortened. It was a rumble preceding the earthquake, the preliminary smoke of the volcanic upheaval. Already, in the late 'nineties, women were going into the City to work there. There were, in some offices, female clerks to use the typewriters and to take down shorthand, although a great number of firms resolutely set their faces against women in the office at all.

If a girl had to work, because of family finance or of bereavement, she could be a governess, a school-teacher, she could teach music, or become companion to a lady. It was all a matter of grade. That was woman's work. Or she could become a nurse. All these jobs were hard and poorly paid. The City and business were men's sphere. Women, argued the men, knew nothing of business—how could they? They did not want to bother their heads about such things, bless them.

But girls were in the Post Office, girls had got into the telephone service, more and more girls were learning shorthand and typing, those two talismans of independence, and calling themselves secretaries. Slowly, almost imperceptibly, but very steadily and resolutely they were sapping the defences and undermining the outworks of that great all-male preserve, the centre of the world's business, the centre of the world's finance. It was what would now be called infiltration, and the girls knew what they were about.

As the years rolled on and the 20th century shook off its babyhood, more and more women were becoming 'Something in the City'.

CHAPTER IX

The Streets of London

THE STREETS OF LONDON, IN THE DAYS OF THE SOVEREIGN, ALTHOUGH they traversed the same route, were very different in appearance and in traffic to the streets of today. Their names are all they have in common.

In the time under review, the internal combustion engine, to wreak so much alteration in life, was only just creeping in—and that was the right word. There were, except for the railways, two means of transport: the horse and one's own feet—which includes the bicycle.

Everybody walked more. They believed in the use of their legs and put them to their proper purpose. Nobody got tired after a few yards' stroll. It was not considered necessary to take a car in order to run a few hundred yards. And, anyway, there were hardly any cars. Nor did a man going a short distance think of hailing a hansom or a four-wheeler or even boarding a tram or a bus. He walked. He was accustomed to walking—it was quite natural to him. And most men carried walking-sticks—or umbrellas. Walking-sticks, then so popular and of so varied design, are almost things of the past. Young men today never carry them. But then young men of today never walk.

If you went from one part of London to another, whatever the purpose, you went by bus or by tram. There were plenty of buses, all run by private enterprise—Nationalisation had not consumed them all and made them all into one pattern. There were scores of different lines of buses and all had different colours. You knew your bus not by a number but by its colour. This not only gave it greater individuality but also gave a greater variety and gayer pattern to the streets. The modern scarlet bus is a brave sight but it becomes monotonous. There was no monotony then.

There were 'The Favourite', 'The Atlas', 'The Royal Blue', 'The Times' and many other bus companies. There was the London General Omnibus Company (an incipient boa-constrictor which was in time to swallow all the others), and the London Road Car Company, whose buses flew little Union Jacks from small flagstaffs. Tillings, Hearn, Balls Brothers (of Brixton), Jones and others all ran buses. There were blue, green, white, yellow, brown, chocolate, red and black buses. It was the same with the trams; they were as multi-coloured as a flower-garden and they made the streets gay.

The buses had two horses. The driver sat on his seat up aloft, where

Dr. W. G. Grace, the world's most famous cricketer and every boy's idol

Tom Hayward, the England and Surrey cricketer, whose batting record has only just been lowered

Lord Hawke, a great cricketer and captain of Yorkshire

By permission of Picture Post Library]

Tod Sloan, the famous American jockey, who introduced the "monkey crouch" style of riding in this country

[By permission of "Topical" Press Agency Ltd.

he could and did talk to the passengers sitting in the front seats. It was a privilege to chat with him. Neither he nor the conductor wore a uniform. They, too, were individual.

The driver was always the smarter of the two. He retained many of the old characteristics of the stage-coach driver. There was a definite touch of 'horsiness' about him, and he was the lineal descendant of old Tony Weller. Frequently he wore a smart fawn covert coat with large pearl buttons and a shiny topper. Or he might have a coat of more sober hue and a bowler, but always he was smart, lively and communicative. And mostly he sported a stock and a buttonhole of large size. He was not the silent, intent person of concentration who drives the bus today. He was a man of the world at large. He saluted other bus-drivers with a twist of his wrist and his whip. He had numerous acquaintances all along his route, who hailed him or whom he hailed. He had a superlative gift of badinage and a masterly flow of original invective if obstacles arose in his path. He handled his team with the air of a four-in-hand and drove well. He was guide, philosopher and friend to country visitors, pointing out the sights with the utmost pleasure.

The best way to see London was from the top of a bus. It still is, but the expert guide is lacking now and the speed is not so leisurely. All the same, there is very little difference in the time of travel between two points on short stages, as compared with today, for there were hardly any traffic jams or hold-ups and no traffic lights.

On one day in the year the bus was made an even gayer sight than usual. It was the custom when one of the Rothschild family—probably Mr. Alfred—sent a brace of pheasants to every bus-driver and conductor in London for every bus-driver to celebrate the day by tying a bunch of ribbons, of the Rothschild colours—yellow and blue—to his whip. Some even displayed the pheasants on the buses, as a sort of triumphal note.

In wet weather the driver wore an oilskin cover to his hat and an oilskin cape. He always swathed his legs in rugs, summer or winter.

The tops of those buses were open to the sky. The seats thereon had undergone changes. There was the old-fashioned 'knifeboard', with long seats running back to back along the centre of the bus, whilst you braced your feet against an iron railing at the edge. Women seldom rode on top of buses in knifeboard days. Then came the 'garden seats', with just room for two on each. The ascent to the top of the knifeboard buses was up a species of ladder, another reason for the ladies going inside. If it was wet, you opened your umbrella and covered as much of yourself as possible with a tarpaulin sheet which hooked on to the seat ends.

A ride on top of a bus was a good bracer and nobody minded the weather very much. The Middle Class of the time were a hardy race, and would not have liked the closed-in tops of today. Inside, you sat facing each other. Half-way down each side there would be a brass dividing rail. The insides were a little stuffy and a trifle musty. The seats were upholstered, usually in green, and were quite comfortable. There was a line of small advertisements along the top of each window, and the fare-board at the end.

The conductor was also a character. He varied in type far more than the drivers, whose 'horsiness' made them all akin. The conductor had nothing to do with horses, but lots to do with humanity, which he understood remarkably well. Some were morose men, who viewed the passengers as necessary evils, but were seldom impolite, even when poked in the back with umbrellas by old ladies and gentlemen wishing to alight. He would remonstrate, it is true, but mostly with real Cockney wit. He started and stopped the bus by pulling a little cord which rang a bell, and he also gave the two stamps of today if he was out of reach of the bell.

Buses in those days would stop wherever the passenger wanted them to. There were regular stops, of course, but you could get on or off at your own request. Sometimes, if the bus was stopped twice in a few yards, the conductor would remonstrate mildly, and beg you to think of the horses.

You never had to queue up at stated places. The bus was at your service. The conductor was at your service and, strangely enough, the standing was not limited on account of the extra trouble to him in collecting fares. That was his job and he did it. He, like his Company, was under the impression that he was there for the purpose of transporting people where they wanted to go and giving them the best service possible. It did not dawn upon him that buses were run for the purpose of employing him at the discomfort of the public. It was quite the other way round. He knew his route too, and you had only to ask to be set down at the nearest spot to your destination, which perhaps you were unfamiliar with. He never forgot to stop and put you on your way.

Some were real Cockney wits and would keep their bus in a roar with back-chat and their amusing sallies with other transport and other conductors. And they, like the drivers, had withering invective too. They wore no uniforms. They mostly wore lounge suits and bowler hats. They had a bag for the change and they had their clips of tickets. Both they and the driver had a numberplate of enamel. If inconsiderate and quarrelsome passengers fell foul of them and threatened to 'take their number' for the purpose of reporting them, they were the first to hold it prominently before aggrieved eyes—and even to write it down for the complainer. But disputes were very few.

The brakes were on the surface of the wheels, applied by the driver's foot, and skid-pans were used down steep hills.

The average wage was 7s. 6d. a day for drivers and 6s. 6d. a day for conductors.

There were pirate buses too, which operated on the same routes independently of the real lines. There would be races between the pirates and the legitimate buses to fixed stopping points, and they would manœuvre to pick up hailing fares. There was war of speed, skilful driving and verbal ribaldry between them. The pirate buses gave no tickets at all.

In some of the outer suburbs very old-fashioned buses survived. In some of these there were no conductors at all. The driver put his hand through a hole in the roof and you placed your fare—twopence any distance—therein. You got in at a back door which, when closed, covered the step. You started or stopped the driver by pulling the bell yourself. Inside, your feet were amongst straw. The outside had two tiers of seats, facing forward like an old-fashioned coach. It was a point of honour amongst men to jump on and off a bus—or the tram—whilst it was in motion, even if bowling along at a brisk twelve miles an hour. The first sign of approaching age was when a man found he was disinclined to do this little acrobatic feat. Buses were much smaller than the monsters of today.

The trams were a different proposition. They, of course, ran along rails, and when a decrepit one is seen marooned in some remote country field in these days, used as a shed, its smallness seems remarkable. In the days of the sovereign they seemed very large indeed. The trams also were two-horse affairs, but if there were hills a trace-horse joined in, ridden by a boy, mostly, both for trams and buses. Trams, somehow, were never so comfortable or intimate as buses. They are not today. They moved along their lines with a rocking movement, the ends rising and falling like a ship at sea facing a head wind. Inside you faced each other and often the seats were not upholstered, but covered with a kind of cane perforated with small holes. The tops were like the buses. There were trams of all colours. George Lashwood, last of the real 'Lions Comique', had a popular song about them.

Neither the driver nor conductor wore uniform, though some of the conductors wore peaked caps. The driver was not smart and neither was he 'horsey'. There was none of the gay raillery of the bus-driver about him. He was, perhaps, the beginning of the machine age, on account of his vehicle being reckoned, in the eyes of the law, a light railway. He wore drab dark clothes, he wrapped rugs around him and he stood on the little platform. At the end of the tram the floor of the roof protruded over his head like a canopy. He could, if he liked, sit on a kind of shooting-stick, a wooden seat fixed on a pole, which fitted into a socket, but mostly he stood to drive. He was cut off from his passengers, with whom he held no communication.

He need not be an expert driver. All he had to do was to start and stop his horses and keep them on their feet. He controlled the speed of his tram by a brake which operated by turning a big steel handle, which he wound and wound until the brakes went on. He had a whistle which he blew to clear the line of heavy, slow-moving horse-drawn vehicles which would stray all over the place.

At the end of the journey the driver got down, unhitched his horses and rehitched them again to the other end of the tram, which of course could not turn round. It was a simple job. The horses were fastened to a kind of half-hoop of steel which fitted into a socket at either end of the tram and to which traces were attached.

Going downhill on greasy days—and roads were greasy then—was the only difficulty the driver had to face. The tram would, unless promptly braked, almost catch up the horses, which really had to trot hard to keep ahead—and the tram was apt to slip and get derailed. It was pushed back by the combined efforts of the conductor and the passengers and willing help from passers-by. You entered and left the tram through a sliding door at one end. There was a door at each end, naturally, but only that of the conductor was used. On the return journey everything reversed. Tram-drivers and conductors got slightly less pay than the busmen and in some cases the fare stages were longer, though fares were cheap enough in any case. You travelled a very long way for a penny. Naturally neither trams nor buses went as far out as they do today. They were urban transport. Somehow or another the passengers on a tram seemed to be of a Lower Class than those on a bus.

Many City men travelled to town on private buses, which were drawn by four horses. It would call at their door in the morning and bring them back at night. These buses housed cosy little coteries of friends. The drivers and conductors had the status of old family retainers and did very well indeed. The whole turn-out was spick and span.

The other means of street transport were the cabs. The hansom cab and the four-wheeled cab, the 'four-wheeler', or the 'growler', as it was called. Of these the hansom cab was the most romantic form of transport ever devised. It was called The Gondola of London. It was smart, it was speedy and it was by no means expensive. Everyone knows what a hansom looked like, but only the elders remember them in their glory. They had a glamour which the taxi has never attained. But what motor vehicle can compete with a horse-drawn one in this respect? These cabs, these buses, even these trams, had individuality which machinery can never reach.

Most hansoms were shining and gay. Their bodywork glistened in the sun; their lamps, their plated axle-trees, and all their metalwork shone brightly. Some had yellow wheels, which added to the gaiety, and most of them had a little vase of flowers inside, which the driver kept fresh and blooming. Certainly the horse was not always in its pristine prime—but for the most part they were good animals enough, and well groomed. There was always a sneaking belief that one rode behind a racehorse— even a Derby winner. It was wishful thinking, which the driver would encourage, but it added to the thrill.

All drivers took a pride in their hansoms. And it was always a thrill to hail a hansom, get in and be driven along, a thrill which never palled however much you did it. Indeed, rich men often had private hansoms of their own, so much was this form of vehicle esteemed. When rubber tyres came in the likeness to the gondola was heightened, for you just floated along, the patter of the horse's hooves and the jingling of its bells being the equivalent of the guitar and throaty tenor—and better music to the Londoner's ears. In summer, little striped awnings covered the roof.

The driver, in his seat up above and at the back, was always very smart. He was smarter than the bus-driver, although they dressed alike to a large extent. But the topper of the hansom cabby was always curlier in the brim and at a more acute angle, and his bowler would be worn on one side. They had a fine command of their horse from their lofty altitude, and the reins running across the roof and over a little metal bridge on the edge gave them great control. It was as well, for if the horse fell down— and it did from time to time, the fare was likely to find himself precipitated out of the cab on to the back of the fallen animal.

At night time or in inclement weather folding doors closed you in, made in two sections, which the cabby or the fare could operate, and in very bad weather a glass window came down to protect you. This was extremely dangerous in case of accidents, and the weather had to be pretty brutal before cautious folk had it lowered. Also the proximity to the rear of the horse had, at times, embarrassing drawbacks. But Londoners were used to this.

To drive in a hansom on a summer day, or through the dusk of a summer night, with one's best girl, with the lanterns glowing on each side, the gaslight making the streets golden, was a thing of joy. The driver communicated with you through a little hatch in the roof. He could keep you under observation if he so desired. If you wanted him, you thrust the lid up with your stick. He was a man of character and understanding. He summed up his fares at a glance and behaved accordingly. He could be, and was, very understanding. He knew without telling if you wanted to go fast or slow, and he would linger along the darker parts of the drive. He had wit, he had humour, he was a psychologist, and he had a great power in bad language when aroused.

There was a thing known as the radius, outside which fares went up. No ordinary man knew the extent of this radius and the cabby always appeared to be ignorant as well, unless his idea of the fare when you paid him differed from yours. Then he was either very abusive or ironically tearful—and in nearly every case you gave him what he asked. His most usual form was to say "Leave it to you, Guv'nor," which made you feel the necessity for generosity. He had a remarkable memory for faces and would frequently say, when hailed, "Have the pleasure of knowing you, sir. I've druv you afore." Under such circumstances the fare was liberal.

A collision in a hansom with a heavier vehicle could be nasty, for maybe the shafts broke and then the whole thing went over backwards with the fare inside, his feet in the air, contemplating the heavens through pieces of broken glass. But drivers were very good, and accidents did not often happen. Always a ride in a hansom was a joy. The taxi is a means of getting you somewhere. The hansom was something which did the same, but also took you for a drive.

The four-wheeler was nothing like so good. It was badly sprung, it was slow, its driver was like itself, oldish and running to seed. Its horse had usually done so already. It rattled and it bumped and the fare was always in a state of vibration, which may have been good for him, but did not make for comfort. It felt damp and it smelt musty inside. The windows would either not open at all, or would not close. They would refuse to answer to the pulling of the strap which was supposed to control them. If they did so condescend they did it suddenly and you bumped yourself pretty badly.

Young people avoided four-wheelers; they were patronized by old ladies and gentlemen whose motto was 'Safety first'. They went up and down the slightest hill at a walk. But if you had much luggage they were unavoidable. There was room on a hansom for hand luggage only—they were the speed-boats of the streets and things of lightness, the very pleasure-craft of London. The four-wheeler carried luggage. It was amazing how much you could pile on to it and how much the horse could move. Often it did not seem possible. But it got you home.

All drivers despised the arriving motor vehicles. They kept up a running commentary on the objects of their despite. They never believed these 'stinking motors' would drive them off the road, a feat which they accomplished with considerable rapidity, once they got a start.

Early motor-buses—Vanguards—broke down often and the jibes of the horse-drivers were something at which to wonder. But the machines beat the horses. The first taxis gave a thrill. The people of moderate means had their first sensation of a horseless ride. It was novel, it was fast—faster than the hansom if the one-cyclinder affair did not break down. It was sixpence a mile then.

In 1905 the motor-bus took the streets. Progressive people hailed it. The *Bystander* of 5th April, 1905, gave a picture of one with an open top—the police refused to allow a type with closed tops. The caption said:

> "The Arrival of the Motor Omnibus; the Vanguard-line just started by the London Motor Omnibus Company. The motor bus has only just arrived but already it has reduced fares by half and can travel its journey in less than half the time occupied by the horse-drawn vehicle. The London Motor Omnibus Company has placed six upon the road between Brondesbury and Charing Cross. The buses on each route will be distinguished by a name. Five Milnes-Daimler motor omnibuses will be delivered to the Company every fortnight until the complement of one hundred is reached."

The gauntlet was thrown down in no uncertain manner. The battle was short and sharp. The internal combusion engine defeated the horse and drove it from the roads. But that airy statement of doing the distance in half the time took no account of breakdowns.

There was another type of omnibus which went about with what seemed to be a furnace glowing under its bonnet and which was wrapped very often in clouds of steam.

It is rather amusing, too, to observe that the same paper which hailed the coming of the motor-bus with so much *éclat* told a different story in another issue. It recorded:

> "While I am very hopeful of the ultimate benefits that the 'mobus' will confer on traffic in general, the actual performances of some of the new vehicles are somewhat disappointing. I refer particularly to the new Milnes-Daimler bus which the London Motor Omnibus Company is putting on the road. A few days ago I got on one, rejoicing in the name of 'Vanguard', which was standing near the Law Courts. After some hesitation, it crawled into the Strand and stopped dead. The driver, who was, I think, hardly *au fait* with his machinery, proceeded, helped by remarks from passing busmen, to empty a packet of white powder on to his clutch. Meanwhile a similar bus came past and, anxious for a ride, I joined it instead. The gears changed anything but well and the low speed made far too much noise. Travelling was slow, and on such an easy gradient as Charing

Cross Road we were easily passed by a horse-drawn bus. Those interested in this new and promising form of traction must take care that the vehicles are kept in good order and that they get thoroughly competent drivers."

Well, that has been accomplished, but it is a genuine picture of the horse *v.* motor combat.

Motor-cars were becoming fairly familiar sights. The time had gone when the man had to walk in front with a red flag. It was now smart to have a car but beyond the reach of the Middle Class, who still relied on their feet or on horses, with an occasional taxi-ride. Those old-fashioned cars look strange today with their occupants perched high in the air. Renaults, Charrons, Panhards, Mércèdes, Napiers, Darracqs, Siddeleys, Daimlers, Benz, De Dions, Argylls, Sunbeams, Thornycrofts, and of course the Rolls, were all early favourites.

As early as 1905 too, the question of accidents in the street arose. It is interesting to note that the police lists of 1903 gave the number of street accidents resulting in death that year as 154. Cabs killed twenty-two people, buses accounted for sixteen, and the lumbering vans and lorries did the rest. All those were in all probability the result of horse-driven vehicles—for the proportion of motor traffic was very small. Compare it with the lists today. 'Progress' would account for that figure in a few minutes.

There was one advantage in the days of the horse: life was safer. It was urged on behalf of the car that it was much easier controlled. It could, they said, pull up in half the distance when travelling at twenty miles an hour as against a horse vehicle at fifteen miles per hour. Small comfort if you had been run down already. The danger of the skidding motor was already apparent, however. But it had come to stay. Did not King Edward use a car? That settled it for everyone.

The thing which annoyed the motorist most was the 'police trap' and being summoned for speeding. Motoring was still a chancy business. You might get there, or you might not. And one dressed specially for it. The men wore immense coats, caps, goggles and leggings; the ladies long coats and veils over their faces and hats. The whole thing still had a joyous uncertainty about it. There was difficulty over the new words 'chauffeur' and 'garage'. Both are anglicized now. But little electric broughams, with the driver and footman perched up in front and looking as though they would tip the whole thing forward, so precarious did it seem, were already about the West End at night and lining up with the carriages when the theatres turned out.

Already the heads of the Fire and Salvage Brigades were dashing about in cars—or trying to—and already motors were carrying some, at any rate, of His Majesty's mails.

The old mail-cart had an air of romance too. Often behind the interior wire grille were dogs to keep off intruders and thieves. The postman, that familiar figure, dressed differently too. Mostly as regards his hat. It varied down the period. It was an ordinary peaked cap early on, with a flat protruding brim. Then it changed to a kind of tureen shape, with a brim back and front, which turned downwards. The postmen of the day said they did not know if they were going or coming. Telegram boys wore a flat-brimmed cap too.

One London type was being driven away by the oncoming cars, and that was the street orderly, a lad dressed in a red jacket belted round the waist who, armed with a kind of dustpan and hard brush, dived about amongst the traffic collecting the horse manure and placing it in metal pillars along the gutters. His job was doomed.

There were lots of types which have gone. Shoeblacks were numerous. Many of them wore red coats too and had regular customers. There was more mud about and boots got dirtier. You stood on one leg, the other foot placed on the shoeblack's stand, and he operated on you very efficiently in the open street at a very cheap price—and what you liked to give him.

Those cab-ranks and little shelters—some still exist for their descendants the taximen. Each rank had its 'tout' who watered the horses and ran errands, a nondescript creature in rags who nevertheless got a living and filled a definite demand in the life of the day.

The roads were of macadam or of granite setts over which wheels and horses made considerable noise, but not so much as today. The very mud supplied a demand for labour. There was a strange race of men, often half-witted or afflicted, and always in advanced sartorial decay, who swept crossings and kept them pretty clean. They would touch their hat as you passed over, and depended entirely on your generosity. But they had a kind of squatter's right to their crossing, and woe betide an interloper. Ragged children sometimes swept crossings and reaped a richer harvest than their adult rivals. It was not at all an edifying spectacle, though a necessary one then, and it marked clearly the poverty which lay under the shadow of the golden sovereign.

The muffin man was very different. On winter or autumn nights his bell was welcomed as he came down the roads crying 'Muffins and crumpets'. He carried them on a tray on his head, resting on a round flat pad. The muffins were covered by a green baize cloth. All children considered that muffins so bought tasted better than when they came from the shop itself. The streets were full of entertainment.

There were men with dancing bears, of a dirty whitish colour, led on a chain. These poor wretches got on their hind legs and did a kind of shambling dance; also they caught the pole in their fore-arms which their trainer, always a foreigner, threw to them. Children found great delight in them. There were piano-organs galore, with smiling, swarthy Italians to turn the handles. Not only children but adults—though never of the Middle Classes—danced to the organs in the streets. The organs popularized the tunes of the day. To get a tune on the organs was equivalent to getting it on the air today. And because it was not heard so irritatingly often it lasted a full twelve months.

Many organs had monkeys, shivering little beasts made undignified and wretched by little red coats and fezzes, and sometimes even light-blue trousers. Hurdy-gurdies had monkeys too. A hurdy-gurdy was a kind of barrel-organ carried by its owner who, when he played, rested it on a wooden leg which folded under it. There was an art in grinding an organ, but the hurdy-gurdy was a hurdy-gurdy and never responded to the human touch.

Some piano-organs had dancing dolls on top, which revolved in a simple dance of the waltz kind no matter what tune was being played. Italian women in full 'contadina' costume, with raven tresses, flashing smiles and yellowish complexions, brought round little love-birds of such talent that for one penny they would pick out your fortune from a little tray of envelopes. The fortunes were all good ones and never came true, but you could not blame the bird for that.

Punch and Judy shows abounded. Acrobats and tumblers, in pink fleshings—which got plentifully mud-plastered on bad days—performed in the roads. Strong men lifted weights, escapologists got themselves out of seemingly impossible tangles of chains. There were chapeaugraphists, whose stock-in-trade was a round piece of black felt with a hole in the middle. According to how they twisted it they became Nelson, Wellington Napoleon, bandits, all sorts of people—even an abbess or mother superior. This was achieved by placing the felt round their face, adopting a vacant—not to say idiotic—expression, putting their forefinger on their chin and gazing heavenward. But they were popular turns, as were the paper-tearers, the itinerant ventriloquists—whose own mouths moved more than the dolls, despite the camouflage of a heavy walrus moustache.

Very popular indeed was the one-man band. This was an amazing 'act'. The one-man band-er lived up to his name. He had Pan-pipes fastened under his lips, he had bells on his head, his arms and round his ankles. On his back he bore a big drum, the sticks being attached to his elbows so that by flapping his arms he beat his drum. In his hands he carried two wind instruments; one was always a cornet, and when he played on everything at once the effect was quite astounding. It would appear to be a lost art, but once there were plenty of such performers.

German bands were a joke, but a manifold joke. Solemn, bespectacled Teutons, wearing peaked caps, gathered round lamp-posts and played. Sometimes there were only three, sometimes half a dozen, but one always played the bassoon and the 'oom-pah-pah' dominated the rest. Sounds of cornets came in gusts and notes of flute were intermittent. Detection of a melody was problematic. Sometimes little German boys accompanied them and sang sentimental German songs which nobody understood. The whole outfit was usually regarded in the light of being spies, but somehow they made a living. There must have been a lot of Germans in London to make that possible.

Men on stilts dressed in bizarre costumes strode about and peeped into high windows whilst playing banjos, to the horror and dismay of nervous children. There were all sorts of solo performers on all sorts of instruments, and also vocalists who made the most dismal sounds under the impression that they were singing. The streets of London were a vast ever-changing free show before the motor made it impossible.

There were beggars of all kinds, from those who just hoped that their extreme melancholy would touch you to one-legged and no-legged men, presumably old sailors, who played musical-boxes or did some kind of endless tatting.

The old street cries lingered too. Men and women hawked their wares, and there was always nostalgic charm when they cried 'Sweet Lavender' and 'Ripe Strawberries'. Men besought you to buy 'Fine clothes-props', or 'A fireguard, a toast-rack—hand-made out of copper wire'. Newsboys dashed about yelling sensational statements of things not always recorded in the newspapers they sold. Often, on dark evenings, raucous men would run along quiet roads, howling " 'Orrible murder—'ere y'are—'orrible murder", and people went out and bought the paper. They were seldom any the wiser for their halfpenny. The swift motor delivery vans which take the papers now to the newsvendors were then men on bicycles with heavy bags of papers slung round them, who threaded their way through the traffic in the most amazing manner at top speed, and they handed out the papers without stopping.

The London cries have gone now, even the catsmeat man had his own then, crying 'Mee-mee-meat' as he went from house to house with his basket full of skewered horsemeat and a train of anxious cats behind him. And the milkman was very vocal and awoke the early morning echoes.

But there still remains a man who sells aprons, braces and other things of that kind in Covent Garden Market, who retains his street cry and brings a memory of old times. He is also a wit and he shouts as he passes by, "I'll serve you right." One is grateful to him, however; it is almost the last street cry of London. And there were so many.

Carts and vans and wagons rolled along in great variety, even great wains of hay. Your beer was delivered to your door by the barrel in a brewer's dray with big powerful horses; big powerful men of might and brawn, matching those dray-horses, carried the beer to your cellar—houses had cellars then. They wore corduroy trousers and white shirts, like overalls, sleeves rolled up to their elbows displaying huge forearms. They had brewers' caps on their heads, knitted caps of colour made of stockingette tapering to a point and betasselled. Across their leather aprons was a leather crossbelt. On this they carried an inkwell and a pen with which they signed your receipt. No fountain-pens then. They were a rich man's toy.

The coalmen have scarcely changed, nor their carts, save that they have lost their horses.

The butcher delivered by means of a cart. It was a species of box between two high wheels. The meat was in the body or box, and there was a door at the back. It was something like a dog-cart. A youth or young man drove a spirited pony and he travelled fast and cut the corners. He was regarded as the peril of the roads.

The dustcarts were open, two-wheeled affairs drawn by one horse. The dustman, who wore a special hat like a sou'-wester, climbed a little ladder and tipped the dustbin into the cart. The dust blew all over the place.

Bakers' vans were the same as now except not motor-drawn, and bakers used little push-carts too.

But the milkcart was a very different affair. You got your milk either horse-drawn or by human traction. The horsed affair was the true and last remaining descendant of the Roman chariot, or perhaps the more deadly ancient British one. In this cart, which was drawn by a good horse, was a big metal churn with brass fittings, and in that churn was the milk. It came out of a tap into little pewter cans, with lids and handles, and so it was delivered direct to the house. All very unhygienic, of course. Milk could be delivered on foot, the milkman pushing a kind of crate on wheels, sometimes four, sometimes two behind and one in front. Again the milk was drawn from a metal churn into the little metal-pewter cans. It was left on your step, it was hung on your railings, until you took it in.

There was more than one delivery a day, and after the early-morning one the milk was often drawn straight into a household jug, rich and creamy. The hand wagons rattled with their cans and churns, but the milk-carts made a brave noise, like a charge of men in armour. It was a pretty noisy affair altogether was the milk-round, for the milkman yelled "Milk

—milk oh!" with all kinds of falsetto yodels and quavers. This milk was much as it had come from the cow; it was not pulverized or sterilized, and it had not undergone the various forms of treatment suffered by milk today before it gets into the glass bottles with the little tinfoil tops.

In some districts, and notably in the West End of London, an even more primitive form of milk delivery lingered. Women, with skirts looped up above their ankles, carried pails of milk around, supported on yokes borne on their shoulders. This was scooped into the jugs of customers by means of metal measures. This could happen from the carts or hand-carts, for there was usually a huge milk can ready filled, and replenished from the churn. You got a pint, half pint or whatever it was by dipping the measure into the milk and just pouring it into the jug. Children liked to have a glass of milk drawn for them by the milkman in that way. It tasted better. Perhaps on account of the germs.

The milkman also sold cream—real cream—either by measure or in shiny little brown earthenware jugs or jars, with paper tops tied on with string. You could have as much milk or cream as you liked. There was absolutely no limit. Some of the carts carried butter and eggs too—as much as you liked as well.

And there was an even more unhygienic method of giving children milk, mentioned before but which bears repetition. There was a real live cow tethered at the entrance to St. James's Park. Milk was drawn straight from it by human hands—a milkmaid's hands—think of it, in the heart of London!—and children drank it with glee and joy, in that primitive dreadful germinous state. And loved it. The writer had many a glass well over fifty years ago—and lives to write today. Strange, but true. We did not know so much about germs then and we cared a lot less.

Another relic of the days before roads were hard ashpalt, cement or tarred surfaces, when the real earth was not treated like a guilty secret, but was given a chance, and when in consequence, in hot dry weather, dust was prevalent, was the watercart. This was a large metal tank on four wheels, drawn by one horse. At the rear end was a large metal pipe affair with holes in it—a kind of elongated spray or rose. By pushing down a lever the driver caused water to spurt out in numberless sparkling jets as he drove slowly along.

The smell of that water on the dust, a real smell of bygone summers, was one of the best things of the time and an ineffaceable memory. They don't use watercarts now. There is no need. It may be better or it may be worse, but one of the best summer scents has gone, and the stink of petrol does not make up for it. Nothing so fresh, so clear or so vitally of the true earth can be smelt today.

One of the big thrills was a fire-engine. This was not a motor affair but drawn by two fine, plunging horses, eager and speedy, who seemed to know themselves the urgency of their journey. The firemen sat along each side of it, wearing gleaming brass helmets and brass shoulder-straps like plaited mail. As they went they shouted 'Fire, Fire, Fire!' and one rang a bell.

At the end of the engine was a large brass boiler with a funnel. This belched smoke and dropped red-hot cinders as the fire-engine dashed along. It was something of a sensation to see the fire brigade turn out. The horses dashed to their places on each side of the shaft pole, the harness fell on them from above, nimble fingers fixed it in a twinkling, the men leapt on, and the thing was off with a dash and a gallop and a grand amount of noise which the modern engine can never equal. It is all much quieter and more dingy today, and it is not all that quicker either.

The engine would be pursued by a running crowd and cyclists would speed in its wake to the scene of the fire. Nobody could resist it. It could be traced by the trail of cinders.

Of all the London street characters, the policeman has changed least, except perhaps that you never see a bearded one today and they all appear much younger. But that may be the observer's fault. The changes in uniform are only minor. The speed 'cop' is something new and alien. He has yet to prove to the foreigner that, like the sturdy, steady old flat-foot on the beat of the Golden Age, he is wonderful. And to prove it to his own countrymen too.

One man has gone for good, a street character who was so typical of the time. Machinery and electricity both have killed him. He was the lamp-lighter. He came along the road at dusk walking briskly, with his pole over his shoulder. That pole had a brass container on the end, something like a cartridge case, but perforated by holes. Inside was a flame, but how it was kept burning was apparently a trade secret, for nobody seems to know. He came to the lamp-post, he pushed the pole through a small hole at the bottom of the gas-lamp and the pole turned on the tap, which set the gas coming through the jet. Then out of his pole darted a little flame, and the gas-lamp flared merrily. Down the road he went, as one watched from a window, and lamp after lamp sprang to life. He left a firmament of flickering stars behind him, illuminating the growing dusk and twilight.

Children watched him eagerly and with a touch of sadness too, for it meant another day was over, and bedtime loomed near. And yet he was a friend of theirs, although unknown. His coming was a daily event, part of the life of their youth. To the grown-ups it meant that night time had come—and it brought relaxation, or the pursuit of pleasure. It was a thrill to watch those yellow lights—afterwards came the whiteness of incandescence—and to see the long street star-studded with them. Today, when it all goes on at once, there is no thrill. It is just machinery.

There are men and women about today, not so very old, who have actually seen a Jack-in-the-Green on May-day in London, and people in the country who have had a visit at Christmas from the Mummers, St. George, the Russian Bear, the Doctor and all.

CHAPTER X

Broughams, Bicycles and Trains

IN ADDITION TO THE PUBLIC VEHICLES, THERE WAS A CERTAIN STRATA OF the Middle Class which had its own private means of horsed locomotion, and there was a very great proportion of it which would hire a carriage for a special event. This hiring was done from the local 'jobmaster', as the man who let out carriages was then described. They abounded in all districts, as do garages and petrol pumps and hire services today. It was a sound and flourishing business, this 'jobbing'. Also it was a very personal one. The jobmaster's 'livery and bait' stable had a great attraction for children of all ranks. There was ample stabling and quite a large array of horses of all kinds and colours. That alone was a great draw to juvenile eyes. The grooms and ostlers could be seen rubbing these steeds down and 'grooming' them, which every young lad wanted to do. The ostlers made rather sizzling noises with their mouths, which every boy tried to imitate. This was said to calm the horses, though few people understood why, and the horses, naturally, could not say.

But the ostlers were busy, expert men, very hard bitten and very horsey. They worked in their riding-breeches and leggings, with their sleeves rolled up, and either wore a waistcoat of horsey cut or just the shirt. They might be bareheaded, they might wear a large cap indeed, a voluminous affair with a peak. And few of them were without a straw in their mouths.

There was always a small crowd of errand boys, or other children, if not at school, to watch the operations and to reproduce it in their own games, small brothers and sisters being the horses and commanded to 'get up' or 'come over' as they underwent the process of rubbing down. There was the indefinable sharp smell of the stables over all, and the grooms, ostlers, and the whole stables were always spotlessly clean, a remark which applied—and still applies—to all those connected intimately with horses.

You could hire practically any sort of carriage you liked from a jobmaster, who lived up to his name. The favourite was the brougham, that closed, solid, respectable carriage so beloved of all. Doctors of any standing had a brougham—or hired one on contract—to make their calls. A doctor who walked to his patients inspired less confidence. And practically every doctor wore a frock-coat and a tall hat, the attire which went with the brougham.

Lawn Tennis in the Golden Age. Miss May Sutton, a champion, in the correct attire for the game of those days

The Bathing Machine—typical of every seaside resort

Off for the holidays. Papa is getting the tickets

The Pierrots oust the Nigger Minstrels—a typical seaside scene

There were victorias, which were open carriages with little doors; there were landaus, which were much the same thing but which had no doors at all. The sides sloped down to a level step, by means of which you got in or out. There were still some barouches. There were phaetons, which were not hired by families unless they were of a sporting bent and going to the country. These were kind of compressed stage-coaches, very smart and very dashing and would hold four and sometimes six passengers, including the driver. It is rather difficult to describe, but it had the driver's seat in front, who would have a passenger beside him and seats for two more at least at the back, facing the same way. They always were of light colour, and were built for speed. They were driven single or tandem, but they could have four horses if one wished.

The Middle Classes did not incline to phaetons very much, except in the case of wealthy publicans or sporting characters. To do the thing really well one needed a tall-hatted, cockaded coachman, tiger—groom—at the back and perhaps a Dalmatian dog to run underneath. These dogs were the usual accompaniment to a dog-cart, which was a lighter affair still, almost like a child's mail-cart, only more so. It was the speediest of all the horsed carriages. It had two seats in front, one for the driver, and two at the back. The occupants of these sat facing the rear, with their backs to the people in front. The wheels were large and high; the body of the dog-cart was a good deal off the ground. This was usually a one-horse affair, although it could be tandem.

Commercial travellers sometimes used a dog-cart for special rounds. But when not in commercial use—and it resembled very much in general make-up the butcher's speedy delivery cart—it had a dog running underneath it. You got in by a kind of stirrup step at the side. Dog-carts were dangerous, and needed expert driving. If the horse went down, so did the passengers, and going up hill was very uncomfortable for the rear passengers, who tilted forward and had to hold on tight.

There were governess-carts, nice comfortable little low-lying affairs, something like a tub on wheels, entered from the back. You all sat round and the driver was usually nearest the horse, usually a pony. It jogged along, and a child could, and often did, drive it. There were other rather nondescript vehicles which were called traps, and often lived up to their name. And there was a waggonette—rather like the phaeton, but holding considerably more, for the seats were ranged facing each other behind the driver, who sat rather higher up. These were in great demand for country outings, picnics, or visits to sporting events—also, in a more cumbrous and covered form, to go to the station with a big family for the summer holidays. But those waggonettes resembled buses.

The brougham was the most-hired carriage by the Middle Class.

It was a comfortable affair, with room for four, though six could squeeze in. It was well upholstered, the insides of its doors were padded, and it was shining and respectable and solid, like the class which favoured it. The jobmaster would often have broughams which looked exactly like a private carriage, but for the telltale enamel plate on the back, with a pair of well-matched horses and a driver in a smart blue coat, white breeches, metal buttons, top-boots and tall hat complete. Ladies wishing to go for a drive in the summer would have a landau or victoria. All these could be one- or two-horse affairs.

For weddings it was always a brougham. The coachman wore a big bouquet, and his whip had a white satin ribbon bow—and the horses were always white—or grey.

The rich people had carriages *de luxe* of all kinds. They had not only coachmen but footmen and tigers. The footman, or the tiger, sat beside the coachman, with his arms folded in a most uncomfortable attitude with the elbows stuck out. In winter all the servants attached to a carriage had long overcoats down to their feet, and often fur capes as well—that is, amongst the rich.

The Middle Class carriages or the jobmaster could not run to that, though some of the best had very good and well-matched pairs of horses, and even 'high-steppers'. This was most greatly esteemed. The horses proceeded at a kind of sustained trot, lifting each foreleg well off the ground as they trotted.

Somehow the motor, however rich and opulent, has never quite caught the extreme smartness and style of a real, first-class brougham, with its coachman and footman and its perfect pair of high-steppers. Middle Class people would go to Hyde Park to watch the riders in the Row— women rode side-saddle then, with little veiled bowler hats or toppers, and a riding habit, well-cut and tight-fitting, with a voluminous and rather flowing skirt to hide what was below. One knee went round the horn of the saddle and one shiny top-boot poked out of the stirrup. A few daring spirits rode astride during the last years of the era, but it was not 'the thing'. And nobody would think of riding a horse in less than the formal attire prescribed for equestrian exercise. But riding was not a general Middle Class occupation at all.

One of the sights of London, which few Middle Class women missed, was the afternoon parade in Hyde Park during the season. There, every afternoon, the carriages of the rich drove round, and the occupants of all of them were—or thought they were—'somebodies'. There you saw horse-flesh—carriage horseflesh—*in excelsis*, with the best carriages procurable, the best-trained footmen and coachmen, and the best of everything. It was a definite part of the day's social round. It was not to be missed.

The Middle Classes sat upon park chairs or stood by the rails and watched the Upper Classes—and the rich—roll by. Every woman wore her best and her smartest. That was where the fashions were studied. Men accompanying their womenfolk in the carriages all wore full dress, top hats and frock- or morning-coats. It was a shining, glinting, dazzling sight of ever-changing colour, when titles—their bearers, at any rate—and opulence showed themselves at their smartest and best, in silks, satins, jewels, hats and bonnets, all very *à la mode*, but without vulgar ostentation, to the lesser people of the Middle Class, who appraised it all, exclaimed at the clothes, took note of the sunshades and the parasols, spotted the celebrities and the reigning beauties and went home really quite exhilarated.

They bowed to each other, these carriage folk, but were oblivious of the Middle Class audience—the invisible barrier of class was there.

Sometimes a carriage might stop at the side of the road, and its occupants might speak to a member of their own circle who was for some odd reason walking—it was always a male who was so favoured. On these occasions the Middle Class would sidle by, with eyes aslant for a close-up of dresses and coiffures, to say nothing of personal appearances.

No such thing exists today. It was the epitome of the age of the sovereign and also of the age of the horse, because it was a very old custom indeed dating from the 17th century. But the motor killed it. A motor crawling along at the prescribed rate has not the same charm, is not the same thing at all. Ascot, and Hyde Park in the afternoon during the season, those were the high spots of the horse and of the Society folk which drove behind it, although they were equally in their glory at Eton and Harrow, or at Boulter's Lock on Ascot Sunday. Also wearing their full Court dresses in their broughams crawling along the Mall to Buckingham Palace Drawing-Rooms, trying to be oblivious of the lesser people who gazed at them as if at a show (and, indeed, a show it was), and who were inclined to be ribald, to make remarks not always complimentary, and to shower badinage on the expressionless coachmen and footmen.

But, of them all, the Hyde Park carriage parade was the best. There was a lesser and more intimate parade on Sundays after church, when some of the great ones even walked through the Park and could be studied at close quarters. Every 'season' the Middle Class mother and her girls would attend these Hyde Park parades as spectators, dragging their menfolk protestingly with them.

Horses then were as much discussed as cars are today. Their points were known, the type of harness was open to argument (its details, in the general run, was the same), but every boy knew all about it. He knew, too, the breeds of horses, and he could tell at a glance a bay, a chestnut, a piebald (which did not get into carriages but could be driven in a phaeton or a dog-cart), a blue or a red roan and all the rest. He knew the difference between a snaffle and a curb, he knew a trace, a bellyband, a bearing-rein, a kicking-strap and all the details of the complicated leatherwork which went to driving a horse.

Of all the scenes of the age of the sovereign, that Hyde Park carriage parade was the most characteristic. It showed the division of society, it showed the difference between the classes. It was a throwback to almost feudal times. It was no good a Middle Class couple with social aspirations getting mixed up in it, they were always spotted. There was a visible difference then. The rich rode by, the carriages went at a gentle trot and the Upper Classes sat in the carriages behind their matched pairs, apparently unconscious of the Middle Class which stood behind the railings under the trees, the chestnuts in bloom, the greenery and flowers all around, the sun of a quieter, richer, more solid London shining down upon them.

They of the Middle Class wore all sorts of things, but the best they had got: summer dresses, blouses and skirts, costumes, their best hats and their sunshades or parasols, too, but they knew the difference between themselves and the people in those carriages.

Policemen stood in the road directing the ever-moving traffic of carriage folk, and there were mounted policemen too, who in those days carried swords. No motor was allowed in the Park. This was the kingdom of the horse. Although the car was taking the road in increasing numbers, although many of those folk who sat in those broughams, those landaus, those victorias, already had cars—they never rode in them in that parade. It could be seen, that amazing sight, right through the London season, in an age which seemed so stable and so enduring, upon which the Boer War had produced only the merest ripple. It was at its height during May, June and the first two weeks in July. Then Goodwood brought the 'season' to a close. Nobody who was anybody could possibly be seen in London during August. So then even Hyde Park's parade ground could become Middle Class.

Henley, with its Regatta, was not really a Middle Class festival, although riparian folk given to rowing went there, and its results were real and important news in the paper. But for the London Middle Class folk Hyde Park and its parades, Carriage and Church, were the great social things.

Some would attend the Four-in-Hand Rally there too, and some would go, on Whit Monday, to that more Middle Class resort, Regent's Park, and see the Cart Horse Parade. It was a very pretty sight, even if it had no social status. But carts and vans and horsed vehicles of all kinds competed for the prizes; coalcarts were not excluded, although there was not a speck of coaldust on them that day! They gleamed and shone as brilliantly as the carriages in Hyde Park, and showed much more colour. Their horses had been groomed to within an inch of their lives. Their manes, their very tails, were gay with plaited ribbons, there was a plentiful show of ribbon everywhere. Cart Horse Parade was a great function and a very pictorial one, indeed. You cannot do that sort of thing with cars.

What the motor has brought in speed and comfort it has lost in picturesqueness and real humanity. At the best, a car is a machine. At its worst the horse is a living creature and a noble thing.

There was one more occasion when the horse had a very big show, and that was at a funeral. Funerals then were very solemn occasions indeed; they were more than occasions, they were pageants. Now the departed Middle Class personage is borne swiftly and smoothly to his or her final disposal by a motor hearse—often a Rolls-Royce—a nice bit of cynicism, for the corpse may never have ridden in one when alive—but then the horse pulled it. Not a horse, but horses—on some special occasions as many as four, but always a couple. These horses were black. There were some genuine blacks, but mostly they were dyed for the occasion, and in third-rate undertaking concerns they sometimes wore a bit rusty. But mostly they were black enough.

They always appeared to feel their position acutely, as well they might, for they bore high, nodding sable plumes on their heads and over their blackened bodies were draped vast velvet rug-like trappings of purple, edged with gold fringe. The horses drawing the mourners' coaches—and there was always a long *cortège*—were not quite so elaborately got up as those which drew the hearse, but still they were beplumed. And either by training or by accident the hearse horses always neighed mournfully when entering the cemetery.

Funerals were serious, long-drawn-out affairs then, slow-moving and very solemn. But the horses usually returned home minus their cloths of purple and at a brisk trot. A horsed funeral could produce a much more depressing effect on the spectators than can be achieved in these horseless days.

There was, if you wanted a Middle Class machine, the bicycle. Most people of the era under notice, if not children, had watched the evolution of the bicycle, as they were to watch the evolution of the car. The bicycle, when it became a 'safety', started a craze, which died down well before 1914, when motor traction drove it off the road as a means of pleasurable riding.

But people then could remember the high bicycle, the Penny-Farthing, a most risky and dangerous means of traction. You bestrode the great front wheel, having climbed into the plain saddle up a curved iron leg at the back, to which the tiny back wheel was attached. The pedals were on the hub of the front—and driving—wheel. It had no gears. It had solid tyres, and it had a brake which, if applied too suddenly, threw you head first over the handlebars on to your head, as did any sudden obstruction, like a large stone in the road. You could attain a high speed, for the size of the wheel provided that. Going uphill was a labour of Hercules—you walked most inclines. Going down was a matter of your own pluck or skill. Daring, expert riders would cock their legs over the handlebars and 'coast' down a hill, recovering their rapidly revolving pedals at the foot with some difficulty. Most men applied the brake gingerly and back-pedalled. No woman rode a high bicycle, but men raced on them on grass tracks and smash-ups were frequent. Few bicycling pioneers but had suffered severe accidents and bore the traces to their dying day.

The smaller high bicycle, the 'Kangaroo', was just a small replica of the older one, but had pneumatic tyres. You mounted in the same way—you had to hop along behind the bike to get the requisite momentum and balance. The Kangaroo was never really popular, and the swift arrival of the 'safety bicycle' killed it. The old boneshaker had been the 'safety's' forerunner, but it was seldom seen at this time, although the original 'safety' could be met with, especially in country districts. Its wheels were spindly and narrow, like those of a perambulator, and had solid tyres. Its front wheel was larger than the back one, and the crossbar sloped backwards too.

Cycling grew steadily in favour when the 'safety' arrived with its pneumatic tyres and its modernity. Women took to the wheel, although their costumes would strike with horror the breeched amazons who, scantily clad and showing much bare flesh, swarm the road today. True, there was the attempt at wearing 'Bloomers'—or Rational Costume—but it never caught on. Derision killed it speedily. In the late '80s cycling swept all before it. Everyone rode a bike. Battersea Park was the great centre. It continued, but not as a craze, more as a means of short distance travel and pleasant exercise, through the early 1900s. And where roads were paved with wood (a new idea), there was the heaven of the cyclist. Up and down they rode, glorying in the smooth surface after the granite setts and the rougher macadam. Every evening thousands of cyclists turned out for a spin.

There were, as there are today, cycling clubs, some serious and purely male, some in which both sexes mixed. People discussed the various makes of bicycles much as they discuss makes of cars today. Every make had its champions. Cycling tandem gave us one of our deathless music-hall songs, 'Daisy Bell', who on account of not being able to afford a carriage, was to 'look so sweet, upon the seat, of a bicycle made for two'.

There were many makes of bicycles, most of which survive today. There were the Rudge-Whitworth, Humber, Premier, Raleigh, Sunbeam (with the little oil-bath, as largely advertised), the Swift, the B.S.A.—makes innumerable.

The Stanley Show, at the Agricultural Hall, was the big event of the year for cyclists, and nearly everyone was a cyclist until it went out of fashion because of the car—to revive again in the inter-war period. Bicycling itself was in every way a thing of cycles. That Show at the Agricultural Hall was a splendid affair—stand after stand of glittering machines, and as much argument and indecision amongst purchasers as there is today over a new car. The catalogues were in great demand, especially by the young, who would pore over them for weeks and almost come to blows about their selected makes.

When a boy got his first bicycle it was a definite step. Much thought went to its selection, and as he rode along the quiet, pleasant suburban roads, to and from school, or after school when homework was done (or evaded), there were few things in life more delightful. He was not harassed by the flood of traffic as he is today. Having mastered his machine he was ninety per cent safe. Around where he lived cars were few and motor-bicycles just as scarce. When evening fell even horse traffic was at a minimum, and a bike ride on a summer's evening was a thing of real joy—especially if there was some wood paving upon which to do it.

Most children graduated by means of a tricycle, a form of wheeled transport which never became really popular. Even the child with a tricycle regarded it only as a step—which had to be endured—before the possession of a real two-wheeler.

There was much cycle racing. Some machines had very high gears and consequently enormous gear-wheels, of such extent that, although the feet and legs appeared to go round quite slowly, the bike sped along. Some machines so fitted had handlebars dropped to such an extent that the rider's nose appeared to be on them. These were the speed merchants, execrated as 'scorchers' by the general public and more normal cyclists. They looked not to the right or the left, speed was their motto. Fowls fled squawking, and often found out why a chicken crossed the road to their cost. Dogs made attacks as the fiends sped by, and policemen delighted in a capture. The scorcher was a public enemy—the original road-hog. But they were comparatively few.

In the earlier days there were no 'free wheels', although they followed not far behind, and plunger brakes were succeeded by rim brakes. American bikes came on the market, affairs of extreme lightness, with cane rims, weighing much less than the average British machine. They were built for speeding, not for hard wear, but many people liked them, even if they were brakeless and the ability to stop depended on the rider's ability to back-pedal. Free-wheeling killed that accomplishment, of course.

Every suburban road had its learner, often its groups of learners, of both sexes, wobbling about whilst the instructor, a man, did his best to keep them upright. Often disaster ensued, and both landed in the dust. But nobody took long to learn, and more and more cycles came on the road. There were no rear lights needed, but you had to have a light in front, either an oil lamp or an acetylene one—and the latter were fitful efforts, given to stinking and going out unexpectedly. Some gay sparks carried a Chinese lantern on the handlebars. It was within the meaning of the bye-law. A little tool-case swung from the rear of the saddle, and a puncture was everyone's dread.

Ladies, having discarded the bloomers (and very few ventured into them), wore quite ordinary clothes in which to cycle, although the skirt was a short one. And what was meant by a short skirt then was one reaching the ankles and with plenty of fullness. They rode only ladies' bicycles, those without crossbars, and the back wheel was guarded by a network of what looked like long black bootlaces or cordage, to prevent their skirts getting caught therein. Gears, too, were covered in by gear-cases. It is the custom of the younger generation to laugh at the dress of their elders in the days of their youth, but illustrations from the papers of the early 1900s, depicting lady cyclists, show little at which to laugh and, from the point of view of grace, a good deal to admire. A picture in the *Sphere* of 1901 shows a young lady in a little round hat which would be modern and smart today, a bolero over a white blouse with a lace fichu at the neck, and an ankle-length skirt—it is a costume, of course— and gloves. A lady on a tandem whose tight-fitting jacket splays out round the hips is not so attractive. But ladies awheel wore veils and gloves.

The *Illustrated London News* of 1903 has a most spirited picture. The caption is "The World Awheel: The continual procession of motors and cycles in Kensington High Street, opposite Holland Park." The great gates can be seen in the background. There are two cars in the picture, one wholly and one in part. They are typical of the period, with their openness, their high seats, their heavily coated and peak-capped driver complete with goggles, and the ladies in long coats, all muffled up, with large veils right over their hats and tied beneath the chin. They do not seem to be enjoying themselves and are as closely wrapped up as if in the Arctic. On the other hand, the cyclists, of which there are several, are carefree. In the foreground is a pretty young lady with an extremely good figure, as figures went then. She wears an ankle-length cloth skirt, a white blouse, the sleeves of which balloon over the forearms, a large straw hat decorated by what appear to be artificial roses, and a light veil. Her male companion has assumed a large check suit, bicycling knickers, and a cap. He also wears a high, stick-up stiff linen collar and a buttonhole. There is a sailor in full uniform and a soldier ditto, who has a girl behind him on a tandem. This is a little bit of artistic licence. The caption continues: "Any fine holiday afternoon or Sunday morning such a scene as our artist has depicted may be witnessed on the road to Richmond. Motors and cycles quite out-number the horse vehicles, which would almost seem to have had their day." Much virtue in 'almost'. The horse died harder than that. But for several years cycling was universal.

The trip to Richmond was the extent of a Sunday outing. Towards the north Potters Bar or Hatfield was the usual objective, and Chingford to the east. Westward a few might attain Windsor. The Portsmouth Road was the popular run for serious cyclists bent on covering the ground, as later it proved to be for motorists, when the Hut at Wisley became quite a rendezvous.

Cycling got into the Army. There were also Cycle Volunteers. One corps, the 21st Middlesex, had most attractive blue uniforms, a bit lighter than Air Force blue, and scarlet centres to their black forage caps. Their white spats completed a very pleasing martial picture, and their efficiency was amazing. They did with their cycles all a cavalryman did with his steed, and more. They tent-pegged, they attacked the Turk's Head, they cut the lemon, they dashed into action, rifles fitted alongside the front wheel, they leapt off, embattled their cycles and fired over them. It was all most inspiring and fluttered the hearts of female onlookers.

But the bicycle was declining in favour as the car became ascendant, and did not regain its popularity until after the First World War, and then not with the Middle Classes.

But a young Middle Class lady in her day cut a much better and far more attractive figure than the enmasculined bifurcated she-cyclist of the present time. She kept her femininity and lent colour and charm to the road, even if she did not get so far along it. She did not want to. Men did not like athletic or masculine women then. And she got her man all right.

There was altogether much more colour in life. Even the railway trains provided it. There were a great many more railway companies, just as there were a great many more banks. Centralization was not the motto, competition was considered a good thing. There was, indeed, a bewildering choice of lines, even if they did not all go to the same places. Today you have only British Railways.

How different in the days of the sovereign! Then the Middle Class could travel by the London and North Western, the Midland, the Great Northern, the Glasgow and South Western, the Caledonian, the Great Eastern, the Great Central, the Cambrian, the North British, the North Eastern, Great North of Scotland, the London and South Western, the London, Brighton and South Coast, the South Eastern, the London, Chatham and Dover, and a great complex system of smaller local lines like the North Staffordshire, the Hull and Barnsley, the North London, the Lancashire and Yorkshire, the Taff Vale, the Somerset and Dorset, the London, Tilbury and Southend, and many, many more. Each had its distinctive type of engine with distinctive colouring, impossible to mistake.

The Midland were of lake colour, similar to the L.M.S. of yesterday. The London and North Western had black engines and chocolate-and-cream carriages; the Glasgow and South Western engines were olive green, the Caledonian prussian blue. The Great Eastern had ultramarine engines; the Great Northern apple green, the Great Central dark green, and the Great North of Scotland black. The London and South Western engines were dark green, which went lighter later in the period. The London, Brighton and South Coast started as green, but went variegated into yellow with orange chrome, burnt sienna and bronze green. In 1904 they were dark umber. The South Eastern were green, and so were the London, Chatham and Dover and the Great Western. The North London, which served the suburbs—going as far as Richmond, which was not north—had queer-looking squat, black engines with driving pistons outside of flashing steel, which made quite a show of power. Their London terminus was Broad Street.

The London, Chatham and Dover was the 'joke' line. A comedian could always get a laugh out of it in the south of England. He would call it the London Smashem and Turnover, he would tell tales of passengers getting out and picking flowers whilst the train moved slowly along, of young boys who became bearded patriarchs before the journey's end.

But the truth was that the railways were run most efficiently. They got there as quickly as they do today, and often, except in the case of very special trains (suspended, anyway, since the Second World War), a good deal quicker, and they were punctual and not overcrowded. You could reserve a seat on the big trains, but you only stood (except on rush hour suburban lines) if you went by excursion train on a Bank Holiday or to a very, very popular resort on a Saturday during August. And even then you got a seat in the second-class—and, of course, the first. Accidents were very rare. Fogs upset the railways more, for the simple reason that we had more fogs then. But they battled manfully.

Some modern comforts were missing, of course. Restaurant cars were —for years—rare luxuries, and were only found on some of the really long-distance trains. So you ordered a luncheon-basket, which contained cold meat or chicken, lettuce, rolls, cheese, fruit, the condiments, butter, and, a little bottle of red wine, with knives, forks, plates, spoons and even serviettes. The price was half a crown.

Some railways had a long stop at a station en route, where you might snatch some food. The Great Northern did this at York, which is a very long station. If the traveller in search of refreshment was in the rear of the train it was a breathless dash up the platform to a very crowded refreshment-room, a struggle for a cup of scalding coffee and a very hot meat pie. He suffered the agonies of Tantalus, for he could neither drink the one nor eat the other before the bell rang and the whistle blew, and he had to scamper back, for a corridor train was a rare thing also, and one had to reach one's own carriage.

That lack of corridors was very unpleasant for people who had certain physical weaknesses. It made travelling any distance a nightmare. Shops near the great termini exhibited kinds of secret travelling lavatories for sale, lengths of rubber tubing covered in brown cloth, which were apparently worn bound round the leg. But nobody one knew had ever bought one. You could not wash in those pre-corridor trains, either. One arrived very much the worse for wear. As late as 1897 a journey to Scotland was a feat of some endurance and physical control, with frenzied rushes out when the train stopped. But corridors soon became general, although not on short journeys.

The degree of comfort as regards seating was much the same then as now, first, second or third, except on suburban trains and certain of the big lines on shorter runs. On these, the third-class compartments had no upholstery at all. You sat on bare boards, and the whole coach was one large compartment, divided into smaller ones by cross walls shoulder high, giving six seats aside. They were primitive and not comfortable, but they were kept clean. The seconds were well upholstered and had five seats aside, the firsts were luxurious, and had three seats aside only.

Men setting out on a longish journey took rugs and changed their tall hats, once in the train, into caps or deer-stalkers, with flaps to keep their ears warm. They could also, before the days of steam heating in trains, get footwarmers, long, flat leaden affairs, filled with hot water which soon got cold. The third class shivered, but the Middle Class, in the seconds, could get footwarmers too.

There was extraordinary little difference in the speed, though stops were more frequent.

Lighting changed as time went on. In the early period the lamps were oil, and the oil could be seen in the glass container, swaying and gurgling as the train swayed along. Then came gas, with little inverted burners, which gave quite a good light. Men walked along the tops of the trains, a pole in hand with a flaming tow on the end, lighting the lamps with a plop and shutting up the projecting little iron funnel with a bang as soon as the gas was alight. There was a smell of gas until the train began to move. Finally, of course, came electric light. But you got in mostly on time, you were not dashed to pieces, you paid a great deal less for your fare, you always got a seat and you always got a porter and a great deal of civility and service. The multiplicity of railways had the wisdom for that. People did not travel to the extent they do today, and they travelled with a purpose. They also travelled well, they did not rush aimlessly about and choke up the corridors, and although there was sometimes a dispute as to whether the window should be up or down, there was courtesy, even if it was the courtesy of silence, among them.

There were no loud speakers braying about the stations, indistinct because of escaping steam just when the bit one wanted to hear was being announced. The porters did the shouting themselves. At every station they bellowed out not only the name of that stop, but every other station the train would call at. They were not good elocutionists in the first place, and long custom and familiarity had made their diction extra slovenly—but they did call out, and loudly too. What you might hear was 'Arngyornsy-woodgrnboparkpalmsgrnmoreillifield'. But there was always a porter to ask.

The majority of the carriages were non-smoking, not the majority as today. It was the smoking carriages which were labelled, not the ones where it was forbidden. Women did not smoke then.

London trains also went underground. Before the coming of the Tuppenny Tube (electric, Bank to Shepherd's Bush, 2d. all the way or any distance, in 1900) it went underground on the Metropolitan, the District, and the City and South London (opened in 1890) by steam-driven trains. This was definitely not so good. It was pretty bad at all times, but when a 'London particular' fog descended, then it was a very fair idea of Hades. Dante or Orpheus would have felt quite at home. It was suffocating, it was filthy, and you breathed a mixture of soot, smoke and sulphur, the memory of which still lingers in the nostrils of those who savoured it. A damp foggy day made it much worse, and then they were plentiful in the winter. You emerged finally in a state which would make a coal-miner rush to a wash-basin.

But, above ground, these underground burrowings caused no small amusement. Along certain thoroughfares, of which Euston Road was one, were large gratings, through which the smoke of the tunnelling mole-like trains was supposed to escape—and did—making a fog of its own. A train passing under these caused a tremendous updraught, and unwary ladies, crossing gratings at the same moment, would find their skirts and petticoats around their faces, to the huge delight of all onlookers and of rude men who, on suitable days, would congregate to see the sights. The only comfort the poor women had was that their skirts obscured their scarlet, shame-stricken faces. There was the Inner Circle and the Outer Circle, though few people knew where one ended and the other began. It was a gloomy, dirty and miserable way of getting about. But people did it, especially those members of the Middle Class who could not run to cabs.

The Piccadilly and Northern Railway—forerunner of the immense system of efficient electric tube railways which now honeycomb the soil beneath London—opened in 1906, from Finsbury Park to Hammersmith. It was regarded as a thing of wonder, and it was. But it never showed such wonders as it and its sister lines show today in the rush hour. The Black Hole of Calcutta was still talked of in the Sovereign Age with shudders of horror. The descendants of the Golden Age suffer torments each night on the tubes compared with which the Calcutta place must have been luxurious comfort.

When the Piccadilly tube first started, the machinery was controlled by men. Men stood in each compartment and worked the doors by pulling levers—no doors opened by themselves. There were numerous sliding gates at the entrance to platforms, which uniformed officials slammed in your face, although the train was still there. The men working the gates called out the names of the stations, and looked after you generally. There were no escalators, you went up by lifts and the rule in them was No Smoking. Tube travelling became very popular, and overcrowding followed quickly upon it. The straphanger was born in the tubes.

Little did any of those travellers, who maybe changed a golden sovereign to pay their fare, dream that the day would come when their descendants, and in many cases themselves, would go down those tubes every night to escape destruction above from hostile bombs dropped by what they would have called Flying Machines—things even then becoming a possibility, a probability, and a fact. But they were disregarded as mere fanciful toys. ("If God meant men to fly," said people, "He would have

171

given them wings.") It was regarded somewhat illogically as flying in the face of Providence to attempt this conquest of the air by such infernal machines. Balloons one understood, but they were at the mercy of the winds. Airships might become a very vulnerable toy. But flying machines, never!

So had spoken the stage-coach stalwarts when Stephenson flung down his gage, so believed the cabbies and coachmen of this very time as regards the motor, and so it will always be. There will always be a disbelief that Science can go any further. Maybe the wish is father to the thought. For it really does seem that it has gone far enough and that further progress, as it is so cheerfully called, must end in the self-destruction of everything, Science itself included.

But those gay pedallers of the bicycles of all kinds, those pioneers whose goggles and hootings and the smell of whose exhausts annoyed and amused the slower-minded and more contented folk, those people who travelled by train, corridor or non-corridor, felt themselves of a stable world, a peaceful world. They never dreamed of what was coming to them, their children and their grandchildren. They never heeded war, it was not likely to bother them. It was a purely professional affair. The Boer War was 'bad for business', and shook confidence in our Generals, but never in Tommy Atkins, be he English, Scots, Welsh or Irish, and never in the boys in Navy Blue—the 'handy men', as it became fashionable to call them.

They were invincible because they were British—nine people out of ten said English. They were invincible because they were islanders whose little island was the heart and the head of the greatest Empire the world had ever seen, and because the standard of their business, and indeed their life, was a real gold sovereign, worth its twenty shillings anywhere within His—or Her—Majesty's realms and dominions, and worth considerably more outside it, even in that foreign country where an amusing race of people spoke nearly the same language and were collectively known as Yankees.

A dollar to a citizen of the Golden Age was a five-shilling piece, a huge, if inconvenient, coin of silver. It did not mean, to him, an American dollar. Indeed, he looked askance at that—and would have died of shame had he thought that the Yankee might one day do the same at his sovereign. But it was not the sovereign which bowed before the dollar, it was the Pound Note. He had no use for them, the subject of the sovereign. They were not English, and if you got one from Scotland you lost sixpence by it. So much for paper money—unless it were a fiver.

The days of the sovereign seem distant indeed.

CHAPTER XI

Sartorial Splendour

THERE SEEMS A FIXED IDEA THAT THE DRESS OF THE MEN IN THE 'NINETIES and the 1900s—before 1914—was dull, drab and dismal. That is a great mistake. It was more formal, true. It was more ceremonious, true. But it had its share of colour, and it was considerably smarter than the male dress of today. For informality was taboo, except on holiday. Men did not wear sports clothes in town and never at business. There was none of the looseness and carelessness which, from clothes, is seeping into life itself. Young men accustomed to the sports coat and grey flannel trousers and bareheaded uniform might think the attire stiff and uncomfortable. But the men of the Golden Age did not regard it as such. Clothes then were typical of a man's standing. Today they are not. The stricter discipline of life (which enforced military discipline of two World Wars seems to have destroyed) made men much neater and far more careful of their appearance. There was a good deal of civilian pride of appearance.

Young men roar with laughter at pictures of their fathers, or grandfathers, as young men. Those worthies would have roared too, not with mirth but with indignation and anger, if the young men of their time had dressed as they dress today. Highly coloured pullovers and corduroy trousers of exotic hue can be just as funny as stiff shirts, high collars and toppers. The absolute necessity of being neat and orthodox in attire kept the mind evenly balanced and amenable to the discipline of commerce and trade. It was not a bad thing at all. But the keynote of everything was dignity, so essential then, so disregarded today.

The great male garment was the frock-coat. That was the outward and visible sign of stability and respectability. It was, of course, also worn by men who were neither of these things, but that had to be endured. It was worn by H.R.H. the Prince of Wales, and it was worn also by him when he became King Edward VII. It had been worn by his father too. It was also worn by his son, King George V, but it finished then, except perhaps for some very special occasions.

King Edward as monarch, and as Prince of Wales, was a fashion setter for men. But he did not set the fashion for frock-coats—that was there before him. It was the link between the 18th and the 19th and even the 20th century. It was the 'square cut'—once of silk and satin—adapted to the needs of the day in cloth. It had another link too with the 18th

173

century. The two buttons at the back, useless in the frock-coat of the 19th century, had supported the sword belt in the 18th.

But, like all British customs, although it altered its form, it still clung tenaciously to some of its past glory. The lapels of frock-coats were silk-faced, and it was, except in its cheaper forms, silk-lined too. Its dignity and decorum made it the correct wear for all responsible men of the age of the sovereign. It was the most apt, the most suitable garment, you could have imagined nothing better. There it was, a real coat, not a jacket. It fitted in to the waist, when there was a waist for it to do so, and its tails, coming to the knee-joint, meant that its wearer was not the sort of person to be hasty either in movement or in thought or deed.

It was the coat for monarchs, princes, noblemen, statesmen, for politicians, merchants, bankers, financiers, stockbrokers, doctors, lawyers, men of science, actor-managers, schoolmasters, master men of all kinds, even down to shopwalkers. It was ordinary wear for a majority, Sunday wear for many more, and you simply could not go to any ceremony of importance unless you wore a frock-coat. It was the stable wear of a stable age. What is more, it suited most men. If they were slim, it became them. If they were inclined to be stout—and most middle-aged men were stout then—it gave added authority to their bulk. It even concealed a protruding paunch.

When the head of a household stood before the fire and spread his legs abroad on the hearthrug he gathered up the tails of his frock-coat under his arms. It was the clear symbol that he, the male, was the master. When, owing to the discarding of the frock-coat, men have been unable to take that stance and make that gesture, their mastery of households has fallen from them. A little thing, but true, and very significant. It was at once a symbol of his domestic ease and a pointer to his dignified garment of mastery. It gave occupation to the hands, for a man held on to his lapels and did not plunge his hands in his pockets.

The frock-coat need not be black, although the great majority were. Even so it could be of smooth sable cloth or have a rougher surface. It could be grey, and although as effective in many ways it had not quite the same power behind it. It smacked slightly of relaxation. The waistcoat accompanying the frock-coat presented a wide field of choice. It could be single-breasted and black, cut high or low according to the fashion. It could be double-breasted and cut to show a lot of snowy, starchy shirt-front. It could be grey even with a black frock-coat. It could also be fawn.

Some men there were, but not of the first flight, who wore red fancy waistcoats, but that was definitely not right. But you could wear a fancy waistcoat of black and white, or with spots, with a frock-coat, and it could be of ordinary suit material, of nankeen, of piqué. And you could

174

have fancy buttons. Sometimes the pockets were plain, sometimes they had braided edges. There were even frock-coats with velvet collars, a hangover from the late Georgian and early Victorian days.

Many men, who wore the black single-breasted waistcoat, wore also what was known as a 'vest slip'. This was a shaped strip of white material, mostly piqué, which went round the neck, and fitted just inside the opening of the waistcoat down to the end of the V, showing just about half an inch of white edge against the black cloth. If properly adjusted —which was by no means easy—this added much smartness and also dignity to the appearance.

The shirt was always white linen, with a starched front and starched cuffs—which were wide and flat. The old-fashioned cuffs, which were circular tubes around the wrist, were Victorian. The real Edwardian had a wide white cuff, which, when he wrote, lay flat on the table at right angles to his wrist. The collar was white linen and starched. It was also high. It could be a straight-up 'choker', it could have 'butterfly points', or it could be of the Gladstone variety, but not quite so all-embracing. Even when double-fold collars came in, they were not considered right by most men for a frock-coat, although young bloods wore them, provided they were high ones. Some men wore low collars which fitted inside the collars of the coat and ended in points which lay upon the shirt front. Professors or nonconforming parsons might perhaps be allowed to get away with this, and even schoolmasters, but not professional or City men—or the Upper Classes. For this garment was worn by Upper and Middle Class alike.

The tie was black, spotted or grey. Coloured ties simply could not be worn with a frock-coat. Nor could brown boots, of course. That was as great a solecism as a red handkerchief with evening dress.

There was naturally only one hat—the topper. You could wear a grey topper with a frock-coat of the same colour. You could even wear one of those hats which seemed to be felt bowlers which had attempted to be toppers and failed.But this was provincial and old-fashioned. You did not wear a grey topper with a black frock-coat, yet you could do so with a morning coat in the summer or at the races.

An Ascot tie was all right with a frock-coat, so was a 'four-in-hand' or a stock tie. The Ascot tie was very becoming and very hard to tie. It was practically a stock. The four-in-hand was often worn ready made. It was a curious cross-over affair of some considerable spread and it demanded a tie-pin in the middle. But most men wore tie-pins then. They were in great variety. They could be jewelled, they could be plain gold, or they could consist of one pearl bead. No jewel was barred, and some of the gold pins bore a single turquoise, which looked very smart against a black silk or satin tie. If you used the ordinary sailor's knot, you could have any tie-pin you liked.

Early in the period it went into the knot itself. Later it went in the body of the tie. Sporting men wore pins with gold horseshoes, horses' heads, foxes, hunting-horns, all sorts of devices. Some wicked bohemian bachelors had even tie-pins shaped like a female leg. There were cameo tie-pins too. A few men wore their ties loosely round their collar and pulled through a gold ring. Few men wore bow-ties with frock-coats. It was too undignified. Yet it could be done with a morning coat.

There was a solid gold watch-chain across the waistcoat—an albert. At one end was a gold watch, a hunter, a half hunter, a repeater. At the other end of the chain was always a sovereign-purse to mark the dominance of the golden coin. These have already been described. But some held both sovereigns and half-sovereigns. There might be a seal or two adorning the middle of the chain in mid-stomach, or a spade guinea. And it was possible that a gold matchbox might accompany the sovereign-purse.

Most men who smoked carried matchboxes. They were not always of gold, they could be of silver and even gunmetal. They held, not wooden matches, but wax ones, called vestas. These were of white wax with either brown or pink heads. They were not eminently satisfactory, they were apt to bend and melt, and the heads often fell off and burned holes in the trousers. And if they bent when being struck, they might burn the fingers too. Their place has been taken by little pine matches which retain the pink heads. These vestas were struck along a groove in the bottom of the matchbox, which had indentations in it to cause friction. After considerable use they got a bit smooth, or clogged with the particles of matches, and the match had to be struck on some other surface. Men of no social pretensions sometimes did this on the seat of their trousers. The usual way was on a rough surface—and a mirror was a good thing. These vestas gave off rather sulphurous fumes and were apt to choke one slightly.

But there was also the 'fusee'. This was really a kind of firework, more than a match. It was the relic of a former age before the dawn of safety matches. The 'sticks' were of browny yellow, of some curious substance which was at once shiny and sticky, and when struck they fizzed, they fumed, they gave off sparks, and it was a matter of some difficulty to put them out. They were not so bad in the open air in windy weather, but indoors they spoilt many a good cigar—and cigars were very good then.

There was another brand of match, which had heads running half-way down the 'stick', starting pink and becoming chocolate-brown. They burned a long time, defied the wind and were useful for pipes, if you did not mind a few whiffs of almost pure sulphur. You could buy small

176

boxes of wax vestas, flat and handy. You could buy very large ones, flat and oblong. You could buy them in little gilt or white metal boxes, with a picture on the top and a place to strike below. You could buy enormous boxes of safeties, and little miniature boxes which fitted into the waistcoat pocket. There were matches of all sorts and sizes and all very cheap. Safety matches cost $2\frac{1}{2}d$. per dozen boxes.

Nobody dreamed of a day when matches would be hard to come by. Why, a public-house gave you a box for the asking. Matches were wanted by men, not only for smoking purposes but for lighting the gas, the commonest form of illuminant for the greater part of the period. But on the question of smoking one could smoke a cigar or cigarette with a frock-coat, but never a pipe. That was as bad as brown boots, or the wearing of a bowler with a frock-coat or, for the matter of that, with a morning coat either. Men carried cigar-cases, mostly of leather or crocodile skin, often with their initials on it in gold or silver. They carried cigarette-cases, of gold, silver, gunmetal or leather. The leather ones were not much good because the cigarettes got bent and battered.

But nobody smoked nearly so much as today and chain-smoking was unknown. There still remained rooms in the house in which smoking displeased Mamma. There were still smoking-rooms everywhere, supposed to be reserved for smokers. And it was not really the thing to smoke in the streets, although the younger men did so freely. But they never smoked a pipe in the West End, and seldom a cigar—they had more respect for the cigar.

The trousers accompanying a frock-coat were of pepper-and-salt, sponge-bag (shepherd's plaid, fashionable for ties too), or striped. Plain grey for a grey frock-coat, of the same material as the coat. These trousers were never turned up. The boots, always black, could be of leather, kid, *glacé* kid, calf, or patent leather. They could be lace-up or button. In the latter case a buttonhook had to be handy. Spats were very largely worn. And the patent boots could have light uppers, of *glacé*, white, yellow or even brown kid. The brown uppers were worn mostly with morning coats or lounge suits. And you could, for lounge suit wear, get black boots with brown leather uppers which were very smart. Men seldom wore shoes, and never with frock- or morning coats, only with lounge suits.

Gloves were worn, and you could suit yourself out of scores of varieties of materials. Almost white washleather gloves were very smart with a frock-coat, morning coat or topper. The handkerchief was either white linen or of silk. It was worn in the breast pocket or in the sleeve, although some old-fashioned men still used a bandana and kept it in the tail pocket; smart men, however, kept those tail pockets empty because

177

of the set of the coat. Fashions changed as regards the cut of coats or waistcoats. It even changed as regards the bands on the toppers. These were sometimes narrow, and of corded silk, at other times quite high and of black crêpe.

Shapes of tall hats varied, too, with the overriding principle of getting one to suit your type of face. Sometimes the hats were rather low of crown and curly of brim, other times they were high in the crown and flattish of brim, and for a while they were almost straight, without a suggestion of a curve. But the fundamental principles of the coat and hat always remained the same. It was a noble garment, even if you had to take care not to sit on the tails and crease them.

The morning coat was mostly worn by younger men, and it was perhaps an incipient revolt against the more abundant frock-coat. But it, too, had a Georgian ancestry. It was the coat which went with the, powdered wigs, the swords, the patches and the snuff-boxes at Bath, although it had shed its silks and satins, save for lining. It sometimes compromised by having braided edges—black braid. But the best people did not wear this. It also varied in fashion as to opening. Sometimes one button only adorned its front, and it cut away sharply as to its tails. At other times there were two or three buttons in front, and the tails were longer and fuller. But as a rule it was kept together by a kind of link, as was the frock-coat.

You did not wear coloured shirts with the morning coat, although towards the end a few brave spirits did this, and even went in for soft white silk double-fold collars. Some artistic souls even tried a low Byronic one. But the real gentleman of affairs or fashion kept to the starched collar. The upright, winged collar was the best with either frock- or morning coat. You did not wear coloured ties with the latter but you could wear a bow-tie of black, grey, stripes or spots. Sometimes as regards bows, the fashion was for short ends, at others for long and pulled-out ones. Waistcoats could be fancy and high or low cut, as fashion decreed. Other appurtenances followed the frock-coat.

Although the frock-coat is a thing of the past, the morning coat lingers as full morning dress—instead of being informal, as it was in the Golden Age. It is now the garment of state functions for civilians, for marriages and for funerals. But there are still undertakers who cling to the frock-coat.

It is a pity that the frock-coat has vanished. It did add stature to the personality of a man, and dignity. A statesman expounding his foreign policy by the Despatch Box in the Commons was a figure of far more authority in a frock-coat than he is in a lounge suit. There is no doubt that he was listened to with more attention by the country in general. But maybe he had more cheerful and heartening things to say.

A good-frock coat could cost you five guineas the suit, even more. But it lasted for years. A morning coat cost you from $2\frac{1}{2}$ to 3 guineas. It lasted too. And you always had two pairs of trousers with both.

The lounge suit was another affair. There again greater latitude was allowed, both as regards colour, material and style. Much, of course, depended on social and financial standing. The average Middle Class man's lounge suits were dark blue or grey. There were numerous shades of grey and numerous patterns, too. It was also possible to wear a black jacket and waistcoat and striped trousers, such as pass for cere-monial dress today, but then were office or daily wear, a mere shadow of the frock-coat.

Younger men had more latitude in dress than had middle-aged men. A middle-aged man—as middle age went then, it was from 37 to 45—dressed more quietly, as became men of some position and importance in the world. Youth was allowed to have its fling. The young man's clothes were more jaunty and more amenable to fashion. He could also wear brown suits, and he did. He could have striped suits and check suits, of a rather noisy nature, and he did. But when he began to be 'Something in the City', in good sooth and with a capital 'S', he mostly took to morning or frock-coats. And toppers. In a more junior capacity, he wore a bowler. That was never an easy hat, and is not easy now.

It is at all times difficult to find a really suitable bowler for one's face. It brings home, as does nothing else, the unalterability of a human face. So far as the bowler goes, it is a matter of brim more than height of crown. But the makers never really seem to make the kind of bowler one really wants, which induces a feeling of oddness and frustration. It is want of enterprise on the part of hatmakers for not being more flexible-minded. But they did not care. In those days a man had to wear a hat, young or old. Today, when young, he goes without. The bowler market today cannot be what it was, but the soft felt hat makes up for it!

Before the young Middle Class man reached the top-hat stage—although he bought one for Sunday use as soon as funds permitted—he wore a bowler hat in spring, autumn and winter, and a straw hat—or 'boater'—in the summer. The straw hat, although light and to some slight extent shady, was not an easy hat, either. It was comparatively simple to get one to suit your face and fit the head, it was another thing to get it to stay there. Straw hats were easily blown off. They were elusive things to chase on a windy day and helpful passers-by often trod on them or transfixed them with walking-sticks and umbrellas with the best possible intentions. So one wore a hat-guard. This was a long black cord, which fastened into the lapel buttonhole with a clip, or was knotted in, and which had a little screw which pierced the brim of the hat and screwed into a little black round metal cap.

Some men wore these little round caps in the back of the rims of their bowlers. The inference was that they were horsemen, perhaps given to Huntin'—when it was necessary to secure headgear. These impostors sometimes had the bow of the bowler band at the back too. Most of them so adorned had never bestridden a horse. But all straw hats needed a hat-guard. In quiet, peaceful weather it could be wound round the brim of the hat, where it merged into the plain black hatband with the bow at the side. The band was often replaced by club colours, and as these were always very variegated and striking, the summer streets were lit up accordingly.

For a long time the brim of the straw was serrated, then it became smooth, which was much better and more economical, for the teeth of the serrated edges had a way of getting broken and your hat was shabby at once. But no young man of any pretension wore his straw hat more than one summer. They cost only 2s. 6d., so there was no need. Clergymen and elderly gentlemen wore black-and-white speckled boaters and some clergymen had all-black ones. The season for 'straws' was from May to September.

When off commercial duty, and in suburbs or country, a young man could wear a cap. This was of tweed, and could be of any hue or pattern. It was not so voluminous as the Cup-Tie cap of the North, and smart young men would have one made to match their suits, out of the same material. Coloured shirts, when they came in, were permissible with lounge suits, and any sort of tie you liked and any colour. You could wear a pink shirt, but this went best with a black silk or satin tie with a plain pearl pin in it. Brown boots also could be worn with lounge suits. Most men wore gloves. And they always wore them in town. They always, also, removed the right-hand one before shaking hands. If caught unawares, they said 'Excuse my glove'.

A man's fashions in suits and in collars changed considerably. Coats were worn long or short. They had vents at the back or they had not. They had long rolling collars, moderate rolls, or the lapels were cut high and almost level with the collarbones. Waistcoats could be cut low, or so high that there was hardly any opening at all for the display of shirt. Sleeves were short or long. Cuff buttons varied in number, so did coat buttons. In the early 1900s, the bottom button of the waistcoat came undone and has never been fastened since. Or hardly ever.

Naturally, ties followed the waistcoats. For the high-cut ones— and for a time they were very high indeed—they were pulled out in a loop and then vanished back again into the vest. On a low-cut vest a tie-pin impaled them on to the shirt. The matter of collars affected the tie as well. The choker called for a certain kind of tie. To prevent the tie riding up there was a loop at the back of the shirt—still there in dress shirts—and to make doubly sure curious little triangular gold gadgets fastened over the tie round the collar to keep it down. Nothing looked more absurd than a tie riding up the collar. Of course it went under the back stud as well, but many men wore studs with a short shank and needed extra help.

The winged collar kept the tie down a bit, but aid was still needed. Little clips were worn beneath the waistcoat to clip the tie on to the shirt. No young man with any pretence to smartness wore a ready-made bow. He tied his own, be it dress or ordinary tie. But ready-made ones could be bought, which clipped on to the stud. Some careless or lazy men, who could not even bother to tie an ordinary sailor's knot, could get ready-made ties of that kind. There was a length to go round the neck, fixed at one end, whilst the other was pulled round and fitted through a hole under the knot, where an ordinary black pin protruded to catch it and hold it. It often caught the fixer's finger in as well—and served him right.

There were several rather vain efforts to popularize the panama which, being a comfortable and sensible sort of hat, never caught on, except with old gentlemen. Trilby hats and soft black felt hats were only worn by devil-may-care fellows like artists, musicians and actors and such-like outlaws of small account. But the day came when King Edward VII wore a Homburg—and a green velour Homburg with a bow at the back. The new fashion swept the country. Young men took it on eagerly, and everyone owned a green velour Homburg with a bow at the back, and some of the more daring had a little bunch of feathers there too. The tyranny of the straw hat was broken. It never recovered. Although it was a long time—years, indeed—before the Homburg or its successor, the soft felt hat, was the right thing of Town or City wear (it took the First World War to do that), an era was in, and it had come to stay.

There was, for a season or two, a quaint custom which concerned straw hats. A craze broke out for wearing little enamel brooches, sometimes of real gold, in the form of flags or burgees, quite attractive in themselves, but why worn, nobody seemed to know. These were pinned on the bow of the boater, but sometimes boldly in front. It probably originated with men belonging to a yacht club, but ninety per cent of the young men following this fashion had never even been on a yacht, let alone being members of a club. It was, perhaps, a rash breaking out in ornamental form on a maritime nation. It did not last very long, but it was popular while it lasted.

181

Men's underclothing was much heavier and far more uncomfortable in the golden sovereign days than it is now. Woollen combinations were much worn, or thick woollen vests with long pants, and often the vests had long sleeves too. Less heavy ones were donned for summer wear. People were accustomed to wrap up and take a lot more care of themselves. And many old-fashioned Middle Class men clung to nightgowns instead of pyjamas, but the nightcap had long since vanished. Flannel nightgowns for winter, cotton for summer. And most men wore bed-socks, although they never admitted it. Central heating was unknown, and a fire in the bedroom was a luxury for the rich and Upper Classes. Stone or earthenware hot-water bottles were in great demand, and even hot bricks wrapped in flannel. The rubber hot-water bottle became popular later on.

Most men carried little silver toothpicks, and it was customary at the restaurants for a small glassful of quill toothpicks to be put on the table. In these days of filled, golden and false teeth you never see them. Short-sighted men wore *pince-nez*, or steel or gold-rimmed spectacles. Horn-rimmed glasses came from America at a much later date and were not really popular until the First World War.

Men wore boots with their lounge suits. A few young men wore shoes, brogue or with American snub toes, and with these went shoe-laces which had big bows and the ends of them pulled out into quite a wide expanse.

Another era started when the double-fold linen collar defeated the 'chokers' and wing collars. These double collars, much as they are worn today, varied in height and shape. At first they were very high indeed, and the two sides of the opening fitted closely together, so that the knot of the tie was lost beneath them, for the knots were then worn inside the opening and not without. One enterprising firm put a collar on the market called 'The Double Event'. This could be used as a straight-up collar, by the simple expedient of tying the tie outside the collar and round the base, or a double collar by wearing the tie between the folds.

High collars were considered very smart. Then revulsion came and they went very low, mere strips of linen like a double dog-collar, a god-send to short-necked men. After a while most men compromised by wearing collars about two inches high.

But in 1906 another collar entered the field, destined to rout the stiff collar altogether in time to come, and to drive it to the last stronghold of full-dress events, evening dress or round the necks of old diehards. This was the soft, double-fold collar. It was Sir George Alexander who popularized this. He was one of the leaders of male fashion, but he never went to extremes. He was always, of his time, the most perfectly and correctly dressed of men. So when he made a tentative start with a soft collar in *John Chilcote, M.P.*, there was a considerable flutter. And when he wore it again in *His House in Order* the deed was done! Men who might have been chary of this informal innovation hesitated no longer. What was good enough for Alexander was good enough for them. The double-fold soft collar swamped the shops of 1906 and sold like wildfire.

It was flannel when it first came in, and striped. It made no pretence to match the shirt. It was straight up and down, like the linen variety, and it was held together in front by the lower corners being linked by a gold safety-pin. It was, however, never worn in town. It was for home or country only. No man of standing, or employee of trust, would have worn one at the office! Nobody would have worn them in the West End! But they were delightful for use when taking one's ease or playing games. White silk ones followed, some with white shirts. Nowadays the soft collar is general wear, on almost all occasions.

The starch having left the collars, or at least one variety of them, proceeded to evacuate many of the shirts. The shirts of younger men became coloured and soft. The cuffs came double, too. They assumed the hues of the rainbow, or they were, perhaps, of one colour only. Sir Seymour Hicks (plain 'Mr. Hicks' then by name but not in appearance) gave evidence in a theatrical lawsuit. He wore a plain pink shirt and a black tie. At once the chests of young men became of roseate hue, and the black tie was adorned with a plain pearl pin, or a turquoise one.

Starch still remained the wear for middle-aged and many other unprogressive men, but others discarded it, save when wearing dress shirts or with a frock- or morning coat. Nowadays people even wear soft collars and shirts with dress clothes. In the days of the golden sovereign they would not have been admitted.

Laundries proved an obstacle to the new soft fashion, and for quite a period returned men's coloured shirts and soft collars resolutely starched and stiff. They put up a good fight but they lost to weight of numbers. Ties underwent changes too, and for a long time the narrow tie kept its popularity. You could get good ones of *crêpe de Chine*, in every colour, for sixpence each. But the broad-ended tie won the day at the finish.

Trousers varied remarkably. Sometimes they were very loose, sometimes medium, and for a period around 1906 they were very tight indeed, almost skin-tight. This was not economical and not ornamental. They could not be properly creased, they speedily bagged at the knees, and if one had rather large feet, these extremities looked much larger still. Tight trousers did not last long and were succeeded by medium ones which retained the crease. Men had trousers presses to keep the creases in, and careless creasing produced bad results. There was an attempt by

Royalty to introduce trousers creased at the sides. With every desire to be loyal, men could not bring themselves to follow that fashion. There is a legend to the effect that the Royal trousers had been pressed that way by mistake. At any rate it was not popular.

'Oxford bags'—vast and voluminous—struck wonder but no wide appeal. Men wore bicycling suits with knickerbockers fastened round the knee and mostly Norfolk jackets. But it was the age of the blazer, and these lived up to their name.

The wear for summer sports was white flannel. No man would play cricket, a very serious game indeed, unless properly arrayed. Certain prominent cricketers even played in stiff white shirts, with the cuffs turned up. But most men wore the cricketing shirt of white flannel, with the lay-down collar attached. And a club tie, to lend colour. They wore white shoes for tennis, often with brown leather bands across toecap and heel. These were also worn for rowing. But for cricket it was white boots, either kid or canvas.

The blazer topped the whole thing off, flaming in its club stripes and making a great splash of colour everywhere. You wore a club cricket cap for cricket, but for the river either a boater or a soft white hat of twill, which was coming in around 1907. George Grossmith, Junior, another fashion leader, made his gallant attempt to popularize the panama in *The Toreador* at the old Gaiety in 1901. He failed. But not before a mass of imitation panamas at about 2s. 6d. each had got on the market. That, maybe, was why it was a failure.

Those flannels were amazingly cheap. You could buy jacket and trousers plain, grey or even with a thin black stripe—the latter for wearing, not for games—for 19s. 11d., 24s. 6d. and 29s. 6d. complete, and ready made. If you wanted a vest as well, this cost, for the entire suit, 21s. and 29s., according to quality. Extra special quality in ready-mades were 39s. 6d. Flannel jackets (coats) were 6s. 11d., 8s. 11d., and 12s. 11d. ready made, and flannel trousers were 6s. 11d., 8s. 11d., and 12s. 11d. ready made.

If you wanted your suit made to measure then it cost 35s., 37s. 6d., up to 44s. 6d. Lounge suits cost about the same, the average price being £2 2s., made to measure. The average price for boots was 8s. 9d. Some men paid as much as 16s. 6d., which was regarded as extravagance. You could have a pair of boots made to measure for £1 1s. Shirts cost anything from 2s. 6d. up to 5s. Collars were ridiculously cheap. Those 'Double Events' cost 6d. each. You could get collars for much less than that, with a reduction for a dozen or half a dozen. Eighteenpence got you a good tie. A bowler could be bought for 3s. 9d.—more of course at famous makers. A tall hat was 10s. 6d. and lasted a lifetime. Gloves were always worn.

Their price varied according to where you bought them, but you got a very good pair indeed for 2s. 6d., and most Middle Class men paid less. Furlined gloves for winter wear cost 4/-.

Socks were mostly black, although coloured socks followed quickly on the coloured shirts and were worn with shoes, the trousers being braced high to display them.

Men who wore shoes turned up their trousers—men wearing boots only turned theirs up on wet or muddy days. When the permanent turn-ups came in it was easier to display your socks. But men who wore black socks mostly had them 'clocked'. That was also a link with the 18th century.

Most Middle Class men wore woollen- or lisle-thread socks, although a few sported black silk socks with their evening dress, with which 'pumps' were worn, if dancing. Otherwise men wore dress boots of patent leather—very apt to crack—or patent boots with kid uppers.

Overcoats varied in fashion and were of many makes. Sometimes they were tight, sometimes loose. There were the Raglans, the Chesterfields, and the Covert coats, the latter short, fawn and a little 'horsey', but much worn in spring or autumn. In winter many men wore ulsters, long, heavy frieze coats, with a belt round the waist and very deep collars for turning up. Chesterfield coats had velvet collars, Raglans never. There was the evening dress overcoat too, a very smart affair, well cut and tight fitting, with buttons at the back, a fine garment.

Inverness coats with their capes had many devotees, and some men still wore the dress cape, the 'Millionaire's Cape', as it was known, with its scarlet lining and the fastening at the neck in the form of a lion's head and chain—easily the most pictorial of all male clothes, and very comfortable too. If you did not wear a tall hat with your evening clothes you wore a 'Gibus'—an opera hat which, made of corded silk, could be crushed flat and put under the seat at a theatre. It often got left behind, but it was a good hat.

There were fashions in walking-sticks and nearly all men carried one when not taking an umbrella. You could have a horn, ivory or deer's antler for the handle, with gold or silver bands. You could have sticks of ebony, with gold or silver knobs, or Malacca sticks, with either metal knob or crooked handle. If crooked it had silver or gold mounts and care was taken, when buying the stick, to see that it had a 'blade'.

There were sticks of partridge cane, with curved handles and mounts. For a while green cane sticks were very popular. You could carry a cane— a rattan cane, with curved handle and metal mounts—there was no end of variety. Some oak sticks had elaborately carved ivory handles. For the country it was an ash-plant, which cost sixpence at any tobacconist's.

But there were special shops then selling nothing but sticks and umbrellas. There are few such places now. The umbrella was much as today but the handle was inclined to more elaboration.

There were rainproof coats and mackintoshes with capes. Few men wore 'goloshes'—they were a joke. A play called *The Private Secretary* had made them so, for the mild little curate in that play—'The Rev. Robert Spalding', played first by Tree and then by W. S. Penley—carried goloshes and was anguished when he lost them. He also wore a 'blue ribbon' in his buttonhole to denote he was a teetotaller—who hears of 'The Blue Ribbon Army' today?—and was made to complain, "Do you know, I've had nothing to eat all day but a bath bun and a glass of milk and I've got such a funny feeling here." This stage character also wore his hair parted in the middle, which gave rise to the idea that all men following that fashion were either 'dudes' or stupid. All brainless young men were so depicted by the artists of the period.

Overdressed men were called 'dudes' and then became known as the 'B'hoys', and finally as the 'K'Nuts'. The 'K'Nuts' had their greatest exponent in poor Basil Hallam, in *The Passing Show* at the Palace. They were not fools, however, but 'young men about town'. They will be met again later.

Although it was essentially a masculine age, many men used scent. This was another old habit dying hard. It had been used largely in the Georgian era, and then Victorians carried it on to hide the odour of tobacco, which ladies 'could not endure'. The scents used were either eau-de-Cologne or lavender water. Men wore 'buttonholes' too, and carried little glass vases in the buttonholes of their coats, filled with water and fastened by a little silver fern-leaf. Some old-fashioned men, in the privacy of their homes, still wore elaborate smoking-jackets and smoking-caps—round caps with tassels. Again the idea was that their clothes should not get permeated by tobacco smoke, nor their hair either.

There were even fashions in the pockets of one's lounge suits. These could be crosswise, sometimes with flaps, sometimes without, and for a time they were vertical. Men wore braces; the trousers which fit round the waist and fasten with a strap were unknown.

And nearly every man wore a moustache, and a fairly big one. Some, of course, waxed the ends, *à la militaire*. Men with large walrus moustaches —quite a common sight—used special cups for drinking, called 'moustache cups', which had a strip of earthenware across them, supposed to keep the moustache from the liquid. This was used for tea, but they didn't bother about the moustache when drinking spirits or wine. Nor soup, which never improved any moustache.

Quite a lot of middle-aged men wore beards—as did King Edward and
186

his son King George V. A few elderly men still had 'dundrearys' or mutton-chop whiskers. Agricultural characters and coasting sailors affected a whisker which left mouth and chin shaven but surrounded the face like a halo. This went right out when the Boer War came along, for Kruger was so adorned. There was a passing phase of the 'Kaiser' moustache, but neither it nor its original were very popular. Only actors, barristers (and not always they) and a few clergymen were clean-shaven. And even so, there were moustached actors like Charles Hawtrey (who failed when he shaved his off and had to grow it again), Sir Squire Bancroft and others.

All Middle Class men then regarded themselves, and very rightly, as gentlemen. That is to say, they behaved as gentlemen, for they had so been brought up. They had 'manners' and they never forgot them. To do so was terrible. A gentleman who forgot himself found it hard to live it down. They were much more courteous all round than today, and their behaviour to women—who were always referred to as 'ladies'—was impeccable. They treated her not as an equal, but as a superior. She was something to protect, to cherish, to serve. They took her flowers, boxes of chocolates, gloves. They sprang to their feet and rushed to hold the door open if she went out of the room. They always removed their hats when meeting her in the street. And often remained uncovered until she gave permission to resume the hat.

Men of special courtesy would uncover in a shop, if ladies were there, and in a lift or such-like places. If strolling along with a lady, he always walked outside. But if there were two ladies he walked in the middle. The popular toast at public dinners was 'The Ladies—God Bless 'Em'. No man swore, was coarse in his remarks, or told a *risqué* story before beings of the 'gentler sex'. He also asked permission to smoke. And, as a hallmark of the entire period, it was always 'Ladies First'.

CHAPTER XII

'The Ladies, God Bless 'Em'

IT IS PERHAPS A SIGN OF THE TIMES THAT IN THIS BOOK THE AFFAIRS OF men have preceded those of women. Let it stand, for men do not get much of a chance in these days of so-called equality of the sexes. It is not a case of 'Ladies First' today. Also, the writer is a man and cannot be expected to be an expert on this subject, although happily married, a father and a grandfather. Despite the fact that his profession has brought him into contact with hundreds if not thousands of women, he still does not feel that he knows much about them, and being of the age of the sovereign himself, still regards them as he did in his youth—when they will permit him to do so, which is not often. What was simple courtesy then, so ordinary as to be unnoticed, is today looked upon either as impertinence or just plain stupidity. This chapter therefore must beg the pardon of what the writer still regards at the back of his mind as the gentler sex, and must be taken simply as his own views on the matter. Few young women will agree with him, if any read these words, but women of his own age may do so, and the men most certainly will. What he now writes is his own observation and his own opinion.

The great thing in those days was that women were individual. Of course they were, in the main, ruled by fashion; they always have been and always will be, but then they still managed to remain individual. They were not the abject slaves to it which they became later on. They kept strictly within the framework of the prevailing mode but they gave their own personality a chance. They never all dressed alike. Their waists were movable, their sleeves were long or short, tight or full, balloon or skimpy. They never wore a full skirt in a tight-skirt period, they never wore a tight sleeve when fashion demanded yards of material. But their main idea was to adapt that fashion to themselves, and to make the most of themselves whilst conforming to it.

Their dresses might go through many revolutionary forms, but their own forms were not affected, for women then were essentially feminine. They had figures, they made the most of those figures. They were not all doomed to slimness—to emaciation. They were feminine, they were women, they wanted to look like women, and they succeeded. The very last thing they wanted to look like was a man. They knew something their descendants do not. They had not tried to alter the architecture of their Creator. They retained the charm of womanhood in their gracious curves.

If those curves were on the ample side, nobody cared, and many men preferred what they called 'fine women'. If a woman lacked curves she padded. Their clothes allowed this. No woman in those days wanted to look just like all the other women. And she never did.

They were women at a time when it was man's job—and pleasure—to revere, respect and protect his women from the dirt and dangers of the world. And to his credit he mostly did.

Women then believed in mystery, and how right they were. Their bodies, and most certainly their legs, were secrets. They wore clothes which were unrevealing but enticing—because they were ultra-feminine. Skirts were long and legs were private property. It was not delicate to mention them, even. Consequently on the few occasions when they were revealed, by accident or design, the effect on men was electrical, not to say devastating.

Even when a directoire style came in—introduced by the musical comedy *Les Merveilleuses* at Daly's, and a few ultra-smart women showed a glimpse of limb through a slashed skirt, it failed to catch on, although the style—minus the slash—was attractive. Daly's gave women the 'Merry Widow' hat too—the stage led fashion then. There was an attempt to get women to wear the harem skirt—loose Turkish trousers—but loud male guffaws and references to 'harem scarem' slew it almost before it was born.

It was the same with hats. There were always fashions in hats. But again the woman of the Sovereign Age adapted the prevailing one to suit herself. Hats might be large or small—and they touched each extreme—but a woman wore a hat which suited her, not just because it was fashionable or because every other woman wore one just like it. Nothing like the period of the *cloche* hat, when all women looked exactly like each other, would have been endured then.

Hats were the pinnacle of the dress *ensemble*. 'Is my hat on straight?' was a woman's first anxious query. And the reason was plain. For the hat depended to a large extent on the coiffure.

Women then, in their desire for equality and freedom, had not cut their hair short. It was not bobbed, shingled or messed about as it has been since. Every woman then wore her hair long. The more she had, the better she was pleased. It was still her crowning glory, as the poet had hymned. It was her pride and her joy, if also a severe and exacting task-master.

The Middle Class woman 'did' her own hair. None but the rich and leisured went to hairdressers. Hours and hours and pounds and pounds were not spent on impermanent 'permanent waves', which need constant renewing, nor on cutting and clipping, leaving a bristly extent

189

of neck like a man's unshaven chin. No, she did her own hair. Friends who were really intimate would 'do' each other's hair and take pleasure in it. There would be long discussions before a customary coiffure was changed, and anxious examinations in the mirror to see if it really 'suited'.

Hair might be worn piled high on the head, or done low on the neck. She bowed to the main rule but adapted it to suit herself again. Fringes came and went—Queen Alexandra had set a fashion there. A certain amount of false hair was worn, and there were things called 'foundations' over which the hair was swathed (another use for these will appear later). These extra curls and often these 'foundations' were made of the woman's own hair, for hairdressers advertised 'Ladies' Own Combings Made Up'. Women spent a long time combing and brushing their hair, and would save the combings in a little linen bag to take to the hairdresser for him to 'make up'. It was about the only money he ever took off them, for his was a male establishment and a preserve of masculinity.

Dressing the long hair meant the use of innumerable hairpins. These were of wire, sometimes quite stiff, sometimes quite thin, with the middle of each leg, as it were, in a series of little squiggles. There were light-coloured hairpins for fair hair and dark for brunettes. These hairpins were often—indeed always—falling out. Pavements were littered with them, and so were rooms. Men liked that, they came in handy for pipe-cleaning. Hairpins were easily shed and could be found everywhere.

A woman washed her hair herself, as she dressed it herself. She put it into curlers at night, if need be. A woman prayed for naturally curly hair, a mother prayed that her daughter's might be. Few of those prayers were granted, it seemed. So on went the curlers, either flexible little metal lengths covered with brown material, or curlers made of steel, something like brooches, the hair being wound around two straight clips in the middle which fastened into a slot in the framework. She wore these all night. And she used curling-irons, which she heated either in a candle or over a little spirit-lamp like a pad used with a rubber stamp, and then curled her hair very tight with them.

Some of the curlers had straight 'blades', convex and flat at the end, others had wavy blades which induced a belief in extra wavy results but did not fulfil it. There was always a slight smell of singed hair in every Middle Class woman's dressing-room after she had completed her real toilette. Her back hair, for nights, she plaited into a pigtail. If she had naturally curly hair she thanked her lucky stars and was inclined to crow over less-favoured women friends, whose hair speedily lost its curl in damp weather. But she always made the most of her coiffure, and was individual in this.

She remained individual in her colour too. She wanted to be herself, not somebody else. There was, in consequence, no going suddenly, dazzlingly, and obviously falsely, blonde, or of suddenly changing from a brunette into a redhead. She stuck to her own colour. There might be a little delicate tinting to hide the ravages of time, when a grey streak made an unwelcome or premature appearance, but that was all. The dyed streak in front hair, common today, would have aroused laughter or disgust. No woman wanted to be piebald. A woman with dyed hair was labelled as 'fast', and that was shocking.

A celebrated novelist of the period was sued for libel by a woman who found herself described, or said that she did so, in the pages of a novel, which spoke of her dyed hair. If memory serves, the damages were one farthing, but it just goes to show what dyed hair meant. A woman with dyed hair and 'make-up' could only, in those days, belong to 'a certain class'. Nowadays it is difficult to tell.

No woman in those days made up her face in public. Indeed, she used little make-up at all. When absolutely necessary, a little rouge was applied in the secrecy of her bedroom or boudoir, a little of what was called 'lip salve', and powder was most discreetly dusted on, to prevent shiny noses or perspiration. Women cherished their complexions. Those with good ones were triumphant. Those with bad ones suffered a great tragedy. They protected their complexions, they wore veils, and they carried sunshades. A woman making up her face in a theatre or restaurant then would have been asked to leave, just as she would if she had lit a cigarette.

A woman's complexion and a woman's hair were her own, in ninety-nine and three quarter cases out of a hundred; and in the other quarter the falsity was only in the same proportion. And on that hair of hers she put her hat. That hat had to be at an exactly right angle, or perfectly straight. It was a matter of great moment and even greater precision, and the fixing of it was a work of artistic skill, for the hat was secured on the head with hatpins. No woman's hat in those days fitted her head. It was not expected to do so. It does so today, as often as not, and by so doing both have lost individuality; even the hatpin has vanished.

Those hatpins were grimly dangerous affairs. They were long, they were slender, and they were very, very sharp. Some had plain black glass knobs, some had coloured knobs, some had quite ornate endings on the non-business end, some indeed had little jewelled hilts, like the stilettos they so greatly resembled. A woman in a hurry, or by being a bit careless, could inflict a severe wound on her scalp, and hatpins were used as weapons by the lower and less restrained stratas of society, with diabolical results. That 'foundation' came in handy here, for the pin could be skewered through it and held firmly in place.

N

191

Women removing their hats, under protest, at matinées in theatres, would fix the hat to the back of the seat in front of them with their hat-pins, and frequently transfix the unfortunate person sitting therein.

There were, in connection with the hair, the 'transformations'—again those 'own combings' cunningly made up came in useful. These were used in front of the hair over the forehead by women whose advancing years meant thinning tresses.

But for the most part women were far more natural than today, when a girl will dodge from blonde to ash-blonde, to carrots, and back to brunette with violent suddenness and no warning at all. A young woman's hair now is seldom its natural colour, her complexion is never all her own, and her nails are painted even more violently than her face. Not content with ultra-revealing clothes, she even favours the world with a sight of her heels and her toenails—scarcely ever things of beauty, even when varnished over. It was not so then.

Next to a woman's hair, perhaps the great feature of the age was the petticoat, that ultra-feminine garment. It was indeed still the era of the 'tempestuous petticoat'. Women wore many petticoats and the better off they were the more they wore of them. They made a foam of lace around her feet and ankles, they gave a swish of silk and a rustle of satin as she walked; they gave her poise and balance, they clothed to perfection the divinity of mystery that was woman. And they had a great effect on men. Women were not given to slimming. They did not want to be 'skinny', as it was then called. And if it was their misfortune to be so, the petticoat helped a lot.

Into the deeper mysteries of her underclothing it is not permitted to probe. It 'was not done' in the Sovereign Age. But there were no 'scanties', no 'panties', no 'step-ins' and the like. A woman never mentioned such things. The garments then in vogue were not even displayed in the shops, except sometimes in the corner, very very discreetly and complexly folded up, something of white silk or cambric and very lacy might be seen, but its use only guessed at. There were corsets, of course, mostly called 'stays'. Everybody knew about them—they were even a joke. They could be seen in shop windows and even in magazine advertisements. But the advertisements in a modern woman's magazine, if printed then, would have led to suppression by the police. If you wanted that sort of thing there was *La Vie Parisienne*.

Those corsets were formidable affairs of silk or other material covering the foundation of whalebone, which were laced up at the back and fastened in front by means of very solid hooks and eyes. They were veritable coats of mail. Whether fashion decreed a woman's waist to be under her armpits or round her knees, and it reached these places during the period, still the real woman underneath relied upon her corsets to keep her true waistline slim and dainty and as wasp-like as possible. She never let it spread, for she valued her hips. Hips had great sex appeal, and, although she never discussed sex, being a woman she was fully aware of its appeal.

Nowadays waists and hips are things of the past. Men were fully aware of corsets—had they been innocent before, the moment they encircled a woman's waist they found out all about it and, indeed, badly fitting corsets were extremely revealing of themselves about the bust. And women believed in busts too. Probably they thought that a whale's chief object in life was to supply bone for their corsets. They were never expected to buy its meat to cook for their husbands, who would not have eaten it if they had.

There was also the 'chemise', which was well known. It was regarded as a bit of a joke, but the mention of it was as far as decency would permit discussion or remarks on underwear of a feminine nature. There was no chatter about 'cami-knickers'. There was, though, one more garment (or should we say 'fixture'?) of femininity which had a great appeal, and that was the garter. The most noble of all chivalric orders was based on this so there was little indelicacy about it, although great allure. They were dainty, delightful trifles then, of ribbons and lace. Most desirable, and things of beauty.

Today they have given place to a species of machine of wire, elastic, rubber and metal which apparently, under the name of suspender, causes more damage by way of dreaded 'ladders' than any service in the way of suspension, and it has no romance as had the garter, especially when worn on a silk stocking above a pretty knee. The other mysteries of women's under attire—garments of enchantment and lace and ribbon— yards and yards and yards of ribbon—were secrets known, it is hoped, only to the fortunate and happily married man.

Skirts were long. Mostly they swept the ground. On rainy days a woman sometimes gathered them up in both hands. Or perhaps she used only one, if carrying a bag or umbrella; she would put that hand behind her, and by a knack and a feminine form of hitch would manage to bring her skirts just off the mud and wet. Now and again, by accident, bad luck or misjudgment, she held them too high and would show quite a length of leg and stocking. Sometimes, even a glimpse of a lacy frill as well. That almost stopped the traffic. Rude men stared, bus-drivers whistled and waved their whips, errand boys shouted and ran, bus conductors cheered, until the lady, apprised of her error, beat a blushing—yes, women really blushed then—and hasty retreat, full of shame and confusion.

Sometimes a lady, in warm and sunny weather, would be deceived as to the thickness of her dress and discard her petticoats. Against the sun she

193

made a most exciting and provoking silhouette until some friend told her. Again confusion and retreat into a woman's shop for the purpose of pinning brown paper or newspaper under the skirt until she got home. Nowadays the full extent of a woman's leg, bared or stockinged, does not turn a single head. Women have sacrificed their mystery and with it much of their grace. If you really want to see a woman of today at her very worst watch her getting out of a modern car. No woman of the Golden Age would have dreamed of doing such an ungraceful thing. She knew much better.

It is not possible to trace the various changes in women's fashions over such a long period of twenty-four years. They were far too numerous. The crinoline had gone, the bustle had gone, but the hobble skirt was to show to what lengths of inconvenience she would go even then.

All that can be achieved is to pick out salient points and generalize. It was, of course, throughout, a period of long skirts. A short skirt meant one of ankle length. Occasionally, very occasionally, in the country, a woman might wear one which reached half-way down her calf, and then she wore gaiters—but not as a rule Middle Class women; but the women of the grouse moors or the pheasant shooting. The ankle length was the usual length for such sports as women then indulged in: lawn tennis, fishing, boating—they punted very often in most elaborate costumes, but they seldom rowed; their place was to steer (mostly into the bank), wearing lacy, diaphanous gowns and big floppy hats—or at golf or even hockey. A few women fenced, but seldom Middle Class women. No women played football or ran races in vest and shorts.

Women wore nightgowns, mostly very charming affairs, and never pyjamas. Those came in with the First World War for women, although dainty little actresses sang songs about them and wore them on the stage. Nightdresses, like underclothing, were white. Colours for such things were considered 'fast', and to be fast was death in the Middle Classes. They had delightful négligés and dressing-jackets—there was quite a large wardrobe needed of such things.

It was an age of blouses and skirts, of costumes, of coats and skirts. And if the day dress was unrevealing, evening dresses were usually the reverse. A woman could be most décolleté, with corsage just covering the bust, bare arms, back and shoulders, and yet be good form and modest. In cold weather, of course, they wore furs, either tippets or stoles, of all sorts of furs, and bear was quite a popular one. And they carried muffs, with entrancing muff-chains to support them. Middle Class women did not run to fur coats as they do today. Mink they knew not, or it was far beyond them. Ermine was the fur de luxe and also out of reach of most

Middle Class pockets. Even the rich did not pay such fabulous prices as rule today.

What most women of matron age craved was a sealskin coat. That was an ambition of them all and it was very often realized. It lasted for a lifetime. But few young women got them, or fur coats of any kind either. They had good thick warm cloth coats, and stoles or tippets. Some had velvet coats with fur edgings, a very attractive fashion indeed, and they fitted tight to the figure. A girl in one, with a deep stole, a little fur cap and a fur muff, could be very fascinating, and knew all about it.

Capes were worn in great variety and looked charming, besides being comfortable and warm. The more mature women wore 'mantles', wonderful confections with frills and trimmings and even jet trappings to them. Bonnets were worn with these, as a rule, and the bonnet was the sign of middle age. You see no such things now, but they could be quite jaunty, with trimmings and whatnots and a wide ribbon tied under the chin or at the side of the face in a big bow.

A woman then, fully dressed, either for the day or the evening, looked like a picture specially painted for a purpose. That was her idea and she achieved it. There was nothing casual, nothing haphazard, it was a carefully thought out and built-up creation, and it achieved its purpose.

The Middle Class girl or woman got few silk stockings. She wore cashmere as a rule. She wore high-heeled shoes of extreme daintiness, and high-heeled boots which were often buttoned and very smart indeed. The Louis heel was the thing in those days.

Now what did all this cost, this fitting out of a divinity of the Middle Class? It is almost staggering to discover.

"Model 374 in Half Guinea Costumes is an exceedingly smart mode in Cheviot Serge. It consists of full wide Godet skirt, with belt, also very neat bodice, with full front and broad box-pleat down centre; trimmed bold silk cord and three fashionable buttons. The collar, cuffs and belt are also edged silk cord and the saddle and sleeves are lined. Price complete, only 10s. 6d. Safely packed and sent carriage paid for 9d. extra."

That is not a bit of fiction or imagination run wild, it is an actual extract from an advertisement in the programme of Earl's Court Exhibition in 1895. You could have the skirt alone for 5s. 6d., containing enough material to make two of the dresses of today. The advertisement also gives a clue to the physique of the women of the golden sovereign days. The stock sizes were 34, 36 and 38 inches round the bust (under arms), the skirts were 38, 40 and 42 inches long in front. If you were an outsize you could be accommodated for 1s. 6d. extra. The colours were black, navy, brown, myrtle, bronze green, electric blue, ruby, dark cinnamon, fawn or grey.

If you came under the heading of 'Young Misses', the costume was yours for 8s. 6d. It comprised blouse, bodice and full-cut skirt. The bodice was lined throughout, and made with high fancy collar, broad box-pleat down the centre, finished buttons and fashionably full sleeves in front, cuffs and collar being trimmed with military braid. The advertisement continues:

"The full Godet skirt has deep hem and is trimmed at each side with fancy pocket, finished military braid and buttons *en suite*."

The colours were the same as the ladies' costumes. But if you were a little girl your mother could purchase a costume for you for the amazing sum of 2s. 6d. This was in Cheviot serge, with saddle top, loose hanging skirt, full sleeves and deep puffs.

"The skirt, cuffs and saddle are effectively trimmed in gold silk braid and the whole garment is well made and finished throughout."

Again, the colours are the same as the ladies' and the misses'.

There was no deception. There were the coloured sketches in the programme, and you were exhorted to look at the posters on the walls of the Exhibition. "There's richness for you," as Squeers said.

Many parents of moderate means took advantage of such offers. But the more well-to-do of the Middle Classes patronized their drapers and dress shops, or had things made up by 'the little woman round the corner'. Large families had itinerant dressmakers call at the house and work there.

Handbags were as necessary then as now. Woman has never been able to achieve proper pockets. At this period the pocket was at the back of the skirt, reached by what was called the 'placket hole' into which a woman groped blindly for handkerchief, purse or other necessary article. She often dropped them, and the system was a godsend to pickpockets, who frequently cut the whole pocket out without the wearer being a whit the wiser. But handbags then cost from 6s. 11d. to 30s. Today they cost pounds.

Blouses, those essentials for women's wear, varied from 6s. 11¾d. to 12s. 11d. Famous dress shops in the West End sold blouses and what they described as 'slips' at a higher price than this, of course, costing 8s. 6d., 11s. 6d. and even 27s. 6d., whilst evening blouses, very ornate, cost as much as 28s. 6d. The price today would be £8 or £9 and the quality nothing like so good.

The same fashionable firms sold coats and skirts at 89s. 6d. The average Middle Class woman paid 2½ to 3 guineas for hers. Hats cost what you liked to pay for them, but the average woman paid about 10s. 11d. Silk stockings, to the Middle Classes a luxury, not a necessity, were expensive at 8s. 11¾d. The cashmere stockings usually worn worked out at 1s. 11¾d. to 2s. 11¾d. All these prices are average, be it understood. A woman's evening gown, in the Middle Class, cost her from 2 to 3 guineas. One at 4½ guineas was super, and other girls envied her. Her shoes cost from 10s. 6d. to 16s. 9d., her gloves were 4s. 11d. to 6s. 6d. You got a serviceable pair of kid gloves, however, for 2s. 11¾d. Long evening gloves, which were so very attractive, cost 5s. 11d., with suède gloves a bit more expensive. All the stuff was good and it all lasted.

Her hairdressing, as has been shown, cost her next to nothing, for she did it herself. Her expense was the cost of the curlers and the very small cost of the ever-vanishing hairpins. Everything was inconceivably cheaper and inconceivably better in quality.

Every woman of the Upper or Middle Classes insisted on being individual. Her one horror was the discovery that another woman was wearing exactly the same hat or dress as herself, or one who, so she firmly believed, had copied her style of hairdressing. The hair was so important to a woman. When her hair went 'up' her skirt went down— and almost overnight she had passed out of girlhood into womanhood.

Women, then, although their age was always a secret and never discussed, made concessions to time in their mode of dress and in their mode of hairdressing. You never mistook, from the back, a mother for a daughter. Adult women never went about with their hair round their shoulders, they abandoned that in their early teens. Here and there an unmarried woman, then referred to as a spinster, or an 'old maid', would try to retain some semblance of lost youth in her dress and general appearance. She deceived nobody. Rather she was either pitied or laughed at. Nowadays women either retain their youth longer or youth vanishes much earlier. It is one or the other, and probably the latter.

Then, young matrons in their twenties still dressed more maturely than single girls ending their teens, and were proud to do so. The status of a married woman was high. And you could always tell the mistress from the maid. A Working Class girl never succeeded in looking like a Middle Class girl. She did not really want to. Some venturesome maids who copied their mistresses were sacked at once.

Glancing down the memories of years, it is possible to recall some facts and phases which have impressed themselves on the male mind.

There were feather boas, which became very fashionable. They were worn round the neck and thrown over the shoulder, they were worn sometimes quite loosely draped around the shoulders and drooping down on the back. They were of marabout, of ostrich, of cocks' feathers—all sorts of feathers and all very charming

There were veils of all colours, to preserve the complexion. Some were plain, some had little velvet spots and some quite large designs on them. To take tea or refreshment or blow her nose the woman had to fold them up, starting from the chin, until they were on a level with her forehead. They fastened round the hat, and the lady, when veiled, twisted the end under her chin. One recalls sleeves which ballooned at the shoulder, called 'leg-of-mutton' sleeves, and others which were very full down to the elbow and then went tight, whilst yet others were tight almost down to the wrist and ended in balloons. Also there seems to have been a period when sleeves were bell-shaped, like miniature sailors' trousers, and boleros were the fashion.

Lace dresses were things of joy to behold, often three-deckers edged with some delicate colour, but mostly pink or blue. And there were enchanting lace coats.

Some hats were toques—and women wear them today but don't realize it. Other hats were of enormous size and height, with veritable bushes of flowers, fruit and foliage. Others, of felt, bore entire birds on their crowns or flat on their brims. Feathers were in great request for hat trimming. The 'Merry Widow' hat, which was so charming, was in shape like an inverted basin. Large hats, middle-sized hats, small hats, a woman always wore head-covering. She never went bareheaded or swathed her hair in a handkerchief—as the exigence of war has forced her to nowadays.

Women surrendered to middle age much faster and drifted into a very placid and dignified old age—but they remained like that for a long time. Clad in black silk, with an apron of the same material, or perhaps a deep violet, with often a little cap on their silver heads, they took their rest, watching and advising their juniors. They ruled like matriarchs, these grandmothers, and commanded respect. There is little or no respect for elders today, and it is largely the fault of the elders, who insist on remaining persistently young. It may be good, it may be bad, it all depends on point of view. But of one thing there is no doubt at all; life was easier and more pleasant for a woman before she got her 'rights', before she achieved what she is pleased to believe is equality. The young people don't know this, because they have never experienced it. But the elderly are well aware.

When the suffragettes started their battle they had very little support and much derision. In the bulk, women were not interested in politics or

198

government. They were interested in families, and that was their contribution to the State. The 'shrieking sisterhood', as they were called, who carried on their violent battle and their antics of assault, battery, dog-whip, sulphuric acid in letter-boxes, screams, kicks, arrests and hunger strikes, eventually brought about the enfranchisement of women—which would have come in due course anyway. Women got the vote and were entitled to it. The world was then told that a new era had dawned. The women's vote would put everything right that the men had bungled. She would, at the polls, bring about peace on earth and good will towards all men. What has actually taken place is a never-ending series of world crises, industrial unrest and the greatest war in history. Nobody blames the women for causing this, but that vote of theirs did not seem to do much to prevent it.

Since a woman became the equal of man there has perhaps been less embarrassment. In the days of the golden sovereign such a thing as a lavatory was never mentioned. It was the guiltiest of guilty secrets. The ordinary natural functions of the body were apparently denied to women, and if members of opposite sexes happened to bump into each other near a lavatory, the embarrassment was extremely and mutually acute. Such a thing, like sex, was covered right up, and the benighted foreigners who were more open about it were regarded as a lot of dirty scoundrels. No girl then would have asked her male companion to wait whilst she went to 'spend a penny', as happens today. She would have died first. If this is, to some, still an indelicate matter, it cannot be helped. It is one of the great differences between the times.

There were tea-gowns, long loose articles of great ease and comfort, with cascades of lace down the front. Women wore them at home when relaxing, and they were very useful when the lady in the golden age found herself in 'an interesting condition'.

Women did not smoke—and even the daring few who did it at home, or as a provocative act in flirtation, never dared in public. Women 'flirted' a lot, and you never seem to hear that word used in these downright days.

There was a thing called a fringe net which kept the fringe in control, when such things were fashionable. It was a very fine net of hair and extremely delicate and easy to break. But as stated already, fringes never lasted for long. Such graceful and dignified creations as the Gibson Girls dealt 'hair-dos' of that kind death-blows. But the Lower Classes of the time delighted in fringes—indeed, they wore curlers all the week to have a fringe like a barbed-wire entanglement on a Saturday evening or a Sunday. They adored frizzed hair and often looked like a lot of fuzzy-wuzzies.

Nobody wore snoods then, they were early-Victorian. Today you see them all over the place and nobody laughs at them. Yet the picture of a Victorian girl wearing one, and the costume which went with it, moves young girls to uncontrollable laughter at the follies of those days. They never seem to realize that women's fashions are constantly recurring, and when they come up afresh they are greeted with joy. They have worn (or will in their time) nearly all the things they laugh at. And liked them.

Some of their button boots went very high up the leg. They did not wear coloured shoes, except satin ones with evening dress. Boots and shoes, like the stockings, were either black or tan. But women in those days when in evening wear mostly carried a fan. This was another survival from an older age and a very charming one indeed. A girl with good hands and arms could make great play and havoc amongst the males by simply putting a fan to its proper use, if she knew how to do so in a graceful manner. And when closed it was very effective for using as a sceptre to enforce her majesty the woman's commands, and for tapping her escort on the hand or arm to bring him to his senses.

The first lesson inculcated into girls was that their behaviour must be ladylike. That meant a modest demeanour, a quiet voice, a general restfulness and no yelling or stridency. They mostly lived up to it. Loud voices were 'common'. A girl in glasses or spectacles was at a severe disadvantage in the marriage market, whereas today it matters not at all. There are even fashions in spectacles now. But a married woman might use a lorgnette, and no more devastating social weapon was ever designed. A lorgnette, properly used, could quell the most daring man, annihilate the bore or the person of presumption, put everyone in their proper place and strike general terror. It was the atom bomb of a drawing-room.

There was not the free mingling of the sexes so general today. There was no frankness between them. There was no exchange of what were then called 'smoking-concert' stories or remarks with double meanings. And anything approaching vulgarity was completely taboo. Decorum, modesty and good manners got the girl to her desired goal—a husband and a home of her own. Women then did not imitate men. They thought that men were to be pitied on account of their severe and plain attire— poor creatures they, who could not wear pretty things.

Yet when woman became what she thought was emancipated the first thing she did was to assume male attire, and the nearer she got to the real thing the better she was pleased. She thought it triumphant to wear the trousers literally, whether they suited her or not. Girls so attired little knew that their mothers and grandmothers had worn them figuratively for centuries, and retained their femininity at the same time. The odd characters of the past generation who adopted male attire were looked upon as abnormal. Geniuses such women might be—George Sand and Rosa Bonheur—but they were immodest and they were not ladylike, so therefore they were outside the pale. It was then social suicide to be bold or brazen or even to stare at members of the opposite sex. It was bad manners as well. So it was doubly terrible.

There seems to be one more fashion which has changed, and that change may be a subtle but certain example of the difference in the times, of the laxity of manners and morale and general ethical backbone. That fashion is the wedding-ring.

In the days of the golden sovereign this was the most prized possession of every woman entitled to wear one. In company with the sovereign it was of gold, broad, solid and strong, typical of the lifelong link of which it was the symbol. It was treasured with pride, it was worn with a deep satisfaction. Very many women, when once it had been slipped on their finger at the altar, never removed it again for one instant all their lives. It went with them to their graves. To show the value they placed on it, they frequently wore what was called a 'keeper'. That wedding-ring was the true emblem of Marriage and its sacrament, which was then deeply regarded by the Middle Classes.

Today that broad gold ring is infrequently seen. The wedding-ring is narrow, attentuated, often removed, and more often than not it is of platinum. Today the marriage tie is not so strong, so indissoluble as it was. It is more of an experiment than a dedication sacrament. Divorce today is so frequent as to be entirely disregarded. What is now called freedom would, in the Golden Age, have been called lack of self-control.

Divorce was disgrace in the Middle Class days of the sovereign. It was seldom practised. People made the best of marriage and found it turned out well after all.

The lack of dignity in the appearance, the wearing and the pride in the wedding-ring is an outward and visible sign. It is no longer a thing which links for life. It is insignificant. It can be slipped off at any time.

But then, it is no longer that same solid thing of gold—with the same stability as that companion the golden sovereign.

CHAPTER XIII

'Every Third Thursday'

IF THE LADY OF THE AGE OF THE GOLDEN SOVEREIGN HAD NO VOTE, NO enfranchisement, no equality with man, she had one thing which went a long way in making up for all those doubtful blessings—she was the undisputed mistress of her home. And a home then meant what it said. The Home was the centre of life, round which the whole Middle Class family world revolved, and the Middle Class housewife was the ruler of the whole thing. No Cabinet Ministers expressed sympathy with her then. There was no need. She was indeed monarch of her realm, with hordes of people at her service, eager for her approval, trembling at her displeasure. She was the queen of the castle when an Englishman's home was his castle. She was the customer who was always right. Money was plentiful and went far. If she had two golden sovereigns to spend each week on housekeeping her family lived in what today would be luxury. At no time did two one-pound notes go nearly so far. The whole of her domestic economy was contained in one word—service. It was, however, subdivided into two parts—domestic service and the service given to her in shops.

The first half—domestic service—was the only thing which set her a problem. There was a servant problem even then. But nowadays there are no servants to make a problem of their own at all. The servant problem was practically her only worry. "My dears," a lady would say, when attending the 'At Home' of a friend (Mrs. Vavasour Smythe, The Laurels, Crediton Avenue, Highgate, N. At Home Every Third Thursday), "my dears, pity me, I'm without." What she meant—and she was understood perfectly clearly by every woman present—was that for the moment she was without a domestic servant. That was quite a serious thing, for in those days there was a lot of work in a house.

Nowadays, of course, practically every housewife is 'without'. Such service as is rendered is done as a favour at a high price, and is referred to not as service, but as 'Help'. It is often open to grave doubt if that is the right word. But in those days there were plenty of servants.

The class from which the domestic servant came went in for large families. It was the regular thing for girls to 'go into service'. It was their destiny, their career. Many of their mothers had been 'in service' before them. Nobody had told them it was derogatory for one human being to work in the house of another for an agreed wage. The word 'service' did

202

not mean slavery to them but regular work in return for board, lodging and a wage. They did not think themselves demeaned. Rather they looked down upon the smaller proportion of female labour which entered factories. They considered themselves a good cut above that.

These girls who worked in factories were a rougher type, who objected mainly to wearing 'uniform'! Later, of course, they all donned a species of uniform under stress of war. Were they degraded by that? one wondered. They chose, however, to work very hard in indifferent factories under very indifferent conditions for indifferent pay, because by so doing they could escape the 'uniform' of the cap and apron and have their evenings free.

Well, they got their evenings free and much good it did many of them. There were no pictures to go to, and few amusements except the local music-hall or theatre—the latter did not attract them very much unless a touring musical comedy was on—and as for the ' 'Alls'—well, it could only be once a week, otherwise you saw the same bill. There was the great joy of walking up and down the local 'Monkeys' Parade' in the main thoroughfare, or in summer in the local park (a monkeys' parade was that portion of the park or main street sacred to the young of both sexes as a promenade and ogling place, its limits being an invisible barrier at each end which was always kept inviolate by every generation), disappearing up a dark alley with a young man (often with unfortunate results), or the pub.

All that, of course, represented freedom and no restraint as to uniform. You could always tell the factory girl from the general servant. The former was never as neat or well dressed. She wore indifferent clothes, a long coat, and a black straw hat with very often her hair in curlers—or she had flashy cheap finery which never improved her looks. The domestic servant, on her evening out, had to be neat, clean and nicely, if plainly, dressed. Her employers saw to that.

Domestic service was the regular calling for a vast number of girls who were a decent, law-abiding, healthy and respectable part of the community. They were a necessity to the Middle Class. Indeed, the Middle Class began to decline and alter when the shortage of housemaids first arose after the First World War. The social importance of the domestic servant was as great as that.

So the Middle Class housewife who was temporarily 'without' was an object of general sympathy. She would not, however, be 'without' for long. The supply of servants exceeded the demand. For the housewife, the problem was quality, not quantity. She would be inundated with applicants from the Registry Office. and if she advertised there would be a flood of replies. What she wanted, however, was not just a domestic servant, but a good one. And eventually she would get one.

It has become customary to think of domestic servants as slaves. They were very far from that. They could, and they did, give 'a month's notice' if they did not like their job with the same ease and freedom as they could receive it from a dissatisfied mistress. They had no union, it is true, so they could not indulge in the popular pastime of a later age and go on strike. Nor would they have done so. Their month's notice and their 'character' was as good as any union. The 'character' was the great guarantee. With a good one, a girl could always get a good job. Without it, she went into a factory.

Mistresses preferred personally-given characters to written ones, but sometimes distance prevented that. And it so happens that most women were quite fair when it came to the question of giving a servant a character. There was sometimes spite and anger in them when a good servant left the employment of a woman for a friend of that same mistress. Old friendships were broken over this, accusations of stealing the girl were hurled, and much bad feeling arose. But spite or bad temper in a reference were easily discerned. No woman, however, could commit a greater crime than stealing a good maid from another. It was the height of what we should now describe as 'anti-social'. But it was done, nevertheless.

That 'character' of the girl was at once her insurance and the guarantee of her employer. All mistresses were not good employers, any more than all maids were good servants. But the law of averages worked out. The bad mistresses got the bad servants, as a rule. A housewife who was frequently 'without' came to be regarded as a bad employer even by her friends, who, experienced women themselves, knew that it could not be the maids' fault all the time.

The number of servants a Middle Class housewife controlled varied according to her means, or the size of the house in which she lived, which was practically the same thing. You could rent a nice house, with eight or nine rooms and a good garden back and front, for £40 a year; £35 a year was as much as most couples starting in life expected—or needed—to pay. You could get houses for £20 a year, but they were small. There were plenty of houses 'To Be Let' and plenty of landlords tumbling over themselves to let them. No need then to start your married life with a mortgage hanging round your neck in respect of a house you had 'bought' on the instalment system for double or treble its real worth. A man with an income of £5 a week could have a £40-a-year house and keep his wife and family in comfort. Rates were negligible as compared with today, income tax was 1s. in the pound, and this was grumbled at, although the allowances were far more generous and the starting tax based higher than nowadays.

The wife of a five-pound-a-week man could have a 'general servant', who was really a maid-of-all-work. What most women liked was to catch one young and train her up in the right way. Often a girl so obtained, when she left to either better herself or get married, would be replaced by a younger sister, for frequently one family served another in this way for years, which led to general understanding, good relationship and comfort all round.

The girl starting in 'service' got a small wage at first, plus her keep and lodging. She had to be 'willing' and clean and respectable. She had to be respectful and obedient and to show a desire to learn. None of these was considered bad or degrading things. She could, and did, as a 'general', rise to £20 or £28 a year. She wore 'uniform', it is true. She did not object to that. This 'uniform' consisted of a print dress (of which she usually had three), with a coarse apron and a small cap for mornings, and a black dress with a fancy apron and far smarter cap for evenings. If, when she started, she had not this equipment and her family had not been able to provide her with it, her mistress did so, and repaid herself by easy deductions from wages due. But quite frequently, especially if the girl's parents were known as respectable, it was a gift.

The girl was usually presented with new caps and aprons for Christmas or birthday presents. She lived in the kitchen, which had a scullery attached, and slept at the top of the house. If it was a Victorian house that kitchen was often in the basement, but even so, it and the bedroom (which was often of a good size and airy) were better accommodation than that to which she had been accustomed at home.

In that scullery would be a sink and a copper, in which the washing, the greater portion of which was done at home, would be boiled. That washing was done by a woman who came in to char and to wash. She got from 2s. 6d. to 5s. for a full day's work, and she did a full day's work too. Compare that with current rates. Yet, so far did money go then that she was better off financially. She also got her meals and usually some food to take home with her. She and her life story would be well known to her employer, who would give her all sorts of odds and ends for the family.

Washing days were times of strenuous activity. The copper fire was lit (it often required a 'knack') and the copper filled early in the morning. There would be clouds of steam and a dampish atmosphere of wet clothes filled the house. A wet washing day was something of a domestic tragedy, for it meant the clothes being dried indoors, on lines slung along the kitchen and on great clothes-horses before the fire.

Cats, however (and most households had one), seemed to revel in washing days, choosing the piles of clothes as ideal sleeping-places, and also the warm top of the copper. Children also delighted in the general confusion and added to it. The sheets, blankets, bedclothes, table napkins, and the whites requiring starch went to the laundry and came back regularly and rapidly. There was a good deal of washing to be done.

The Edwardian houses began to discard the basements, but retained an indoor coal-cellar. The kitchens were large rooms as compared with their modern counterparts. The kitchen table was of deal and was always being scrubbed down. There was a tremendous amount of scrubbing everywhere in Golden Age households. A mangle or wringer was in every home.

The general servant had one evening a week and every other Sunday as time off. The rest she spent in her kitchen when her work was done, although she usually managed to find some jobs to occupy her. She was just as well off there. There were few amusements open to her, and only the streets in which to walk about if she had had every evening off. There were too many at home for her to put in much time there, and often she came from the country.

A good cook got £40 a year and could deal with anything from an egg to a full-course dinner, and would turn out those marvellous dishes now only known in the pages of the great 'Mrs. Beeton'.

A servant getting what she considered a 'good place' did her best to keep it. She became almost one of the family; she gave loyal service, and often real affection existed between mistress, family and maid. Some housewives made a rule of 'no followers'. The girl in that case conducted her wooing *sub rosa*, but most housewives turned a blind eye, unless the suitor made too great inroads on the family larder. Some girls, of course, 'got into trouble'. That was not peculiar to the age of the sovereign. But the standard of morality was very high then, and a girl in that condition was bundled off at once, with her little tin box containing all her personal belongings, but without her 'character'. That was gone for ever.

Often, however, girls who had behaved retained close touch with their employers all through life and would rally to their assistance when needed in crises of illness, etc.

One thing from which mistresses protected their maids was the blandishment of salesmen who, calling at the side door, tried to get the girls to buy things on the instalment system. Most girls desired a sewing-machine, then part of the equipment of every woman who ran a home. But the girls often got one and failed in the instalments, which resulted in them being dunned and worried out of their lives, and often made them dishonest.

The sewing-machine was an integral part of every home. The older

"Up the River"—which also shows the boating costumes of the period

A popular item of the summer holidays which still exists, Donkey rides on the sands

The Great Wheel at Earl's Court—a famous landmark of the Golden Age

ones were affairs with treadles, which were worked by the feet, heavy and cumbersome, but the more modern ones that came in, which stood on the table, and worked by hand, were moderately portable and far more efficient. Most women then were experts with the needle, and made a whole lot of things for the home. With the 'machine' they would run up new curtains, clothes for the family, and often for themselves. They took pride in it, and there were not so many outside distractions.

But domestic servants had no idea they were slaves. They would have resented the idea if told so. They thought they were well off. They took pride in their work, their idea of service contained no thought of slavery.

There was, of course, plenty to do. The rooms were of good size, and there was a lot of furniture and far more ornaments and knick-knacks than today. You could furnish a house on £100. Those who spent £300 had the very best. In nine cases out of ten the purchase was outright. And they bought for quality and purchased stuff which would last. First-class chairs cost £1 each from the best makers. You got a good carpet for £12 10s. A suite of furniture cost less than one piece does today, and was very much better made, so there was plenty of it. The older-fashioned heavy Victorian style was going out and the lighter Edwardian idea was coming in. Horsehair furniture, saddlebag and mahogany were *vieux jeu*. Fumed oak, a bit 'arty crafty', was the more modern trend. The young people starting life had been brought up in very solid, heavy surroundings.

Their dining-rooms had gleamed with mahogany and satinwood against a red, patterned wallpaper. There had been a very high and ornate overmantel, with many brackets and shelves, all elaborately carved and decorated and plentifully besprinkled with ornaments. In the middle was a large mirror. The mantelshelf was also full of ornaments, and had a marble clock—rather like a sarcophagus—in the middle. There would very likely be bronzes as well, either Roman warriors with spears, riding prancing horses with such assured horsemanship that they did not require reins or stirrups, or rather nude gentlemen leading horses of great size and having a good deal of trouble with them.

There would be an immense sideboard, also with a mirror at the back, possibly to double the display of food and bottles placed upon it. And on that sideboard would be a tantalus. They were usually wedding presents, used in the first excitement of a new home, but gradually kept for ornament only. They still linger here and there.

The dining-room chairs, usually mahogany, upholstered in leather or —later—high-backed oak, were ranged round the table, usually oak too, but covered, when not used at mealtimes, with a chenille velvet or plush tablecloth, with tassels or little balls dependent from the edge. There was a valance, similarly decorated, over the mantelpiece too. The fender was a marble curb, or a brass one, with steel or brass fireirons, and there would be a coal-scuttle, from which it was always a matter of great difficulty to extract any coal. For the fires were all open coal-fires. Gas-fires, comparatively new, were regarded as unhealthy and dangerous. They very often were.

The pictures were either big steel engravings or large oil-paintings by unknown artists, in very large gilt frames. Few people, except visitors trying to be polite, ever looked at them. Lighting was by a pendant chandelier, which hung from the ceiling and had several gas jets with globes on them. These were mostly of metal, but memory recalls a very lovely one which ended in a genuine Wedgwood china bowl, with lamps to match.

The drawing-room was a maze of furniture. It was lighter in tone than the dining-room. Often it was yellow in colour scheme, with a large patterned paper; furniture of lighter texture, and often of black wood with yellow upholstery; plenty of chairs, rather spindly; always a cabinet, often black lacquer with mother-of-pearl inlay, which contained all sorts of treasures and curios; and a host of small tables, smothered in photo frames and ornaments, all on little mats, which made progress in the room very difficult.

The overmantel was there, the valance was there, but there might be an ormolu clock (which never went) under a glass shade. Some of these were very nice and the reason for their immobility was mostly because the keys were lost. Before the window, in the drawing-room, was usually a stand of aspidistras, and the window alcove was heavily curtained with either serge or plush curtains, which drew across, the windows themselves being swathed in lace curtains—full length, none of your skimpy casement idea.

This arrangement was common to both dining- and drawing-room. No fresh air was allowed to enter. Across the division between the upper and lower window-panes lay long 'sausages' of turkey-red twill, filled with sawdust, to prevent draughts, the fear of all good Victorians, and there were curtains or *portières* on the doors as well.

The drawing-room walls were covered with pictures (it was just as well, for the wallpapers, although good, were very ugly). And there was a draped fireplace, with perhaps a couple of little banner-like objects, to shade complexions from the fierceness of the fire. The fender and fireirons were brass. In summertime the open grate contained coloured paper, a fern, or a fan.

There was, of course, the piano. This would be of rosewood or ebony, and mostly an upright grand with a kind of fretwork front masking pleated silk, the colour of which matched the room. It had two curly candlesticks projecting from it, and the top was covered with a yellow silk runner, on which stood as many photos in frames as could be crowded upon it. When a guest was asked to play they were all removed and the top was opened. The piano-stool was a circular seat which revolved by means of a screw on a pillar, with three feet at the bottom. Every household had stacks of sheet music. The piano might be of almost any make, but in Middle Class circles they were mostly by Collard and Collard, Brinsmead, Justin Brown, or Broadwood. Those candles in the candlesticks were wanted because the chandeliers were very high and the gas was obscured by fancy globes, so you needed more light to see the music. The candles themselves were coloured and spiral—often they had blobs of gold paint on them.

There were always hearthrugs, mostly skin—bearskin frequently, or of some fur dyed black, always very thick and a little musty.

The door furniture was either brass or china. Some artistic souls decorated their drawing-room curtains with enormous and bloated-looking spiders with long legs, stuffed with cotton wool and covered with some shiny material—a very repellent sight indeed.

Drawing-rooms were cold places, a little lonely and remote, for they were only used on special occasions.

There was heavy oak furniture in the halls and very big hatstands.

The best bedroom had enormous wardrobes and a vast dressing-table, often with china sets, little boxes, pin-trays, and a curious upright china prong, like a deer's antler, on which the lady hung her rings. There would also be a washstand with a marble top and a double set of toilet utensils—running water was not laid on to bedrooms then. The bed was vast, double (nobody used twin beds), and of brass. It could be all brass, or iron enamelled black, with brass knobs on the uprights, which (except in the best bedroom) had a habit of getting dented and of even being unscrewed and lost, which lent an immediate air of shabbiness.

Again the heavy curtains and the exclusion of air—indeed, it was quite usual for the bed to have a *ceil-de-lit* and side curtains which could swing in or out, to ensure further cosiness. Their exclusion of air never seemed to affect the later Victorians, who carried on in this style in Edwardian days. They were a strong, healthy race. That best bedroom was sacred to Papa and Mamma. Most of the children were born there, and unless their ends came suddenly or violently the parents died there too. It was indeed the cradle of the family—and very nearly of the race. It was certainly the cradle of the Middle Classes.

There was an enormous amount of metal everywhere. It all made work.

There was plenty for the general servant to do. She had to be an early riser. And she had a pretty full day. There were plenty of stairs, and stairs make work.

It got less, however, when the Edwardian houses arose. They were smaller, they were lighter, and there was not nearly so much impedimenta. The long lace curtains went, the heavy plush curtains went. Less furniture was used than in Victorian days, but it was always kept bright and polished. The lay-out of the houses was much the same, although the basements vanished and two storeys was high enough. Victorianism ran to three or four. Some Victorian houses had really no ground floor. There was a basement and then the ground floor, so far as earth level went, in mid-air, approached by stairs inside and a vast flight of stone steps without. Large flags then made a path to the front gate, some distance away, or tiles or tesselated pavement.

These all had to be kept clean, but the servant did not do that. That was the job of a female called 'The Step Girl'—a calling now vanished. She came once a week; she supplied, as often as not, her own hearthstone and her own cloths, and she washed down those steps and front, leaving them shining and spotless—but they did not remain so for long during the winter. She was of any age, often quite young, dressed in a slatternly manner, and wore on her head either a man's cap or a gents' black straw boater. The remuneration was sixpence. The maid would sweep the steps down each day unless it was very wet.

Those massive flights of steps went out in Edwardian days, shrinking to a mere two or three. Those the maid could, and did, tackle.

But there was all the metalwork to keep bright and polished, the grates to blacklead, the fireirons and fenders, the front door-handle, bell, letterbox and knocker to polish, the rooms to turn out, the place to be swept and scrubbed, the paintwork to do, the windows to clean— and most of the windows were sash windows, although the casement type were creeping in. Vacuum cleaners naturally did not arrive until electricity became general, and that was not until the century was getting into its teens. But there was the Bissell, which was looked upon as marvellous.

The coals had to be fetched from the coal-cellar, which held anything from two to ten tons, and it was easy to fill those cellars, for coal merchants competed for the job. You got the finest possible coal for 20s. per ton, delivered promptly the day after it was ordered. Yet fires in the bedroom were a luxury only indulged in when illness occurred.

The hot-water system worked from the kitchen range, that vast metal affair which also had to be blackleaded and polished—for some of it was shiny steel and demanded emery paper. Ranges were temperamental, and so in consequence was the hot water. Baths were a matter of timing, and very hot baths of good luck.

Gas-stoves were in use for cooking. But a whole lot of it was done on the range, and the mistress and maid had to understand the oven.

Earlier in the period there had been 'meat jacks', which really roasted the beef, mutton or the poultry and game, and did not bake it. These stood in front of the roaring fire in the grate, on four legs. They were of metal and about four feet high. They were half closed in, but naturally the front was open. From a hook at the top hung a thing shaped like a solid bell which was wound up; from that again suspended the joint. It then revolved before the fire until it was perfectly roasted. The gravy dripped into a receptable at the foot and the joint was properly basted. Only those who have tasted roast beef cooked that way know what roast beef really is—or any other joint or bird, for that matter.

For most of the period gas was the main illuminant, and that meant gas globes—something else more to be cleaned and, if the maid was unlucky (or what was known as 'a smasher'), to be broken. 'Smashing' is today an adjective of praise, then it was a word of horror.

Yet glass and crockery were amazingly cheap and very decorative. Even gas globes were ornamented, and you could have them with pink uppers fading into frosted white below, and all engraved and patterned. That yellow tulip-shaped gas-jet, with its blue heart flecked with golden spots, warmed as well as illuminated. It could be turned down to the merest blue crescent of a glimmer. The kitchen lighting was a central one, a long pipe with a circular curl in the middle and an upright burner, usually without a globe. Most maids used a candle in their bedroom, so that gas should not be wasted.

Then incandescent mantles made their appearance and the light grew white and bright until the mantles, very fragile indeed, got broken. The first mantles were upright little spires, like diaphanous candle-snuffers. You burned them when you first put them on, before you lit the gas. The inverted mantles were better from every point of view, and stronger too. To have electric light installed, even as late as 1911, was to be very modern and go-ahead.

Knives had to be cleaned by hand. There was no stainless steel. To clean a knife you had a knifeboard, a long piece of board with a semi-circular end, pierced to hang it up when not in use. On this board was a coating of some brown material. On that material was spread knife-powder, a reddy-brown gritty substance, and on that you rubbed away with the knife until it shone again. The most popular powder was named after the Duke of Wellington. The powder got all over the place. Then the patent knife-cleaning machines came in. You stuck the knives in slots, turned a handle, and there you were. That was very modern and very efficient. But, with either board or machine, it was always a little difficult to get the 'shoulder' of the knife properly polished, and mistresses were particular about this. Boots were mostly cleaned with blacking. But when kid and other substances began to replace leather the cream age started. Some families employed a boy to clean the knives and boots.

Work went on at high pressure during the morning. In the afternoon the girl was expected to wash and change into her black dress with cap and apron. The lady of the house dressed in the afternoons as well. Any caller round about the hour of half-past three or four was most unpopular —except on special days.

The maid worked hard and mostly worked well. If she did not, she went—and as the supply of labour exceeded the demand, she never wanted to go. She did not have very much leisure, it must be granted, for there was the evening meal—often supper, not dinner—and it had to be laid, served and cleared away—and washed up. Then she went to bed. Such leisure and spare time as she got she used either for sewing or reading highly spiced and sensational novelettes—*Forget-Me-Not* was a favourite series—which dealt with the doings of aristocrats who were evidently well known to the author from the intimacy displayed in their life stories and methods of living, but whom nobody else had ever met.

The maid always 'answered the door' and dealt with callers. Tradesmen came to the side door, and their daily visits—yes, daily visits—were occasions for back-chat, badinage, brief flirtations, giggling and a good deal of head-tossing. The mistress of the house was 'Mum' or 'Madam', the head of the family either 'Sir' or 'The Master'. Most Middle Class housewives called their servants by their Christian names. There was a sprinkling of snobs who used the surname, but nobody was impressed by them. In most cases the girls were well treated, or they did not stop. Familiarity was not encouraged, but light conversation on the doings of the neighbours—and all the maids knew all about the neighbours—was freely indulged in during housework hours.

The housewife's job in the house was mostly giving orders and supervising. She dusted the precious articles, and she dusted 'the tops'— that is, the places where dust was most readily visible. The maid did the rest with casual assistance from a 'char'. And those chars stopped in a family, often being succeeded by their daughters and grand-daughters to the second and third generation.

The lady of the house might also, on occasion, wash some of the more precious china. And a 'best' tea-service was always kept, often a very charming set indeed. The maid 'did' the silver. There was a lot of plate, and there were things called 'dish-covers', large concave covers which were put over the joints to keep them warm, very like extremely concave breastplates. They were usually in sets, from very big to very small ones. They also had to be cleaned inside and out, a pretty long job. And always there were vast numbers of plated and silver articles acquired as wedding presents: entrée dishes, cruets, toast-racks—scores of things, for it was a metal age. It all had to be cleaned.

The lady did little of the actual housework beyond what has been stated and perhaps lending a hand in making the beds. Daughters helped too, if there were any.

There was a good deal of entertaining at home. There were little dinner-parties, there were musical evenings, there were little card-parties and whist drives. Entertaining at home was one of the things the home was for. The family, male and female, were encouraged to bring their friends home. It was considered so much safer. The husband would pay no greater compliment to a business friend than to ask him to dine in the bosom of the family. That was the supreme act of courtesy and friendliness—much more intimate than a dinner at a restaurant. Another reason for the seeking of recreation at home was that transport was far more limited and the Middle Classes were thrown more on their own domestic resources.

When the sons grew up it was always considered most desirable to keep them at home. If there was a room large enough, and there usually was, a small billiard-table was purchased, half or three-quarter size, and this was considered the final inducement, for billiards was regarded as a dangerous game, one of the portals to ruin if indulged in outside the home, and all young men were presumed to have a passion for it. It ranked with cards, racehorses, drink and wicked women as one of the usual reasons for a young man 'going wrong'.

Billiards is, in itself, a pretty innocent amusement and demands a good eye, a steady hand and considerable skill. It is not easy to see evil in it. But the reason for the fear in which it was held was because about the only place you could play it was in public-houses. Every Middle Class mother knew what that led to. No Middle Class woman with any pretensions to respectability ever went into a 'pub'. That was *not* done. And all barmaids were regarded as sirens of the most fiendish variety. Even the Middle Class husband was careful who saw him going out and coming in at the 'local'. But he went in all the same.

The highspot of the housewife's own entertaining was the 'At Home' day. That was the time when she sat in state and received her friends, when formal calls were paid, as against mere friendly 'dropping in' of intimates and near neighbours. The lady had her 'At Home' day printed on her cards, 'Every Third Thursday' or 'Second Tuesday', as the case

213

might be. It was a matter of considerable social discrimination and tact when two ladies who knew each other, and possessed the same circle of friends, had the same 'At Home' day. It was all right for the friends, they could go to both, but the ladies who were 'At Home' never got a chance of seeing what each other did in the way of entertainment. They only knew from hearsay and gossip. Gossip was the chief attraction of the 'At Home'.

There was a special clean-over on 'At Home' days, a special polish and a special dust. The best service was out, the silver (or plated) salver, the ditto cake-basket, the ditto milk or cream jug—or both—and the silver teapot. The mistress and the maid were ready early, the one in her new dress, her hair done as near perfection as she could manage, the latest additions to the home displayed carelessly but prominently, and special cakes and extra thin bread-and-butter cut in great quantities. The silver hot-water jug was ready too, the silver apostle teaspoons; kettles crowded each other on the hob or the gas-stove, all on the boil. The tea-caddy was ready and open—tea was plentiful and cheap. Sometimes the thin bread-and-butter was done up in little rolls, most attractive to childish callers. It seemed to taste much better that way. There would be trays of sweets too, of all varieties. No such thing as rationing had been dreamed of. The three-tier cakestand of brass, wood or wicker was crowded on each plate with very attractive cream cakes, cream buns, éclairs, plain cake; everything in plenty, very fresh, tasty and very nice indeed.

Brown and white bread-and-butter, of course, and sometimes in winter hot toasted scones, teacakes, or muffins or crumpets. Not a great supply of these, because they were a little messy and buttery to eat, and might drip on clothes or gloves.

All would be ready before the appointed hour. The lady of the house would sit, quite satisfied with her preparations, in her drawing-room.

This was a much lighter room than the old Victorian one, and more frequently used. The younger people of the Middle Classes in the 1900s went in for plain wallpaper, very often brown for the dining-room, with green carpets and upholstery to the upright chairs and sofa, brass or copper fender and grate furnishing, green lampshades, oak furniture—the heavy sideboard replaced by a Welsh dresser, and sepia engravings of classics on the walls.

The drawing-room might be grey, green, white or pink, with everything to match. Gone were the heavy curtains of previous years, gone were the draught-protectors, gone were the ornate overmantels and the plush hangings and tablecloths. Gone were the multiplicity of tables and stools and ornaments. It was lighter in every way, furniture as

214

well, and quite tasteful. Pictures in the drawing-room would be coloured prints or water-colours with perhaps an oil or two. The curtains in the drawing-room were net, with a pelmet, and heavier curtains, often of corded silk, for drawing at night.

The blinds were of material, although the old-fashioned and troublesome venetian blinds, those slats of wood operating on a cord, so liable to go wrong and so difficult to get level when pulled up, might still be found in some rooms. The slats rested between the webbing rungs of two webbing ladders and were raised or lowered by a cord, which was wound round a brass hook to secure it at the desired level. Quite complicated, and the maids found 'they made a lot of work'. You did not find them in drawing-rooms, where the windows were generally french, leading on to the garden. Here again were net curtains.

When the callers arrived they were received by the maid and ushered in by her with a suitable announcement. They sat on the chairs and they chattered. They did not remove their hats. Fifteen to twenty minutes was the conventional stay. The lady of the house poured out, enquired as to tastes in sugar, placing the requisite number of lumps in each fragile cup out of a silver sugar-basin with silver tongs (or plated, as the case might be), and asked if the caller preferred milk or cream (there was always plenty of cream).

The maid handed round the tea and the bread-and-butter and cakes. Sometimes tea went round on trays, the callers sugaring, creaming or milking to taste. If there were daughters, they helped too. If it was a very busy day, a great friend would also lend a hand. The ladies removed their gloves, or, if wearing long ones, undid the buttons and turned the hands of the gloves back over the wrist. They partook as largely as possible, and the maid ran about fetching more hot water, more tea and more milk and handing the cakes. But after a while she would retire and the general gossip would turn to the two all-important topics, obstetrics and domestics. Forthcoming happy events would be discussed from all angles, the virtues and faults of current domestics passed in review and the lady who was 'without' would dree her weird and get advice and perhaps recommendations. Dress, too, and fashions were discussed.

Callers not intimate with the household would leave their card in the little tray provided for that purpose in the hall. Everyone wore their best and smartest. Everyone took everything in: details of dress, food and drink. Those coming from other 'At Homes' would bring the latest news, those going on to other 'At Homes' would depart with their quota of fresh stories. The teacups were held in the hand, the eatables either balanced on the saucer or on tiny plates. Two cups was the general rule, and little fingers were curled fashionably whilst it was being drunk. All the news of the neighbourhood was passed around. A popular hostess had crowds of callers, an unpopular one a very sparse gathering. The Middle Class suburban housewife soon found how she stood socially by virtue of her 'At Homes'. Books were talked of, plays discussed, with squawks of admiration for the matinée idols.

Forthcoming events and plans were passed under review. Every woman loved 'At Home' days, her own or other people's. It was indeed a very social affair and it made friends for newcomers and enlarged the circle.

There were usually some nice little bits of scandal to hear. Sometimes two ladies at loggerheads would meet accidentally at an 'At Home' and the atmosphere go chill. Neither would go before the other; she was not going to be driven from the field by that Mrs. So-and-So with her jumped-up airs. It called for considerable tact on the part of the hostess when such a thing occurred. But it was all done with the most terrific politeness and good manners.

Those were the days of good behaviour, and that is what the 'conventions' really meant, not a dull, drab, squashing super-respectability, as a younger age imagines. Such things as visiting-cards—and no man or woman was without them—such a thing as tea-drinking in crowds and talking—these were neither foolish nor dull. They were very lively indeed, and a visiting-card is now compulsory under its new name of Identification. Only you have to keep that and not give it up. A visiting-card was the sign that you were a householder, a person of standing with a permanent address. You were, indeed, an individual, and not a telephone number. It was the address—the home—that mattered, not the 'phone number, which is the least individual of things in itself.

There were special card cases, often of silver and even gold. There were even little metal cases of silver—or gold—in which you carried your postage stamps. They were made like miniature envelopes and frequently got lost. It was an age of metal gadgets.

The wallet had not assumed its modern importance—the paper money thrust that on it. A woman kept her money in her purse, usually a much larger thing than today, fastening with two interlocking metal knobs.

The 'At Home' day was the highspot of the housewife's month and she would, when it was over, congratulate herself on its success and probably praise the maid, who, as a reward, got some of the cakes which had been left over.

The 'At Home' day was one of the housewife's greatest domestic pleasures. The other great pleasure was . . . shopping.

CHAPTER XIV

The Customer Was Always Right

YES, THE GREAT PLEASURE OF THE LADY OF THE MIDDLE CLASSES IN THE DAYS of the golden sovereign was to go shopping. She knew nothing about queues, about rations, about points, about dockets, of what came to be called B.U.s. She knew nothing about things being 'Under the Counter'. Everything was on the counter, and in the windows, in glorious array. The idea of the tradesmen in those days was that they were there to please the customer. A complaint made them tremble, a threat to take your custom elsewhere brought them figuratively to their knees, with abject prayer and apologies. They could not do enough. The housewife was their living, their prosperity, their very existence depended on her favour. They actually believed it was their job to please her, and they did their best to do so.

A shopkeeper was selling his goods in competition with many others. He had to please you or you withdrew your trade. He was not your master, you did not cringe and beg for favours. The boot was on the other leg; he did the cringing. On moving into a new district, or when a couple of newly wedded Middle Class young people entered their home, there was a state of siege. Tradesmen of all kinds came to the door, begging their custom. They waylaid them and solicited their favour. They almost came to blows over a potential customer. It was possible to live for a week on the free samples which poured into the house. And civility was the rule. Let a person in a shop be rude—a customer was lost for ever.

They delighted to give credit, they did not demand spot cash. They liked the housewife to run a weekly account—a 'book', as it was called. They felt that a customer with an account—and they did not mind it running on for a bit—was bound to them by a stronger link than one who paid for everything she bought on the nail. It was necessary to check those books pretty carefully, for accountancy was not the strong point in those shops. Imaginary items might creep in and mistakes were always on their side. There were humble apologies and assurances that 'it shan't occur again, Mum'. And for some time it would not.

Of course this credit system sometimes hit the shops, for all Middle Class people were not honest, and there were always the few who 'shot the moon', that is, decamped one night, leaving the rent and other trifles owing, and then the tradesman would ask the neighbours if they knew where the defaulters had gone, and bewail their fate. Perhaps that

217

accounted for some of the little errors in the books of the people who paid. But they certainly gave service, and they gave it with civility.

The butcher could not do enough for you. He stood before his shop in his blue or white overall, his straw hat (summer or winter a straw hat) on his head, his 'steel' swinging round his waist over his blue-and-white-striped apron like a species of dirk, and he shouted his wares. "Buy, buy, buy!" he exhorted in stentorian tones. He had plenty to shout about. The whole front of his shop was packed with meat. Whole sheep hung headless, vast sides of beef showed red and yellow richness. Massive joints lay on the slab, there were the choicest chops, the thickest, juiciest steaks, the best cutlets on which to feast the eye in a preliminary canter of appetite. There were wing ribs, sirloins, best ends, scrag ends, stewing steak; there were kidneys, liver and hearts—nobody called it offal then. There were pigs, very pale and still satisfied-looking, although they were split open and their throats cut; there were festoons of oxtails; there were sausages with plenty of meat in them, and herbs too. There were saddles and shoulders, forequarters, lamb or mutton according to season. There were gently resigned calves' heads with lemons in their mouths.

And the great bulk was English. Foreign meat was so marked. The Middle Classes did not eat foreign frozen meat. It was no good to them. The English meat, home killed, was plentiful and wonderfully cheap. The butcher was most anxious to oblige. He cut or trimmed your joint himself, he shouted his orders to the cash desk, he pushed the meat aside for the boy to deliver to your home.

That butcher sold poultry too. And at Christmas-time whole curtains of turkeys, score upon score, veiled the whole shop-front. It was usually an open front at the butcher's. The meat was displayed to the winds of heaven. And nobody thought it unhygienic, nor was ptomaine poisoning rampant.

The butcher also had trays of scraps and odds and ends of meat which the Middle Classes had spurned, the trimmings of their own super joints, or odd bits unsaleable to them. These the poorer people bought for a few pence—almost for nothing on a Saturday night. And eager fingers turned them over and over, time and again. Not healthy, of course, but what the eye did not see the heart never grieved about. People survived. That straw-hatted butcher (though why he wore the hat was a mystery to the Middle Classes, if they ever thought about it) was your humble obedient servant, and so were his staff.

The grocer was just the same. He did not stand outside his shop and shout. He stood behind his counter in a white apron, in his white shirt-sleeves, their starched cuffs turned back to his elbows, a pencil behind his ear, and he took your orders, also with civility and respect. "And the next thing?" he kept asking, very politely. You simply could not order enough to please him. He would draw your attention to new lines, he would give you a biscuit to taste. He was very anxious to please a good customer. And his shop was a real delight. There were mounds of dried fruit, chests of romantic Oriental appearance, with strange black marks on them in some Eastern language, lined with foil and crammed with tea of all qualities. Tea mingled its aroma in the mixture of scents which went to make up the particularly rich smell of a grocer's shop. Or you could, of course, have it by the packet, in wrapper of silver foil, as like as not. There was any amount of it, at 2s. or 2s. 9d. the pound, or almost any price you liked.

There were hundreds of tins of biscuits, their open tops tempting you to indulge. There was sugar galore, castor or lump or even sugar-loaves. You bought your lump in the packet and sometimes the moist too, but on occasion you bought it loose and the grocer would make a piece of blue paper into an inverted cone, like a dunce's hat, and pour the sugar in. A deft twist or two and it was completely wrapped. Almonds, raisins, currants, sultanas, flour, candied peel, cheese, eggs, vinegar, oil, marmalade, jam, pickles, chutney, even some forms of cakes and sweets, you could get them all at the grocer's, and so you could certain brands of spirits and wines.

It was a nice, ladylike way of buying such things. It never looked too well, a lady considered, to be seen going into the wine merchant's or the off-licence too often. The grocer's brands might not be the best, but there was a well-known name on it and it was quite cheap. And over the whole mixed richness and mouth-watering smell of the grocer's hung the delightful aroma of fresh, roasting coffee. It was delightful at the grocer's, and he was always such a very civil man.

The fishmonger was your servant. He would pick you out the best, he would fillet anything. Nobody took their own paper to the shop and carried home their own fish. He, like everybody else, delivered to the door. Some fishmongers wore straw hats as well. The slabs were crowded with fish; there were more bloaters and kippers than you would have imagined a whole nation could eat. And, just to make things fair, there were aquariums in which goldfish swam, rejoicing, no doubt, in the fact that they were considered inedible by an enlightened people.

The provision merchant also had curtains of poultry and game masking his shop-front. He and his men wore white overalls, and again a straw hat could be seen out of season. Poultry then cost per bird about what it now costs per pound. Pheasants were 6s. 6d. per brace, for in-stance, when it came to game. Hares hung upside down, little buckets over their noses to preserve their gore and make the 'jugging' rich.

Ostend rabbits were in hordes, rather pitiful-looking objects, all skinned and a little purple; skewered up, and always presenting the appearance that they held their arms akimbo. Wild rabbits were despised by the Middle Classes.

The provision merchant's shop always had a nice, clean, sharp smell. Before the First World War new laid eggs were 12 a shilling, 'guaranteed' at 16 a shilling, and cooking eggs (unguaranteed) at 24 a shilling. The shop cat frequently took a nap on the eggs and never broke any—but nobody would have worried much if it had, they were so plentiful. There was the widest possible selection of bacon: lean, streaky, back, gammon—what you desired. For most of the period the man cut it for you himself. "Fine piece of bacon, that," he would assure you, as the sharp knife severed it into lovely rashers. There were positive mountains of butter (1s. 2d., 1s. 4d., 1s. 6d. per lb.—and salted if you wanted it). It was a treat to see it cut, if not bought in pats, each with a picture embossed on it, and a treat to see how dexterously it was handled between square wooden bats with handles, something like ping-pong rackets.

Later, bacon was cut by machine, as it is now. There were piles of hams—and York hams too. You bought a 'quarter' or as much as you wanted. There were tinned goods, both here and at the grocer's, but the Middle Classes rather mistrusted tinned goods other than ox tongue, and that it preferred in glass bowls. Why, indeed, should they bother with tinned goods when fresh goods could be obtained, when there was a cook or a maid who was a 'good plain cook', or even the lady herself who might like to do it? Tinned goods were suspected of making one ill, too. A Middle Class housewife, on being told her husband intended to bring someone whom she didn't like home to supper, would utter her direst threat, "If you do, I'll buy a tin of something and give him that."

Nobody dreamed of the day when corned beef would be a luxury; it was rather despised then. There was cheese in bewildering variety, English and Canadian, but most people bought the English. The man cut it by means of a wire with a little wooden handle at each end. Children loved to see a whole cheese being divided up that way into large wedges, and the amount the man cut was amazingly near the amount desired.

You could get real ox tongue, either whole (and you always had a whole one at Christmas) or by the usual fractions of the pound. Lard and fats of all kinds were in huge supply. Delicious foreign cheeses too—and everything good and cheap.

The greengrocer usually sold flowers as well, as he does today. But the price of his goods was staggeringly different. Strawberries were sold in punnets, very attractive indeed. You did not have to buy something you did not want in order to procure the very ordinary thing of which you stood in need. Peas sold by the peck. The main point was the cheapness and the quantity; potatoes, greens, cauliflowers, all the fruits and produce of the market garden were reckoned in pence, and not many pence at that. In the early days of the period bananas were a rare fruit, strange as it may seem.

The bakers knew nothing of bread queues. They baked their bread, and one of the world's most delicious scents could be savoured. Most of the loaves were of the old-fashioned cottage shape, a smaller dollop on top of a larger one. The square or oblong shapes were referred to as tinned loaves.

There was a mouth-watering array of cakes and confectionery, iced cakes, marzipan cakes, seed cakes, tennis cakes, pound cakes, madeira cakes, sultana cakes, fruit cakes, sponge cakes—either the small ones or large ones shaped like blancmanges—buns (halfpenny and penny ones, the latter of amazing size), Scotch buns of great richness and consistency, shortbreads (the English variety with the single cherry on it), mince-pies, fruit tarts, rock cakes, almond cakes—sorts far too numerous to mention. Jam tarts, Banbury cakes, Eccles cakes, tarts of great flakiness in two layers with jam between them and a twisted scroll on top. Open jam tarts, cheese-cakes, maids of honour, lemon curd, jumbles, doughnuts, and jam puffs light as air but a little deficient in jam. And you had hot rolls delivered in the morning. . . .

Haberdashers were much the same as today—only now they call them gentlemen's outfitters and the prices are about ten times as high, the selection being twenty times less.

Wine merchants had a wonderful variety of cheap wines to sell, and a courteous way of doing it. They would handle the bottles lovingly as they sold them, as if they were of rare vintage, and compliment the customer on being a good judge of wine. There were clarets from 1s. 6d. to 2s. 6d., burgundies from 4s. upwards, and white wines in the same ratio. Many Middle Class people drank Australian burgundy (Emu brand) sold in flagons, and liked it.

Whisky was 3s. 6d. per bottle, all famous brands, and if you wanted it twelve years old it cost 4s. 6d. You got a crate of beer (six bottles) for 1s. 3d. And the wine merchant sent it all home by errand boy.

The music shops sold music and musical instruments. The gramophone and the radio had not knocked that all sky high. Piano-tuners were on the staff and very busy. But here and there a thing called a 'phonograph' was coming along, although they were mostly sold in bicycle shops. They were machines, you see, not musical instruments. The first phonographs (called talking-machines by old-fashioned, conservative people of the Middle Class, who disliked new-fangled ideas), were naturally very primitive.

They were of iron, the base being in the shape of a lyre, which was practically the only sign of music about them. On this, fixed by an upright, was a zinc drum, over which you put the wax cylinder of chocolate brown, which was the record. You wound up, and the drum revolved by means of cotton, string or elastic. The horn was like a trumpet of tin. The needle was a thing like a piece of gum stuck on a circular plate from which an arm fitted into the horn. As it travelled along the record you had to raise the side of the phonograph with a screw to keep it level, otherwise it slipped along, making a screaming noise. Nor did you hear very much when the thing worked smoothly. You detected the words 'Edison Bell Record', and you knew which tune it was because it said the name on the little tubular cotton-wool padded box in which the record lived.

After a time you got to know it by contant repetition. But speech was always difficult to detect. Vocal recordings were bad, but certain instruments like the banjo, guitar or mandoline came over quite distinctly. Very soon the method of preventing the slipping came in and the horn and its needle travelled along a little bar, the needle lying gently on the record. They wanted a lot of attention and a lot of winding did those early phonographs. They were always running down, and the records were always getting broken.

Furniture shops had plenty of well-made furniture at prices which would today seem absurd. Warings and similar firms would completely furnish a house for £200.

The toyshops were much cosier than those of today, and were mostly in the hands of elderly people, fatherly and motherly, who took the greatest interest in the children. There was more of a jumble, and things were not orderly in toyland, but the quantity and selection were there. Some nice shops sold toy soldiers singly, to the delight of small boys.

There were fewer multiple stores then and far more individual shops, as became the age. That made the service more personal and the contact more friendly, for each shop was the head office and branch in one—you dealt with the boss, not with underlings. The governor was always about.

Sweetstuff shops were mostly run by women. Sweets have been dealt with, but it remains to mention that array of jars, that bewildering assortment, and those acid tablets or drops of such terrific strength —they took the skin off your palate—and to reiterate that a farthing was never despised in a sweetstuff shop. And there were pigs made of white, sugary stuff, very sweet and sickly, which were seldom entirely consumed.

They were not Middle Class but they were London " 'Arriets" on Hampstead Heath

The Court of Honour at the White City—a pleasure ground of the Golden Days

The Muffin Man, a popular
figure

A Hurdy-Gurdy and its
player

There were not so many tea-shops—many confectioners did a small trade in teas in a parlour at the back. But some of the larger catering establishments had large refreshment rooms attached to their shops. Here you could have tea, coffee, cakes, tarts and all sorts of light refreshments, even lunches. And these establishments had a licence for drink as well. Ladies of the utmost respectability could, therein, sit and have a glass of stout, a drop of sherry or a small port (ladies did not drink much spirits), without losing caste or being thought any the worse of. It was not, you see, a public-house. It had not the lowness of a bar—even a saloon bar. It was a refreshment room. So middle-aged ladies, somewhat florid of face, in mantles and bonnets, would roll up their veils and sip their stimulant, which no doubt the doctor had ordered, with complete freedom and ease. Hypocrisy? Not a bit. Merely a sense of the fitness of things. There were no such things as cocktails, and no lady ever got 'tight'. Had she done so, she was no lady.

A lady out shopping seldom called at the dairy unless she purchased her butter or her eggs there. The milkman called at least twice a day. But she might pop in to order cream, which would come in a nice little stout brown earthenware jug: rich yellow cream, and as much as you liked. Devonshire cream too. The more you ordered, the better you pleased the milkman.

Ladies, of course, seldom went to a tailor's, unless their husbands took them to their own place so that they could have a real 'tailor-made costume'. Tailors' shops were much the same then as now, but there was more dignity and far more personal attention. Your tailor knew you and he looked after you. With his coat off and his tape-measure round his shoulders, he displayed his superfine cloth. He had roll upon roll of it.

He insisted on several fittings, and even though the customer might think the thing a perfect fit he would still find room for improvement. He gave his best attention and his personal service, even though that suit cost only £2 2s.—or, with an extra pair of trousers, £2 12s. 6d. or £2 15s. Today it costs over £30. You could only upset him by offering him cash. In this he saw danger, even insult. He expected, he almost demanded, to give credit. You usually paid for the old suit when ordering a new one. And you usually ordered two suits at once, and a light and winter overcoat in season. It was made and delivered in a week, if you wanted it.

There were, as there still are, many big establishments where you could purchase either ready-made clothes or made-to-measure. Boys were fitted up there at a very small cost. One of these establishments of many branches had a large and spirited coloured picture of Alexander the

Great standing in a chariot displayed permanently on all its premises. The firm was Alexander the Great Tailors.

These large outfitters specialized in outfits for boys and youths. Overcoats for little boys, with fur trimmings, cost 12s. 11d. to 25s. 9d. What was called a 'Rugby' suit, consisting of jacket, vest and knickers (the jacket cut high right up to the neck) was from 9s. 11d. to 16s. 11d. in tweed, 19s. 11d. to 34s. 6d. in West of England cloth or Scotch Cheviot, with 'All Wool Black Diagonal' at the same price. Eton suits ran between 24s. 6d. to 35s. 6d. ready-made, or 39s. 6d. to 45s. 6d. to measure, tweed suits according to quality ranged from 8s. 11d. to 39s. 6d., overcoats from 4s. 11d. to 39s. 6d., with cape overcoats from 4s. 11d. to 16s. 11d. Those horrible 'mortar-boards', sold as college caps, cost 4s. 11d., sailor caps from 1s. 6d. to 3s. 6d., white shirts with linen fronts and cuffs 2s. 6d. to 2s. 11d., flannel cricketing shirts 2s. 6d. to 5s. 6d. according to size. A full-grown man could get a felt hat from 1s. 6d. to 3s. 11d. or a travelling cap from 1s. to 1s. 11d. Boys' lace-up boots varied from 4s. 11d. to 7s. 11d., girls' from 3s. 11d. to 7s. 11d.

No wonder the Middle Classes could have families, and did.

A gentleman could get a fur-lined overcoat from £10 upwards, if he so desired, ready to wear, or to measure in a few days. If a lady visited a fur shop she could get a cape of genuine sable for any price between £100 and £500. Naturally very few of the Middle Classes ran to that. Mink was 25 guineas to 45 guineas, and Kolinsky sable £20.

Jewellers' shops have altered little, except that the prices are 100 per cent up.

Few men penetrated into a draper's. That was woman's preserve, and a man would have been horribly embarrassed at what might be on view, but there was a pomp and dignity about a drapery establishment then which has now departed. This was because of the Shopwalker. He was a man, but he never felt embarrassed. It would have been impossible to embarrass him or put him out of countenance. He had the dignity of an old English butler, retainer of a noble house, and the demeanour of an ambassador. It was the frock-coat that did it.

All shopwalkers wore frock-coats, and so did some of the male assistants in the material departments. The shopwalker lived up to his name. To say, however, that he walked the shop is to understate the case. He progressed about the shop like a not-so-minor royalty. He was mostly middle-aged and big. Short men were no use. He had a 'presence'. There were some young and handsome shopwalkers who caused quite a flutter, but mostly they were middle-aged—for safety. As soon as a lady entered a shop the shopwalker, with a beaming smile, bore down upon her and bowed. "And what may we have the pleasure of showing you?" he would ask. The lady would tell him, and he would precede her to the desired department, place a chair for her with a flourish and issue his command, "Miss Brown, forward." And Miss Brown had to 'step on it' and come forward with alacrity.

He supervised the whole place, he superimposed himself on customers and employees alike. He it was who, in response to a call of 'Sign, please', would step forward, scrutinize the proffered bill in its duplication book, and affix some sort of a signature—initials, one presumes, although never legible. It was a mere formality, surely, for he could never have remembered the exact price of everything, but it gave the customer a feeling of security. He was a martinet with the counter-hands. He ruled with a rod of iron. He kept them on their feet, ready to jump 'forward' all day long, and quite late at night too. And he would escort the lady customer off the premises, bowing her out.

Whilst so doing he would insinuate to her notice any special line the shop might have to offer, a great novelty and bargain, according to him, but which, if truth were told, was a bad bargain to the shop, and hanging fire. He would very often effect a sale, for his salesmanship was considerable and skilful. The shopwalker was one of the highest ranks towards which a drapery assistant (called improvers when very young, possibly because there was so much room for improvement in their style and work) could hope to rise, short of having a shop of his own—always a cherished ambition. The shopwalker was always well dressed and his manners were impeccable—to the customers.

Nothing was too much trouble to the assistants, male or female. Hundreds of things would be fetched out, yards of material in heavy rolls, partly unrolled and displayed over the arm. The Middle Class lady of the period knew what she wanted and was hard to please. It all had to be put back afterwards. However small the purchase, there was a terrific and lengthy inspection of stock. Memories of drapers must come from small-boyish days when the young male accompanied his mother. He would sit on a chair and watch with great fascination the scores—nay, hundreds—of cardboard reels of ribbon, most attractive, being shown to the lady, the dexterity with which the assistant measured off along a brass foot-rule on the inside edge of the counter and the accuracy of judgment which went to the cutting of material. The assistant would take the roll of material, unfurl it and spread it out. Then taking scissors in hand, which usually hung suspended from the waist in the case of a girl, or in waistcoat pocket if a man, the desired length would be cut off. Cut off? No, it was far more exciting than that.

These assistants were experts. They did not cut with their scissors as did ordinary lay folk. Opening them wide, they put the joint between the blades at the edge of the material and appeared to propel it right through the stuff without any effort. It was not a push, a slash, or a cut. It was just that the scissors, without being open or shut, went through that material like a knife going through butter. And there was never a rough edge!

Favourite drapers' shops (favourite, that is, with small people) had a method of getting change which was also fascinating. Taking a large wooden ball, the assistant unscrewed it. Then she placed the bill and the money in the cavity within and, screwing it up again, put it in a kind of upright shoot. She either pulled something or worked a lever. The ball shot up the shoot, and by means of a kind of 'points' system (a pair of wooden arms) it found itself on an overhead railway track along which it travelled to a cashier perched high above the world of drapery. It never lost its way, be the shop never so large. It returned, eagerly watched throughout as much of its journey as was within eyesight, and it fell, after a momentary hesitation, into a little net at the bottom of the shoot. The employee took out the change and the entrancing experience was over. It was one of the joys of going shopping with Mother. It outweighed the boredom of waiting in the shop. It can still be seen here and there, giving delight to mechanical-minded children of the machine age. But they doubtless know how it works, and don't get the same thrill as did the small boy or girl born under the sovereign.

Another curious thing in drapers' shops was that everything cost so much and three farthings. You seldom got the farthing change, you received a packet of pins instead. Drapers' windows, like all shop windows of that time, were packed rather than dressed. The idea was to get as much in as possible. There was some attempt at art, of course, but quantity was the main thing. The shopkeeper then put his goods in the window, not under the counter.

All shop assistants worked much longer hours and had far less rest. There was no closing for an hour or an hour and a half for lunch. There was no going off to get a cup of tea. The shops did not close at dusk, they remained open until seven, eight, or even nine at night. The assistants got a much smaller wage and worked three times as hard. Discipline was severe and strict. And even when the shop was closed there was folding up, covering up and putting away. This was never done whilst a single customer remained. And customers were not at all thoughtful. The customer was always right, and the slightest rudeness, pertness or impertinence led to dismissal. And when Early Closing came in, shopkeepers saw the ruin of themselves and the country fast approaching. Shop windows were not lit at night, but closely shuttered.

Tobacconists were numerous and far more individual. There were the multiple shops, like A. Baker, Salmon and Gluckstein, etc., even then, but most tobacconists were as individual as their clients. A man was a friend of his tobacconist—and of the young lady who sometimes served therein. Women seldom went into such shops. Few smoked. For the few who did there were 'Ladies' Cigarettes', of small size and incredible mildness, with either gold tips or coloured ones, whilst some had folded round the ends what the tobacconist assured you were rose-leaves, often of a deep magenta. Such cigarettes were mere toys and not to be taken seriously. Women smoked them for bravado and choked the while. They were discarded after a few tentative puffs.

But a man could get gold-tipped cigarettes too, if he wanted to be ostentatious. Some men even had their cigarettes specially made for them, with their name printed on the paper. Some cigarettes could be got which had cherry-wood tips, but they never succeeded. There was a far greater demand for Turkish and Egyptian cigarettes then. The First World War killed this taste and led to the general adoption of 'the gasper'. There were cork-tipped cigarettes then too, one brand known as 'The Belted Earl' having the cork tip surrounded by two little belts of silver paint.

Most tobacconists sold not only their own mixture of tobacco, which many of their customers swore by and would smoke no other, but also their own brand of cigarettes, mostly described as 'straight' or 'silk' cut. Some places even had girls seated in the window making them. There was a fashion, too, for cigarettes rolled in rice paper.

Cigarettes could be purchased by weight as well as by number. These were kept in glass cases and weighed out on scales. You did not get the popular brands that way, but what the tobacconist assured you was something special—and you got more for your money.

Many brands of tobacco and cigarettes have vanished, or, at any rate, are not generally seen today. 'Guinea Gold' was a very popular brand, manufactured by Ogden. They were in white packets with two golden guineas printed on the front. The cheaper variety of this form were known as 'Tabs'. There were 'Park Drive', 'Bandmaster', 'Cinderella', 'Winfred', and many more, as well as the brands sold today. There were scores of Turkish and Egyptian blends, such as 'Quo Vadis', 'Neb Ka', 'Au Bon Fumeur', 'Snake-Charmers', 'Du Perfex'—many, many more. And the same applied to pipe tobacco.

One of the multiple firms boosted a cigarette called 'The Dandy Fifth'. A copy of the poem was given away with every box of fifty or a hundred. It recalled an episode in the American Civil War when a regiment so nicknamed did a deed of valour. Advertisements depicting a

227

languid kid-gloved soldier in a peaked cap, very smart and point device, were shown everywhere. The poem was recited by practically every amateur reciter, who thus turned his smoking to practical use and who became an active advertisement as well.

But the great thing about all forms of tobacco was its cheapness. Players were 2½d. for 10, 5d. for 20; Gold Flake 3d. for 10, 6d. for 20; Woodbines were five a penny. You could buy them in packets, in cartons, in cardboard boxes, in flat tin boxes or circular ones. 'State Express' were 6d. for 10 and 4s. 9d. per 100. Nowadays the same cigarettes cost over 2d. apiece. Pipe tobaccos were the same as now (except as to price), but there were more brands. There was a run on Craven Mixture when J. M. Barrie, not then knighted, allowed it to be announced that it was the 'Arcadia Mixture' of 'My Lady Nicotine'.

Cigars were plentiful and cheap. Havana cigars, regarded as dear then, were obtainable anywhere, and any brand was procurable. You got a very good one for a shilling. There were cheaper brands of cigars, such as Flor de Dindigul and Marcellas ('known by the narrow red band' was their slogan), which cost only a few pence. And there was a kind of cigar known as a 'tuppenny smoke'. And dear at the price.

Pipes have not varied much, but those were the days of the meerschaum for proud smokers, who coloured them by their consumption of tobacco and cherished those of deep hue. Calabash pipes tried to get popular, but without much success, but quite a lot of men smoked cherrywood pipes.

The Middle Classes did not smoke clays, or even churchwardens. Pubs gave a clean clay pipe to any customer who asked for it.

There were cigarette-cases of all kinds, but few Middle Class men boasted a gold one. Silver was the usual metal, although gunmetal had its devotees. Some men used leather ones, but these only caused the cigarettes to get squashed and bent.

Everyone smoked less than today and chain smoking had not become a habit. Lots of men still looked upon cigarettes as effeminate, even though women had not acquired the habit.

The barber's shop was a barber's shop, not a hairdressing establishment. Nearly all the barbers were Germans and were regarded as spies. Yet most people talked to them freely. Haircutting, shaving and shampooing were much the same as now, except that there was less use of the clippers and men used cut-throat razors with a strop to keep them sharp, thereby giving barbers a good income by having the razors reground and reset. Safety razors did not really get into general use until during and after the First World War.

There was, however, a feature of barbers' shops not met with today.

That was the mechanical brush. It was a large and circular brush with a handle on each end like a rolling-pin. It fitted into a long endless rubber band which went round a wheel in the ceiling of the shop. This revolved mechanically and so therefore did the brush, the barber holding the handles at each end to guide it. It was pretty fierce and nearly brushed your head off. It may well have accounted for the prevalence of baldness in the generations which knew its use. It being an age of moustaches, these had to be trimmed, as also had the beards. Haircutting cost three-pence or sixpence, according to the place in which you had it done. A shave was twopence or threepence and everything else in proportion. Few men had manicures, and fewer still went in for hot towels and face massage. Barbers' shops always had the painted pole, although they no longer 'bled' you (except when they cut you in shaving).

Many shops which made things carried on their work in the window: a watchmaker with his magnifying glass in his eye; a shoemaker repairing shoes in full public view; a saddler working at his craft was a popular sight in the Haymarket; whilst opposite, at Loewe's, a famous pipe shop, men plied that mystery in the window.

If window-dressing, therefore, was not so artistic, it had far more of the human element. There was a shop in the West End, possibly in Regent Street, which sold a preparation for the beautification of ladies' hair—not dye, be it understood, but the female equivalent of hair oil. In that window sat a row of pretty girls, their backs to the public but displaying heads of hair of wonderful texture and shade, and of amazing length. They drew crowds of both sexes to see what 'Harlene' could do for the hair.

Chemists and apothecaries always had the huge bulging glass jars filled with green, blue, red and yellow liquid. A hairdresser or barber of the better kind had a wax bust of a man—who got rather sallow by exposure—but who rejoiced in a marvellous head of hair, moustache and whiskers, although the mode of dressing them was out of date. Sometimes there was a woman's bust too.

Even your butcher, once a year, had a living display. Early in November the Cattle Show was held at the Agricultural Hall in Islington. Here beasts of an astounding fatness were shown. Butchers bought some of them. They would display these wretched animals before slaughtering them, the pen in which they were contained being decorated with the rosettes denoting awards.

The sheep were usually quartered in the hall of the butcher' house— he always lived above his shop and his front door was next to it. There they stood, these doomed animals, or there they reclined, gaped at and poked by curious people, with the dead bodies of their species within a few feet of their noses as an example of what the immediate future held. This display always seemed the start of Christmas, somehow, although that feast was some weeks ahead. But London filled up the Cattle Show and places of entertainment did a roaring trade. It was the forerunner of that later annual invasion, the Motor Show, and held pride of place until machinery won the laurels.

No shopkeeper or tradesman would hear of you carrying home your purchases unless they were very small parcels. Even then he always enquired if he might have the pleasure of sending it home for you. On being asked when the errand boy was starting, he always replied, "Now directly, Mum." He was a bit optimistic, maybe, but it always got there. Ladies who wanted their stuff—small handy stuff—at once carried it in string bags or shopping baskets. But ninety-nine per cent was sent home.

Butchers' boys dashed up in their swift dog-carts, or other butchers' boys in blue overalls and striped apron, like their master but without the steel, carried the meat on queer things on their shoulders, scooped-out trays of plain wood, oblong in shape and with two straight handles at each end like a wooden stretcher. It was borne over the shoulder. Few butchers' boys wore caps and their heads were very shiny. They were said to apply suet to it, and may well have done so.

Fishmongers' boys used a similar tray to the butchers', but sometimes baskets as well. They did not wear a striped, but a plain, apron. Bakers' boys and grocers' boys had baskets. These were used for seats on which the messengers sat to read their 'penny dreadfuls' as a breather from their onerous job. They watched every sight in the street: men digging, a fallen horse, anything at all out of the ordinary—and the streets had many free shows. They all were addicted to piercing whistles. They all conversed with their friends in loud, raucous shouts. Cries of 'Wait for us' were vociferated down the whole length of the street as a result of a shouted conversation as to destination at a distance of well over a quarter of a mile. But the stuff got delivered and there was always plenty of time.

Itinerant merchants with well-stocked carts called at the houses too, and did a fine steady trade, calling on regular days. Men came to grind the knives, to mend mats, to sell baskets, to offer carpet-beaters, brooms, dustpans, brushes, all sorts of things. Pedlars, male and female, with baskets of haberdashery and odds and ends of drapery, such as cotton, thread, darning wool, needles, tape and other necessities, were always calling round. No need to run out of anything. And always, perpetually, men delivered circulars, thrusting them under the door or through the letterbox.

No housewife need carry anything back from the shops, and middle-aged Middle Class ladies nowadays, staggering home in rain and slush, laden with things far too heavy for them, remember these days of ease and comfort with a sigh. But times have changed. Those were the days when nobody minded working, when work was not regarded as a part-time occupation between the pictures and other pleasures. Those were the days when a person worked—or starved. And as these words are being written it would appear that problem is imminent again. But the service in the shops, the relations between tradesmen and customers, are never likely to return to the days of the sovereign. Something has intervened, something which we are told is Progress. Of course, it is possible to progress in either direction.

So shopping was always a pleasure to the Middle Class lady who had golden sovereigns or silver coins in her purse. And a special treat was going up West to make some purchases and have a look at the shops. This was quite an adventure. She dressed in her best and her smartest for these trips, which were nothing like so frequent as today because transport was different. But if it was more roundabout and slower, it was at least comfortable, and if the bus, tram or train was full a gentleman always gave a lady his seat.

Up to the time of the tubes the lady had to go to one of the termini and take a bus from there. Few took cabs, for women then, as many do still, always economized on travelling. But when she got to the shopping centre she would walk round, in and out of the big shops, gazing, staring, pricing and making a few purchases, and having what to her was a gorgeous time. She seldom went alone—even in daytime.

A woman alone was likely to be accosted in those days in certain quarters of the West End by wicked men who should have known better. And no woman went about the West End alone at night; indeed, she very seldom went there without male escort. But after an afternoon of shopping she would have tea at Fullers, or later at Slaters, The Cabin, or Lyons' Pop., now a broadcasting studio, and, later still, at the Corner House—or perhaps at the St. George's restaurant in St. Martin's Lane, or Eustace Miles's place in Chandos Street—both the last-named were vegetarian establishments, although the former did good egg dishes and delicious coffee—and so home, before her menfolk arrived for their meal. Few of the big shops had restaurants then.

But she would have had a lovely time, even if she was a bit tired. She had seen the shops, the latest fashions, the different life of the West End, and she had money to spend—money which went so very, very far. She could relax in the evening, the servant would do the work. She would

231

listen to what her 'hubby' had to say, she would hear her children's news, she would read a book, or do her sewing—she seldom looked at a newspaper unless it were the *Daily Graphic*, or, later, the *Daily Mirror*—and she felt happy, safe, and supremely comfortable. There was no major cloud in her sky, the sun of which was that golden sovereign which made her shopping a real joy.

CHAPTER XV

Up West

THE MIDDLE CLASSES OF THE SOVEREIGN DAYS WENT 'UP WEST' WITH A sense of adventure. For the 'West End' was still the 'West End'. It had not become commercialized to the extent it has today.

The true West End then reached from the eastern end of the Strand to the extreme west of Kensington. Mayfair and Belgravia were still the living-places of the aristocracy. Offices had not swamped Berkeley Square, Grosvenor Square and so many of the others. The smart streets were still residential, not commercial. No theatrical agent or film agent would have dared ply his trade in that quarter. Shops there were in the right places, but of very select quality, going in for no show or display, caring little for the custom of the Middle Class or the passer-by, but having the names of the 'quality' on their books.

Nowadays the houses are shops or offices, the dwellers in that once exclusive domain crowd into flats. Where Edwardian horses were stabled, now people pay high prices to live. There is no real West End today, as there was in the days of the sovereign. Here and there a stronghold stands grimly—the clubs defend St. James's Street and Pall Mall, but all the last bulwarks are crumbling in the fusion of all ranks, and the Blitz—undreamed of in the days of security—has brought shabbiness and ruin where once was the glory of paint, window-boxes ablaze with flowers, the glow of footmen's liveries, the golden light pouring down red-carpeted staircases for a great party, and the ripple of the horses' hooves tap no more, silenced by the grind of the motor-bus and lorry.

But that was not the West End of the Middle Classes. They might go to Hyde Park to see the 'Smart Set' (as they called it) against whom Father Bernard Vaughan thundered in fulminating tones—and oceans of publicity—from his pulpit in the midst of their camp. They might go to see the *débutantes* in the Mall *en route* for Buckingham Palace Drawing-Rooms, but for them the West End was more circumscribed. For the woman it was a shopping place—Oxford Street, Regent Street, Piccadilly (the eastern end), and Stagg & Mantle's and Russell's in Leicester Square.

Their other West End jaunts were to the Queen's Hall for concerts—and ballad concerts—to the museums with their children, sometimes the Albert Hall, the theatres, of course, and an annual visit to the Royal Academy in Burlington House.

Every Middle Class person with any claim to culture went to the

Royal Academy. They bought a catalogue, they stared at the pictures (they did not examine the nudes too closely), and they looked at what they knew was 'the picture of the year'. They had read about this in the papers, they had heard about it at 'At Homes'. Often it was a 'problem picture' by the Hon. John Collier, who specialized in such things. There was 'Indeed, Indeed, Repentance Oft I Swore'—which showed a beautifully gowned lady on a not-very-comfortable settee (but of obvious period and valuable) leaning hand-clasped on a cushion and gazing into the fire. The problem of what she had been up to intrigued them greatly. They hazarded a shrewd guess in their minds.

Other such pictures were 'The Cheat'—an evening-gowned lady standing up at a card-party whilst her partners surveyed her. But who was the Cheat? You worked that out for yourself. And 'Sentence of Death', a man staring straight out from the canvas whilst a distinguished-looking specialist, profile at his desk, gazed at him thoughtfully. That caused a shudder. There would be portraits by Frank Dicksee, Seymour Lucas— pictures by him as well—Solomon J. Solomon and Sargent. There would be pictures by Sir Edward Poynter, P.R.A. (classical nudes mostly), by Wyllie (seascapes), Farquharson (sheep in the snow), landscapes, interiors, nudes by Tuke, Herbert Draper (often allegorical), H. G. Riviere, Alma-Tadema (Romans or Greeks and marble), G. A. Storey, Alfred East, David Murray, W. W. Ouless, and many more.

The Middle Classes were not very interested in the portraits; they liked the pictures. Perhaps they did not understand too much about Art—their descendants do not really know much more—but 'they knew what they liked'. And they liked pictures which they could recognize at sight. Cubism, Surrealism and suchlike meant nothing to them, not even a name. They understood a clear subject and a lot of colour. Not bad judges either, when they demanded that a picture should represent what it was called. They would buy a publication which reproduced photographs of many of the important pictures, and they would look at it at home and keep it. They enjoyed that as much as the Academy, at which they mostly developed a headache and were grateful for 'a nice cup of tea'.

Those artistic souls who derided the Royal Academy and its pictures had at once their scorn and sympathy. It was the Royal Academy, was it not? Very well, then, the pictures must be the best that this country could show. Of their generation they were quite right. It was customary to go to the Academy in full dress—men wore frock-coats and toppers. You did not go in a lounge suit and tall hat, except after the 'Season' was over, even if you came from the suburbs where 'seasons' meant railway tickets.

But for men the West End only mattered when night fell. That was the time of the male, for to all Middle Class men the West End meant the Night Life of London.

In those days the people of the Middle Classes did not need myriads of electric lights or flashing sky-signs to make their nights bright—they did that for themselves. They did not rely upon mechanism for anything, they made their own fun. There was plenty of choice in the way they could spend their evening. Nobody finished work much before six o'clock, unless they were in banks, insurance offices or the Civil Service, and most Middle Class men were 'Something in the City'. But from that hour onwards, when the offices disgorged their workers into the City streets, the West End beckoned.

They went 'Up West' with a feeling of adventure. They went 'Up West' with a golden sovereign, a golden half sovereign or a few shillings in their pockets and they had a good time. A day visit to the West End meant formal dress and gloves. No man would appear there in a cap or a sports suit, as such things were understood then. He wore a topper, a bowler, or in summer he could wear a straw hat. He would always wear gloves and he would never smoke a pipe in the West End streets. At night he need not wear the topper, the frock-coat or the morning coat. He would wear a 'lounge'. But he mostly wore the gloves, he carried a stick or an umbrella and he did not smoke a pipe.

He could choose many ways of enjoyment. He could go in the gallery or pit of a theatre for 1s. or 2s. 6d. respectively. He could have 1s. 6d. worth of pit in a music-hall. He could smoke his pipe there if he liked, so long as it was not the Palace, Alhambra, or Empire (the prices were higher anyway); he could have his drinks at the bar and watch the show at the same time. The lights were bright in music-halls, and life was gay. There was no sitting crouched up in the dark whilst highly magnified voices brayed forth American accents, which appears to be his descendants' idea of fun.

London then was an English city, speaking English, and if it spoke with an accent it was at least the accent of its own streets, its own soil. It borrowed from nobody, it lent to all. That great and friendly nation whose grammar is the same as that of England, but whose speech departs further from it year by year, was something extremely foreign in those days. The infiltration of the film had not begun.

But later in the period, when the pictures, as he called them, had come silently in, he might drop in for a bit. Not in the West End, but in his own suburb. But up West, if he felt so inclined, he could for a while combine the cinema with instruction. He could go to Hales Tours. There was one of these side-shows in Oxford Street, opposite Frascati's. The building, of a temporary nature, was in the form of an American railway observation car (there were no such cars here). The door was up a few steps to a kind of verandah, where the entrance fee (either threepence or sixpence, probably the latter) was paid at a paybox and you went apparently into the long, narrow car. At the far end was the screen.

When the place was full (it filled rapidly) the lights went out and the lecturer—dressed as a guard or 'conductor'—started the picture going. He pulled a lever and the 'car' adopted a kind of rolling motion in simulation of a train travelling at speed. And there you sat and ascended Mont Blanc, had a trip through the Scottish Highlands, or the Rocky Mountains, the Black Forest—all sorts of lovely places. The illusion was excellent and very cheap at the price. You got half an hour's picture travel for your money. It was, however, only an incident in an evening 'Up West'.

But this did not appeal to many; there were powerful counter-attractions. There were the pubs and the so-called cafés. For this, Leicester Square—a different place from today—was the spot from which the night life radiated. Leicester Square was the epitome of naughtiness. Men winked as they mentioned it. Women, except to visit its two great drapers, Stagg & Mantle and Russells, avoided it as something not quite nice and definitely indelicate. Indeed, no woman could walk across Leicester Square after nightfall without running the risk of being taken for what she was not, and being accosted in consequence.

She ran a similar risk in daytime but not so great a one, because in those days the difference between a lady and a 'lady of the town' was apparent at a glance, complete and obvious. But at night, any woman alone in the Square was classed as belonging to the 'unfortunate' strata of womanhood.

The fame of Leicester Square and its gay night life was world-wide. Foreigners grinned and leered as they spoke of 'Li-ces-ter Square' as they called it (one pitied them, of course, but forgave their misfortune in not being English), but they knew all about it. They had heard.

Leicester Square today is a respectable place filled with cinemas and milk bars, its two drapers merged into one as becomes a lesser age, but in the Golden Sovereign Age it had all the allure of wickedness.

It was a bit raffish by day, but at dusk it became a place of adventurous appeal. There stood the Empire, the Alhambra, its twin giants, the Gog and Magog of the West End, adjacent was delectable Daly's Theatre, the Hippodrome, and so many other theatres and halls were near by.

Just to walk across the Square was a thrill. The hansoms tinkled along, the carriages rolled by, the occasional motor snorted and chugged smokily, a four-wheeler might make its somewhat sombre way, but it was a kind of Pleasure Preserve, for no buses or public vehicles, other than cabs, ever crossed it. Indeed, they do not today, but charabancs park there and there is no romance in them. But Leicester Square then had more than these things. It had places of night resort. It had pubs and restaurants around it galore.

If you wanted to see 'Life'—which in those days meant the underworld—this was the place. You could go downstairs to the Café de L'Europe. You would find yourself in an enormous room, with mural decorations of German gnomes. The air was filled with tobacco smoke and trembled with noise. There were hundreds of little tables, nearly always full. At those tables sat the ladies of the underworld, the *demi-monde*, with their temporary escorts. They talked, they laughed, they quarrelled, they chattered and they drank.

Waiters—all German—were everywhere. They carried amazing quantities of beer mugs with frothy tops, either lager or the home-brewed variety. How they served them without dropping and spilling was a mystery. They took your order, which you shouted as they sped by, without seeming to hear it. But you got your drink with astounding speed, and you could have any drink you liked—and any quantity of it. Nobody ran out of liquor in those days. The whisky was threepence a go and the soda (if a 'splash' from a syphon) was free. You could, if you so desired, get drunk for half a crown, and many availed themselves of the opportunity. There was a great deal of drunkenness in sovereign days, for the pubs were open all day and up to midnight.

The L'Europe never altered, night after night it was always full, it never lost its appeal. About half-way up the wall, in a little gallery, a uniformed but very unmilitary and numerically small orchestra discoursed sweet music, heard only infrequently above the babel of sound rising from below. Their dress suggested they were Hungarians, but they were really Teutonic, as were most things about the Europe, except its name.

The manager walked about in a frock-coat. He was a German. That nation provided most of the night life for London, as well as our barbers, and a large proportion of the street-walkers too. The Middle Class had a hearty contempt for it in consequence, to be rudely shaken later on. At intervals a hush would fall over the place, as a police inspector and a couple of sergeants walked through on a routine visit of inspection. The din broke out again as soon as they had gone. There is still a Café de L'Europe on the same site, but it is a very different place nowadays—a well-conducted, excellent restaurant of complete respectability and efficiency.

If you wanted to meet sporting people, jockeys, professional backers of horses, and the like, you went to the Queen's Hotel. You would find them, with a goodly sprinkling of actors, in the Long Bar, or downstairs in the small bar by the Grill. It was the unofficial Turf rendezvous and amazing characters frequented it. One professional backer, who operated in thousands even in those days, had a suite there when in town, and always brought his solid silver dinner service with him. The jockeys liked it because it was near the Turkish Baths by the Alhambra and in Jermyn Street, and the Queen's Hotel still stands.

There was the Leicester Lounge at the other end of the Square. This was upstairs; up a lot of broad stone stairs carpeted, it is true, but with a broad brass nosing on every tread. There again you met the 'ladies', but the atmosphere was clearer and the noise less deafening than in the Europe, except perhaps on Saturday nights, when 'Rugger Roughs' invaded the town. They made for the Lounge, they created scenes of high-spirited exuberance, and when their absorption of external spirits or beer—and remember that all liquors were of greater potency then—persuaded them that they were again on the football field, and to commit excesses and breakages and make the ladies squeal—then very large 'chuckers-out' in light-blue uniforms would bounce them down those stairs into the street. Many a young Middle Class man's anatomy made acquaintance with those broad brass nosings, and those stone stairs, though carpeted, were extremely hard too, but they were none the worse for it, neither the stairs nor the men.

On the east side of the Square, next to the Alhambra (which Oriental building disproved the point about East and West never meeting, for it was one of the focal points of the West End), was the Cavour Restaurant. Here, amidst a Bohemian atmosphere, you could lunch or dine amongst actors, music-hall performers, artists and writers, and the cooking, service and wines were admirable. The prices, from today's standpoint, were remarkably cheap. The choice of food was amazing. The Cavour Bar was a sort of public Green Room. You met all the top-liners there.

On the corner stood the 'Provence'. This was, to all intents and purposes, and to the cursory eye, an ordinary public-house. So it was—until you went downstairs to the basement.

Then you got as near to Hell as it was possible for a human being to achieve in London at that time—or since. Women of a lower type than at the Lounge or the Europe; men, mostly foreign and even lower in type than the women on whom they preyed, vile and unprincipled, people who left no doubt in the mind of the Middle Class man who went there to see 'Life' as to what was meant by 'the criminal classes'.

The procedure was much the same as at the Europe, although there was no orchestra and none of the brightness and glitter (meretricious but still glitter) that place possessed. The voices were louder and more strident, the noise more metallic and harsh, the atmosphere more sinister

—the whole place was a threat. It was like sitting on the brink of a volcano, and eruptions frequently occurred. Female screams and shrieks would rend the air as a couple of 'daughters of pleasure' went for each other with their fingernails or their hatpins. Sometimes a woman would attack a man, sometimes a man would bash a woman. Glasses crashed, tables were overturned, and those near by found themselves involved in a general *mêlée* as friends of the contestants rallied to the cause.

The frock-coated manager (they all wore frock-coats) would push his way through, swearing in guttural German, and the waiters were all expert chuckers-out. But the police were often needed. Then a procession went across the Square heading for Vine Street police-station, the ring-leaders yelling and struggling with the stolid bobbies, and their partisans streaming like a slimy snake in the rear. All that vanished years ago. The place became most respectable.

In Bear Street was another pub. To savour this in full you went up-stairs, not down. You found yourself in a small room packed with small tables, and jammed with men and women. The latter predominated and were all of 'a certain class'. There were ferns and aspidistras (how they survived was a mystery but perhaps they were frequently renewed), there was tobacco smoke like a London fog, there was the heavy, overpowering smell of cheap but powerful scents, the fumes of liquor of all sorts and no air at all. This was called 'The Cosy'. Inexperienced young Middle Class men venturing into this delectable haunt of pleasure, under the impression that they were desperate dogs who knew a thing or two, usually emerged minus their watches and any other valuables they might have had about them, and went home sadder, wiser and poorer men. That could not happen now.

A little further along Coventry Street was Challis's Buffet, soon to be absorbed by Lyons's Corner House, but its bar to retain the name. This was another actors' haunt, but mostly a male rendezvous, an informal Green Room Club. You got a marvellous long glass of lager there for $1\frac{1}{2}d$. One dashing fellow caused a stir by ordering in bravado the dearest drink they had. It was a Grand Marnier at $9d$.

Near by, also in Coventry Street, but vanished now, was the old Globe Restaurant, a gay place to which you took the ladies who would not have been welcomed at your Mamma's 'At Homes'. The lights had a habit of failing, and there would be battles royal with rolls as missiles, and much laughter in the dark and scrambling. . . .

Further along, led to by a turning on the corner of which stood a silversmith's of ancient foundation with wonderful Sheffield plate always in the window, was Arundel Street, now submerged altogether by the Corner House. It led to a little square in which were little hotels. Furtive

Q

couples went up that street, for the hotels were not particular and you got a room for 10s.

If you wanted to chat with a friend, have a drink and listen to a good orchestra playing well-chosen light music, you went to Oxford Street to Frascati's. There you could sit around the central floor in almost a Continental atmosphere and have your drink without being pestered. In the centre or on the balconies you could lunch, dine or sup remarkably well at a very reasonable price, and at Christmas there was always an enormous Christmas Tree. Frascati's carries on.

The actors, the music-hall folk, the men of the theatre and the Middle Class man who knew his West End would take their dinner at Stone's, in Panton Street. This was an old English eating-house whose fare was plain but magnificent in quality. It was of the Dickensian type but it went back to the 18th century. You could sit at the bar to eat your food, in which case you were waited on by a red-haired Welsh girl called 'Tommy', who served you between serving the drinks. She was there for years, but she never altered and she seldom spoke. But she knew all the regulars—casuals were not much wanted at Stone's and treated accordingly—and she wore a complete air of detachment and a perpetual Mona Lisa smile.

The Coffee-Room, with its old-time, high-backed compartments, was presided over by Charles, a great figure. He was the English waiter *in excelsis* ; it is a pity Dickens never saw him, to make him immortal. He was tall, dark and silent—he was good-looking too. He, too, wore a smile around the corners of his mouth under the curled black moustache. He never hurried. He moved about by some means of locomotion known only to himself, for he never seemed to walk like ordinary mortals.

He knew everyone of eminence, or what was to him the same thing, the real regular customers. For others he had a cold, studied politeness which they found embarrassing, for they felt that they only just came into his scheme of things because they had strayed into Stone's, and that otherwise they were nobodies. He took your order with care, but you often got something very different to what you had selected. A request for roast mutton might materialize as a grilled sole. You never protested. Charles knew what it was best for you to have. The steaks and chops at Stone's were sublime, and in season they gave you peas as big as marbles which you could never get anywhere else.

The manageress was Miss Hubert, whose respectability of demeanour and dress and general appearance was almost beyond belief. But with her about nobody ever dared make a fuss, not even the rowdiest reveller; the quarrelsome 'drunk'; nobody created a scene or misbehaved in any way. Her mere appearance was sufficient to quell any roysterer. Yet she was a warm-hearted, kindly soul, and when the First World War changed everything for her and everyone else she wrote regularly to many of her regular customers who were fighting in France, sending them good cheer in the form of words—with a strong spice of religion and what was equally, if not more welcome, supplies of cigarettes as well.

Stone's was destroyed by a bomb in the Second World War. Nothing else could have shaken it, for it seemed that there time stood still. Its atmosphere was unalterable, age never seemed to touch its staff or anything connected with it. The very butcher who supplied its vast quantities of meat was a man of great age, yet as spritely and fresh-complexioned as his own joints. It was impossible to guess at anyone's age—they did not appear to have such a thing. Stone's is to be rebuilt. You cannot rebuild that atmosphere, for it even withstood the passing of the age of the sovereign before it passed itself.

Stone's had its rival, but in the Strand. This was Gow's. The name of this restaurant or chop-house survives elsewhere as a first-class modern restaurant, but otherwise there is no trace of the old days. In its Strand days it, too, was of the 18th and 19th century and kept its air of olden days with perfection. A man entering one of its boxlike compartments would not have turned a hair at finding Dickens or Thackeray at the table.

Its waiters were as English as its fare, and a good English waiter of the sovereign days had no equal. Those waiters at Gow's knew everyone who came in and they knew what their patrons liked. They took the deepest interest in them and their good. They gave messages of importance from one customer to another without any mistake and in complete confidence. They had apparently Christian names only. They kept places for their own customers, who would never have dreamed of sitting elsewhere. Gow's was a man's place, plain but superb, and a very good place it was too. The modern tenant of its name is good too, but in such a different manner. You never hear the ghostly chink of a sovereign there.

In Maiden Lane, Rule's catered for dinners and especially for suppers. Here, again, the Middle Class man saw 'The Profession'. If he was very lucky he took a Gaiety Girl to supper there himself. It still retains its atmosphere of older and better times in every sense of the word, and it is still a first-class place. The customers have changed, but Rule's has not.

There was Romano's in the Strand, another gay place where money flowed with the champagne, where good food could be enjoyed—and where Gaiety Girls went too. You would meet all Bohemia there, at 'The Roman's', people like Phil May, who knew his London as well as he drew it; Arthur Collins of Drury Lane, who went there to lunch every day and was frequently still there talking when they served dinner; Horatio Bottomley, who was once horsewhipped outside it; and life therein danced like the little bronze cupids which now deck the portico, beneath which nobody enters one of the golden haunts of the Golden Age. The site has been sold for offices.

Simpson's is still there, but it had an unlimited supply of vast joints then, of a size which it cannot get today, and the carvers trundled them round on great trolleys and showed the customers how an artist uses a knife. They still do so in these rationing days, but although the quality is still there the quantity has perforce gone, but Simpson's retains its unique atmosphere.

There was also the Sceptre Chophouse in Warwick Street, just behind Regent Street, which has now passed away entirely. Again the food was wonderful to eat and wonderfully cheap to pay for. It was run by a family who made the regular customers feel they were part of it. There was no chromium at any of these places, and the Sceptre was no exception. They did not try to create an air of gaiety by bright colours. The customers were happy people who provided their own brightness. What they wanted was good food, and that they certainly got.

The Sceptre had one strange customer. He was tall, military, distinguished and silent. He was also a marvellous drinker in an age of drinkers. Frequently he started his day by falling down the marble steps of the Club in which he lived. The servants would pick him up and turn his face in the direction they knew he wanted to go. It was always the same way and it led to the Haymarket. He never appeared before the hour when a gentleman could show himself about the well-aired streets. He would walk in silence and preoccupation to the Pall Mall Buffet, in the Haymarket—a small but very select bar next door to the Haymarket Theatre and actually containing some of the wall of the original Little Theatre in the Hay—and there he would have his morning draught. Then he would lunch and drink at the Sceptre, often falling asleep there—nobody would disturb him—until it was time to wake, dine and drink in the evening. He then passed on to other haunts.

Nobody ever spoke to him, knew his name or what he was. He had plenty of money. Once he fell off the top of a bus as it turned from the Haymarket towards Piccadilly Circus—no one-way streets then. People rushed to help him, but he picked himself up and walked to the Sceptre quite unperturbed, and quite unharmed. Men were men in the golden days.

Most young Middle Class men who knew their way about 'Up West' would have a meal at one of the places mentioned—half a crown would cover it. Or they might partake of a steak or a chop at the 'Lord Belgrave' (first-class still)—world-famous then for its steaks, which the customer selected himself. This was eaten in a little room just off the bar. Nobody much went upstairs then.

Or perhaps the young man would go into Soho and for 2s. or 2s. 6d. have a seven- or eight-course dinner—any course of which equalled weekly rations for two today. They would have a bottle of wine for 1s., 1s. 6d. or maybe as much as 2s. 6d., according to their means. The richer and more epicurean would visit Kettner's and have superb food and wines in quiet surroundings with little red-shaded lamps on the tables, whilst soft-footed waiters carried rich dishes and wonderful wines to perfectly appointed tables. And perhaps there would be a slight and quickly stifled stir and movement as a bearded gentleman in overcoat and evening dress passed through the vestibule and up the stairs—a Very Exalted personage indeed who, like the Middle Class man, was 'Up West' for the evening. It was tactful not to notice.

Cheaper but quite excellent other places were numerous, but memory lingers over the Florence, the d'Italie, and Ristorante Il Commercio (still going strong), where the veal and the *zabaglioni* were so astounding. In earlier days there had been the Continental, and the St. James's—known as Jimmy's—wonderful places at night.

There was also Verrey's, in Regent Street, with an atmosphere of Paris, and the Dieudonne, the Trocadero, the Café Royal, Oddennino's, the Rendezvous, the Gambrinus, the Comedy, and other places which —like them—still remain. There is still a link with these days, for at Kettner's now is Martini, once of the Dieudonne, and later of the Rendezvous—a link with old times.

There were many famous bars besides those recorded. Entering the West End from the Strand there was the Gaiety Bar, next to the Gaiety Theatre, a very delightful place indeed, for you saw the Gaiety folk there. There was the Bodega in Bedford Street, where the old actors were said to congregate and punish the free cheese. Short's, also by the Gaiety, with port wine of wonderful vintage and a curious sort of heavy fruit bun with great power of absorption. There was the little Adelphi Hotel, just off the Strand, Yates's Wine Lodge—lots of them. Some still remain, but the potency of the goods they sell departed with the golden sovereign. It is no fault of theirs.

In Shaftesbury Avenue was an upstairs bar, the resort of men whose curious habits were then kept very much under the counter, but have now become a music-hall and even a radio joke. The Middle Class man, if he knew about it at all, went there just to take a look and to hurry out after a hurried drink. He did not feel at all at home or happy.

There was a famous pub called the Prince Rupert, with an amazing lot of glass and mirrors about it, at the corner of Rupert Street. At the Long Bar at the Trocadero you met all sorts and conditions of men, from crooks to geniuses, and also at that other little bar round the corner, but still of the Troc, in Windmill Street. A very severe old lady, who looked like an Italian gypsy in a black silk dress, presided over this. The Long Bar at the Criterion too was quite a famous resort in those days, and there was the Spatenbrau in a cellar under the London Pavilion Music Hall where you got lager which tasted very much as it did in Germany.

The Trocadero then, as now, was a first-class place for food, so was the Criterion Restaurant, a fashionable place, but where the Middle Class man could venture. The Monico was another celebrated restaurant which still exists. The clientele in those days was a box of allsorts, but the fare then, as now, was of one quality—only the best.

Other places deserving a memory are the Villa Villa, in Gerrard Street, a restaurant still, but then with a most striking line in tomato soup—you never seemed to get it quite the same elsewhere. The house had once been that of Dryden, the dramatist, and bore a plaque to this effect—as it does still.

Maxim's and Pinoli's, both in Wardour Street, the latter the oldest established and with Pinoli himself, small, brown and keen-eyed, to superintend the terrific amount of food you got for the small amount of money you paid, the Boulogne round the corner in Lisle Street and the Monte Carlo. These and many others still flourish, as does De Hem's, noted for stout and oysters. There, at the counter, with the walls covered in oyster shells, as was the support of the counter itself, you sat on stools and partook of the fattest and most succulent of what hack writers then described as 'the succulent bivalves' and washed them down with a balloon of stout. Of course, there was plenty of lemon and brown bread and butter then.

There was Rayner's at the top of the Haymarket, a public-house where the company was also very mixed, but where there was one of the best snack bars in the whole West End, always crowded with steadily feeding Middle Classers. For some time this was presided over by Arthur, a young man with an absolutely incurable cheerfulness which never deserted him at any hour of the day or night, and whose ever-ready smile actually won him a prize when an evening journal set out to find the happiest smile in London—and nearly all Londoners wore a smile in those days, as did London itself.

Arthur never forgot a face, a name, or a taste in food. His recommendations were perfectly made and timed, he served with the speed of lightning and he never made a mistake—even in your change. Sand-

244

wiches of every known variety: lobsters, crabs, cold joints, ham, tongue, poultry, prawns, salmon, potato salad—any salad in fact—great bowls of hard-boiled eggs, pies, Eccles cakes, sweets and cheese, you got it all from Arthur of the smile and civility—and he never was familiar or took a liberty in any of his badinage or jokes.

If you wanted a drink, a tall, thin waiter in evening dress brought it from the bar behind you. It was noisy, it was crowded, but it was supremely good. You can still get excellent snacks there—but the quantity went when the rations came in. Also the company in the bar is far more respectable. It was not so in the Golden Age. There is a story about a barmaid there who had her watch stolen. She believed she knew the man who took it and consulted the police. They asked her to their Black Bureau and showed her their picture gallery, in case she could identify her man. She took a look and fainted. She recognized in that Rogues' Gallery all her regular customers. Well, it is not like that today. Those gentry have been moved on.

But then you met the shabby but well-brushed gentleman who was 'The Major'. He may have once worn Her Majesty's scarlet, but all that remained of it was in his nose. He would engage in conversation, say that he had not met a man he liked so much in years, feel in his pocket to buy you a drink, explain that his purse was on his dressing-table and how embarrassing it was, solicit the temporary loan of the ridiculous sum of half a crown, his cab fare to his club, give you his card and depart. The card, of course, had no address on it. 'Confidence men' abounded at certain of the places named. They lived well, and many were never caught. Their belief was that 'one was born every minute' and their careers proved it.

Further down the Haymarket on the opposite corner to the stately Her Majesty's—afterwards and now His Majesty's—Theatre, was the Waterloo Tavern, a comfortable, old-fashioned place where there was good food and drink and good professional company. It got itself rebuilt in the pound-note age and then vanished. But across the way and next to the Haymarket Theatre was the Pall Mall Restaurant, another first-class place where the Middle Classes could and did go.

As regards the hotels, the Middle Class did not frequent the Savoy or the Carlton, but they 'used'—as the phrase was then—the Metropole and the Victoria, the twin giants of Northumberland Avenue, the Grand Hotel in Trafalgar Square, and the more remote Holborn Restaurant. They also went to the Hotel Cecil in the Strand, but mostly for public dinners. They would have drinks at the Golden Cross, opposite Charing Cross Station, and recall memories of Mr. Pickwick. They fed, too, at the Ship in Whitehall, where Nelson and the old sea captains dined and where now stands the Whitehall Theatre. The Ship moved over the way.

Some few restaurants had orchestras. For the most part, people liked to eat in peace in those days and give their full attention to it. They could never have dreamed of jumping up to dance—or crowd round on a tiny floor—thus spoiling a good dinner and a charming exercise.

Eating and drinking then were eating and drinking—dancing was dancing. Never the twain should meet! People were altogether more restful and more serene. They enjoyed one good thing at a time and disliked a gallop and a rush. Indeed, they considered it vulgar.

At tea time—ladies' time in town—as already stated, there were the Slater shops, the Cabins—built to resemble the cabins of ships—and Fullers'. Stewarts' had its devotees, and women Up West did not go to the A.B.C. depots—it was too much like home. But they welcomed Lyons's Popular Restaurant when it opened, and enjoyed sitting there eating their cakes and drinking their tea and listening to the band. There were 'No Tips', of course. And when the fresh and tasteful Waldorf Hotel opened in Aldwych in Edwardian days and a shilling tea was served in the Court—well, that was magnificent and all the Middle Classes flocked to it.

Rumpelmeyer's in St. James's Street was a little bit beyond the average Middle Class—but one went to see what it was like—and boasted a little about it.

Many of the places mentioned still maintain their quality as highly as the times will let them, wonderfully well indeed considering all things, but nearly everywhere the clientele has altered. It may well be that other restaurants flourish today bearing the same names as those mentioned in this chapter, but it is the old places to which this chronicle refers—not those of today.

Although the West End was always gay, the night time was the bright time. The crowds were great, but they were happy crowds. The streets were indeed always crowded from dusk until the small hours of the morning. People—happy, laughing people—with money jingling in their pockets, out for a good time, and pretty well dressed too, were in and out of the pubs, the restaurants, the night resorts. They were care-free. No siren was to affright the air and send them to shelter, no whistle of bomb, rending explosion and crash of masonry meant sudden, unexpected death. There were no 'Leave Trains' to see off at Charing Cross, Waterloo or Victoria, no long hospital trains to bring in their maimed and torn sons, husbands and lovers.

The newsvendors shouted of the latest cricket scores, or of ' 'Orrible Murders', and called you 'Captain', the piano-organs played, the hansoms trotted by, their lights a golden glow like fireflies along the length of

Piccadilly, and the gas-lamps flickered or the new-fangled electric globes shone bluey-grey over the pleasure-seekers of London—largely of the Middle Classes—as they went along the Strand, across Leicester Square, up Regent Street, down the Haymarket, and along Piccadilly, a gay, care-free, light-hearted throng, whose tomorrow would be as today, as yesterday. No rations, no coupons, no restrictions, plenty of everything.

The crowd might thin slightly when the theatres began at eight and thicken as they poured out their fresh mob of pleased, excited people at eleven and after. The press of carriages became thick and the policemen had all they could do to direct it.

And swimming with that stream of pleasure, in it but not quite of it, a little detached and watchful, in and out amongst the men, eyes eager, a smile—mechanical, but a smile—always ready when eyes met, moving with a deliberation and a somewhat feline tread, slow yet personal, purposeful and with a good deal of panther-like grace, and the unmistakable gait of their trade, went the Ladies of the Town, the Daughters of Pleasure, who ministered to their side of London's night life, who sold their favours and their smiles, who whispered, " 'Allo, dearie"—painted, powdered, scented and with a raffish smartness which was perhaps a bit bedraggled, very unlike the other women around her—but still she was part of the scene, an integral part of that London of the night. She was there, the lady of the *demi-monde*, trying to earn some of that thing which was being plentifully spent all around her—the Golden Sovereign. And she, too, was in full view, not Under the Counter.

247

CHAPTER XVI

Home, Sweet Home

THAT NOBLE BALLAD 'HOME, SWEET HOME' WAS SUNG LARGELY BY THE Middle Classes in the sovereign days, and it was indeed their own particular National Anthem. For, as this chronicle tries to show, they were born in the home, they lived in the home and they died in the home. That home was the centre of their being and, in spirit, all Middle Class homes were exactly alike. It varied in appearance, it altered in contents and economy as the age wore on, but it was, and it remained, 'The Home' —until that war came which killed the sovereign and killed the old idea of home—and gave its death-blow to the Middle Classes, for the end of that Class dated from the departure of the golden sovereign. It did not die then, it was far too strong, too vital, but it got a mortal wound which festered, which bled internally and produced a wasting disease for which there was no cure—today the Middle Class is small and middle-aged, even old. It is, indeed, on its death-bed.

When that brave new world comes along there will be no Middle Class—until in the fullness of time the winter of the world dies away and spring comes again. Then the Middle Class will reappear like the leaves on the tree, like the flowers in the hedgerows. For, in the end, the Middle Class always turns up to provide the balance, the *bourgeoisie* is never beaten. Because it is adaptable it bends, but it does not break. And in this country, being so essentially British, it absorbs its opponents without them being aware of it.

But in the Golden Age—and one repeats again that the Golden Age refers to the coinage only, being too well aware of the blackness and pain which lay without its pale—the Home was the thing. The Middle Classes surrounded the Upper Classes in the districts they inhabited as the Lower Classes surrounded the Middle Classes by hanging on to the outskirts in each case.

Thus, in London, the Middle Class domain began in Regent's Park and St. John's Wood and travelled out from there in circles. There were patches of London where its caravan had rested and moved on, patches which were decaying rapidly, where the houses had not been lived in long enough to give them characters of their own, patches which the prosperity of the times had made only temporary resting-places, or patches which had once been the abode of rich city and professional men who had quickly moved further out. It is still going on, or it would be if

he result of scientific progress, as exemplified by war, had not halted the
building of homes and reduced most classes to the status of unwelcome
lodgers or dwellers in one room. It is not even so cheap today to live in
one room, back or front, as it was in the days of the sovereign, when the
song ran:

> Why did I leave my little back room in Bloomsbury
> Where I could live for a pound a week in luxury?

Also the result of an ill-advised venture into matrimony, at Trinity Church,
led a couple of people to a top back room, a terrible blow in the days of
plenty. Those were Music-Hall songs, and the Music-Hall told the
truth.

The lodger was one of the country's stock jokes. It was a sign of
poverty to take a lodger, of course, and few Middle Class people descended
to it. Music-Hall songs were full of him, however, and the havoc he caused
in the home. Today most people who have a home are, in effect, lodgers
themselves. A flat is really some hired rooms in a building owned by a
third party, with common entrance and stairways and sometimes communal feeding-places. A house may be owned by a landlord, but it is a
private place, a home, in its own little plot. It is all that is left of the
Englishman's castle, and these castles are getting as few as the old baronial
ones, it would seem. When a lodger comes in that sense of privacy which
the Middle Class cherished is all over.

However, in those days when everyone, except the unfortunates who
had gone to Trinity Church, had a house, there was always a best room
in every house and a best road in every suburb.

That best road was something like a road. It would consist of houses
—no, mansions—large and of brick and several storeys high. They might
even have towers and gables, or billiard-rooms with glass domes. They
always stood in their own grounds of considerable acreage and had a
carriage drive. These were, of course, Victorian. They had a carriage and
stabling, they had a domestic staff and often a butler. They had green-
houses, kitchen gardens, green lawns, flower-beds, shrubberies, possibly
a tennis- or croquet-lawn and they were embowered in fine trees.

Nobody liked being overlooked then. Neighbours were nice, of course,
but after all an Englishman's home was his castle, and privacy was the
thing. When the Garden City movement started the idea of a more communal life, and garden walls were abolished, it was not long, one observed,
before rose bushes and similar vegetable defences grew up as hedges by
degrees, but none the less steadily, until those little home patches were
established once more. The communal idea is not easy in this old country

249

and old race which has shaken off the tribal spirit for many centuries. 'What's mine is my own' was the motto then.

But that best road was the pride of the neighbourhood. Visitors were walked along it to admire its architecture, its wealth and its lovely trees. It was often the local church parade, where folks took a constitutional after the service, to bring their minds back to earth and their bodies in train for the substantial Sunday meal. One bowed to one's friends, and the ladies observed each other's dresses. Young couples walking together along its length on a Sunday thus made a tacit avowal of a forthcoming engagement. It was every housewife's ambition to live there—and some of them who had started more humbly eventually got their desire.

But when they did, it was not the same. For a suburb never stands still. It reaches a certain height and then it decays. She found also that the houses, big and imposing as they were, were extremely difficult to work, and, as time went on, that servants did not like them very much. They were Victorian houses, the product of the zenith of the Industrial Age. The water supply was never too good. It came mostly from a cistern, and those cisterns were in need of constant cleaning, for they usually had a few dead birds in them—but nobody seemed the worse for it.

The large houses were useful in case of infectious illness, which were often dealt with at home, rather than at the hospital. The Middle Classes then had a horror of hospitals and did not believe in nursing homes, of which there were not nearly so many. The general impression was that only fatal cases went to nursing homes, and that going there was the first step to the grave. Hospitals also were not for them, but for the poorer classes.

So in cases of infectious illness, even scarlet fever and diphtheria, the patient would be rushed to the top of one of those big houses and isolated there. Disinfected sheets hung across the stairway. One of the family went into isolation too, to do the nursing, although there might be a trained nurse, or an untrained old family retainer, as well. Meals were left on the stairs and the empty plates collected. It was all very primitive and rather gruesome, but it was quite usual.

For such things as the minor maladies—measles, chicken-pox, whooping-cough and the like—the mother, if she found one of her children sickening for them, would run it right through the family and get it over. It was a terrible nuisance, of course, but it finished the thing quickly. Sometimes it finished the children too, but the stronger came through. Life, indeed, was a question of the survival of the fittest, and viewed coolly and dispassionately—not such a bad thing. Anyhow, it led to a very tough race of people. Infant mortality was high, but it was caused naturally.

Today, when so much more care is taken over even small diseases, the balance of mortality is made up by death on the roads. So the average is maintained. Children are dashed to pulp in the roadway instead of dying in their beds. Measles was not taken as seriously then as now; its after-effects were ignored. Many a child suffered all its life from the neglect of ignorance. But smallpox was soon dealt with. It was already a dying scourge, though one constantly saw Middle Class people dreadfully pitted—such a thing is seldom seen today. Vaccination has done for that and immunization gives the little people of the Paper Age a better chance than their little forerunners of the Golden Age.

Nowadays those 'best roads' are sad sights of dereliction or have surrendered and become flats. But whether the Middle Classes were of sufficient standing to live in the best road, or in any other, the home was still the centre. It was home, birthplace, hospital, playground and death-bed all in one—it contained the whole circle of life.

It was, as has been pointed out, also the centre of much of the amuse-ment and entertainment of life, for the Middle Class people were very social and entertained a great deal in their homes. It was not simply a question of the housewife's 'At Home'. There were parties of all kinds: dinner-parties, card-parties and musical evenings, to say nothing, where space permitted, of private dances.

Card-parties vary little save now that bridge is played in place of the then universal whist—and there is not so much to eat and drink.

The dinner-parties, however, were far more formal. Quite a long invitation was issued—there was no ringing up and asking friends to drop in. The preparations were on a grand scale and everything was done in style. The housewife and the maid—also the cook, if there was one—would spend days, if not weeks, in preparatory discussion and planning. The main differences between a dinner-party then and one now was the table, method of service and the food itself.

A Dinner Engagement was sacred. Once accepted, only death or serious illness was a sufficient excuse for non-attendance. The casual method of today would have meant social ostracism. It is difficult to get an answer to an invitation in these days, let alone to ensure the arrival of guests. But then a formal acceptance on a printed card or a sheet of letter-paper (with address embossed) in the third person would be received by the hostess in response to her own formal invitation.

The day would come, and the housewife, however experienced, would be in a twitter. All the resources of the house and the kitchen had been mobilized. Prayers were offered up secretly in the hearts that the oven might behave itself, and the housewife spent most of the day preparing for the feast. The husband would lay in a couple of bottles of wine or so. He might have claret and burgundy and perhaps a Sauterne,

251

for the ladies were known to like a sweet wine. No Middle Class woman then knew anything about wines at all. The cost, however, was negligible.

If there was a cook, then she saw to the cooking; if the maid could be described, as they sometimes were, as a 'cook-general', the lady felt she need only 'keep an eye'. If the domestic were the ordinary general—who could nearly always do plain cooking, then the housewife was her own cook as well. A dinner-party meant a whole lot of work and anxiety. The silver was specially cleaned and all the treasures were on view. The house was given a special 'go-over'.

The great thing was the dinner-table itself. It might need extra leaves in it if the guests were many. So before he went to business the husband found the handle which operated the table—it was usually quite a search, for such things were always getting lost. The handle was very like the starting-handle of a car. It fitted into a screw at the end of the table which expanded mechanically to the turning. Then an extra leaf or leaves (all dining-room tables had them) was or were fetched from the corner in which they were stored, put into place, and the table screwed up tight again, much enlarged in size.

The housewife covered it with one of her best white damask table-cloths, such as were used only on special occasions. These were heavy cloths of snowy whiteness. They were seldom plain, they had very often lovely designs on them, how achieved only the manufacturers knew. The best dinner-service was put into commission, mostly of real china and quite charming in colour and design. Every Middle Class wife had a best service, as well as the one she used in the ordinary way. It was a very large service too. There were soup tureens, and plates, dishes for fish, small plates, large plates, dessert-plates, vegetable-dishes, gravy-boats, sauce-boats, all to match. A typical one would have a blue rim to it, with a narrow gold line on each side and on the base of the plate a bouquet of flowers, often roses.

The idea was to crowd the table. A big epergne went in the middle, of silver and cut-glass or of plate (a wedding present, of course), or perhaps a very large flower-vase of silver and glass with a main vase in the middle and smaller vases sprouting from the long, curving supports. Flowers were used in profusion. The silver cruets—there were always several—were put out, and silver salt-cellars also. Even the knife-rests were of silver. Very often a large flat mirror was laid on the table upon which the centrepiece rested, either epergne or vase, and on this mirror, presumed to be a lake, were china swans, who bore little ferns between their wings. The epergne bore either flowers or fruit, according to its construction.

The Middle Class hostess of the Golden Age was a great believer in smilax. Festoons of this graced the table, around the centre and might even stray to the sides. Each guest had the fullest complement of cutlery and silver, all shining and bright, and the fullest complement of glass-ware too. There would be a tumbler and wine-glasses, sometimes several wine-glasses. The host might want to cut a dash and serve suitable wine with each course, so there would be a wine-glass for each. The wine-glasses might be of plain glass or engraved and fluted. They might even be coloured, either ruby or green, which added a distinct dash of colour. Memory seems to whisper that claret was served in green glasses and burgundies in red, but it may have been the other way about—there was some sort of convention as to this.

Little silver trays bore salted almonds in the best houses; there were also little glass dishes of olives. The table-napkins were folded into shapes; they assumed the device of mitres, of fans, or what were called swans, although the resemblance was not striking, and as often as not a roll was placed in their folds. Each place bore a card showing who was to sit there.

When the hot and perhaps flustered housewife finally surveyed her fully-laid dinner-table she saw a very striking sight indeed, and one of considerable beauty. In these days of labour-saving utility, when a refec-tory table has a runner down the middle, there is as little of everything as possible; such a display of personal possession and pomp is never seen. But the housewife desired to honour her guests by giving everything of the best—and also to let them see for themselves how large were her own possessions, for property was something which mattered then—as John Galsworthy has told in his immortal Saga.

The Middle Class dinner-table was a resplendent affair and reflected the spirit of the age and its class. If there was a salad, it was in a crystal bowl with appropriate servers, or in a silver-mounted oak bowl, bearing a china one inside it. In that case the servers were of silver with oak handles to them. The Master of the House, who was to carve, would have a meat-carver and a poultry-carver, and a fish-slice for the fish. Dinner was a ritual then and needed serving properly. The silver entrée dishes were in use, the wedding presents came in handy, but everything gleamed and shone with metal, china, glass and flowers—and even the napery shone too.

The husband would come in early, see to the wine, decant the claret into the cut-glass and silver claret-jug, place the burgundy near the fire (if in winter) or into a bowl of warm water (if summer)—all men knew then how to serve wine—see that there were cigarettes in the silver cigarette-boxes, put an edge on the knives and generally fuss about. He would be told not to smoke by his wife, who was in all her finery of dinner-dress (not *décolleté*) and ready for the fray, although with half her mind in the kitchen, where preparations and some bustle were plainly audible.

She would murmur a prayer that the soup would not get burnt, the fish dropped, that everything would be nicely served, and that Maud—or whatever the girl's name was—would keep her head and remember to hand the things properly, in their right order and on the right side. She had rehearsed all this beforehand.

She and her husband would wait in the drawing-room. There would be a ring. The first guests arrived—it was seldom evening dress, although some snobbish and superior Middle Class suburbans went even that far. The maid would answer the door and the guest step in. Usually they knew at once what was for dinner. It was difficult to stop the smell of cooking pervading the house when of medium size, and coming events cast their aromas before them. But it was polite to be unaware of this. To say, "Ah, I smell you've got turkey!" or some remark of that kind was vulgar. The maid would announce the guests and show them into the drawing-room, or the host and hostess might go into the hall and give them a hearty welcome—hailing their safe arrival, as though the people from round the corner or next door had crossed deserts and floods, to say nothing of mountain ranges, to achieve the meal.

The hostess took the lady to the best bedroom to remove her cloak and tidy up, the man left his things in the hall—the hatstand and the table had been specially cleared for action. If the maid remembered she would take his things for him and hang them up, but not many 'generals' remembered that. The men would stand or sit about and talk perfunctorily until the ladies descended, when, if sitting, they would both leap up and place chairs. There would be a buzz of light conversation, quite formless, and the host would suggest a glass of sherry and serve it himself. This happened until all the guests were assembled. The hostess would be glancing at the clock, as were some of the guests too, and the smell of dinner was by this time making itself very felt, for dishing-up was in progress, when the maid entered and announced, "Dinner is served."

The guests were ushered into the dining-room, seated according to plan, and the meal proceeded. It would be soup (the salted almonds and olives served for *hors-d'œuvres*), fish, entrée or joint or game or poultry, perhaps a savoury, sweets and cheese—and dessert. Everyone was pressed to take more. Everyone refused. Mostly it went without a hitch—for the servant or servants were on their mettle and a housewife seldom attempted anything elaborate if she could not rely on her domestic staff. Even the fingerbowls were handed—if the equipment ran to it—and then the ladies either retired leaving the men to their port or, if it was a modest affair, everyone went into the drawing-room for coffee.

254

It was then permissible to smoke. Nobody smoked at the table, least of all between courses. In the drawing-room, if the host was of a facetious nature, he would offer the ladies a cigarette and cause laughing refusals. Towards the very end of the period a few women might accept. The coffee was served in a special coffee-service, and conversation, now that food and drink had loosened tongues and the housewife's cares were lifted, ran riot. The host might press cigars on his male friends—having got permission from the ladies—but most men stuck to cigarettes. They were, mostly, judges of cigars and doubtful about those handed round on such occasions. If it were a box of a good brand they probably fell for them, but otherwise—cigarettes.

Then there might be cards, a little music and the evening passed very pleasantly. Before they left the men got a drink—a whisky or brandy-and-soda—and they usually had quite a few during the evening too. There was plenty of it at 3s. 6d. for the Scotch and 6s. for the brandy. The ladies might be prevailed upon to have a glass of port—to keep out the cold on the homeward journey. About eleven o'clock the guests departed, saying that they had never enjoyed themselves so much, to discuss and criticize on their homeward way, whilst the host had a final drink and the mistress went into the kitchen to send the staff to bed and to distribute praise or censure. The couple, quite tired but very satisfied, discussed the matter as they turned in. They always decided it was a big success.

Those were days of formality and courtesy. Therefore it was customary for the guests to pay a call within seven days, to return thanks for the hospitality shown them. Why, having been once, they should have to come again, and partake of further, if light, hospitality, few, if any, of them ever knew. But that was the custom and they did it. And, by the way, an invitation to a dinner-party went out three weeks in advance of the event. Everyone had plenty of warning.

There was, as well, the other function of entertainment at home, the Musical Evening. Much fun has been poked at this by people who never went to one. It was much more of a Victorian institution than an Edwardian one, but it persisted for many years. It was, it must be confessed, more of a social than a musical event. But everyone was supposed to be fond of music, every home had a piano which had to be used, every young lady and quite a few young men could play the piano, the violin—some even played the flute or the harp (although that died out with Victorian times and few, very few, Edwardian young ladies underwent the strain of taking their harps to a party); and many, many more were under the fixed impression that they could sing, and that their singing gave pleasure. So there were musical evenings.

R

A very large number of Middle Class people really did like music and appreciated it. They went to concerts, they went to hear Gilbert and Sullivan, they went to the Opera, though usually in that case they attended when the Moody Manners, the Royal Carl Rosa, the Joseph O'Mara, or the J. W. Turner Opera Company came to the local theatre—and nearly every locality had its theatre then. Only the real musical fiends went much to Covent Garden. For one thing the season was limited, and it was expensive too. They did not want to sit up in the 'gods' amongst the foreigners. They went to musical comedies, too, with avidity, and to any performances of Offenbach or *opera bouffe*.

There was no radio, the electrophone was the perquisite of those who had telephones (a small minority), the phonograph was not yet regarded (and very rightly at that time) as a musical instrument, so being individualists, accustomed to doing things themselves, they made their own music.

The Musical Evening had nothing of the terrific ceremony of the dinner-party. It was a much more free-and-easy affair. But most people accepted the invitation, and, of course, brought their music with them in a little music-case, mostly of patent leather. This they left in the hall with their hats and coats, or in the bedroom with their wraps, according to their sex. They seldom took it straight into the drawing-room with them. It was not good form to show that they were eager to perform, though it was the deadliest insult if their hostess forgot to ask them; they never went there again.

Many of the people present on such an occasion were devotees of the Ballad Concerts, then held at the Queen's Hall. At these concerts there might be one or two instrumental items, but the staple fare was ballads, and lots of them. They were well sung by the most eminent of vocalists, and the reception at these concerts of the songs themselves showed the publishers whether they had launched a success or not.

There was no song-plugging then as it is understood now, for there was not the means of doing it, but let a song be encored or doubly encored at the Queen's Hall and you would see an advertisement in the *Daily Telegraph*—columns of advertisements in fact (for there was no rationing of paper and consequent shortage of 'space')—that Mr. Thorpe Bates and/or Mr. Harry Dearth, or whoever it was, would sing 'Little Grey Home in the West' at the Queen's Hall, and then a list of other vocalists who would be singing it at concerts on the same evening all over the country.

The same applied to the sopranos and contraltos. If Clara Butt sang a song it became famous at once. Singers got well paid for popularizing

256

songs. That was the plugging of the day. But it was mainly the reception at the Ballad Concerts which was the acid test, and there were very often surprises. 'Little Grey Home in the West' was regarded by Thorpe Bates, before he sang it, as a song which had no chance. He was encored so much that he had to give up. The Middle Class adored songs about the home—it was something very near and dear to them.

The same singer underwent another surprise of the same kind when he first sang 'The Floral Dance'. That also was a world-beater. There were hundreds of other instances.

Born at the Queen's Hall Ballad Concerts, ballads went into the repertory of every singer, professional or amateur, and into the drawing-rooms for the Musical Evenings.

These usually opened with a pianoforte solo by a lady or a gentleman, and then the concert started. They were all there—tenors, baritones, basses, contraltos, sopranos, mezzos and instrumentalists as well. Usually the instrumentalists were the worst. Quite a proportion of the people sang acceptably, and some quite well. Some needed a little persuasion before they performed—they had brought their music with them all the same—others leapt into the breach and were difficult to stop.

Sometimes there would be a man or a woman who could accompany well, sometimes the accompanist was not so good—no good at all—but nobody minded except the singers. The lucky ones played their own accompaniments. A gentleman of social mind, but no musical knowledge, would volunteer to 'turn over'. He stood beside the performers, got into their light and watched for the nod which meant that he must turn the page, and then he often knocked the music off the stand in so doing.

But little things like that did not matter to the audience, however annoying they might be to the singer. The culprit would laugh heartily and beg pardon, thus further interrupting the song. If there was an encore, the recipient either turned over for him—or her—self or chose a number they knew by heart. Attractive young ladies had a bevy of anxious assistants at this game, and would make quite a havoc amongst the hearts of their admirers when making their choice. *Fiancés* were instructed in this turning-over art, and mostly did it pretty well.

There were fashions in ballads. For a while the lugubrious and melancholy ballad had a great vogue and indeed never entirely died out, but it reached some heights—and depths—in its time. However, it was popular. The singer would plunge his audience in gloom and they liked it. Some were even affected to genuine tears. The singer would warble of the motherless child who spoke to her 'Daddy', which was the title of this particular song:

257

Take my head on your shoulder, Daddy,
    Turn your face to the west,
'Tis just the hour when the sky turns gold,
    The hour that Mother loved best.
The day has been long without you, Daddy,
    You've been such a while away,
And you are tired of your work, Daddy,
    As I am tired of my play . . .

and so on, until the child bid him a long good night, several times over.

This was most popular and heartrending. There were songs about little crossing-sweepers who, with their brooms, stood amongst the crowd. Nobody would sing that today because crossing-sweepers have vanished, but people understood it then. Any song about children or a home had a universal appeal, and orphan children and motherless homes had a double pull.

There was a very popular ballad about rich children playing in a beautiful garden. It was called 'The Children's Home':

They played in a beautiful garden,
    The children of high degree.
Outside the gates the beggars
    Passed by in their misery,

which is sufficient to show what sort of a song it was. There were scores of them. There were songs of gentler melancholy too, like 'In the Gloaming', Tosti's 'Good-bye', 'The Last Rose of Summer', 'Love's Old Sweet Song'—hundreds of them.

There were light songs with some approach to comedy, many of them very charming. Ballads were pleasant things when they shook off their misery. There were the geographical songs, about British topography, not American. There was a perfect outbreak of songs in praise of Devon (very justly so). 'Glorious Devon' was the most famous, although there were plenty more like 'Red Devon by the Sea' and others. There was 'Killarney', still a classic. Indeed, Irish songs were much more popular than Scottish, although 'Loch Lomond' held its place and other Scots airs remained always in the repertoire. But although Ireland was always a thorn in the side of this country and vexed its politics—doing indeed to the English what they begged the Creator to do to their enemies by confounding their politics—nothing gave the English greater joy than to sing songs in praise of Ireland. One recalls hearing a whole barful of men singing:

258

Then they sprinkled it with stardust
Just to make the lakes so grand,
And when they had it finished, why—
They called it Ireland!

at a time in 1916 when British soldiers were being shot down in the streets of that very country's capital city. A strange race, the English.

A list of popular songs which would be heard at the Musical Evenings may recall memories. 'The Slave Song', 'The Green Isle of Erin', 'Maire My Girl', 'Nirvana', 'O Dry Those Tears' (a favourite one for burlesque), 'Daffodils are Blowing', 'Because', 'Indian Love Lyrics', 'In Sympathy', 'Love's Coronation', 'The Cuckoo', 'I Hid my Love', 'I Know a Lovely Garden', 'My Memories', 'Parted', 'If I Built a World for You', 'My Ain Folk', 'Thora', 'The Rosary', 'Rose in the Bud', 'My Dear Soul', 'Sink, Sink, Red Sun' and, by contrast, 'Arise, O Sun', 'My Old Shako', 'Tommy Lad', 'I Hear You Calling Me', 'A Sergeant of the Line', 'Stone-cracker John', 'Where my Caravan has Rested', 'Drake Goes West', 'Every Morn I Bring Thee Violets', 'As I Go Down the Vale', 'Border Ballad', 'Until', 'The Old Superb', 'The Bedouin Love Song', 'Valley of Laughter', 'The Skye Boat Song', 'Mifanwy', 'The Floral Dance', 'Little Grey Home in the West', 'I Love the Moon', 'When You Come Home', 'Bird of Love Divine', 'Up From Somerset', 'Friend o' Mine', 'Shipmate o' Mine', 'In an Old-fashioned Town', 'Love's Garden of Roses', 'The Little Irish Girl', 'Devon, Oh Devon'—that is to name only a few.

Tenors would tackle the Gilbert and Sullivan gems, baritones would sing of 'Long Ago in Alcala—Tral-lal-la, tral-lal-lal-a-lal-a la', and they would sing patriotic songs too. 'Land of Hope and Glory' was over-whelmingly popular. Basses shook the whole room with their hearty bellowings, proclaiming 'A Giant am I', or the song 'Simon the Cellarer' or 'Drinking'. Sometimes they fell back on very old songs indeed of a nautical flavour, one very popular song being 'The Midshipmite', telling of a budding naval officer of the rank of 'snotty' who had spiked the Russian guns during the Crimean War at some long-forgotten engagement. He did his act of valour and his friends 'with a long, long pull, and a strong, strong pull' brought him to shore and finally:

We'll drink tonight
To the midshipmite,
Singing cheerily, my lads, yo-ho.

That went down very well with a maritime nation as audience.

Rather arch young ladies would sing about:

> If no one ever marries me,
> .And I don't see why they should,
> For nurse says I'm not pretty,
> And I'm seldom very good;
> If no one ever marries me,
> I shan't mind very much,
> I shall buy a squirrel in a cage
> And a little rabbit-hutch . . .

very often with fears in their heart as to their own personal position, knowing full well that the sentiments they sang were far from being their own. Or they would tell tales of a nice young couple who, as children, measured themselves in the garden to compare heights:

> Jack said I was only a silly,
> As there we stood back to back.
> He used to be shy,
> Though no one knew why,
> For I was taller than Jack.

However, the young lady lost her superiority in height and won the heart of her Jack, and would hasten to assure her audience in the end that:

> He used to be shy,
> Much shyer than I,
> But now I'm shyer than Jack,

which statement of suitable maiden modesty always brought the house down.

A full-blooded baritone would sing a song about Claud Duval and the famous dance on the heath—the saraband of romance, when the lady had complied with the highwayman's demand, not for her money or her life, but for just the dance in the moonlight, a touch of her hand, the rose —it was always a rose—which she wore next her heart, which he swore to cherish always. The song ended:

> Whilst he to the end of his desperate way
> To rifle or plunder, perchance to slay,
>   Rode on—to the end of his desolate track,
>   His heart to the maiden still wandering back.
> And lady, believe me, when Death played its part,
> The rose which she gave him was found next his heart!

This last line was repeated twice, with a dying fall, and always made its effect.

Patriotic songs reached their zenith in the Boer War, of course, but many of those ballads were things of great charm. Haydn Wood gave so many beauties, and later Herbert Oliver was to contribute his 'Songs of Old London' which, apart from musical evenings, deserve their place in the folk songs of this country. They are now classics, and justly so.

There would be a reciter at these drawing-room concerts as well, and he—or she—usually inflicted considerable emotion on the listeners, not always of the type desired. The recitations were often far too long, and too hackneyed, no matter if they were dramatic or humorous. The elocutionists were very hard on Tennyson, whom they punished severely. 'The Brook' and 'The Victim' were perennially mishandled. Kipling, too, came in for trouble, and 'Gunga Din' was told he was a better man in all sorts of ways—and tones. 'Dagobert the Jester', 'The Jackdaw of Rheims', 'Fra Giacomo' and a long affair about a soul in Purgatory, who had a shabby trick played on it by an angel who allowed it to return to earth and see the man it loved married to another, were evergreen and ever-long items.

The same applied to a description of Rubenstein's piano virtuosity. Duets, both instrumental and vocal, had their place, mixed, all-female and all-male. 'O that We Two were Maying' drifted out into the winter fog, and a tenor and a bass became 'Peace and War' and debated the point at some length. There was the musical monologue too, mostly about a watermill—though Corney Grain and George Grossmith had many amateur rivals.

There were also the comedians. These gentry still abound; the gay, high-spirited, lighthearted gentry who elect themselves the life and soul of the party. Then they were just as numerous. The trouble at Musical Evenings was that they did not restrain their humour for their own 'turns'. Indeed, they must have dissipated it altogether by that time, for when they 'obliged' with a song of Chevalier's, the more suitable of the popular music-hall comic ditties, or something like the First Lord's song; the Major-General's song; or the Nightmare song from *Iolanthe*, they usually proved most indifferent. But all through the evening they had kept up a fire of witticisms, if not wit; they had pulled funny faces, they had endangered their chance of being invited again by performing comic business with ornaments or articles of furniture dear to the heart of the hostess. And they had told innumerable 'funny stories'.

They went very well indeed with the ladies, but the men held them in contempt. Some even clenched their fists and most murmured amongst themselves that "Old So-and-So thinks he's very funny, don't he? I don't see any virtue in misbehaving like a clown," or, "The man is getting insufferable. He wants kicking." Of course the host, who disliked him as

261

much as the rest, had to pretend to be highly amused and laugh uproariously, but in his heart he considered that the fellow was taking a
liberty—and the hostess held him in abhorrence for some side-splitting
remarks about a china dog or some other valued trifle of hers never till
then insulted.

The trouble about the comedian was that he was usually in such a
position locally that he could not be excluded, and the ladies all declared
that he would be the death of them. He was very often near death himself
at the hands of the gentlemen present, had he only known.

But by and large the much-derided Musical Evening was an excellent
effort in self-amusement by a community who had to amuse themselves.
Most of the people there thoroughly enjoyed it, and all those who performed did enjoy it to the full, without any question at all, and, as they
were in the vast majority, a 'happy evening was had by all'. These affairs
are often burlesqued in broadcasts devised (that is the word of power, or
'edited'—an even stronger charm or talisman) by young men or women
who were never present at such things.

In these things the tenors are all throaty, the baritones out of tune, the
basses husky, and the instrumentalists strike wrong notes. It was not at
all like that. It was good amateur entertainment and never pretended to
be more. Some of the more efficient were told that they were so good
that they ought to go on the stage. Some of them, carried away by local
success, actually did so—and learnt the lesson of the gulf between the
best amateur and the worst professional. But even so, some succeeded
in reaching professional—and even high-professional—standard. And
going on the stage was a desperate thing then; it amounted for a long time
to social outlawry.

But there was more than mere music at a Musical Evening. There
were light refreshments—or what the people of the Golden Age called
light refreshments. These were served in the dining-room, or the break-
fast-room downstairs, if there was one. Positive mountains of sandwiches
—ham, tongue, beef, egg, egg-and-cress and paste (which were usually
left and eaten by the servants), little patties and meat pies, tarts and cakes
of all descriptions, some home-made and highly praised, custards in
glasses and tiny plates of jelly, to be washed down with tea, coffee, lemonade or claret-cup.

During the evening the gentlemen in small batches had received
a nod and a wink from the host. They understood this quite well, and
went out of the room. Then, in stealth and silence and in a dimly lit
room, they partook of whisky-and-soda. There was no need for this
secrecy, but it was still considered not quite good form to drink when
ladies were present—much reticence there is now when the ladies partake

as freely as the men!—and the surreptitious nip of spirits had a much better taste for it, and each nip today would represent a double-double, so strong was the drink.

And finally there would be the chatter of good-byes, the light laughter, the assumption of shawls and fascinators, of hats and bonnets, of coats and wraps. If it were cold, there would be a cup of hot soup as a final strengthener against the rigours of the climate—and a stirrup-cup for the men out of the whisky bottles. It was not called 'one for the road' then, it was either 'the final', or, after Harry Lauder came into fame, 'a Doch and Doris'—said with a strong, if faulty, Scots accent and roars of laughter and giggles. The guests would go, expressing their thanks, and again the host and hostess congratulated themselves on having given their friends some pleasure in an age which, if inclined to individualism and privacy, at least understood sociability—and behaved itself whilst partaking of communal entertainment. And well over sixty per cent of those present had either sung, played or made some contribution towards the evening's pleasure. Could a similar congregation of the Machine Age say the same?

CHAPTER XVII

The Theatre, the Halls, and the Cinema

IN THE DAYS OF THE GOLDEN SOVEREIGN THE MIDDLE CLASS WERE GREAT supporters of the Theatre. There was a cleavage, however, for a portion of that class, of strict upbringing and with old-fashioned parents, still regarded the theatre as a place of evil and never entered its portals. Some went only to see the plays of Shakespeare, which were always considered moral and uplifting. But it was the Middle Classes, none the less, who filled to overflowing the cheaper parts of the playhouse and who, if they were theatre-goers, were playgoers of the greatest possible enthusiasm.

If anything is wanted to prove the stability of the age of the Golden Sovereign, the Theatre can do so, for that institution—one of the most precarious in the world—reached a condition of quality and stability during the '80s, '90s, and 1900s which had never been attained before nor has it since.

This was largely, if not entirely, due to the actor-managers of that period, who had their greatest patrons and supporters, their most faithful admirers, and what we should now call 'fans' in the members of the Middle Classes.

The theatre-going public then was not so large, especially so far as the West End was concerned. Apart from those—the quite considerable number—who regarded the playhouse as not respectable, if not, indeed, a place of sinister aspect, there were enough playgoers for each suburb of any importance to have its own local theatre which could be reached with a minimum of trouble and expense, and where prices were cheaper. It says much for the actor-managers that they commanded so large a following. But the Middle Classes were always the staunch supporters of Quality—and the actor-managers certainly had quality, and gave it.

The actor-managers—wise men who knew their business and were men of the theatre first and last—catered for the Middle Classes. They knew they would get the stalls and boxes, because it was part of the social life of the time to go to the play, and because during the 'Season' it was also a social duty. One had to see the plays and be seen there. For London had a 'Season' then, when all the great ones of the land were in town and entertained. They gave much the same sort of entertainment as the Middle Classes, but they engaged professionals instead of doing it all themselves. Money flowed from their well-lined pockets into the tills of those who catered for amusement, and into the pockets of the

264

shopkeepers as well, who could not do enough to serve them and reap the golden harvest.

Although the Middle Classes had no 'Season' they knew all about it and what went on. They followed the Upper social life very closely.

But their value to the actor-manager was that they always went to the theatre in and out of season and not just for a few hectic weeks, except during the general August exodus. So the actor-manager shut down shortly after Goodwood, and did not reopen until late in September. If he had a determined success on his hands he put in another very good actor to play his part and went off for a holiday.

But most London theatres were shut during August and early September, and exhibited bills saying, 'Closed for Preparation of Autumn Production'. The Middle Classes did not affect the stalls or boxes to any great extent, although they would venture into the dress circle on special occasions.

To sit in those parts of the house meant wearing evening dress. Nobody presenting themselves at the theatre for admission to the more august seats would have been admitted unless so attired. That was inconvenient for the Middle Classes, who worked longer hours than they do today and had not the same transport facilities. So they went into the Pit, the Gallery—or that half-way house, the Upper Circle.

The Upper Circle had the benefit of being reserved. There you got a seat for five shillings or four shillings—according to the row in which you sat. There was no entertainment tax. True, you might have to dodge a pillar, but you went in comfort and leisure; the lady wearing a special blouse, but not wearing a hat. Even this was allowed at some theatres in the Upper Circle; and with that strange conservatism of the playhouse, you might read on the programme, 'Upper Boxes (bonnets allowed)'— the theatre had no cognizance that the boxes had vanished, or that already 'bonnets' were only worn by old ladies.

The man wore his best suit, and he and his lady sat entranced, ate Neapolitan ices in the interval (sixpence each) and consumed vast quantities of chocolates. The programme-girl carried a huge assortment of these on her tray—sixpence, a shilling and upwards—and in dearer, reserved parts of the house it was not 'the thing' to bring your sweets with you. You bought them from the programme-girl for the lady you accompanied.

But this was not necessary in the Upper Circle. Nobody looked askance if you bought your confectionery outside, although the cost was the same. The gallant male would often prefer to cut a dash, and buy a box of Fuller's (wrapped in plain white paper with the firm's remarkably well-written autograph in red on the front) for his *fiancée* or wife in the theatre itself. The programme-girl would thank him as he motioned her to 'keep the change', and he assumed the proportion of a wealthy and generous male. It 'looked much better'—appearances then counted for a good deal—and the lady preferred it. A half-crown box provided a luxurious feast and left plenty for the next day.

If you went to a theatre with an actor-manager in charge, for the greater part of the golden period your programme cost you nothing and your cloak-room was free. The actor-manager studied his clients and was fully aware of them. He was in personal touch and in full sight (if you paid to see him). Nowadays it is a wise theatre that knows its own management. But the whole atmosphere then was one of politeness, respect and, above all, of dignity.

The actor-manager, too, showed his awareness of his Middle Class patrons by catering especially for them. In nine cases out of ten he put on an entertainment for their special delectation. This was known as a 'curtain-raiser'. It was a one-act play performed before the main entertainment. It was also a part of the evolution of the Theatre, which was emerging from the Georgian and Victorian theatre which, in the earlier days, gave shows lasting for many hours and offered three plays during the evening—two shorter ones and one entirely full-size; and when you could go in half price at nine o'clock and still have a full night's entertainment.

That, of course, had gone; but the curtain-raiser survived. It was seldom seen by the Upper Classes, who arrived late then, as now; but it was seen and enjoyed to the full by the Pit, Gallery and the Upper Circle —who did not come late and who revelled in every moment of their playgoing. Those curtain-raisers were excellent, and gave many a rising playwright, actor and actress a chance to show their paces. And sometimes even the actor-manager himself would appear in them.

It was doubly appreciated by the Middle Classes because, if they went to the theatre regularly, they did not go as often as they do now. That made it all the more enjoyable. A visit to the theatre was anticipated with pleasure, enjoyed to the full before the glamorous hours spent in the playhouse, and discussed for weeks afterwards. It was not something to forget whilst still on the way out, or to be eradicated by an immediate visit to the films.

It was not so easy to forget those productions, anyway, for you not only got full measure, but magnificent quality of acting and presentation. Yet the cost of running a play and producing it was less than half what it is today. The Pit was the Middle Class rendezvous. It cost 2s. 6d. and, again, there was no tax. That was the standard price; and there was a fine row at the St. James's Theatre when Sir George Alexander tried to make it three shillings.

The Gallery was also Middle Class in the West End, but on a slightly lower scale. It cost a shilling (no tax).

But two of the great theatres, where two of the greatest actor-managers held sway, would supply the Middle Classes with a magnificent reserved seat for less than the price of the Upper Circle. At the Haymarket you got a fine reserved seat for 2s. 6d.; and at His Majesty's, in the great days of Tree, for two shillings. You saw the finest stage productions of their kind ever witnessed in this country for that small sum, and you got your cloak-rooms and programmes thrown in.

Yet of recent years it has become the fashion to sneer at the actor-managers. That is perhaps another sign of the elimination of the true Middle Class, who knew them and appreciated them—indeed, the actor-managers were of the Middle Class themselves. They were the aristocrats of the Stage, and they behaved like it and looked like it. They, too, wore the frock-coat and the tall hat, and their appearance and personality left no doubt at all of their very great celebrity. But their birth was not of the aristocracy of life, but of that sound, solid Middle Class which ran the country for the country's good. Nor did they persistently grab all the limelight. They surrounded themselves with the finest casts available.

You queued for the pit and gallery. Before the queueing system was introduced there was a fine old rough-and-tumble and free fight when the doors opened, but the queues stopped all that.

In those happy days the theatre was the only thing for which the Middle Classes had to queue—and they enjoyed doing it. The length of the wait was according to the success of the play and the popularity of the actor-manager appearing in it. Many waited for hours. They took refreshments, they read magazines, periodicals and the newspapers. They read novels and they talked 'Theatre' to their neighbours. Many friendships were formed, and even marriages made, in the theatre queues. If the entrance at which they waited was in the main street, they watched the life of London pass by—a much more interesting sight than now, for then ninety per cent of the people in the West End were well dressed.

Once inside the theatre they gave themselves up entirely to enjoyment. There was the curtain-raiser provided by the actor-manager. This was not always a play; it might be an entertainer at the piano, or sometimes it was a select and clever concert-party. Even if there was no curtain-raiser there was always a first-class small orchestra of living performers who contributed well-chosen and well-played musical programmes during the entr'actes and before the show commenced—curtain-raiser or not.

267

These were listened to and applauded by the Middle Class playgoers, who did not have music laid on to their homes like water by means of the radio, and so reach the saturation-point of what is known as 'background listening', which really means hardly listening at all. That Middle Class audience listened to that orchestra which was part of the show they had come to see, and they appreciated it as such.

But the great thing they had come to see was, of course, the actor-manager. They knew they were going to get quality, and they knew also the type of entertainment with which they would be provided. For theatres in those days had policies. They supplied branded goods and the public knew exactly where they were.

George Alexander—afterwards Sir George—was the idol of the ladies. He ruled at the St. James's Theatre and he fitted that very exclusive quarter of the town perfectly. At the St. James's you got High Comedy, and there you got the works of Pinero.

At the Haymarket there was Cyril Maude, giving lighter comedy, as a rule, in a playhouse of perfection, with all the perfection it required.

There was Charles Hawtrey, who had no theatre of his own, but who frequently appeared at the Prince of Wales's or the Comedy Theatre —if at the former he was presented by Frank Curzon, who had himself been an actor and who was a splendid manager—and sportsman, who eventually won the Derby. There is no actor today quite in the same street as Hawtrey, who was a combination of ease, personality and acting ability which seldom comes to pass. He was the greatest stage 'liar' of all time; and the Middle Classes adored to see him lie his way into difficulties and out again.

You could see Arthur Bourchier at the Garrick: a big burly man whose wife, Violet Vanbrugh, was a much better actress than ever he was an actor. He specialized in 'rough diamonds' who had amassed fortunes and were at war with 'The Smart Set' who were trying to ruin the honour of his wife. The Middle Class loved that sort of thing. Bourchier was a much better actor under other people's management than under his own, and did splendid work with Tree.

At the Criterion or at the New Theatre, or at the theatre which bore his name, would be Charles Wyndham, who became a knight, as did Hawtrey, but not Bourchier. He was an actor of charm and mellowness, and with him would be Mary Moore, afterwards Lady Wyndham. They were an ideal stage couple.

For a portion of this period, too, Sir Henry Irving could be seen at the Lyceum, still writing that page of glory in the annals of the British Theatre, and Ellen Terry too. They were the popular idols, and both were revered and loved by the Middle Classes. Survivors of those days, and their children and grandchildren, flocked in massed crowds to St. Paul's, Covent Garden, to pay homage to this lovely and great woman when her centenary was celebrated in 1947. They packed the church, and although the winter was the bitterest for generations, they stood bareheaded in the deep snow outside the church to hear and see what they could and to do homage to her gracious memory. What actress of the Paper or Machine Age will command such respect or veneration?

But the ladies gasped and swooned with joy, and the men pulled their moustaches and sat up, when Lewis Waller took the stage. Here was the romantic actor *in excelsis*. Handsome, dashing, masculine to a degree; golden-voiced, perfectly at home in the 'costume parts' in which he had —and has—no equal, he was a hero—he was Romance. To see his 'Monsieur Beaucaire', his 'Henry V', his 'White Man', his 'Brutus'—for he was a Shakespearian as well as a romantic—the Middle Class queued for hours and hours.

There were Fred Terry and Julia Neilson, that wonderful pair; there was Martin Harvey (also to be knighted); there was Forbes-Robertson (to receive the accolade as well), Oscar Asche and Lily Brayton, Sir John Hare, Weedon Grossmith, Miss Compton, H. B. Irving; Laurence Irving—sons of Sir Henry, and worthy sons—Aubrey Smith (another knight), Henry Ainley, rising to fame, and Godfrey Tearle doing like-wise, H. V. Esmond, Eva Moore, Mrs. Patrick Campbell, Edith Wynne-Matheson, Lena Ashwell, Marie Tempest, Lilian Braithwaite, Irene Vanbrugh and hosts of others, some of whom—like Irene Vanbrugh (now Dame of the British Empire)—are still delighting the Middle Classes.

In the earlier period one could still see the Kendals, and the Bancrofts had not long retired. Charles Frohman was running the Duke of York's Theatre with distinction and producing new stars constantly. Matheson Lang was over the horizon and a star in his own right. Names like Edward Terry, Lyn Harding, Fisher White, Holman Clarke, Sydney Valentine, Dawson Milward, Margaret Halstan, Constance Collier, Louis Calvert and Lionel Brough were assurances of splendid performances. Ethel Irving and C. M. Lowne were drawing all London to see a new play by a new author named Somerset Maugham.

A young actor named Dennis Eadie had graduated from musical comedy *via* Frohman's company at the Duke of York's into leading parts. So had another young actor, this time from His Majesty's, whose name was Gerald du Maurier. Both were to become actor-managers of the Golden Age and make history. Greatness strode the stage, and you could see the giants.

You could also see such actresses as Winifred Emery and Kate Rorke.

Kate Rorke was one of the great figures of the Victorian and Edwardian stage—a woman whose character was as fine as her art—and that was very fine indeed. She would, at a later date, have been hailed as something marvellous (as indeed she was). But she walked with the giants, and her stature was not so marked as it would be now. Still, she was fully recognized as one of the great ones, and she gave magnificent service to the Theatre, spending many of her later years training the aspirants to the profession she so much adorned at the Guildhall School of Music. Her name will strike many a chord.

Dramatists abounded: Pinero, Henry Arthur Jones and J. M. Barrie leading the way; with such people as Sydney Grundy, Hubert Henry Davies, Comyns Carr, Stephen Phillips, Edward Knoblock, Rudolf Besier, Haddon Chambers and Alfred Sutro as their companions. Out at the Court Theatre, J. E. Vedrenne and H. Granville Barker were starting something new with the works of a new dramatist with a red beard and revolutionary ideas whose name was Bernard Shaw.

And Granville Barker and Lillah McCarthy were to do fine work after that. There was life and movement everywhere. In Manchester, Miss Horniman was heading a great movement which gave many precious things to the Stage.

Frank Benson and Ben Greet—both to be knighted too—carried the banner of Shakespeare all over the country. It was indeed a Golden Age for the Theatre. It progressed more during the Sovereign Age, or that part of it under notice, than it had done for two centuries.

And at the apex of it all stood the mighty figure of Herbert Beerbohm Tree, the actor-manager *in excelsis* and one of the great personalities of our Theatre history. At his beautiful theatre—His Majesty's, opened as Her Majesty's so fittingly in Diamond Jubilee year, that highest point of the age of the golden sovereign—he gave the loveliest and most stupendous productions of Shakespeare and other plays our Stage has ever seen. It was to all intents and purposes a gigantic repertory theatre, for Tree was a great creator, and would never keep a play running just because it was a success. He always wanted to be doing something new —and he did it. He gave London marvellous Shakespeare Festivals, glittering with stars, every Easter. He trained the young generation to be the stars of the next generation.

He became Sir Herbert Tree, and never was knighthood—stage knighthood—better bestowed. A great—a very great—character-actor, a great producer, a great artist and a great man, he was typical of the theatre of the Golden Age. He gave the Stage a dignity and a breadth which passed when he died—and he died with the golden sovereign, or very shortly after. The Stage has had no such leader since. His work and

270

ALLY ON THE "TRI"

"Ally Sloper", the great comic figure of the age. Many people believed
he actually existed

The first challenge to the Carriage and Pair

The motor arrives as a means of travel and added adventure to a trip

his personality was as sound, as brilliant and as valuable as the sovereign which ruled his period.

If the Middle Class wanted to see musical shows—and they did!—they were catered for royally. For the one and only George Edwardes was in command at the Gaiety, at Daly's and elsewhere. Later he took over the Adelphi, where, earlier in the period, William Terriss—whom everyone called 'Bill'—had ruled, and drawn all London to see melodrama, before he was so foully stabbed to death by a madman.

George Edwardes had invented musical comedy. He gave shows which for quality, polish and workmanship cannot be matched today. Their memories and their music live on—the tunes of Ivan Caryll, Lionel Monckton, Sidney Jones, Paul Rubens and the rest of them, who filled the Golden Age with melodies which, if not classic, at least rank as true and chimed as melodiously as the golden sovereign itself.

Edwardes had stars whom he made himself, and whom he fitted with parts which suited them to perfection. Above all, he glorified femininity. His 'Girls' were world-famous—and the Gaiety Girl had a lure, a glamour, an attraction which has never been achieved since. Those Edwardes galaxy of stars will stir middle-aged Middle Class memories today as they stirred the pulses when young—Evie Greene, Gertie Millar (what a joy!), George Grossmith Junior, Edmund Payne, G. P. Huntley, Hayden Coffin, Huntley Wright, Marie Studholme, Joe Coyne, George Graves, Gabrielle Ray, Ruth Vincent, Lily Elsie, W. H. Berry—a very firmament of stars—indeed, of planets.

There was also that amazing couple Seymour Hicks and Ellaline Terriss. Seymour was then an actor-manager, who not only played parts in the shows but wrote and produced them too. Ellaline was everybody's sweetheart, worshipped from afar. Both of them shine with perennial youth today. There was golden-voiced Isabel Jay—wife of Frank Curzon—and Bertram Wallis, who caused a flutter in feminine hearts greater than any film star from Hollywood achieves, and who was—and still is—a real type of true British manhood. There was Edna May, who came here with *The Belle of New York*, bidding London to 'Follow On'—which they did for years. There was Pauline Chase, Gracie Leigh, James Blakeley, Billie Burke (still as delightful as ever), Gladys Cooper, Zena and Phyllis Dare (both still flourishing), and a host of others.

The Middle Class playgoers adored them all; but there was no familiarity which breeds contempt. The great ones of the Stage lived a life apart, separated from the everyday world by the footlights. Nor did the Middle Classes wish it any different. They were more sentimental, more romantic; they liked their divinities to remain divinities.

But the Middle Class wrote for their autographs; waited for hours at the stage-door to see them come out; bought picture-postcards of them by the million; vied with each other in snapping up new ones as soon as published, kept them in albums to gaze at entranced, sent them to each other, swapped and exchanged them—such was the thraldom in which the Theatre and its people held them. They bought real photographs of them too, 'cabinet' size, which they cherished. If they saw one of their revered stars in the street it was something to talk over for months. The 'mummers' had mystery then—'ballyhoo" had not stripped it from them.

The provinces had their own stars, and saw the London plays performed by players they knew and liked, under the banner of George Edwardes or of George Dance, the Napoleon of touring companies. Prices in the provinces were five to four shillings for stalls, and downwards in proportion. The gallery was sixpence and the pit a shilling, with 'early doors' extra. Most people patronized the early doors. Every city and town had its theatre or theatres, and every important suburb as well. Going to town to see the actor-managers was quite a journey—but worth it. It meant a train to one of the termini, a bus to the nearest point to the theatre, and a bus back with a fine scramble for the last train. But the Middle Class people sat in that last train and mused on the glories they had seen and the joys they had experienced. The programme was read all over again. They knew little of back-stage life and thought it all marvellous.

Theatrical companies went all over the kingdom, taking the drama in all its forms—even to the smallest villages. These had 'fit-up' companies, who played in small halls, fitting up their own proscenium arch to make the platform a stage. And there were portable theatres which were built up at a small place—they were made of wood and, after the performance had been given, were pulled down again, put on the carts like a circus tent, and went on to the next place. The actors did the putting up and pulling down, besides the playing. Prices suited the pockets.

West End prices were: Stalls, 10s. 6d.; Dress Circle, 7s. 6d and 6s.; Upper Circle, 5s. and 4s.; Pit, 2s. 6d.; and Gallery, 1s. There was no tax at all. The benefits of victory had not been experienced then.

Then there were the music-halls. That was a definite phase of the British life. They have departed altogether. One or two places remain which call themselves by that name, or describe themselves as 'theatres of variety', but they are no more like the true music-hall than is the popular Saturday item of that name on the radio. The music-hall cannot live today as it lived in the days of the sovereign. It was the entertainment of the people by the people for the people. The people themselves are different, so that the music-hall they knew has gone. Fundamentally the people may be the same, but they are not so by habit. The music-hall was typical of the age of beef and beer, of high spirits, of deep drinking, of money to spend, of cheap prices, and of a fearless outlook and a peaceful land. It was a place for a man with a song in his heart—and in his mouth as well. It had no place for reticence; it was downright, it shouted, it made a noise, it enjoyed itself and it made the people enjoy themselves as well.

In an age which believed in delicacy, it was indelicate; in an age when refinement was practised, it was unrefined. It was the contrast which kept the balance. Its appeal was essentially male. It had come from the 'pub' and the tavern, and whilst it retained something of that atmosphere, it prospered. For even in the Middle Class there were myriads who wanted a night out, a night off from conventionality; a night when they could let themselves go and have a fling.

That was where the music-hall came in. It was down to earth; it was the real true atmosphere of the old bar-parlour—and all men of the Golden Age liked that. Here was a place where they were not expected to be the courteous escorts of their womenfolk; here was a place where they could be a man amongst men. The music-hall had its regular devotees, for it was a club to the clubless. It gave the people, not only the Middle Classes but the Lower Classes as well, what they wanted in the manner in which they wanted it, in a way they understood. It sang and it pattered of the unpaid rent, the mother-in-law, the lodger, the broker's man, kippers, unfaithful swains and faithless damsels, erring wives and husbands—the wife who carried on with the lodger and the husband with the barmaid or a lady from 'Gay Paree'. It joked about physical violence, the seaside holidays and beer. It jeered at foreigners, it glorified this country. It gave the people their patriotism in doses hot and strong—and people were patriotic then. It could be incredibly sentimental in a senti-mental age—it could exalt marital bliss, as it did in the classic 'My Old Dutch'. It could show the yearning heart of the exile, as it did in 'The Miner's Dream of Home'.

It was vulgar, but openly vulgar. Its vulgarity was vulgar in the real meaning of the word. It could be coarse on occasion, but with honest coarseness. It was very, very seldom 'blue', as that azure tint is known today. It would have drawn the line heavily at many of the jokes which today convulse audiences of both sexes. It was, above all, a friendly, homely place, with no 'side' and no pretence of being other than what it was. Many of its greatest performers never cracked a 'blue' gag in their lives: men like Harry Tate, Eugene Stratton, George Lashwood, Arthur

Lennard, Dan Leno—scores of them. A few earned reputations for being very naughty. It was mild to the 'naughtiness' of today.

The traditions of the naughtiness of Marie Lloyd grew up because gentlemen with lewd minds who invented smutty stories—reputed to come from the Stock Exchange—could father them on to Marie. "Heard Marie's latest?" they would ask. But she never told them. The supreme artist, whom Sarah Bernhardt considered the finest performer in this country, could—and did—express much with a look, a wink, a turn of the head, a most ravishing smile. But read her old songs, sing them, and then attend a cabaret of today. Or a so-called music-hall. The result will be astonishing.

The music-hall folk were different in every way from the stage folk. In the music-halls the provincials and the Londoners saw the same stars. To a music-hall top-liner there was no difference between London and Liverpool, Mayfair or Manchester, Ealing or Exeter, Brixton or Birmingham. They were 'dates' to be worked. On the halls they were 'performers', not actors or actresses. They did not 'play'—they 'worked'. The difference is subtle but important. There was no false art or hybrid culture about the halls or its people. They were highly skilled individuals in an Individual Age, relying on themselves and their talent. That is why the music-hall was so great.

Middle Class ladies seldom, if ever, went to the music-halls. They did not go until the music-hall had made itself respectable, had forgone its drink licence, and taken to referring to its stalls as 'fauteuils', and sacrificed its old-time raffishness to velvet and gold paint. That was, naturally, near the end of its life. Ladies might go to the Palace, in Shaftesbury Avenue, which had started as an English opera-house and failed, which had become a Theatre of Varieties and succeeded—thanks to the magic touch of Charles Morton, the Father of the Halls; indeed, their creator. The Palace was the smartest Theatre of Varieties the world ever knew. 'Boiled shirts' and bare shoulders filled its stalls—but it purveyed Variety, not Music-Hall. Marie Lloyd herself nearly failed there. One song, however, saved her.

The ladies might be taken, under very heavy male escort, to see Zanfretta, or Genée, dance at the Empire, or Leonora 'posture' at the Alhambra, for these two halls were the strongholds of ballet then.

At the Empire, Katti Lanner and Wilhelm (British, despite his name) reigned, and when Genée danced 'Coppelia' the lid blew off London. So it did, in a different way, when Fred Farren—one of the greatest male dancers and mimes of the world—danced the Apache Dance with Beatrice Collier.

The ladies were never allowed to penetrate into the Empire

Promenade. Women were there, but not ladies. The Promenade was, except for its main attraction, a male preserve. And the attraction was the cream of the frail beauties of the town. That place has no counterpart. But Middle Class young men rejoiced to pay their 5s.—a lot of money—to have the daring and bohemian thrill of a night spent in the Empire Promenade, to watch the wicked ladies as they floated—none of them seemed to walk—to and fro; wonderful women wonderfully dressed, noiseless on the rich carpets, overwhelmingly alluring in their known 'naughtiness', yet rather frightening to youth as well, in an atmosphere of rich, blue cigar-smoke, frangipane, patchouli and the heady scent of champagne, whilst the sound of a wonderful orchestra from below made a fitting background.

Some of the more daring Middle Class young men would engage the sirens in conversation and even buy them a box of chocolates (which they immediately sold back to the girl behind the chocolate bar). They would observe, however, that after the first few words they were not very successful in holding the wicked lady's attention and that her eyes would roam elsewhere. Those women were quick in summing-up anyone who meant real business. But the young men would boast of it for weeks, and be regarded by their less reckless companions as desperate blades who knew life and were regular Don Juans. But very little harm came of it for the young man.

The Empire Promenade was often attacked. Mrs. Ormiston Chant led a determined onslaught, but overdid it. The mass of the public were against her, especially the Middle Class and even the aristocratic youth of the day. She did not succeed in closing the Promenade, but she became the most popular 'Guy' of the year on Guy Fawkes' Day. To placate the Puritan outcry the management tried to put up a sort of screen, and enclosed some of the bars with a sort of wooden filigree work. The young men pulled it down. Active in this kind of protest was a youth since destined to lead his country through great dangers. He was not perhaps of the Middle Class, but many of his supporters were.

The 'bill' at the Empire troubled few. It was the Promenade that mattered. The ballets, however, were always watched, save by the regulars who used the place as what it called itself in its own sub-title— 'The Cosmopolitan Club of the World'. And so it was. What prudery and puritanism could not do—and how could it when Middle Class men of mature years and terrific respectability would admit with pride that in their young days they had been 'chucked' from the Empire?— the disappearance of the Golden Sovereign soon accomplished. Very soon after paper money came into being—in 1916—that Promenade was closed—and closed for good. It also was of the Sovereign.

The Alhambra, though older than the Empire, never had quite the same glamour, or the same exclusive richness. It was more the true music-hall. The women in its promenade were not so surely the aristocrats of their ancient profession. But it was a delightful place and, despite its Moorish design and decoration, it was very British indeed.

Yet, for all its strength, it was the music-hall which let in the cinema and so helped to dig its own grave. The first cinema peeped into London at Olympia in 1895, as a side-show run by the great Sir Augustus Harris of Drury Lane. It got into the bill, first at the Empire and then at the Alhambra, in the year following. It was the last turn, and was described as 'The Bioscope'. From that humble position it emerged. It spread into empty shops without projection-boxes, where the film was shown in the open and the reel ran down into a basket, and the risk of fire was immense.

The Middle Classes did not go to the pictures much then, except as an experiment, to see flickering figures jerking along with extreme velocity in what appeared to be permanent tropical rain. But the cinema had come to stay. It got into halls, it invaded small suburban theatres, like the Parkhurst in Holloway. It was cheap at 3d., 6d. and 9d. It had a pianist who pounded away all the time, suiting the music to the action and having set tunes for situations—'Hearts and Flowers' always accompanied a sad or sentimental scene. Captions told the story—'Came the Dawn', they said. Trains dashed headlong at the audience; there were exciting chases.

To attract female custom, the cinema proprietor afterwards gave away free cups of tea and biscuits to their patrons. Of course, the films were silent. The first stars were anonymous, but the public got to know Max Linder and John Bunny—the fat man with the cheerful face. Shortly before the end of the era it had established itself in the West End. It had become a habit. And the spearhead of the victorious attack was a little music-hall comedian called Charlie Chaplin.

But the music-hall itself was as boisterous and hearty as the generation it served. They loved it and they believed in it. It was something of their own. They cheered when it told them, 'You Can't Beat the Boys of the Bulldog Breed Who Made Old England's Name'. They yelled approval when it stated, 'A Little British Army Goes a Damn' Long Way'. They had implicit faith in 'The Navy, a Fighting Navy, That Keeps Our Foes at Bay'. And were not they, and the music-halls, quite right?

You could smoke in a music-hall, but not in a theatre; you could have your drink and watch the show at the same time. You could sing your head off with English songs on English subjects—and you did. The Middle Class man who spent his evening at the music-hall for a very few shillings got full value for his money. There was a quieter atmosphere at the London Coliseum, where Sir Oswald Stoll created a family theatre of varieties by really putting music into the music-hall, and making it very refined indeed. It was a great success.

But the men preferred the places where they could smoke and drink; they saw twenty star turns, so they saw variety; they heard songs, and joined in those which have become the new folk-songs of this land, which the children of the Paper Age have come to know as well as they did. They saw, for a shilling in the gallery, one and sixpence in the pit and three to four shillings elsewhere (and about half those prices in the provinces and suburbs), the greatest individual artistes the world has ever known, giving their performances with consummate skill—individuals in an individual manner, the true exponents of the individual age.

Pantomime improved beyond all measure when Sir Augustus Harris imported the music-hall people into Drury Lane, the home of pantomime —there have been no pantomimes since like those of his and Arthur Collins's; and no melodramas either, for that matter. The people who would never dream of going to a music-hall saw its stars, like Dan Leno (the greatest of them all) and Herbert Campbell, at Drury Lane, and thought them marvellous. They did not know these artistes were just the same at the London Pavilion, the Tivoli, the Oxford and elsewhere.

But the man who went to the music-halls knew all about that, for he could see Dan Leno, Herbert Campbell, Gus Elen, Albert Chevalier, Harry Champion, Eugene Stratton, Harry Fragson, La Milo, Ernest Shand, R. G. Knowles, Little Tich, Marie Lloyd, Harry Randall, Florrie Forde, Vesta Victoria, Victoria Monks, Clarice Mayne and 'That' (James W. Tate), the MacNaughtons, the Poluskis, Harry Bedford, Joe O'Gorman, Mark Sheridan, Harry Tate, Chirgwin, Cinquevalli, Joe Elvin, George Lashwood, Harry Lauder, Vesta Tilley—the superb!— Phil Ray, Fred Karno's wonderful sketches, Arthur Lennard, Paul Martinetti and his shows, Charles Coborn, the Brothers Egbert, George Robey—the Prime Minister of Mirth himself—and hundreds more.

He could roar out songs which are still sung today; he could marvel at the acrobats, the tumblers, the wire-walkers, the Riseley Acts, the Trampoline Acts, the jugglers, the contortionists, the performing animals, Diavalo looping the gaping loop and other acts too numerous to mention. And the songs he sang were true British songs, English, Scottish and Irish, though seldom Welsh; songs of the people who loved them and cherished them too. He could have, and did have, wonderful value, good drink, plenty of tobacco and a night of enjoyment in gay surroundings such as he cannot obtain today.

And when it was over he went out into the streets where the lamps were all alight, where the 'pubs' were still open, in which he could get whatever he chose to order for a few coppers, and he could whistle or sing the songs he had just heard, with his pal, as they jogged home on their horse-bus, or later jerked along on their 'Vanguard'. No black-out, no austerity, no fear of tomorrow, and the certainty of some of those golden sovereigns at the week-end; those coins which, like the 'Little British Army' of the halls, were so small but which went such a 'damn' long way'!

And he and his friend parted with a cheery, happy 'Good night' and the exhortation not to be late in the morning.

They were not late, either. They worked as well as they played in the days of the sovereign.

CHAPTER XVIII

When Britain Held the Championships

DURING THE ERA OF THE GOLDEN SOVEREIGN GREAT BRITAIN WAS
supreme in sports. It held practically all the championships, except the
heavy-weight boxing title. The reason was not far to seek. It was almost
the only country in the world, with the exception of America, which
devoted itself to sport.

This country is still devoted to sport. But the Middle Class people of
those days were to a far greater degree participants and not onlookers.
Every young man worthy of the name played games. The small proportion who looked on were regarded as slackers.

The reason was that it was very largely the age of the amateur.
Professional sport, although steadily creeping in, had not reached the
dimensions of today. Nor did sport, with the exception of cricket and
racing, figure much on the programme except on Saturdays. There
were, of course, no Sunday games.

But on Saturdays the youth of the country girded themselves for
cricket in the summer and football in the winter. As regards the latter, it
was divided between Soccer and Rugger, although even then more
played the former than the latter. But the Rugger players regarded themselves as the aristocrats of this game, and rather looked down on the
players of Soccer.

Golf had not assumed the general appeal it now makes; it was regarded
as an expensive game and the general run of the Middle Classes did not
play it. They got plenty of walking exercise in the ordinary way, for
everyone walked more and rode less.

But so great was the preoccupation with sport that the Poet of Empire,
Rudyard Kipling, gave terrific and widespread offence when he assailed
the 'flannelled fool at the wicket and the muddied oaf at the goal'. It
was worse than his *gaffe* about 'The Widow of Windsor'. The whole of
the country was affronted. Had not the Battle of Waterloo been won on
the playing-fields of Eton? That was firmly believed. It did not matter to
them that Old Etonians were in a very small minority at that particular
bickering, and that the rank and file who stood the hard pounding had
never been there; indeed, few had been to any school at all.

But the idea was good enough for them, and they resented Kipling's
attack. There was even a special verse about it in that great topical song,
'Peace, Peace', which Rutland Barrington (who did those things to per-

fection) sang in *A Country Girl* at Daly's Theatre. But, having shaken an admonitory finger at the great Anglo-Indian who, as he sang, 'had poured out his soul on the oaf at the goal, and the flannelled fool at the wicket', he went on to say, "We'll forgive all his rails, if he'll tell us some tales of the beautiful valley of Bhong." Kipling did that, in effect, and all was peace again.

Professional football was strongest in the North of England, although it received great impetus in the South when, in 1901, Tottenham Hotspur won the Cup, beating Sheffield United by 3–1, after a draw. Cup Ties were then played at the Crystal Palace, and the gates were nothing like so big, nor the arrangements so expert, as at Wembley.

It was not until 1914, however, the very last year of the Golden Sovereign, that a monarch attended a Cup Final, and that was King George V. The professional game had been steadily growing since 1895, although the Middle Classes still thought it rather *infra dig.* and exalted the amateur status, as represented by the Corinthians, the Casuals, the 'Varsities, the Civil Service, the London Caledonians and such clubs as those. Tottenham Hotspur gained much support because for some time it boasted an amateur centre forward, and a very brilliant one, in Vivian Woodward. There were some great names, however, amongst whom Steve Bloomer gleamed. Now, football may claim to be the national game of the country. Its season lasts almost the whole year round. In fact, that incorrigible jester of the theatrical profession—Lauri Wylie—asserts that there are now five seasons—spring, summer, autumn, winter and football.

Young men of the Sovereign Age who in winter did not play football played hockey, which girls played too. There were mixed teams, though why hockey should have been considered ladylike is extraordinary. It is a rough game at which one can get badly hurt. Girls never played football then, and the sight of them in jerseys and shorts would have caused a riot. It would also probably have led to their arrest. They played hockey in short skirts—that is, half-way down the calf and sometimes to the ankle—and they mostly wore tam-o'-shanters on their heads, with woollen blouses and woollen stockings. Men were very gallant, and seldom did their best when there were women in the game. It was not considered sportsmanlike to do so. The ladies must have a chance. Today the Amazons give as good as they get. But of course femininity was of importance then—the line between the sexes was very strongly drawn.

Some young men played lacrosse, but it was never really popular. Football was the great winter game. It was never played in August. Professional football began on 1st September and amateur football early in October. The cricket season died hard in those days, and September usually seemed to be a delightfully mellow month.

There was a great deal of cross-country running, paper-chases and a lot of pedestrianism, which reached its height when the Stock Exchange started their walk to Brighton. Everyone started to walk to Brighton. An actor attempted the feat in full evening dress and dancing-pumps. He did not finish the course, but he finished the pumps. Indeed, he nearly finished himself.

There was a little beagling around the London suburbs, for the country was very near the town then, and hares ran where now crowds and motor-buses roar. Indoor sports included gymnastics—there were many gymnasiums, one of the leading clubs being the German Gymnastic Society, with its hall near King's Cross Station. It had, despite its name, a preponderance of British members. Its premises were, by irony of Fate, destroyed by a German bomb in the First World War. Its great rival was the Orion Gymnastic Club, and the contests between these two societies were 'needle fights'. Boxing—amateur boxing—was very strong, and fostered by the Amateur Boxing Association. There were many excellent clubs, like the Belsize, the Polytechnic, Fulham B.C.; and amateur boxing was extremely popular and very good. The championships were held for years at the Alexandra Palace. They lasted from 10 a.m. to 10 p.m., and some of the contestants had plenty of fights during the day. Professional boxing was still regarded as mere pugilism. It did not come out into the open and attract great crowds until the era was nearly ending. It still, however, had an aura of some romance left over from the Regency period, and the names of the giants of the prize-ring days were remembered.

Professional boxing, so far as London was concerned, was confined almost entirely to the National Sporting Club, which was founded in 1892. The sport received tremendous new vitality from Lord Lonsdale, the *beau ideal* of British sportsmen, when he instituted the Lonsdale Belt in 1909. Yet this country, the true home of boxing, had only held the Heavyweight Championship once since the days of the prize ring, when the Cornish-born Bob Fitzsimmons beat Jim Corbett in 1897, to lose to Jim Jeffries in 1899.

The Middle Classes, by and large, had not much to do with the National Sporting Club. They did not begin to take much interest in professional boxing until the great ballyhoo which began in 1910–1911, with the exploitation of Billy Wells, Tommy Burns, Jack Johnson, Joe Beckett and the magnificent Frenchman Georges Carpentier. Then the craze for fights spread through all classes, and the Albert Hall and Olympia could be filled to overflowing.

Although we lacked heavyweights, we had other splendid boxers like Dick Burge, Dick Smith (a most unlucky boxer), Jim Driscoll, Johnny Summers, Johnny Basham and—most wonderful of all—Jimmy Wilde, a true world champion. But only the males of the Middle Classes went to fights before the First World War. They were not the thing for ladies.

There were plenty of old fighters about who had battled and won titles in the days of the 'raw 'uns'. There was old Jim Carney, who could neither read nor write but who had, in his last fight, gone seventy-two rounds with the skin-gloves against an American champion, and beaten him. Modern boxers would die at the thought. They nearly made old Jim die, too. He would spit on the ground in contempt when he could be induced to go to a contest.

There were recurrent crazes for roller-skating. At one time Olympia became a vast roller-skating rink. Both sexes took part in this exercise—or sport.

The game of ping-pong burst upon the Middle Class in the late 'nineties and became a perfect furore. Table-tennis, which developed from it, has become a game of great speed and skill. But ping-pong was a very different game. It was played in all Middle Class homes, and—at the start—on the dining-room table, denuded of its cloth for that purpose. This did not please the housewife until she, too, surrendered to its charm and excitement.

It lived up to its name, when it first came in, by being played with an old-fashioned kind of battledore, with vellum instead of strings, like a little banjo with two sides. This provided the 'pong', the 'ping' being produced when the celluloid ball struck the table. There was a lot of excitement when the ball bounced off into the open coal-fire and vanished in a whiff of flame and smoke. There would be disputes as to the rules concerning this, and the general impression was that, like back-garden cricket, 'over the wall' was 'out', and that the striker lost the point, even if he or she had cleared the tiny net across the table. There are professionals at this game now. Then, they were all amateurs.

Croquet was played by ladies, old men and curates—who were usually experts.

Bowls was an old man's game and had nothing like the widespread popularity it now commands; nor did women play it. But there was an indoor species called 'Carpet Bowls', played with china balls bearing distinctive stripes and about the size of a cricket ball.

There was a lot of amateur athletics, and the Amateur Athletic Society was its central figure.

Tennis, so universally popular today, was lawn-tennis. This was a game at which both sexes could play together. It was a much gentler, more leisurely game than it has now become and nothing like so strenuous. That speed came from abroad. Young men did not devote themselves to it as they do today. It was the more middle-aged men who were the backbone of the numberless clubs. If young men played, they did so as a change from cricket, or to please their sisters and *fiancées*. They looked upon it as a little effeminate. The hard court had not arrived—it was always played on grass, except in some public parks, where asphalt courts were provided for damp weather.

For many years the championships were held, if not entirely by this country, at least in the British Empire; and it was a great Middle Class game. It did not cost a lot, it was excellent exercise, it had a good social side, and it was also a good stepping-off place for that marriage which was the career of all Middle Class girls. There were—as there still are—clubs all over the place; perhaps not quite so numerous as today, but plenty of them.

There was not only lawn-tennis at those clubs, but strawberry teas, dances and concerts. The girls looked nice in their tennis-kit—their ankle-length skirts, mostly white; their coloured belts; their blouses and their shady hats. Many wore straw hats like 'gents' boaters', either black or white. The game showed off a pretty figure and a pretty arm, and there was no 'make-up' to run, and worry about, on hot days. There were flirtations too, between the 'sets'. The girls did not wear shorts or trousers. The young men looked athletic and debonair in their white flannels, their club belts, ties and blazers. And it was not too athletic for the ladies, either.

The great names in tennis in those days—amateur again—were the Dohertys, A. W. Gore, Wilding, Roper Barrett and N. Brookes, and as regards the ladies there were Mrs. Hillyard, Miss Cooper, Miss Douglass, Miss May Sutton and Mrs. Lambert Chambers. After the golden sovereign had disappeared in the vortex of the First World War, France was to send us dynamic players of both sexes, including the amazing Mademoiselle Suzanne Lenglen, who revolutionized the game with Gallic volatility. Tennis was never the same again. . . .

One of the great sporting events of the year which held complete sway over the Middle Classes was the University Boat Race. The Middle Classes themselves did a bit of rowing, but not very often at the 'Varsities. They belonged to Rowing Clubs, or they just went 'up the river'—the 'River' being understood by all as the Thames—and enjoyed it to the full. The river was a great resort then; it had not been spoiled. The upper reaches were peaceful solitudes, for they had not been invaded by the motor-car in its annihilation of distance. It was as leisurely as its own stream. There were no motor or electric launches until the era was ending, but the steam-launch was there, and regarded with considerable disfavour. You rowed (or sculled); you punted or you canoed, and you took it easy. You wore your whites, the girl of your choice reclined in the back seat (if it were a skiff) on lots of coloured cushions and, charmingly if unsuitably gowned, made a pretence at steering.

There was no hurry, and gentry who were inclined to put their heads down and their backs into it and get up speed were politely but sternly requested to "Look ahead, sir!" when collisions seemed imminent. The locks themselves set the pace, and you could not indulge in speed as you sat in your boat, the hitcher ready, as the water ran either out or in, and you sank down or came to the top; and the lock-keeper collected his dues.

It was all a nice, gentlemanly, Golden Sovereign Age recreation, with no vulgar hurry about it at all. If you were an energetic or restless soul who recoiled from the temporary imprisonment of the locks, you hauled or pushed your boat over the rollers. That, of course, meant the disruption of everyone in it, who had to get out and embark again when the boat had negotiated the iron rollers that took her up the incline.

There were lovely little backwaters, with willows for complete shade and screen for 'spooning' couples, where the roar of the weir made music, and swans floated by, moorhens scuttered and ducks bobbed about. The banks were flower-decked, and there were mists of forget-me-nots, flowering rushes, or purple loosestrife, according to season—and water-lilies too. Pike basked, and you could watch the fish amongst the weeds, and the water-voles plop into the stream and paddle across. And all that within a very few miles of London, where the banks are now modernized and cemented.

An evening on the river or a deep summer night, with the moon shining, with a gaily-coloured Chinese lantern in the prow, and a banjo playing somewhere from a flower-embowered houseboat, is something unknown today in the way of restful, soothing enjoyment.

Henley Regatta was never a truly Middle Class event, although its results were scanned with interest. And the nation was shaken when a foreign team won the Grand Challenge Cup at Henley in 1906; the club Nautique de Gand (Belgium) beat Trinity Hall, Cambridge, paddling home by an easy three lengths and taking the coveted trophy abroad for the first time. It shook English rowing circles to their core, and confidence was only restored when, in September of the same year, Cambridge beat Harvard over the Boat-Race course by two lengths. Cambridge, it was said, could have won by much more, but kindness of heart prevented them.

That was the sort of sportsmanship which obtained under the Sovereign.

However, if the Middle Classes did not go to Henley, they went to the smaller, Saturday afternoon Regattas like Molesey, etc., and thoroughly enjoyed themselves.

But so far as boating and the river went, the rowing event of the year was the Boat Race. The Middle Classes were as deeply enthralled as though every one of them had been to one or other of the Universities. This obsession started in early youth. Suddenly in the first days of spring the youth of the country broke out into a rash of blue, either light or dark. It was worse than measles, and far more violent. Boys at school suddenly found themselves in the opposite camp to their bosom pals. That nice boy next door, who had seemed a 'decent chap', although he did not go to your school, became either a firm ally or a desperate foe. Former friends became deadly enemies. For the Light and Dark Blues had a hearty contempt for each other.

Why they were supporters of the sides they cherished they could not tell you. They just knew instinctively they were Oxford or Cambridge and let it go at that. Probably it was hereditary, and family influence accounted for it; there was very seldom a personal reason at all. But they were firm, even grim, partisans of their colours. The Boat Race occupied their minds completely.

The names of the crews, their colleges, the weights—all were well known. Chances were discussed, even fought over, and every boy, and most girls, wore their favours. You wore a light- or dark-blue monkey made of some kind of fluffy velvety material, with a bushy tail, on a pin; you wore a leaden medal with the Arms of the favoured University on it, suspended on a ribbon of the right colour which was fastened to a safety-pin at the back of a leaden boat and two crossed oars. You wore a rosette, or one of those 'buttons' printed with a light- or dark-blue flag. There were a multitude of favours. As the day of the race grew near, excitement reached fever-heat. Although only the tiniest proportion ever saw the race, it held them fast in its toils. Some of the more fanatical children even included a plea for their favourite's victory in their nightly prayers.

There were rival chants, like the incantations of witch-doctors, or maybe battle-cries, which one side hurled against the other. The Oxonians would sing:

> "Oxford, Oxford, rowing on for ever!
> Cambridge in a matchbox floating down the river,"

to which the Cantabs would reply:

"Cambridge upstairs, eating all the cakes—
Oxford downstairs, washing up the plates!"

The result was awaited with breathless anxiety. There was no radio then to give a running commentary of the race and to make the result known as the winners passed the post. It took much longer for the suspenseto be lifted. But there was a day of jubilant rejoicing by the victors —and then it was over for another year, the badges put away and feuds forgotten until another spring.

It was noted that girls inclined to favour Cambridge, possibly on account of the colour. For a long time during the Sovereign Era the Dark Blues had it all their own way—for Oxford won from 1890 to 1898 inclusive. Cambridge got a look-in in 1889 and 1900, Oxford won in 1901, Cambridge from 1902 to 1904 Oxford in 1905, Cambridge in 1906–7-8, and then Oxford were out on their own from 1909 to 1913, with Cambridge winning in 1914, the last year of the Golden Sovereign. Sixteen wins to nine in favour of the Dark Blues.

Horse-racing in those days was 'The Sport of Kings'. Except to the Derby, the Middle Classes went little to racecourses. Transport and time off were the bar. Racing was an affair of professionals and the Upper and Liesured Classes. The Middle Class man might go on a Bank Holiday, because there were always meetings near town; or to "Ally-Pally" to a Saturday afternoon meeting, but that was the extent of it in general.

Women of the Middle Classes seldom went racing at all.

That is not to say that the Middle Class man did not have his bet. He most certainly did. But he did his betting away from the course. It had a strong hold on him. Preachers inveighed against the amount of gambling. Compared with today, with its Dogs and Football Pools, the amount was negligible. But the Middle Class man gambled. He read all the news in the papers about racing. He studied 'form' and consulted the 'Naps' as he does today. And he lost his money just as easily. He helped to enrich bookmakers like Dicky Dunn, an outstanding figure of the day. He knew all about horses and the jockeys at second hand, even if he seldom saw them. He knew all about Tod Sloan, who revolutionized racing by riding on his horse's neck with shortened stirrup-leathers, whereas the English jockeys had always ridden with a long leather. Men like Loates, Cannon, Madden, Trigg and the Reiffs were the star jockeys.

When the King won the Derby—or any big race—the whole country rejoiced, even if they were the losers. Herbert Jones was for years the Royal jockey. King Edward VII won the Derby three times during this period—twice as Prince of Wales, with 'Persimmon' and 'Diamond Jubilee', and once as King, with 'Minoru', which went by the post in a

A day's outing before the Motor Coach arrived—the Char-a-banc of the Golden Age

The horse tram—a leisurely method of leisurely days

The "Growler"—a four-wheeled cab

The Fire Engine of the pre-motor days

desperate finish with 'Louviers'. People held their breath, but the King raised his hat, and the cheers followed it. The verdict was a short head. One would have liked to have seen a 'photo-finish' of that race.

His Majesty was surrounded on the course by his enthusiastic subjects, who patted him on the back in the most democratic manner and cheered wildly.

There was a tremendous sensation in 1898 when 'Jeddah', ridden by Otto Madden, came in at 100—1; and again in 1908 when 'Signorinetta', a filly, won at the same price. It was owned and trained by Signor Ginistrelli, and it was the only horse he had. It also won the Oaks—but at 3—1. 'Sunstar' won in 1910 after going lame during the race.

There was tragedy—double tragedy—in 1913, when Suffragettes interfered with the race, and one of them was killed. Her sacrifice did little to endear her cause to the racing fraternity. Also 'Craganour', first past the post, was disqualified and the race awarded to 'Aboyeur'—a most unpopular decision. 'Craganour' was favourite, 'Aboyeur' was 100—1.

Other great horses were 'Tagalie' (first grey to win the Derby), 'Spearmint', 'Orby', 'Cicero', 'St. Amant', 'Sceptre', 'Pretty Polly', 'Rock Sand' and 'Flying Fox'—although not all of them won the Derby. The great owners were the King (Edward VII), the Duke of Westminster, Lord Rosebery, L. de Rothschild, Major Loder, the Joels and Robert Sievier, whose horse 'Sceptre' won the Thousand Guineas, the Two Thousand Guineas, the Oaks and the Leger, whilst Major Loder's 'Pretty Polly' won the Two Thousand Guineas, the Oaks and the Leger. George Edwardes, of Daly's and the Gaiety Theatres, was a popular owner of good horses, the best being 'San Toi'. The 'Profession' backed the 'Guv'nor's' horses to a man—and woman.

Derby Day on the road was a far more picturesque thing then than now. It was the true day of the Horse. All the vehicles for the greatest part of the period were horse-drawn. The roads to Epsom were thronged with four-in-hands—the smart way of going—whose drivers had veils twisted round their 'toppers' and often little dolls in them; there were carriages of all kinds, phaetons, charabancs and brakes with a concertina or cornet accompaniment; dog-carts, tradesmen's carts of all kinds with the family sitting on chairs taken out of the house—every form of vehicle. Costers in gala attire, with their 'Arriets in all the glory of enormous feathered hats, drove in 'donkey-shays' and supplied wit, back-chat and vituperation. Whips were decorated with the colours of favourite runners. There was good-nature everywhere, and a real holiday mood. Children ran alongside yelling, "Throw out your mouldy coppers!" and the Epsom-bound complied.

T

This throwing out of coppers was a custom. Lord Mayor's Show Day had this demand as well, but mischievous people in offices would make pennies and halfpennies almost red-hot before throwing them, and enjoy the yells which this caused among the scrambling children.

There were no hot pennies on Derby Day—when all coppers were regarded, for some unknown reason, as being mouldy. The little beggars kept up a succession of cartwheels beside the coaches until the 'mouldy coppers' were showered.

There was a big boom in physical culture brought about by 'Sandow' the strong man, who ran a college devoted to it, and whose exercise machines and developers had a big sale. And there was also a boom in wrestling. This was a purely professional affair of experts in the Graeco-Roman style. It was exploited by showmen—and not the least among them was Sir Charles B. Cochran.

The great figure of professional wrestling was Georges Hackenschmidt —the 'Russian Lion', as he was described on the bills. He was a quite charming man of immense strength and very considerable skill. The Graeco-Roman method was a lot slower than the popular 'Catch-as-Catch-Can'—which might have brought the displays to a too speedy conclusion and been bad for the box-office. Hackenschmidt conquered challenger after challenger, and then was matched with Madrali, the "Terrible Turk"—an enormous man of enormous physical strength. But there was not much that was terrible about the 'Terrible Turk' when the 'Russian Lion' got to grips with him. He went out of the ring with a broken arm, head first, in less than no time.

There were quite a lot of these mountainous wrestlers with arms like the cables of battleships—one was Zbysco—and they were all 'Terrible' Somethings—'Terrible Greeks', 'Terrible Bulgars' and the like. Georges Hackenschmidt—who was never billed as 'Terrible'—was the master of them all.

There was also a rage on Ju-Jitsu, introduced here by Bankier, whose professional name was 'Apollo', another star of the physical culture movement. He brought over a tiny Jap called 'Yokio Tani', who, by means of this then quite new system of 'grips' and 'locks' reduced people much bigger and stronger than himself to complete impotence. It swept the country. It appealed to everybody, for it was a means whereby the less muscular of the community could be on a par with the Samsons thereof. There was a lot of money made out of it.

Lord Roberts—the beloved 'Bobs'—started a movement for rifle-shooting. He went about the country pointing out how unprepared it was for war, and trying to found 'A Nation of Riflemen'. Miniature

Rifle Clubs sprang up everywhere—helped by a serial in the *Daily Mail* about the invasion of England.

Fencing, quoits, pigeon-flying, whippet-racing—all had devotees, but none of them was a really Middle Class sport. Nor was skittles—and the dart craze was not born. Skating was indulged in when occasion served. But the greatest and the most absorbing game at that time for the Middle Classes—and all the other classes as well—was Cricket. This was the truly National Game, and we were unrivalled at it, except for the Australians. That did not matter because they were, in the parlance of those days, 'Colonials'—people of the same blood—which made it different. The same was felt when New Zealand sent the 'All Blacks' here to shake British Rugby prestige—once again it was 'in the family'.

Every man followed cricket, although no woman ever understood it. Boys of all ages knew the batting and bowling averages by heart. They could tell you who made the first century of the season; who was the first to amass the first thousand runs; to capture the first hundred wickets. These were important items of news, as indeed was every outstanding incident in the County Championship. Contents bills of newspapers at midday simply chronicled 'Lunch Scores' and later 'Close of Play'. That was what really mattered. Special editions were rushed out with sensational bills like 'Surrey Collapse', and men dashed to buy.

The Middle Classes thought cricket, talked cricket, watched it when they could—and played it too. Test matches produced marvels of ingenuity in the way of excuses for absence from the office. The position of the counties in the Championship Table was a matter of the greatest moment to all. Cricket was the English standard. If a thing was 'not cricket'—it was not done.

Cricket suited the times. There was no hurry about it; it is a leisurely game always, except when some hurricane hitter gets busy with a burst. It was not etiquette to hurry to the wickets to bat, nor to dash from the field when out. It was not etiquette for the ingoing batsman to appear on the field before the outgoing one was lost to sight in the shadow of the Pavilion. It stopped for lunch, and it stopped for tea.

Boys on holiday asked for nothing better than a day at Lord's or the Oval. Men often spent their treasured fortnight's holiday watching the game.

And there were giants in the land. W. G. Grace's burly and bearded form still dominated the game—he had his own club, the London County Cricket Club, at the Crystal Palace and people went for the sole purpose of seeing him. At fifty-eight, in the year 1906, he scored seventy-four in the Gentlemen *v.* Players Match, and put up a wonderful bowling display too. No wonder he was called 'The Grand Old Man of Cricket'. Kent won the championship that year, and there was a discussion as to whether C. H. B. Marsham ought to stand down as Captain and give place to the younger J. R. Mason. Partisanship ran high, and the example of Lord Hawke of Yorkshire was quoted, and the fact that Surrey had not done so well since the retirement of its veteran captain, K. J. Key, was stressed by the champions of Age and Experience over the Youth which must be served.

It was indeed an age of giants. There was C. B. Fry—that amazing man who was first-class at every sport and is still so brilliant today; there was 'Ranji', the Indian Prince and one of the most expert batsmen who ever faced bowling; Abel, Hayward, Len Braund, J. T. Hearne, Lord Hawke, Lockwood, Richardson, C. J. Burnup, S. M. J. Woods, L. C. H. Palairet, Archie MacLaren, 'Plum' Warner, H. D. G. Leveson-Gower ('Shrimp'), Arthur Shrewsbury, the Gunns of Nottingham, the Quaifes of Warwick, Hirst, Haigh and Rhodes, Tunnicliffe, Tyldesley, Hornby, the Fosters of Worcestershire, Perrin and the Rev. F. H. Gillingham of Essex, A. O. Jones, J. W. H. T. ('Johnny-Won't-Hit-Today') Douglas, and Gilbert Jessop ('The Croucher').

Later came J. B. Hobbs. There was B. J. T. Bosanquet, who invented the 'Googlie', Tarrant, the Hon. F. S. Jackson, N. A. Knox, Mead, Woolley—scores more, who were all household names to the Middle Class males. And heroes too. In 1906 Hayward made more runs than anyone else had ever made in one season (his record has only just been lowered) and Hirst made 2,000 runs and took 200 wickets (a few more, actually, in each case). There was a dispute as to what W. G. Grace would have done in his prime if he had had such excellent wickets to play on as then obtained.

Cricket was a class-conscious game. It had professionals, of course. One of the great matches every season was 'Gentlemen v. Players'—a bit of nomenclature which always seemed a little hard on the 'Gentlemen'. But the apex of the season were the Test Matches, either here or in Australia. If over there, they were played during winter-time on this side, and there was the additional joy of being able to have an interest in cricket during the 'off' season. But wherever they were, Test Matches were affairs of breathless interest. The Middle Classes had not the advantage of a radio ball-by-ball description of the match; they either—a lucky minority—saw it themselves or they read every word about it in the papers—many-paged affairs then—which gave a Test enormous space.

Excitement always rose to fever-heat, but it seldom boiled over to the extent it did at the Oval during the last Test Match in 1902. It was played on August 11th, 12th and 13th, and so many schoolboys were able to be present, and one amongst them, who saw every ball bowled, will never forget that day. Australia won the toss and batted first.

Craig, the 'Surrey Poet', raced round the ground, shouting the news. This colourful character, who was something of a showman, used to harangue the crowd and sell his doggerel verses about cricket. He would keep in with both sides during a County Match, like a veritable 'Vicar of Bray' at cricket. "Surrey, the county of my birth!" he would proclaim: "Yorkshire" (or whatever side it was) "the place of my adoption!" He must have been adopted many times. Everyone knew him and he did very well. His poetry was terrible.

But when it came to a Test Match, then he was English to the backbone. Australia scored 324 in the first innings, with 42 from Victor Trumper, 52 from M. A. Noble and 64 not out from Hugh Trumble. England made a disastrous reply with 183. Hirst was top scorer with 43, J. T. Tyldesley next with 33, Braund and Lockwood made a useful 22 and 25 respectively, L. C. H. Palairet made 20, MacLaren (Captain) made 10— and the great Tom Hayward a 'duck'. Australia, in the second innings, came to grief as well. They could make only 121. Trumper was run out for 2. The only decent score was Clem Hill's 34, with a 21 from Warwick Armstrong.

The English heroes of that innings were Lockwood, the Surrey bowler, who took 5 wickets for 45 runs and bowled 6 'maidens', and Braund, who got 2 wickets for 15 runs. Trumble had accounted for England's first innings downfall with 8 wickets for 65 runs. This tall Australian had a curious delivery. He would take a fairly long run and come to the bowling-crease in a species of curve with his head leaning on his shoulder, appear to totter and then deliver the ball. He was a magnificent all-rounder. England was thus left with 262 runs to get—a pretty stiff proposition on the first inning's showing.

They made a terrible start. MacLaren was bowled by Saunders for 2, Palairet—a beautifully stylish batsman as a rule—fell to Saunders for 6, and the same bowler dismissed the reliable Tyldesley for a 'duck'. Tom Hayward—England's tower of strength—failed again, scoring only 7, and again it was Saunders who got him. The Hon. F. S. Jackson had come in, but with four of England's best out with only fifteen runs between them, the position was pretty desperate. Jackson was now joined by Gilbert Jessop.

The Australians had a poor opinion of this stocky, immensely strong Gloucester amateur, this forceful and unorthodox player, who adopted a curious crouching stance, but who could hit on occasion like a hurricane, and would always have been worth his place in any team for his fielding and change-bowling alone. But the Australians now regarded the game as being 'in the bag', and there was Homeric laughter from a detachment of Australian soldiers (over here for King Edward VII's Coronation) as this player went to the wicket with his rather sailor-like gait. But Jessop showed them what he could do.

As in war, so in cricket. England's hour of need produced the man. And in this case the man produced the sorely needed runs. Jessop did as he liked with the bowling, good as it was. If the field went deep, he hit them short and ran singles. As the field closed in he hit the ball right over their heads. And to the boundary. They could never get even with him. He hit a six and ran it out—and had to wait for Jackson to stagger round the wicket in an endeavour to recover his breath. He hit everything that came his way, no matter who bowled it—and that Australian team were almost all 'all-rounders'. Trumble, Noble, Saunders, Armstrong—it did not matter to 'The Croucher'. His eye was in, his mouth was set. He was 'showing' them.

Once only during that innings he 'played' two balls in succession, and the crowd, on its feet now with excitement, laughed uproariously. Jackson was out when he had scored an invaluable forty-nine—it was desperate bad luck to miss his half-century, and he felt it too, for he swung his bat round in exasperation. But he had been of the greatest service. He had stopped the rot.

Thick-set George Hirst joined Jessop. It was a time when this typical 'Tyke' was at his best. Jessop went on hitting. He never gave a chance; he scored 104 in seventy-five minutes, and when he was caught by Noble off Armstrong he went back to the Pavilion with such cheers ringing in his ears as only a crowd of English enthusiasts can give—and then only to a man who had turned a rout into a possible victory. He had completely nonplussed the Australians; but those soldiers who had laughed at him when he came in joined wholeheartedly in the applause as he walked off—the idol of the hour, and leaving also an imperishable record in the history of the Tests. Braund of Somerset—a grand 'all-rounder' whose flannels always had a tinge of yellow—could make only two; Lockwood made the same amount; but Lilley, the Warwick and England wicket-keeper, contributed sixteen valuable runs. The last man came in when there were still fifteen runs needed for victory.

That was an ordeal for any man. But the man was Wilfred Rhodes of Yorkshire, played then entirely for his slow bowling, but in years to come to be one of England's opening pair of batsmen. Rhodes, with his long face calm, and his demeanour as phlegmatic as if he were just going to the nets, joined his brother Yorkshireman, Hirst. Between them they fought it out. Grimly and carefully they fought it out, with the crowd going absolutely mad as, run by run, they closed that gap.

It took forty-five minutes to get those 15 runs—but they got them. When the hit was made, productive of a single, which made the match a draw, a clergyman in the crowd—whose excitement had made him miscount—thought that victory had been achieved. He rushed on to the field towards the wicket, cheering wildly. He was 'fielded' himself and crept back to his place, with the crowd in fits of laughter. But that must have been a pretty bad minute for those tough Tykes at the wicket—their nerves taut with suspense.

It fell to Rhodes to make the winning hit. He made it; ran a single; touched down with his bat—and raced madly for the Pavilion, which he was facing. Hirst had to run the other way, of course. In an instant the Oval turf was black with people, as a crowd of over ten thousand rushed to acclaim the heroes. They got Hirst before he could escape, and carried him in, in triumph. His '58-not-out' had been a superb knock. Rhodes had made 6 not out, equal to a double century under ordinary conditions. His calm determination, Hirst's splendid cricket, Jackson's mastery and Jessop's fearless brilliance—together with the superb bowling of Lockwood in Australia's second innings—had given England the victory. It was a victory of team-work, maybe, and there had been eleven extras. But to the boy who stood before that Pavilion cheering with the rest, the picture of Rhodes's calmness and Jessop's terrific attack were the two things he has remembered best of all.

That great excited crowd yelled itself hoarse outside the Pavilion; and then dispersed, glowing with pride and exultation, to tell the story to envious friends all over the town; in 'pubs', in saloon bars, in clubs, at home, at the office next day, to eager groups of less lucky schoolboys; a story of great cricket in the days of so many great cricketers—a memory which has outlasted by many years the golden sovereign, and the golden days which ruled at that time.

CHAPTER XIX

When the Sovereign Shone Like a Diamond

THE GOLDEN DAYS OF THE GOLDEN SOVEREIGN REALLY REACHED THEIR zenith on the 22nd June, 1897, on which day Queen Victoria celebrated her Diamond Jubilee.

Such a thing had never happened in the history of our country before, such a thing can never happen again. King George III had, indeed, occupied the Throne of England for a similar period, but there had been sad occasions in that time when he cannot be said to have 'reigned'. But with Queen Victoria it was very different. For every moment of that long and vivid sovereignty she had been Queen in every sense of the word; and for a portion she had been Queen-Empress, as she was on that sixtieth anniversary of her ascent to the Throne. But she was the last who will do so, for it can never happen again. However long a King or Queen of England may be sovereign-lord or lady, never again will a man or woman sit on the Throne who will reign over so vast a tract of the world, or so vast a number of people.

Never again will come such a display of Empire, such a gathering of Royalty, such a red-letter day in the lives of that majority of British lieges —the Middle Class. For never again will there be such an Empire in the terms of the thing which then existed, and never again will there be a Sovereign who held such sway over the imagination of her subjects— ninety per cent of whom had never seen her, and that figure is probably an understatement!

Such remoteness is inconceivable in these days. For now all people hear their Sovereign's voice over the air. The whole country can follow Royalty almost wherever they go, by means of the cinema, but more closely by means of the radio. They can hear every rustle, every sound, every syllable which accompanies a Coronation; they can hear the soft "I will" of a Royal Bride at the altar. The voices and tones of the entire Royal Family are well known to all classes, to all races, if they choose to listen in. Indeed, the Sovereign and the People are very close together.

But in the days of the golden sovereign there was no radio, and only towards the end did such a wonder as wireless telegraphy begin to come into people's minds. The remoteness of Royalty was complete; they were, indeed, a thing apart. Yet Queen Victoria held the thoughts, the admiration, the love and also the veneration of all of her people, of whatever race or colour, creed or cult, in a way which was quite unique. Also she

294

was the first monarch of this nation to hold Imperial rank—she was a Queen and an Empress.

That small, secluded figure, living a life of almost complete retirement, seen more often by the village folk around her country residences than by the myriads in her capital, was nevertheless very real to everyone. Her portrait hung in nearly every home—not only in those of the Middle Class, but in every class. It might be a photograph, an engraving, or a lithograph on a calendar presented by a tradesman, but there it was, and in every form it signified 'The Queen'. More than that, for people spoke of her as 'The Dear Queen'—and meant it.

Elderly ladies, readers of a pink-covered periodical called *Modern Society*, which enjoyed a tremendous circulation, understood all about her and that terrific spider's web of complicated relationship which spread all over Europe and of which she was the heart and head. So long had she then reigned—sixty years—that only people of advanced age remembered anyone else sitting on the throne, remembered any other image on our coinage. Only people of, say, sixty-five—an advanced age then—with very good memories, or aged people of seventy, could really recall it.

Sixty-five is not old nowadays at all; it is middle-aged only, which is perhaps one of the few ways in which the days of paper and machines score over the days of the sovereign. But then people grew old gracefully and, by spending their days peacefully, managed to live a long time. Men could retire from business at forty or forty-five with considerable fortunes, so prosperous had the golden sovereign made them. And they associated in their minds the prosperous golden sovereign with the almost legendary figure of the Queen. It was under her suzerainty that England had grown to its greatest height and power. She and the golden sovereign were joint sovereigns.

There was a deep and unswerving loyalty to that small female figure of the Queen which passes modern belief. Thus when the announcement was made that there were to be great celebrations in honour of her Diamond Jubilee the whole nation—and especially the Middle Class— was thrown into a fervour of excitement. The Middle Classes were the faithful subjects of Queen Victoria to a man, woman and child. It never dawned on them there could be any other form of government possible than a Constitutional Monarchy. And maybe they were right.

In 1897 the prosperity and security of this country were at their height. No doubt had arisen about its complete perfection. There had been no continental war in which it had been involved since the Crimean. There had been many small affairs with the Lesser Breeds Without the Law, of which Kipling told us—that poet of Empire who had managed to offend the Queen. There was a nasty, if hazy, memory of a defeat at Majuba Hill, but that was almost forgotten, and was considered not so much a defeat as a mistake in judgment which, along with the death of General Gordon, could be blamed on Mr. Gladstone.

These were blemishes which could soon be rubbed away, the Middle Classes felt, when the time came, and indeed they were right; for Gordon was avenged in 1898, the year following the Diamond Jubilee, and the Boer War came in 1899 to darken the last days of the aged Queen, but to wipe out Majuba Hill for the Jingoes and, ultimately, to open up a new and glorious era for South Africa and add a great nation to the Commonwealth of Nations which succeeded the Empire.

But in 1897 the Middle Classes were not worrying about these things. There was to be a Diamond Jubilee—an unprecedented event—and the beloved and revered Queen was to ride in procession and be beheld by her intensely loyal subjects. She had done it before—ten years before, when she had celebrated her Jubilee. That Jubilee showed the expansiveness of those days.

King George V was given a Silver Jubilee after twenty-five years of sovereignty. The old Queen ruled fifty years to attain her Jubilee. Things were done in a much bigger way then. It was a day of full measure, not makeshift and skimpiness.

The fact that there would be Diamond Jubilee celebrations was known in 1896, and for the ensuing twelve months it was the matter of prime interest in thought and conversation amongst the Middle Classes.

They were determined to make this the event of their lives. They—and the entire nation—succeeded in so doing. In March 1897 it was announced that the Queen would go in procession to St. Paul's Cathedral, there to return thanks amongst her people, or as many of them as could crowd into the Churchyard, for the blessings of her long life and reign. That Churchyard, when the time came, was packed to suffocation. Those who could not get there were unable to listen in, as they could do today, but they were there in spirit all the same. A whole nation, a whole Empire —a fifth of the globe—was with its Sovereign in thought and spirit that day, just as closely as radio or television could bind them in modern times.

Vast preparations were made at once. London, which had seen so many great sights, mighty cavalcades, and which had staged so many pageants during its centuries of life as a city, decided to make this its greatest. It had never had such an opportunity before. It will never have such an opportunity again. Kings and Queens had given thanks at St. Paul's Church and at St. Paul's Cathedral on many occasions. Another Queen—Elizabeth—had met her people there and joined in praise for a

296

great danger averted, a mighty enemy overthrown by the aid of Providence—that Providence which seemed to take such a favourable view of this small country. But never had such an occasion or such a Queen as this had such a celebration. It must outshine all else.

The Corporation of the City of London voted £25,000 for its Decoration Fund. It is estimated that £250,000 was spent in the decoration of London as a whole for that glorious day. And beyond that every house, every cottage, decked itself and vied with its neighbours; and every person of every class and age did the same.

London really let itself go and became a City of Flowers, for Venetian masts swathed in, or painted, red, flags and real flowers were the main embellishments. There were flags and banners by the tens of thousands; there were emblems of all kinds, trophies of every sort and vast triumphal arches, spanning the streets. It was amazing. Every man, woman and child sported their red, white and blue; every whip of every cart was so bedizened, every horse had its mane entwined with the national colours; every bicycle was a flashing replica of the Union Jack. Staid, bewhiskered City Fathers, tall-hatted and frock-coated, of immense wealth and respectability, of unbending integrity, all had a red-white-and-blue rosette or a small Union Jack in their buttonholes.

But more than mere decorations went to the making of the greatness of that occasion. Joseph Chamberlain—who was Colonial Secretary—had a genuine brainwave. He would show the English—the British people—what their Empire really meant, on this most auspicious and suitable opportunity. Few people understood it; few knew much about it. They knew they had an Empire; they knew that Empire was composed of Colonies, lands growing rich and prosperous under the aegis of the golden sovereign. The Middle Class knew they did business of vast proportions with those lands, the people of which were also loyal and loving subjects of that other Golden Sovereign—Queen Victoria. They had the haziest idea as to how these Colonies had been acquired. Some of them, of course, had been shown the error of their former ways by means of conquest; some had been taken from the French; others had actually been discovered—by adventurous members of the Middle Classes. However, they were quite sure in their own minds that all these places were far better off under the dual Golden Sovereigns than they would otherwise have been. Maybe they were right.

Joseph Chamberlain decided that the British Middle—and other—Classes should see concrete examples of these lands of theirs which had the same Queen as their own and flew the same flag. So he invited all the Premiers of the British Colonies to be present at the Diamond Jubilee—they were Colonies then; only Canada was a Dominion. And those

297

Premiers came, were duly honoured, were part of the Show and brought home to the people of this country something of the immensity of the Empire in which they and their Queen were partners.

Everyone wanted to see the Diamond Jubilee Procession, so the Queen gave her people a special Bank Holiday for that day. Everyone was to have an equal chance of seeing her, and business would come to a standstill. That did not matter under the Sovereign, when everyone worked, and there was no talk of 'drop in output' or 'targets' to be reached.

The preparations for the Diamond Jubilee were enormous. There was a tremendous influx of visitors from all over the world. Long before the day the streets were thronged with crowds all anxious to see what was being done. And they had much to look at. London burst into an eruption of timber—no 'timber shortage' then. That timber was being made into grand stands; timber covered with red cloth—the colour of the Empire on the maps of the world. It flowed everywhere then all over the world—the flood has receded nowadays.

It looked as though timber was going to swamp London. Churches disappeared from view under great tiers of seats; vast blocks of offices were lost to sight. Charing Cross Station vanished under a thousand-seater stand. Forests must have been hewn down, and many sovereigns flowed into the pockets of timber merchants and those who supplied the upholstery.

There was a huge stand in Whitehall, opposite the Horse Guards. It took six weeks to erect (a very long time then, if a bagatelle now!), and the Office of Woods and Forests (very aptly, for there was a small forest in the construction) received £7,000 for the rent of the site; £6,000 was the cost of its erection. It had 4,000 seats, priced at from four to twenty-five guineas. It was built upon solid concrete foundations, three to six feet deep; it contained a hundred and fifty tons of timber and fifteen tons of forty-five-foot steel girders. Five thousand chairs were bought for use upon it—imagine trying to buy chairs in that quantity today!—and amongst its amenities it included promenades, reception-rooms; a luncheon-room to seat four hundred at a time, ladies' rooms, a smoking-gallery—and even a telephone.

Another giant stand was at St. Martin's Church, Trafalgar Square. This one also contained 4,000 seats, priced at from one to fifteen guineas, and cost £4,000 in rent. One hundred and twenty men took five weeks to build it, using 175,000 cubic feet of timber and twenty tons of ironwork.

That is how they did things in the days of the golden sovereign.

There were, of course, attempts at profiteering, which was by no means unknown in those days. Gentlemen of the Golden Age 'spiv' variety rented a site in St. Paul's Churchyard as a speculation. They even pulled down buildings to erect a stand. They offered seats at fabulous prices, but the business-like and level-headed Middle Classes did not bite. The 'spivs' went broke, and the stand sold at moderate prices.

There were, however, other smart gentlemen of a more ingenious turn of mind, who opened offices in provincial cities and remote suburbs. There they displayed plans of lovely stands in advantageous positions, and sold thousands of seats at very cheap prices indeed. The only trouble was that, when the ticket-holders turned up, the stands were not there. Nor were their vendors. They had gone with the wind in a shower of sovereigns. But big sums were paid for good, genuine accommodation at real places of vantage.

The route spread over seven miles, and so well were the arrangements carried out that, except at one or two special points, there was very little congestion and remarkably few accidents. No ugly incidents marred the day. Yet millions went to see that show and every Middle Class person who could do so was there to see, to cheer and to weep tears of pride and real sentiment at what was—although they did not know it—the culminating spot of their age.

For days before the actual event London presented a holiday aspect, with its mobs of sightseers, its constantly growing sea of red cloth, its forests of masts, its dominating triumphal arches spanning the route, its millions of glass globes for the illuminations, all going into place as the result of the work of an army of men. North-country mills worked day and night to turn out the cloth required for the decorations and nobody went on strike—or even thought of it. Great festoons of evergreens, huge baskets of real flowers, swung between the masts, alternating with banners bearing loyal sentiments, and each mast was capped with the Imperial Crown in gold.

Whilst every street was beautified, perhaps the palm went to that ancient and aristocratic thoroughfare of St. James's. There were two massive Corinthian pillars at either end, their gilt tops bearing vast globes, and all around their bases palms and glowing flowers. Fifty Venetian masts stood on either side of the street, and from mast to mast, across and between, fluttered evergreens, flowers again, birds, apparently in full flight, whilst amongst the blooms and foliage were glass globes of red, white and blue, to light up at night. Never before had London looked so gay, so colourful—and never has the ancient city looked so wonderful since. Practically every street was edged with palms and flowers, like a great garden. People walked the whole length of the route, exclaiming as they went.

The story of the actual day is best seen through the eyes of a boy—a schoolboy at that time—who was there, who saw all there was to see on that day and before it, and who has never forgotten one iota.

He saw the ever-growing army of troops encamped in the Parks; he saw them arriving and detraining; he saw the actual rehearsal in St.Paul's Churchyard by climbing on a window-sill. He has never ceased to be grateful to his people, who took him to every big event in his youth: in fact to every event of the slightest importance. So, of course, they took him to the Diamond Jubilee. He had not seen the Jubilee of 1887; he was not sufficiently developed in body and mind then. But he did see the Diamond Jubilee of 1897, and thus he saw the greatest event in the age of the golden sovereign, and something which can never occur again.

Seats had been secured in a window in St. Paul's Churchyard itself, so not one detail of the whole thing—including the Divine Service—escaped him.

He was awake with excitement nearly all the previous night, and needed no second bidding to get up and dress at dawn. There was a hurried breakfast and then, in a brougham hired for the occasion, he and his elders set out towards the City. It was met at a point as near to St. Paul's as it could penetrate by the 'Good Uncle' who had got the seats and who, to see everything was right, had stopped in town overnight to be on the spot and ready.

That uncle understood small boys, for he had purchased a collection of every favour and every so-called medal and every 'Official Programme' the hordes of hawkers were selling in the streets. That boy kept them all until middle age, when, moving into a bigger house and a plea that there would be no room for such rubbish, led to their swift sacrifice before he realized it.

Under the escort of the uncle, the party proceeded to the coveted seats. There was a handsome basket of food and drink, there was everything that could be desired, including an unimpeded view. As they went, they saw the crowds on the kerbs who had been waiting all night.

The Great Day had begun, and it was as yet only 7 a.m. But there was much to see. The troops in their scarlet and bearskins were lining the Churchyard; there were officers walking about very importantly and having little conferences. There was a constant coming and going of messengers, there were short, sharp military commands; and there was a cart loaded with sand which its occupants strewed on the road—and got cheered heartily. There were Civic dignitaries, in all the finery of their age-old historic dress, to stare and wonder at. The only doubt was the weather. For even in the Golden Age that was a gamble.

The week preceding the event had been inclement and stormy.

Grave fears were expressed about this. The 'dear Queen' had always been favoured with what was known as 'Royal Weather'; she was wonderfully lucky in this respect. Was she to be cheated by the elements on this, her greatest day? For the 22nd June had dawned dull and overcast—only the uniforms of the troops and the gay decorations supplied any colour. The whole multitude in the streets, as one person, hoped and even prayed that the sun might shine on that day of Diamond and Gold. The boy of the Middle Classes was not worrying much about this; he left that to his elders. He was more concerned with seeing the Show. He had, indeed, seen the Queen twice before, being a strangely lucky young man.

His greatest joy, so far, had been the sight of the Lord Mayor, in full robes, mounting a white horse upon which to ride to the Law Courts where once had stood Temple Bar, the gateway to the City, to greet the Queen-Empress at the City's western boundary. His Lordship was not a very experienced horseman, and he was greatly handicapped by his robes.

The horse was not so impressed by the importance of its rider as it should have been. It was disposed to be restive, and when the Lord Mayor had finally got into the saddle it had taken him for a canter—almost a gallop—right round the Churchyard, during which unexpected ride His Lordship's hat had come off.

But that Lord Mayor—a man of the Middle Classes—was made of the right stuff. He got the better of that would-be fiery steed. He brought it to a standstill before the steps of the Cathedral after one circuit had been made, and he resumed his hat amidst the hearty and appreciative cheers of the populace. And nobody cheered that involuntary descendant of John Gilpin more loudly than the small boy, as the Lord Mayor rode off on the now chastened and possibly slightly ashamed horse with the due pomp and ceremonious dignity that became not only a citizen of credit and renown, but the Chief Citizen of the greatest City of the Greatest Empire the world had ever seen, upon which the sun never set and where the very golden sovereigns themselves were minted—and which was the stronghold of that Middle Class of which he, too, was a member.

At eleven-fifteen the crowd seemed to still, and its murmurs hushed. It was the hour at which the Queen was to start her drive through the serried ranks of her subjects, and something seemed to silence that vast throng.

Over the still, hazy, dull air came the thud of a distant gun. Her Majesty had started.

And, as if by magic, the sun came out. Away went the mist, away went the greyness, the threat of rain, and the summer sun—the sun of mid-summer—lit up London in all its finery. It was as if the sun had realized that, if it could not set upon this Empire, it could at least shine upon the microcosm of it that day enshrined. It rode the sky like a golden sovereign itself.

Out upon the steps of the Cathedral, before the eager eyes of that small boy, came the throng of honoured guests and the great ones of the Church. There was a mass of Indian Princes, Maharajahs, Rajahs, in their gleaming silks and their dazzling jewels. There was a choir of five hundred singers; there were bands. There was the Marquis of Salisbury, with his leonine head—looking every inch a Prime Minister of Empire—the slim, tall figure of the Rt. Hon. A. J. Balfour; the keen, alert, sharp-nosed face of Joseph Chamberlain (who had done so much for that day), in frock-coat and the inevitable orchid; there were very many others.

There was the Dean and Chapter in green, gold and white; there was the Bishop of Winchester in the deep blue robes of the Garter. There was the Bishop of London in yellow cope, a figure of gold. And there were the Archbishops of York and Canterbury in magnificent purple Coronation Robes. It was a sight of pageantry to remember. From afar came the sound of cheering, distant as yet but giving that thrill which only a multitude of human voices can provide. That boy, and the whole of the spectators, were keyed up with almost breathless excitement. Nearer and nearer came that roar, growing steadily in volume and intensity; the roar of a multitude of happy people greeting a very great day, a very great event—and a very great Queen.

There were sharp commands. As one man, the troops lining the Churchyard came to attention. The sun gleamed on their fixed bayonets, made the scarlet glorious and their buttons shine like so many sovereigns. Then, in excitement hardly to be borne, the Diamond Jubilee Procession came into view.

This was the day of the Horse. No mechanical, ugly vehicles growled and rattled along, with men more like mechanics than soldiers on board, grinding the roadway and giving off black, smelling vapour. No. This was a Cavalcade in the true meaning of the word. Here were horses and horses—rows and rows of them, their hooves making music, their harness jingling an accompaniment and in tune with their riders' accoutrements, their skins shining like satin, their manes like silk, full of consciousness and pride, themselves, in the part they were playing; a noble sight which boys of the Paper Age can never see in full measure. And there passed before the eyes of that boy of the Sovereign Days the full might of that Age, in all its splendour and its glory.

The Colonial Troops led the way on this day of Empire and Gold. A roar of cheering greeted them. They were something new and something fine for London to see. Canadian Dragoons, Hussars and the Canadian

302

Mounted Police, men of great romance only known till then from story-books, but now here in full sight and better than the pictures of themselves. It was a fairy-tale come true. New South Wales Mounted Rifles; New South Wales Lancers—what glamour that lethal weapon held, with its point of shimmering steel and its waving pennon—Victorian Rifles; magnificent men, these Australians, magnificently mounted, and in many cases wearing that strange new thing called 'khaki'—which Middle Class taxpayers were seeing for the first time but with which they—and the small boy—were to become so familiar and know only too well.

Men from New Zealand, Queensland, South Australia; Maoris; men from the Cape, Natal and other parts of South Africa; from the Crown Colonies; from all over the world. Men of dark skin and red fezzes from Cyprus; tall Sikhs; small green-clad Ghurkas; magnificent Indian Lancers from Bengal and other parts; Chinese troops with yellow, impassive faces from Hong Kong, with curious white helmets like inverted pudding-basins on their heads. Coal-black but magnificent Hausas; white-turbaned, zouave-coated and blue-trousered troops from the West Indies, their black smiling faces brought into relief by their turbans, their black boots shining (like their countenances) beneath their white spats. Men from the North, South, East, West—every quarter of the globe—escorting their Prime Ministers, and greeted with true British cheers.

But a special roar of welcome had gone up for the small figure of the horseman who led them, in his brave Field Marshal's uniform, with his cocked hat and plumes, and his Marshal's baton on his thigh. He was riding on a grey pony, and was acclaimed by all in a frenzy of welcome as 'Bobs!' Small in size, but great in achievement—Field Marshal Lord Roberts, V.C., himself . . . the idol of all.

That was the vanguard; and now came the Royal Procession.

If that army of Colonial troops had been wonderful, this fresh legion was a thing of colour and glory. It was the Boys of the Bulldog Breed—it was the 'little British Army that went a damn' long way'. It was the Soldiers of the Queen themselves.

And all the bands played that famous song, which rose to its true value that day of almost a second National Anthem; that stirring, inspired song, so typical of its age, composed by the genius of Leslie Stuart.

There they were—the Soldiers of the Queen—the men who had always won; living up to their name by escorting their Sovereign on her Diamond Day. And at their head rode Captain Oswald Ames, six feet eight inches of him, in his resplendent Guards uniform; his steel helmet and his breast-plate making him look like a hero of the days of Chivalry.

He was followed by the Royal Navy, a detachment of picked sailors with gun-carriage. They would appear strange today, for they wore those big, round straw hats with the turn-up brim, which were on a smaller scale the headgear of most children of the Golden Age in summer who were, so far as their attire went, all in the Navy. The crowd greeted the sailors frantically—and that boy joined in, for he, too, had worn that hat, and rejoiced to see it on the real sailors. It made him feel kindly towards it and a little proud that he had worn it too. All the nice girls—High, Middle and Low Class—loved the sailors, and that day their cheers showed it, their male escorts being no less enthusiastic, for Britannia really ruled the waves then, and these were the men who, for years, had kept the peace of the world.

Then followed the Army—horse, foot, and artillery—in all the dazzling colour of full-dress uniforms of that time. Horse Guards, Life Guards, Dragoon Guards, Hussars, Lancers—all looking like heroes of romance—scarlet, blue, green; white plastrons, red plastrons, steel breastplates, steel helmets, helmets of fur—black or brown, yellow and gold braid; sabres flashing, lances gleaming, pennons waving; brown horses, bay, chestnut, black and grey, a marvellous sight. The Royal Horse and the Royal Field Artillery, with their gun-teams and guns—no mechanism, but the best flesh of man and horse—and then the Infantry. The Foot Guards moving like one man; the Regiments of the Line; the Rifle Brigade; the Highland Regiments and their pipers, kilts swinging, bearskins shining in the sun—scarlet, blue, dark-green, uniforms of various hues—all the soldiers of the Queen of whom the bands played and for whom the crowd roared itself hoarse—and that small boy was hot, excited and a little hoarse too.

There was, however, still something in reserve.

The Royal carriages followed and the Royal personages—a host of them, all glittering, colourful figures—the members of our own Royal Family all known and picked out; the Empress of Germany, the children, the grandchildren and the great-grandchildren of the great little Queen —all come to do her honour. The excitement was breathless. Riding three abreast before the central figure of it all, as though in escort of the Most Royal of All Royalties, came the Kings and the Representatives of Foreign States; and then another tiny figure in Field Marshal's panoply, baton in hand, riding by himself immediately before the Queen, Field Marshal Lord Wolseley, who was always so correct and so successful that he had given the nation the saying, 'All Sir Garnet!'—for 'Garnet' was his name.

The great moment had come. She was there. The Royal House of England was around her; Kings made her retinue, as they were to do once more when she travelled the streets of London between the serried ranks of her people for the last time—but She was there at that moment on the

Diamond Day and all eyes were on one figure alone—what had gone before was as nothing, and the previous cheering was mere silence. But it happened then, a wave of sound, a roar as of all the oceans of the world thrown together, as that figure drove into view. There were tears in the eyes and a catch in the throat which was nevertheless overcome and swallowed, as the British Public let itself go for the Queen who was their Sovereign.

It was such a tiny figure as it sat upright in its open carriage, bowing its head from side to side. Amongst the riot of scarlet and gold, of shining steel and all the colours of the rainbow, that tiny figure was in black—yet not entirely in black, for there was grey and silver, and a touch of white. In case the folk of today want to know exactly what a Monarch of the Golden Age wore on her Diamond Jubilee, it was a dress of black *moiré* silk with panels of pale grey silk embroidered in silver; a cape of black chiffon with white lace insertion and silver embroidery. Not even on this day did she forget that she mourned her husband—the man with whom she had made her home, like any ordinary Middle Class woman—she was still the widow and she kept his memory green; no doubt he rode beside her in her thoughts.

No crown was on her head but a black bonnet, ornamented with jet and silver, trimmed with white acacia and ostrich feathers; the one gesture to queenly rank being a diamond aigrette. She carried a simple white sunshade, and her old face was a little drawn, a little grave, and perhaps a little strained, as if she were keeping emotion in tight check. She seemed so much alone amidst that great throng of colour and glitter; she was surrounded by the aloofness of Royalty. Yet there was nothing between her and her people but the line of soldiers along the kerb; nothing else was needed, for every one of those people were her guardians too.

She seemed alone, but she was not. She was in the hearts of everyone who saw her—and in those of the millions who did not—and their roaring welcome went out to tell her of their love. No wonder she was moved. It was a marvel she did not break down. And practically all those who acclaimed her as no monarch has ever been acclaimed were seeing her for the first and only time in their lives.

The carriage halted before the great steps of the great Cathedral. The Thanksgiving Ceremony was mercifully short. A *Te Deum* was intoned by the massed choir, whilst every head was bared; a Benediction was pronounced by the Archbishop of Canterbury; the Old Hundredth was sung—and then the National Anthem, in which the multitude joined, with tears streaming down almost every face. The old Queen's head trembled and her mouth tightened. Then the singing died away and, as if by inspiration, the Archbishop called for "Three cheers for Her Majesty!" The sound of those cheers still rings in that small boy's ears—and he watched that cavalcade move on, which still passes through his memory as clearly as if his eyes still beheld it . . . and the Queen-Empress, her thanks given to God, went on her way home. . . .

But that was not the end for that Middle Class boy. He stayed in town and saw the illuminations. The whole of London glowed like a vast living jewel. From almost every building gas-cressets flared; and almost every building was outlined in golden flame, either with gas-jets or fairy-lamps. The Bank of England was a mass of light; and over the main entrance, in letters of fire, blazed the words, 'She Wrought Her People Lasting Good.' The pillars of the Royal Exchange and the Mansion House were swathed with countless wreaths of brilliant tiny lights; on the Mansion House alone 35,000 gas-jets were ablaze.

Nobody knew anything about fuel restrictions then. The grey austere centre of the City was gleaming like a jewel, as became its own richness. On some—indeed many—buildings all over town, vast glass globes, illuminated from within like magic opals, gave glowing radiance to the Royal Arms, and the letters 'V.R.I.' blazed in flame everywhere. Nelson's Column was a pillar of fire and festoons of coloured lamps linked it in great arcs with its nearest buildings. Across the streets hung coloured globes, red, white, blue, green, amber, gold, lit from within like jewels suspended in mid-air. It was full of the glow of the Golden Age, not the cold modernity of flood-lighting. Yet, to surprise the moderns, flood-lighting was there too. That new thing, the Searchlight, was in action, seen by most people for the first time. Searchlights shone on the dome of St. Paul's (at a cost of £1,400), which rose like a mountain of pure silver from the sea of golden flame below.

All over the country it was the same; hardly a mountain summit or hilltop but had its bonfire. Beacons blazed again on old sites which had once kindled them as warnings of danger, but now sent a message of rejoicing and peace throughout the land. . . .

The night wore on; the Great Day was over. The children of the Golden Age had seen it, and had seen the greatest day of their time and the greatest night too.

These men and women of England—Britain—the Empire as a whole, wherever they were—lived that day on the crest of a wave; they lived a day which can never come back; a day of might and glory.

That Middle Class boy whose memory records these things now recalls it all so plainly, so vividly. He was to see many more sights; he was to see that Golden Age go down in war, and another less stable, less prosperous age succeed it until war burned that up too. He was to see and experi-

306

ence war, and many other pageants of peace, to meet and speak to great personages, to Royalty of all nations. But it was never the same thrill.

He knows now what he did not know then—that he witnessed on the 22nd June, 1897, the very summit and topmost pinnacle of the age of the sovereign, of the greatness and grandeur of his country. Many more years were to pass on, years of richness, plenty and security, before the end came; before his class was numbered amongst the things which had been—but he had seen, and remembers, that day of days when a great Sovereign rode amongst her people, and when all was as golden as that golden sovereign which gave the nation peace, security and might—which passed from it slowly but surely when that coin, which was the standard of England, died in the first shock of the First World War, when the whole world changed for ever.

CHAPTER XX

'Fifty Thousand Horse and Foot'

THOSE SOLDIERS OF THE QUEEN WHOM THE CROWDS AND THE MIDDLE Classes had acclaimed at the Diamond Jubilee were, very soon after that parade of peace, to be called upon to show their mettle. Nobody doubted that mettle for one instant. They had shown it often when Britain had gone to war—to that remote war which professionals fought in the distant parts of the earth. Some of those wars had not been too glorious, if the truth must be told. There had been battles when victory had not shone on the British arms. But the Soldiers of the Queen had always won in the end. It was not their fault they had not won in the beginning, for the men were all right. The Higher Command was all too often inefficient, and the Government too ill informed or too indecisive to grasp the nettle Danger with a firm hand.

In the true British way, they always seemed to underestimate the enemy. Thus very small bodies of British troops, cumbered with heavy equipment and in most unsuitable attire, would find themselves opposed to hordes of very unfriendly 'natives'—as every human with dark pigment in his skin was then called—and either fought with desperate valour to extricate themselves or died heroic and quite unnecessary deaths.

But it is a peculiarity of the British that they make victories of their defeats or reverses and send them down the pages of their history in almost brighter colours than those which paint their real successes. British forces had been cut up in India, in Africa, but always, in the end, the Soldiers of the Queen won. They opposed rifles, machine-guns and artillery to the spears and swords of undisciplined fearless *impis* or armies, and they won. It often took quite a while, but victory was certain in the end.

Twice, however, they had not won. They had lost at Majuba Hill to a lot of undrilled farmers who were dead shots and who understood mobility and speed. The British stood fast in their red coats, a perfect mark, exposing themselves as they had been trained to do, and the end came.

They had not succeeded in rescuing General Gordon from the howling, fanatical Dervishes, urged on by their Mahdi, who had encircled him at Khartoum. Egyptian campaigns had been many, the Sudanese sand had soaked up a lot of good British blood. But each time it had been in the main the fault of the Government, who had hesitated, shilly-shallied and never taken real forceful action. Not even Sir Garnet (later Lord) Wolseley had cleaned up the Egyptian mess, in which the nation, with the best of intentions, had become involved. Britain had gone into Egypt to clear up corruption, to put the house in order. She had done so in part, but outside the tidy portion in that mysterious Sudan were grim, dark figures who made things most unpleasant and would not see the force of adopting the blessings of British Rule—or that was how it seemed to the Middle Classes.

Gordon, a brave, gallant soldier—even if a bit headstrong—had been sacrificed, according to them, when he should have been saved. They were quite right about that. A most popular ballad, of singular mournfulness, was still sung which declared it was 'Too late, too late to save him'. It had been much too late. He had met his death bravely like the Christian gentleman he was.

The British—and most certainly the Middle Classes—were determined that revenge should be taken, and that pretty soon. The opportunity came in 1898, when the glories of the Diamond Jubilee were still vivid in the mind.

This time there was no mistake, no indecision, because the man on the spot was a great British soldier and a man who stood no nonsense from anyone. The Government and the high-ups knew all about him, but until 1898 he was not very greatly in the public eye. Then, however, he became an eyeful. He had a title strange to British tongues—he was 'The Sirdar'. He had reorganized the inefficient Egyptian army and made it into something of a fighting force—a better thing than it had ever been before, Camel Corps and all, armed with Maxim-Nordenfeldt quick-firers, nine- and twelve-pounder field guns and Martini breech-loading rifles— and bayonets. He had brought order out of chaos and he was only forty-eight.

His name was Major-General Sir Horatio Herbert Kitchener. He had Nelson's name and some of the Nelson touch, but otherwise he was far different. He stood some inches over six feet, he looked imperiously over the heads of most men with his straight-gazing, enigmatic eyes of blue, he was as straight as he was tall, he was deliberate but accurate, he seemed a thing of tempered steel. He had dark hair and heavy brows, full, red cheeks and a large moustache which draped his strong, determined mouth.

His face was austere almost to harshness, yet it was handsome too, and he was indeed the *beau ideal* of a British soldier as understood at that time. He not only looked it, thank heaven, he was it too. He was a Royal Engineer. He knew the East and all about it. He knew Egypt and he knew the Sudan. He had fought there. He knew the Egyptians and their Khedive, and he stood no nonsense from them. He knew, too, the

Mahdists and Dervishes, and he was not going to stand any of their nonsense, either. He knew that the Fuzzy-Wuzzy was, as Kipling had sung, a first-class fighting man who had broken the British Square, but he was perfectly sure that the Dervishes were not going to break him. On the other hand, he was going to break the Dervishes—and he did, once and for all.

It seems strange that only fifty years ago the British Square was still the great ideal of British arms. It was thus they had fought and won at Waterloo. It was thus they fought—and won—many campaigns afterwards. Men stood in a living square and fired at the approaching enemy; then, when it came to hand-to-hand combat, they fought it out with the bayonet. Waterloo was still the criterion of battle. Those squares were popularly regarded as unbreakable, a rock against which a less determined and tenacious enemy dashed himself to pieces. It never occurred to the British, or to the Middle Classes, that it required great bravery to charge such a square, just as much bravery as to stand in it. But these Dervishes, drunk with religious fanaticism, had actually broken a British Square, and dealt death all around with their long, ancient swords and broad-bladed spears, whilst the British soldiers with their bayonets fought back-to-back in resisting them. One regiment still wears a cap badge back and front, to celebrate such an occasion. Well, the Sirdar was not going to have anything like that.

The Sudan was in flames again. A personage known as the Khalifa had begun again where the Mahdi had left off. He was getting—had indeed got—out of hand and had to be dealt with. The Sirdar was going to do it too.

This great machine of a man, the Sirdar, was perhaps a better Proconsul than a strategist, a better organizer than an actual fighting man; but those were the very qualities needed. He had risen to fame in the Sudan and in Egypt, and he was going to rise even higher. It was said at the time that so great was his organizing ability that he would have made a perfect manager for the Army and Navy Stores.

He never did that, but the time was to come when he was to manage the shop which controlled the Army—the War Office in Whitehall. He had never lost a fight. He had brought the Khedive of Egypt to heel when that petty potentate had insulted every British officer in his so-called realm. He was never in a hurry and he had the power of striking terror into opponents' hearts. He was relentless in gaining his end. He trained men hard, but he made them efficient and as steel-like as himself. He tolerated nothing slipshod or careless. But his men believed in him and trusted him, and they were right.

His lieutenants were men of his own training, his own picking. Some of those names became famous and popular, some went down in disgrace in the war which was to follow. Major-General Archibald Hunter was his right-hand man, and there were Lieutenant-Colonel Hector Archibald Macdonald, Lieutenant-Colonel Maxwell, Lieutenant-Colonel Lewis and Major-General Gatacre.

Hector Macdonald became known as 'Fighting Mac'. He had been promoted from the ranks for conspicuous bravery in an Afghan war, taken prisoner at the fateful Majuba; he was a very brave, hard-bitten, stocky Scot of amazing personal bravery, and he caught the imagination of the multitude. He was always where the blows were hardest, the bullets thickest. His end was then in the mists of time—a sordid tragic end brought about by his own hand to evade disgrace.

Hunter, too, was a man of fearless bravery in face of the enemy, and a very shrewd, far-seeing, organizing soldier. He was trusted by the Sirdar.

Gatacre had already built up a big reputation which the coming campaign was to enhance. He was of the most restless and nerve-racking energy; he was everywhere at once, he wanted to do everything himself, and he worked his men like machines. They loved him, but they called him 'General Backacher'. His fame was to fall, with so many more of his generation, in the Great Boer War—as it was called when it was fought.

Kitchener, the Sirdar, set out to teach the Khalifa what the might of Britain meant with an army of twelve to thirteen thousand and fifty-two guns. That was looked upon as an enormous army. It was considered that they would have to face an army of round about twenty thousand, possibly more. But Colonel Wingate, who was the very efficient O.C. Intelligence, thought everything was all right. The Army marched and marched and marched. In those days an army really marched on its feet, it did not ride in transport vehicles, and this army marched over sand under a pitiless burning sun.

Crawling up the Nile beside them went the section of the Fleet which was to take part. 'Gunboats', they were called, white with one funnel, deck piled on deck, but drawing next to nothing, a gun forward, a couple amidships and a couple of Maxims on a shaky kind of platform. Had not Beresford taken one of them into sight of Khartoum in the effort to relieve Gordon? They were propelled by a wheel at the stern.

The Khalifa proved coy. He knew his game, a waiting one. The cavalry kept up constant reconnaissance, but they could not find him. Not at all nice, those jaunts through sand and scrub, with needle-sharp, dagger-like thorns. They finally flushed him at Atbara, or thought they had. Actually it was a chieftain called Mahmud; the real culprit with most

311

of the men was away off in the desert. But Mahmud had 16,000 men behind a *zareba*, a thick thorn defence with trenches inside and out.

The Sirdar attacked him. He was shelled first, pretty soundly as shelling went then, but he did not respond to treatment and come dashing out. He skulked behind his *zareba*. So the little British Army went for him. No square this time; a long line of khaki-clad men, British and Egyptian, with the Union Jack flying in the middle, with bands playing and pipes skirling, moved to the attack. The officers went in front of the men, and three of the commanding officers actually led the attack—yes, led it, on horseback. They were Hunter, Macdonald and Maxwell. The *zareba* fell, the motley crew of the enemy took to flight—they were not true dervishes in that bickering, and Mahmud was captured. It was a famous victory.

The losses were 24 killed and 104 wounded, of whom 20 died later. The Egyptian force lost 57 killed and 365 wounded. The enemy lost well over 3000. The battle lasted two hours and had taken place on Good Friday, 1898.

The Sirdar stayed where he was during the summer. He had wiped out one of the great enemy strongholds, now he would refit. The Guards came out, the Rifle Brigade, or part of it, the Field and the Garrison Artillery sent detachments, the Royal Irish Fusiliers came along and there also came two things of wonder: some amazing guns called 'howitzers' —tubby guns capable of firing a 5-inch shell, an enormous projectile then—and those shells contained a new explosive named lyddite, looked upon as the last word in death-dealing horror in those days.

There were also detachments of many celebrated English and Scottish regiments. The Sirdar was going to make a job of it. He was going to get Khartoum and to get the Khalifa. He got him at Omdurman.

This was the last great fight with Mahdi-ism and the Sirdar was taking no chances.

In the British force were the Rifle Brigade, Lancashire Fusiliers, Northumberland Fusiliers, Grenadier Guards, Warwicks, Seaforths, Camerons and Lincolns; there was the Artillery and the Cavalry; and in the Cavalry was a young, new regiment of Lancers—the 21st—who were to win fame that day; and there was also a young man named Winston Churchill, who dearly loved a fight. There was the Egyptian Brigade as well. There were no more squares; the Army was in line, flags flying, drums playing.

The Dervishes—the true Dervishes—attacked. Masses and masses of them charged the British line, which, on this occasion, was not a thin red one, as it had been for so long, but a khaki one—the red-coat had gone from the field for ever. Volley after volley crashed into the advancing mass

312

of Dervishes, shrapnel and machine-gun bullets ploughed amongst them, the lyddite made great yellow gashes of death, but still they came on. They died, and wave after wave succeeded them. The British were suffering too. They fired until their rifles were red-hot, and still that brave, obstinate and ill-armed army attacked. The new Lee-Metford rifles were in use.

At last the wave receded, leaving a carpet of white-clothed dead thick on the ground, and the British line advanced against a body of Dervishes which stood fast, awaiting them. The British advanced across mounds and piles of dead bodies. The Dervishes sprang a surprise, with a nice little outflanking movement; but it did not come off. Dervish reinforcements threatened the Egyptian Division—a very different thing to an attack on regular British troops. It was the opportunity for the new regiment, the 21st Lancers, and they took it. They charged, and they charged into a trap.

Hidden in a ravine was a mass of fresh Dervishes. Three thousand bloodthirsty men arose out of the earth to challenge the 400 Lancers. The Lancers went slap at them; over dreadful ground, with gullies in all directions, they charged. Their lances pierced black body after black body. Foemen lay on the ground to hamstring, swords were out, revolvers cracking; the Colonel was down, and up again; but the 21st Lancers rode right through and took terrible toll.

The maiden charge of that young gallant regiment in its baptism of fire is on the scroll of famous British cavalry charges, with the Light Brigade, and the Heavies at Waterloo. Few regiments made such a distinguished *début* as the 21st Lancers.

Then they dismounted and let the Dervishes have it with the carbine. They wanted to charge again, knee to knee, as they had done before. That the Colonel forbade. But they routed the foe in one of the most dashing of British charges ever made against odds natural and odds human.

The Sirdar meant to get between the enemy army and Omdurman. He did it, and in the end the Dervishes melted and broke. A last desperate attack failed, and it was over. The power of Mahdi-ism was broken. A British victory had been won—there had been tough moments, but it had been won. Discipline and weapons had conquered fanatical odds—sometimes at the rate of four to one. The Soldiers of the Queen had done it again.

The Dervish, magnificent in battle, was magnificent in defeat. They met death facing their conquerors with calmness and fortitude. They struck their last blow, threw their last spear, and waited to be mowed down. Eleven thousand of them died so; 16,000 of them were found wounded and helpless; 4000 were taken prisoner, nearly dead with shame. A British Army of 22,000 had beaten over 50,000 first-class fighting men. But the losers were not disgraced. The British casualties were, including Egyptian forces, 131 British, 256 natives killed and wounded. The 21st Lancers lost 24 killed and 74 wounded out of this total.

The Sudan was reconquered. The British people walked in pride. And, fourteen years after he had been killed, Gordon was avenged. The Sirdar and his Army entered Khartoum. The British flag was run up again, and the Guards' band played 'God Save the Queen'. The Sirdar called for three cheers for her—and the troops gave them with a will.

Then they gave Gordon his real funeral. The Guards' band played the 'Dead March' in *Saul*. The Egyptian band played 'Toll for the Brave'. Minute-guns were fired. Four chaplains—Roman Catholic, Anglican, Methodist and Presbyterian—conducted the service. When they played the General's favourite hymn, 'Abide with Me', the men said that even the Sirdar's eyes were misted. The bugles shrilled out the 'Last Post' and 'Reveille'—and Gordon's funeral was over. It took place in what had been his own garden, a green oasis he had loved, and the Union Jack now fluttered once again where he had defended it, on almost the actual spot where he had been cut down facing his foes alone, Bible in hand.

A smear upon the brightness of the British shield had been wiped away. Gordon of Khartoum had been avenged by Kitchener of Khartoum, for that title the Sirdar took when rewarded with a peerage.

The British Empire rejoiced in victory, but another little cloud was in the sky. It was small, but it was menacing.

There was victory in the north of the African Continent, but there was something sinister brewing in the south of it.

The old Queen's last years were not to be peaceful. The trouble was in the Transvaal, once a British colony, but before that a Dutch Republic, and then free again from British rule after the Majuba Hill episode. Gold had been found in the Transvaal. Outsiders pushed in to get riches. The Boers, who had promised to remain under British suzerainty after Majuba, threw off the last pretence of this when wealth accrued. They had at their head a wily and clever man named Kruger, who became their President. Opposed to him in South African political games was Cecil Rhodes, who was called 'Empire Builder'. It was his genius and perhaps his ruthlessness which had made South Africa so largely British. Rhodes wanted the Transvaal back now that gold was there. He did not mind so much about the other republic, the Orange Free State. That had no gold.

The Boers did not give the gold-seeking invaders much of a life of it. These adventurers were called '*Uitlanders*'—and it was they who, in reality, made the Transvaal prosperous. Kruger sat back and took the profits, whilst the men who did the work were denied every civil right, and even refused education for their children in their own British tongue. Or that was the story the British were told. It was Cecil Rhodes's chance. He tried to organize a rebellion inside the Transvaal, and a small and remarkably irregular striking force was ready to raid the place, and join hands, when the flame flared up.

But that little force, under Dr. Jameson, made a mess of it. They, about 300 strong, made their raid; but there was no rising in their support. They fought well, but they were soundly beaten. The survivors, taken prisoner, were sent home for punishment, tried and imprisoned. It was a deplorable affair and did nobody any good. It left a festering sore which was bound to erupt. And erupt it did.

War-clouds gathered, armies gathered, war material poured into the Transvaal through Portuguese Lourenço Marques. The Home Government dithered once more. British troops and Generals concentrated at the Cape, in Natal and in the Colonies all around the Transvaal. All through the early autumn of 1899, whilst the 19th century went towards its end, war drew nearer and nearer. Then, with what every true Briton regarded as amazing effrontery, Kruger delivered an ultimatum to the British Government on the 9th October demanding the immediate withdrawal of all troops from the Transvaal Border; the immediate stoppage and recall of all reinforcements, and the setting up of a Committee of Arbitration.

There was a roar of rage from the nation. That a parcel of farmers should dare! It was all because of Majuba! That business had got to be finished.

Kruger's demands were not complied with and war broke out on 11th October, 1899.

The Colonies rallied to Great Britain. Australian troops sailed for South Africa. The nation at home had the worst attack of war fever they had ever experienced. But the weight of European opinion was dead against this country. France was against it. For France smarted. There had nearly been war between France and Great Britain. A French force under General Marchand had been found in the Sudan by the Sirdar where no French force should have been. The Sirdar dealt with that in his own way. Marchand marched out. In the hands of a lesser man this might have led to war, but Kitchener was not a 'lesser' man by any means.

Open sympathy with the Boers was expressed all over the Continent —and by many at home, who were promptly called 'Pro-Boers', pelted, and had their windows broken by patriotic Englishmen—and boys. The Emperor of Germany—the Kaiser—with that lack of tact and gentlemanly feeling which so distinguished him—sent a friendly telegram to Kruger, which was the first seed of the First World War—the war which

315

was to alter the world. Only Austria, the sprawling Middle-European Empire which included Hungary, under its aged Emperor Franz-Joseph, was Britain's friend. Scandalous cartoons appeared in Continental newspapers. A naked Queen Victoria, like a naughty baby, was pictured across Kruger's knees, being soundly spanked. The whole thing was really shocking from every point of view. But the British did not mind.

They were invincible. They knew it. They had their Navy, which kept the foes at bay, manned by the boys of the bulldog breed. They had the Soldiers of the Queen, and they had the Queen herself. They would have that gold in the Transvaal to make into more sovereigns before the year was out. Old 'Kroojer', as he was called, was derided and cartooned. He had a face for a cartoonist, a figure too. In his funny tall hat, his ill-fitting frock-coat—very unlike the smart English variety—and his fringe of white whiskers under his clean-shaven chin, he looked what the British imagined him to be, a thorough-paced, sanctimonious old humbug. Actually, he was a most astute statesman and a father to his people, although he did take on more than he could manage—and did a bolt in the end, reputedly taking the national cash-box with him. But that end was not yet.

England—Britain—went to war with a fine martial spirit, shouting songs, and drinking oceans of beer, and full of sentimentalism. The Union Jack was cheered everywhere. London Road Car buses, which flew it, found the flags missing and being carried at the head of processions of cheering patriotic men and women—and boys. Enterprising firms flooded the market with Union Jack pocket-handkerchiefs, Union Jack ties, khaki and Union Jack ties, and little miniature flags. Everyone bought them. This was the Khaki War. Everyone grew learned about khaki, and the strange things soldiers now had to wrap round their legs, called puttees, borrowed from the Indian Army. All the troops dropped their peacetime uniform, except the Household Cavalry, and went into khaki. They had khaki helmets too.

The Highland regiments revolted. It was ordained that they should sacrifice their tartan kilts and take to khaki. They would not do it. British compromise stepped in, and they were supplied with khaki aprons to wear in front of the kilts. The Boers were known to be fine marksmen and those kilts were conspicuous. So the aprons went in front. No need for them at the rear—the British Army, let alone the Highlanders, never retreated.

Certain highly placed Members of Parliament objected to the war. In their view it was just a war for gold, for possession. They got into serious trouble. Campbell-Bannerman, leader of the Opposition, was in great odium; a young man named David Lloyd George was denounced as a traitor, and had to don a policeman's uniform to dodge his infuriated pursuers. Later he was to lead the nation, which then thirsted for his blood, through one of its darkest hours to triumphant victory.

The nation then put its faith in Joseph Chamberlain, ex-Radical, then Unionist and apostle of Empire. "Joe knows how to treat 'em," it said.

The slow-moving ponderous British war-machine got slowly into motion. The Boers lost no time. Intensely mobile, knowing nothing about drill and caring less, mounted on good horses which they knew how to ride, they had the temerity to invade British soil. They wore wideawake hats, slouch hats, bowler hats—even high hats—tailed coats, loose jackets; they had bandoliers slung around them and carried rifles with which they were dead shots. They travelled light and in companies they called 'commandos'. Later this put a word into the British language, and a military formation into the Army.

The British Army gathered. General Sir Redvers Buller, V.C., was in supreme command. He was a son of Devon, from Crediton, near Exeter, and the nation believed in him. A man of tried personal bravery, a good Cavalry commander, Redvers Buller was not the man to command big armies (as armies went then), nor was he the man to match wits with the wily, unconventional, rule-disregarding Boers. But the British believed in his bulk and his bulldog look. It would be all over by Christmas, they said. The Boers would have a lesson, and Majuba would be avenged at last.

Fighting began. There is no need to trace that campaign through all its long-drawn-out muddle, mess and agony in chronological form. It was not the Boers who were surprised, it was the British. That word 'reverse' appeared in the newspapers. It appeared again and again. The British rubbed their eyes. What was this? *What* was this? 'Reverse?' Someone had blundered, was blundering. That was true. It was not the poor unfortunate Soldiers of the Queen. They were doing their bit. It was the High Command. Generals with great reputations fell—some fell on the field and saved their names, others fell into the disgrace of error and consequent defeat, and were recalled home.

Strange words appeared in general use—*kopjes*, *spruits*, the *veldt*, *laagers*. Small British forces got besieged in small towns hitherto hardly known, but to achieve world-wide importance. General Sir George White was besieged in Ladysmith; General Kekewich in Kimberley, the diamond town; and a Colonel Baden-Powell, entirely unknown then, got himself besieged in a small place of tin houses and shacks called Mafeking. There was great dispute over the pronunciation of this: some said 'Mafe-king', some 'Ma-feck-ing', but the majority just called it 'Mafficking'.

Now, being besieged was a game the British understood better than the Boers. It was a question of holding on, of bulldog tenacity, not an affair of tip-and-run, of volleys of well-aimed fatal rifle-shots and a swift gallop away. It was not crouching behind boulders and picking off soldiers, acting by the 'book'. Those three small towns held on grimly. The nation demanded their release. Buller set himself to relieve Ladysmith. He kept crossing and re-crossing the Tugela River, losing many men in his desire to preserve them. He succeeded in losing the son of Lord Roberts, who died a gallant death. 'Buller Across the Tugela!' screamed the head-lines, and the populace cheered. 'Buller Re-crosses the Tugela' moaned the headlines, and the entire nation groaned.

Gatacre fell. Penn Symonds fell. Wauchope, who had won fame in the Omdurman campaign, met his death with many of his Highlanders when General Lord Methuen met with disaster at Magersfontein, trying to relieve Kimberley. Fights like Eelandslaagte, Spion Kop, with its gallant Highland charge, Wagon Hill, with its deathless Devon heroism, filled people's mouths. Armoured trains crashed to disaster. British prestige fell. A young war correspondent named Winston Churchill got taken prisoner and escaped.

The people at home grew grim and determined. The old Queen sent out a message that there was no dismay or despondency in her house-hold. The nation cheered up. The old Queen sent every serving soldier in the field a tin box of chocolate for a Christmas present—a flat box, with her head embossed on it. Everyone acclaimed this. Young men joined the Forces—enlisted for the Front. They flocked into the Volunteers. For the first time the Middle Classes went into the Army. The Colonies sent reinforcements—cartoons showed the Lion-Cubs coming to the aid of the Lion. Britannia welcomed them, a crowd of eager young men offering their help.

That poet of Empire, Rudyard Kipling, in association with Sir Arthur Sullivan, made his contribution. He knew and understood the British soldier of his day. He gave him a new name—'The Absent-Minded Beggar'—and his poem was very much to the taste of the British public. It hit the nail on the head. It drew attention to something which had been overlooked, and a sentimental nation rushed to put it right. Never had so large an Army gone forth within living memory, and Kipling said so. He also took a smack at the ultra-patriotic screamers, but they swallowed that Perhaps they did not even see it, for everyone either recited the poem or sang the song. . . .

It will be well to recall it, for it is a perfect picture of the time.

> When you've shouted 'Rule, Britannia',
> When you've sung 'God Save the Queen',

When you've finished killing Kruger with your mouth,
Will you kindly drop a shilling in my little tambourine
For a gentleman in khaki ordered South,
He's an absent-minded beggar, and his weaknesses are great,
But we and Paul must take him as we find him.
For he's out on Active Service, wiping something off a slate,
And he's left a lot of little things behind him.
Cook's son, Duke's son, son of a belted Earl—
Fifty thousand Horse and Foot ordered to Table Bay.
Each of 'em's doing his country's work—
And who's to look after the girl?
Pass the hat for your credit's sake, and
Pay, Pay, Pay!

And the country paid. Mrs. Tree—as she was then—wife of Herbert Beerbohm Tree, and a fine actress, recited it at the Palace Theatre. The house showered money on her. She was hit in the eye, which was blackened, by a badly aimed half-crown, but she did not mind. Silver and golden sovereigns rained on her. The Girl, the Missus and the Kids profited from 'The Absent-Minded Beggar', as they should. Those scenes were repeated all over the country. In the summer, districts and towns held carnivals. Long processions of men and women in fancy dress marched down the streets with triumphal cars amongst them, most of them depicting crafty Boers showing the white flag and shooting down the British soldiers whilst so doing; Boers being transfixed by British lances (extremely popular, this!); wounded British soldiers in blood-stained bandages being cared for by the prettiest girl available, arrayed in spotless uniform as a nurse; 'Krooger'—also called 'Oom Paul'—being severely ill-treated by small boys in what passed for British uniforms, and even Britannias and—yes—replicas of the Queen herself. It is to be hoped this never came to her notice, for she would not have been amused.

She was, however, a very old lady, nearing her end. One of the royal cousins, out of the host of cousins, got himself killed. Casualty lists of extreme length filled the papers. Women in black went to the War Office, and wept whilst scanning the lists which hung there. Stocks fell, business suffered and merchants were ruined.

The British were having a shock. Their generals were not invincible even if the common soldiers were. More and more young men of all classes joined the Colours. The City Imperial Volunteers departed for the Front in a roar of patriotism and beer. And still those three little towns held on. And still the patriots at home wore khaki and red ties, and Union Jack waistcoats; still they killed 'Kroojer' with their mouths, and settled among themselves that Cronje—they also made a hash of that name—Botha, Smuts and a cunning devil named De Wet should all go to St. Helena, where they had sent a much greater opponent who answered to the name of Napoleon Buonaparte.

That had been a good while ago, and there did not seem to be a Wellington in the South African field to cope with the pastoral-minded but bonny fighters of the Transvaal and the Orange Free State (which had very naturally joined in). The patriots wore little buttons in their coat-lapels bearing photographs of the British generals. Popular brands of cigarettes grew even more popular by including cards with these heroes' portraits and war scenes in their packets. Every boy collected them.

The Navy went ashore in South Africa. Immediately they became the 'Handy Men'. They took ashore with them naval guns of incredible size which were 4·7s. Nowadays a 15-incher is normal equipment and out of date.

Still the country as a whole did not think the war was its active job. Men from all the Colonies were at the Front now. But it was still a long way off, and really a professional affair.

It had got serious as month followed month, and general after general failed. A cavalry leader named French was the only man to add glory to his name, except the gallant besieged defenders. And of these Baden-Powell began to rise in stature. He was a smart fellow, and a showman. Dispatches told of clever surprises which outwitted the Boers, of gallant and successful sorties, of home-made shells and bombs, of entertainments to keep up morale in which he took part, of siege newspapers he edited and even of emergency stamps bearing his head. Queen Victoria did hear of this, and was far from being amused.

But things were in a mess. The music-halls did their best to cheer people up. Warlike ditties of attack or sentiment filled the ears. English singers blared of Irish patriotism to the cause:

> "What do you think of the Irish now,
> What do you think of the boys?
> You used to call us traitors, but on my soul,
> You read the names on Glencoe's death-roll!"

they bellowed, and also:

> "Bravo, Dublin Fusiliers,
> You're no craven mutineers.
> You stormed and took Glencoe's dark height—
> Put four thousand crafty Boers to flight—
> Oh, the grand and glorious sight—
> Bravo, Dublin Fusiliers!"

The Dublin Fusiliers had done that. But nobody hymned the deeds of the English 'Tommy Atkins' who took the brunt of it all uncomplainingly. There was:

> Good-bye, Dolly, I must leave you,
> Though it breaks my heart to go.
> Something tells me I am needed
> At the Front to fight the foe.
> See, the soldier boys are marching—
> I can no longer stay.
> Hark, I hear the bugles calling!
> Good-bye, Dolly Gray;

and:

> Good-bye, my Bluebell,
> Farewell to you.
> One last long look into your eyes so true.
> By camp-fires gleaming, 'midst shot and shell,
> I shall be dreaming of my own Bluebell.

There was, in the true British way, an immediate parody to this which ran:

> Good-bye, my Blue Bell,
> Farewell to you.
> One last look into your eyes like glue.
> When on the treadmill
> Think of me well—
> I shall be boozing at the Old Blue Bell.

That was very popular with the troops. The British Army marched to war to the tunes of the music-hall.

There was a young hero named Bugler Dunn, a gallant lad who blew his bugle and stuck to his post though wounded. He also swam a river with his arm broken. He became national. When he appeared at the Royal Military Tournament he was cheered to the echo, his hand was nearly shaken off and money showered on him. That Middle Class boy who saw the Diamond Jubilee shook Bugler Dunn's hand, and gave him half a crown collected from a kind aunt. He envied the bugler. Being a well-grown lad and looking more than his years, he tried to enlist, and got his ears boxed by the recruiting sergeant. It hurt him too, and that is his own personal and private memory of the Great Boer War, untold until now.

Something had to be done. The great news was announced. 'Bobs' himself was going out to take charge, with Kitchener—no longer the 'Sirdar', but Lord Kitchener of Khartoum—as his Chief of Staff. The whole nation cheered up. And well they might.

The tide turned. The generalship of Roberts, the vast reinforcements, the application of lessons learnt, and the amazing organization of Kitchener, took immediate effect. Good news appeared. A nation heard with heartfelt relief that Dundonald had relieved the gallant Sir George White and his starving defenders of Ladysmith. The Handy Men and their 4·7s helped in this, beating the German-manned 'Long Toms'. And then French, the dashing Cavalry man, thrust his way up the centre, helping Plumer to relieve the brave Devonian Kekewich in Kimberley. Still Mafeking held on.

Those towns, and Mafeking in particular, had held up British prestige from falling flat, had sustained it when it most needed sustaining. The fall of Mafeking could not have affected the course of the war, or its final outcome, one iota; but its gallant and brilliant defence, with its supremely British improvisation by its funny-hatted defender with the equally awkward name, was a cornerstone of British prestige during the blackest period of the portion of British history of which this country has the least reason to be proud. Most people called this gallant Hussar 'Barden-Pow-ell'. Some said 'Bayden-Pow-ell'; few knew or cared that it was 'Bayden-Pole'.

But, one Friday night, news came upon London like a thunder-clap which sent it wild with delight. Mafeking had been relieved. Shows were interrupted to tell the news; the whole city—the whole country—went mad with enthusiasm. Strangers were clapped on the back and stood drinks; the 'pubs' were filled to overflowing and people danced in the street with others they had never seen before, without a thought of introduction. There had been mild rejoicings when Ladysmith and Kimberley were relieved, but not like this. The Middle Class decorated their houses—they had started to do this every time a victory was announced. And on the Saturday morning that Middle Class boy and his people went down to town again to see the sights.

They saw an eyeful. They saw a packed mass of frenzied humanity outside the Mansion House cheering without ceasing. They saw processions going along with loaves of bread on tops of broomsticks labelled 'Food for Mafeking'. They saw soldiers being carried shoulder-high, and maybe grateful for it, for they had been bought so much free beer that it is doubtful if they could have walked. Everyone in khaki was a hero—he might have defended Mafeking, if he had had the luck to be there. They took the will for the deed. 'Ticklers' were thrust into their faces as they went along—and 'ticklers' were full-sized, full-length peacocks' feathers of considerable nuisance value. They received squirts of water all over them from little leaden tubes—another strange way by which the British showed their joy and pleasure.

Buses with decorated whips were filled with men and women singing patriotic songs, and the inverted pleasure of riding on the roofs of hansom-cabs was everywhere indulged. London had burst out into bunting, and it was a City of Carnival. Its inhabitants were engaged in putting a new verb into the British language—the verb 'to maffick'. But rowdy and noisy as the occasion was, it was all good-tempered and well-intentioned fun. There was horseplay, but with humour. There were none of the screaming disgraceful scenes of mass-hysteria witnessed at the arrival of American film stars at shows to be graced by Royalty. Yet that Mafeking crowd had really something to rejoice about.

That Middle Class boy and his family had an object in view. They had looked up in a directory (not the Telephone Directory) the home address of the Hero of Mafeking, and they thought they would go and have a look. They congratulated themselves that in this they would be alone, owing to their astuteness, and they set off—if memory serves—to Knightsbridge. They soon discovered that they were by no means alone, and that tens of thousands of other Londoners had been smitten with the same idea. In common with a great mass of people, they filed by that quiet, tall house which had a determined knot of 'cheerers' stationary before it, and saw the family of the man of the hour acknowledging the plaudits from the steps.

And so to their own home, tired but happy.

Lieutenant-Colonel R. S. S. Baden-Powell—to die Lord Baden-Powell —made that hat of his world-famous on the heads of his Scouts, a movement which spread all over the earth. Thus from the tin shanties of Mafeking under the sniping of Boer Mausers came one of the best training movements for youth the world has ever seen.

Later still that Middle Class boy was to meet his hero and help materially in one of the greatest rallies Scouting ever held.

But meanwhile the Great Boer War went on.

CHAPTER XXI

The Face on the Sovereign Changes

THE BOER WAR WAS THE GREATEST MILITARY MESS AND MUDDLE IN WHICH Great Britain had ever been enmeshed. Everything was mismanaged until Roberts and Kitchener went out. The Boers had been entirely underrated, the method of warfare misunderstood and the preparations were entirely inadequate. The British generals, in almost every case, proved unfitted for their task. Experience gained at Aldershot, or in the little campaigns against unorganized coloured races, was of no use against this enemy. Nor could the generals even handle armies of the size required, although they were small enough by modern reckoning. That 'Fifty Thousand Horse and Foot' seemed a force of unimaginable magnitude. But it took a lot more to finish the job. They had tried to fight a cavalry war with infantry.

Casualties were serious, but the worst enemy was sickness. Enteric was a deadly foe, more fatal than Boer bullets, well aimed as these were. The medical service could not cope with the task. It was Alfred Fripp, afterwards knighted and whom a later generation remembers as the founder of 'The Frothblowers', who did much to remedy this state of things. There were not enough nurses, and although there were plenty of volunteers, they were untrained and almost useless. At first the 'Blimps' objected to women nurses at all. The question of commissariat was one gigantic confusion. It was only matched by the strategy and tactics in the field. It took the combined genius of Lord Roberts and Lord Kitchener to pull things together.

The attitude of mind of the great mass of the British public towards this war is extraordinarily difficult for young people to understand. Since then two wars have smitten the world, in both of which this country was a chief participant. In the First World War, although air raids were suffered, they were known to the few and not the many. But death was very near, just across the Channel in France; indeed, death sat on the doorstep, and the best of our youth went to it quietly by train from the London termini, seen off by loved ones who hardly expected to set eyes on them again. Troops moved in secrecy in darkness under the cover of night. The whole nation was in it and suffered in every respect. There was no pageantry about it, no romance, nothing but dirt, filth, maiming and blindness for those who were not sucked down into the whirlpool of extinction which swallowed so many bright young lives.

In the Boer War, it was not an affair of the whole nation at all. It was an affair for the Army, with assistance from the Navy. It was an affair for the Government and the politicians, or statesmen, whichever you liked to call them. Many families suffered bereavement, and for the first time this happened to many Middle Class homes because the sons had volunteered.

But the war was so far away as not to be envisaged. All that was seen of it at home were detachments of troops marching to embarkation, with colours flying, girls encircling them, bands playing, and men in mufti marching alongside as proudly as might be, with the Field Officers still on horseback, and all the panoply of war except the scarlet coat.

It was still war as waged at Waterloo, still an affair of code, of honour, a gentleman's game. It still had glamour and romance. The Middle Classes never saw the dirt, although they did on occasion see wounded men in hospital blue being given an outing, and promptly tried to retard their recovery by making them drunk.

War was an affair of flags, bands, marching, carnivals, giving money to charity, wearing a flag in one's buttonhole, or a tie of patriotic colours. Of displaying photographs of our generals prominently in the home, of doing a bit of knitting for the soldiers—which seldom reached them—of sitting on committees, of singing patriotic songs and cheering at every loyal sentiment. War was only brought home to the vast majority by the rise in income tax (a very slight rise as things are today), the fall in Consols and bad trade in certain quarters.

They saw nothing of it, they knew even less, and then only what the newspapers told them—always one-sided, naturally—and they got their chief ideas from the weekly illustrated papers and the *Daily Graphic*. Here again it was very secondhand, for the pictures were hardly ever photographs; they were either rough sketches, 'drawn by our artist at the Front'—the artist was often very far behind the Front through no fault of his own—or highly imaginative, very popular and extremely spirited pictures drawn by well-known black-and-white artists like René Bull, Stanley L. Wood, Hal Hurst, George Soper and R. Caton-Woodville.

These showed the bravery of the British and the treachery of the Boers. British cavalry with swords flashing, riding horses of impossible speed and action, pursued flying Boers, who fired ineffective revolver-shots over their shoulders whilst being cut down. Boers in full flight whilst Highlanders plunged bayonets into them. A severely wounded and hatless rider, on a steed much fresher than its master, reining up at a cottage door through which peeps a bearded man and his wife, whilst the bloodstained man, pointing with his right arm, pants, "The Boers are coming!" Gordon Highlanders charging downhill—surely a mistake?

325

—whilst an officer points the way with his sword (in case the soldiers did not know) and a piper plays as he runs, with the caption 'The Devils in Petticoats'.

The Boers were always shown as unkempt bearded rascals and the British as glittering heroes. Sometimes sentiment and sadness strikes a note. A nurse in spotless uniform writes on a pad on her knee by candle-light whilst a dying soldier dictates. In the background stands an officer with bowed head (but wearing his helmet), and a second nurse is apparently taking the pulse of another patient but paying scant attention as she gazes over her shoulder at the pathetic scene. It is called 'His Last Letter'.

Another picture shows an upright soldier extending his hand to take something from a badly wounded man in khaki who crawls towards him, and it is 'The Last Cartridge'. There is a picture of an aged white-bearded Boer lying on the ground whilst a Gordon has a bayonet against his chest. The old Boer says: "Kill me, I am satisfied. I have killed five of you *rooineks*." Does the Gordon kill him? He does not. He may be only a private soldier, but he is a gentleman. Gunners serve their guns in the open, without any cover, whilst Boers pour rifle- and shell-fire amongst them from the shelter of *kopjes*. Horse artillery gallop with the guns in and out of action amidst tornadoes of shot which, if the Boer marksman-ship had been all it was cracked up to be, would have annihilated them completely.

Always the British are paladins and Galahads, keeping their wounded captains safe during the bullet-filled nights, sharing the last drops in their water-bottles like so many Sir Philip Sidneys, rescuing everyone in sight who needs rescuing and always seemingly on the attack and victorious. Yet it took such a long time to final victory, a thing which never struck the public (who devoured these pictures with their eyes). Many Middle Class people immediately subscribed to a weekly publication called *With the Flag to Pretoria* when war first broke out, but let their subscriptions languish when the flag took such a terrible time in getting there. But that was the sort of idea the British public was given of this war.

When Lord Roberts got to the Front the artists in imagination had a fine time. Mr. Stanley Wood contributed a remarkably good drawing of a wounded soldier (wounded in the head, as apparently from the pictures that was the only place Boer bullets ever struck—good marks-manship again) lying beside a rock. Mounted Colonial cavalry sit by, with plumes in their slouch hats, and nobody is doing anything for him.

But stay, the figure of a small man with a white moustache, a tiny white chin tuft, who wears a regulation helmet, has dismounted and is approaching the casualty, water-bottle in hand. Yes, it is! It is Field Marshal Lord Roberts himself, Commander-in-Chief, who is doing this kindly deed; and the Tommy is so astounded (as well he might be) that he lifts his hand to his forehead in salute, breaking Queen's Regulations because he is not wearing a hat. Below the picture it says, ' "Bobs" and One of his Beloved "Boys" '.

You see what an advantage a black-and-white artist has over a mere photographer. No photographer ever got a picture like that! And there was another drawing which was amazingly popular. It showed a remarkably tidy interior (for a house in the field of war). In it sits Lord Roberts, with a dear little golden-haired girl on his knee. He is showing her a picture-book. An aide-de-camp comes through the door, his expression anxious, and obviously important dispatches in his hands. "Go away," says the Commander-in-Chief, "can't you see I'm busy?" Prints of that picture had an enormous sale, and that was the sort of idea the Middle Classes had of the war.

But Roberts and Kitchener got busy and cleaned things up. Buller was broken and sent home. His Devonshire supporters never forgot and never forgave. Years afterwards, when Lord Roberts went to Exeter to make a speech, he was booed heartily. Buller has his statue in Exeter today. He was a fine soldier, but not a fine general.

The Boer War was a Jingo war—with the great bulk of the nation as Jingoes. They could not conceive how a foreigner dared to stand up to this country—they never asked themselves against whom war was to be waged, if not foreigners. It made them mad to think that what they regarded as a pack of farmers could make this great Empire go all out to win and inflict serious defeats upon its arms. But such was the case.

Lord Roberts had broken the main resistance by 1901. The war was then in its second year. He returned home full of glory, leaving the rest to Kitchener. And 'Bobs' went to see the old Queen, to tell her personally about her soldiers and that they had won again. He saw her on 2nd January, 1901, when he told her that the war was practically over. It had clouded her last years, this war, which she had never liked, and an interview with the conqueror of her enemies was almost her last function. She received him again on 14th January. She had conferred an Earldom and the Garter upon him.

At that last interview between ageing soldier and aged Queen, whom he had served so well, the two took farewell of each other. On 18th January she could not take her customary drive. It became known that she was seriously ill. The family gathered at Osborne, Isle of Wight. The Duke of Connaught hurried home from Berlin, and the German Emperor came with him. This nearly wiped out the memory of his telegram to

Kruger. But at any rate he was her grandson. At half past six on the evening of 22nd January, 1901, in the heart of her family, with her son and heir by her side, the great Queen passed away and the Victorian age was at an end.

The nation was stunned at the passing of the Queen, and that is not too strong a word. She had seemed so permanent, she had seemed to be timeless, immortal. Few people remembered anything different, for she had reigned sixty-four years.

She had stood for the security, the rocklike firmness of British life, for its stability, for its invincibility, and for its morality as well. There had been no shadow of reproach, she was almost inhuman in her altitude above suspicion. She was the embodiment of the home and the mother which was the ideal of womanhood, at least to the Middle Classes. She had seen her century through and died on the threshold of a new one. And now she had gone. Could it ever be the same again? people asked each other. In many ways it was not. A definite era had come to an end. History may repeat itself, but an era cannot.

The Victorian Age went to its grave on Saturday, 2nd February, 1901. It accompanied the body of its progenitor across the Solent under guard of her Navy the evening before, when the remains rested at Portsmouth. The following morning the coffin and its great little lady came to her capital. The Queen was to drive through London for the last time.

It was a cold, biting misty morning, cheerless and grim, as though the elements mourned the passing. That Middle Class boy who had seen the Queen on her day of diamonds stood in Hyde Park with a myriad of other people. He had been there since 6 a.m., and he was in the front row immediately behind the soldiers. That vast crowd waited in silence, numbed with the cold and with genuine grief and the utter solemnity of the occasion. Other well-loved Sovereigns have passed that way since, sincerely mourned, but not with the complete sorrow that existed for this one.

Except when the police ordered too-eager sightseers out of trees or a branch snapped under the undue weight, there was hardly a sound, and not a speck of colour. Everyone wore black. The scarlet of the troops was hidden by their greatcoats. It was sombre, it was wonderful. Then faintly, and in the distance, came the music of a military band, and the waiting crowd heard those muted notes of incredible sadness, of soulful melancholy, which Chopin put into his Funeral March. There was a hiss of intaken breath. She was coming. There was a sway, but a noiseless sway, as the crowd moved closer to the roadway.

The band drew nearer and nearer, and the first mounted men at its head were passing by, when that Hyde Park crowd of Londoners gently but firmly edged the line of troops aside and lined the route themselves. There was no fuss, no noise, no struggle. They were determined to be as near her as possible when their Queen passed by for the last time. And right in front, standing next to a soldier and with a policeman on the other side, was that boy.

The Queen had left word that she was to be buried with military honours, and military honours she had. The soldiers and the sailors, horse, foot and artillery, were there again, as they had been at the Diamond Jubilee. But the march was slow, the eyes downcast, the weapons reversed. After today, they felt, they would be Soldiers of the Queen no more. The great cavalcade went slowly by, the bands expressing the sadness of the whole multitude. Then, like a shock, came some scattered cheering. A small man on a large horse sternly flung up his hand, and the cheering stopped immediately. It was Lord Roberts, and they had acclaimed the man who had brought them to victory. But only for the moment.

And the Queen came by, as all eyes gazed upon her—or what represented her on that mournful occasion. What had been Queen Victoria lay on a gun-carriage drawn by horses who seemed grief-stricken themselves as they pulled that incredibly small and light burden which had in life represented so much majesty, so much greatness. She lay under her flag —hers and the people who paid her homage, with heads bared and with tearstained faces. Not tears of joy this time, but tears of genuine sorrow. They did not bow their heads, for they wanted to see the last of her. They saw the pall, they saw the flag, and in imagination they saw the Queen as they had known and loved her. Once again she rode with an escort of Kings. Five Kings (including an Emperor and many Crown Princes and Royalty) followed that dead Queen-Empress, that true British woman, on her last ride.

That boy and that multitude looked at their new King, but he seemed still the Prince of Wales, for She was still present. They looked also at the menacing but striking figure of the German Emperor, the Kaiser, who, they saw, was looking at them. He gazed at that British crowd with steady stare, looking across a sea of heads and faces. And that British crowd gazed back at him. He and his were to meet that British crowd again, and it was to take his might and majesty from him. But nobody thought of it that day.

In silence she passed through her capital and entrained for Windsor, there to lie beside her husband, whom she had so deeply loved and mourned and with whom, no doubt, her spirit was already united. And as that tiny coffin went into the Royal Vault at Windsor the Victorian Age passed.

329

The Victorian Age passed and the Edwardian period began.

There was a new face on the sovereign now, a new face of a man whom the nation knew and loved. He had pleased them as Prince of Wales. He had become one of themselves. He had mixed with them, he had been a man of the world, he had been tremendously democratic in an undemocratic Court. He was universally known as 'Teddie', but nobody would have dared to take a liberty like that near him. For he was Royal, and he showed it. There was a humanity about him which everyone liked.

Some severe Victorians shook their heads over him, but the Middle Classes loved and respected him. He was a Man and he was a Sportsman. There was no higher praise. He understood them and they understood him. They knew, too, that he would stand no nonsense from the foreigners. His voice might not be a typical English voice, but it was the Voice of England none the less.

There was great curiosity to know what name he would elect for kingship. He was christened Albert Edward. There had never been a King Albert—it had not the hallowing tradition of English royalty. But still . . . However, he announced his title as Edward VII, and everyone was delighted. The royal names of England went on, nothing was to be imported.

Preparations went ahead for his Coronation and his people prepared for a gala day. Then, like a thunderbolt, came the news that he was ill. He was to undergo an operation. He had a new illness called appendicitis. The operation was performed and he made a fine recovery. The national spirit went sky-high again. They loved King Edward and his beautiful Queen Alexandra.

He was crowned on 9th August, 1902. The new century had brought a new sovereign, and the golden one would shine as brightly. Everything was *fin de siècle* for a couple of years prior to this, now the new century was an accomplished fact. But there was a lot to get used to. It was E.R. now, not V.R. That latter cypher was still on all the pillar-boxes and the usual places of display. It still lingers here and there, though nearly half a century has passed. The deep impression of over sixty years takes a deal of eradication. So, in odd corners, you may still see a letter-box bearing V.R. upon it. There is one outside Theatre Royal, Drury Lane.

There was a new head on the stamps. Victoria had been the first Sovereign to have her head on a postage stamp. There was a new face on the coins. It was now the Soldiers of the King. It was strange to have to say 'Send Him Victorious', to speak of K.C.s instead of Q.C.s in referring to legal luminaries. It was strange to get the masculine note into what had been so essentially feminine for so long. But by the time the Coronation was due most people—and especially the very loyal Middle Classes—were getting accustomed to the new order.

A Coronation in August upset the regular London season. Instead of nobody being in town in that dead month, everyone was there. Gaiety resumed its sway, for with the passing of the old Queen there had been a gradual loosening-up. The pace of life quickened imperceptibly. The old stern discipline became easier, the girths were loosened, the rein was freer on the curb. And also imperceptibly the old-fashioned Victorian moral regime was passing away—to take with it so many things characteristic of this country and its Middle Class.

One of the Coronation songs of the music-halls gave the direct example of this. Everyone sang it, and the chorus went:

> On Coronation Day, on Coronation Day,
>   We'll all be merry,
>   Drinking whisky, wine and sherry;
> We'll all be merry
> On Coronation Day.

Simple, silly if you like, but symbolic. Nobody had sung of being merry on wine and spirits on the occasion of Queen Victoria's Diamond Jubilee. The Victorian bonds were off, and the Edwardian days were in full flood.

The Coronation of King Edward, though a splendid affair of regal pomp and dignity glittering with gold and diamonds and marked with the novelty of all beholders of the crowning of the Queen Consort as well—nobody thought of her as anything else but Queen Alexandra, 'The Sea King's daughter from over the sea', as old Victorian Lord Tennyson had called her—did not seem so impressive as the Diamond Jubilee either. There was all the glory and all the flags and all the Royalty —but not such a thrill by a very long way.

But the nation cheered from its heart, for it loved its new King. It took a deep breath and moved along a lot faster. A man was at the helm now, a man sat on the ancient throne. Things could be robust, more hearty, more in tune with the King who went to the races, frequented the Theatre as a regular patron and was well known in the haunts of even the Middle Classes. On with the dance, let joy be unconfined! The sovereign was worth its full twenty shillings under the male Sovereign. And the Middle Classes were as stable and as strong as ever.

Out in South Africa the war had come to an end at last. It had been finished up by the super-efficient Kitchener. He caught most of the enemy generals in his net. Cronje, the Boer Napoleon, followed his

331

greater prototype to St. Helena. But they could not catch De Wet. Often reported caught, he was always reported on the run again.

The public and the Middle Classes began to have a kindly feeling for him. This game of hare and hounds began to have more the appearance of sport than war. Old De Wet was a sportsman. Lord Kitchener was having great drives and rounding up most of the Boers, but De Wet always slipped through. But at last the game was up, and he and Delarey sent word they wanted to come in. Kitchener's mopping-up was complete.

There was a very different spirit abroad now as regards the Boers. From dastardly traitors of the most treacherous doings, from the cruel torturers of the poor blacks, they had come to be looked upon as beaten enemies. Therefore they were, so far as the British went, practically friends. That was the British way, the Middle Class way, the way of cricket, the way of the sportsman. There is little doubt that the tactful hand of King Edward himself had a good deal to do with the final settlement which took place. The first Boer offer of terms had been a little cheeky and had received the curtest of treatment from Kitchener. The second, negotiated by Generals Smuts and Hertzog, led to a final settlement. The Transvaal and the late Orange Free State became British. It was all over. And the King-Emperor included them in his Dominions when he was crowned in an Empire at peace, as was fitting for the man who was to be known as Edward the Peacemaker.

The long-drawn-out war ended in June 1902. There were some peace rejoicings, but little of the fierce spirit of Jingoism remained, everyone had had enough. The Soldiers of the King had won, but British eyes had been opened to the tune of a list of defeats longer than they had ever suffered, and 4,188 officers killed and wounded and 93,000 N.C.O.s and other ranks. Cecil Rhodes had died in March 1902. He never lived to see the end of his dream realized.

Now the dance of the Edwardian life began in earnest. There was a much faster beat to the rhythm. There was much more expansion. Royalty spread from the homeland to visit the realm overseas. The man who had been Duke of York and was now Prince of Wales, and his wife, Princess May, went for a world tour amidst great enthusiasm. Science, which had made great strides under Victoria, made bounds forward under the new King. The internal combustion engine began to take its place in the world it was to revolutionize. King Edward bought a motorcar. The aristocracy naturally followed him. The Middle Class did their best to follow the lead, and if they did not own motors at least discussed them.

Money began to be spent in much greater freedom than under Victoria. People opened their pockets and entertained. The country was overpoweringly rich and unbelievably prosperous. There did not seem a cloud in the sky and pleasure-seeking grew more and more fashionable.

The Middle Classes followed, as the Middle Classes always did. If they had got together, if they had combined and become a solid whole presenting a solid front when clothed in the armour of the golden sovereign, the whole course of history might have changed. But they did not. Neither then nor at any future time did they, by combined effort, take the power which should have been theirs.

The reason was easy to discover. Nobody with money would admit that they were of the Middle Class, for under the new regime the possession of money was becoming as important as the possession of birth and blood. It had not been so under Victoria. But it was becoming so now. And as none of the Middle Classes would ever admit they had not plenty of money, they never got together. In their hearts they knew they were Middle Class, but they could not bring themselves to blazon it abroad. It was a fetish of the Middle Classes that they were always individually a little better than the others of the same class. It led them to what has followed. They did not know that Union was Strength.

But Labour was becoming a power. There was a Labour Member elected to Parliament and people gasped and talked of a revolution. That man Keir Hardie, a marvellous fellow, stood alone in the Finest Club in the World, as the House of Commons was then called and regarded, and others came to join him. Labour was disputing about its rights. The Middle Classes thought that a bit difficult to understand, and the Upper Classes thought it rather beneath their notice. Parliament was still a most exclusive place. It was still possible to have a Prime Minister who was in the House of Lords, although the last two were the Earl of Rosebery and the Marquis of Salisbury. There were still great figures in politics.

Home Rule was the main issue: should Ireland look after her own affairs or not? That question vexed the nation, interfered with far more important business and even split families. Liberals were in favour of Home Rule; Gladstone, the Grand Old Man, now dead, had been its great champion. The Conservatives were dead against it, so much so that it was now the thing to call it the Unionist Party. There were all sorts of subdivisions too, and quite a lot of Liberal-Unionists.

Things in the House were not nearly so clear-cut as they are today. But there were great names, men who made history, men like Lansdowne, Goschen, A. J. Balfour, Joseph Chamberlain, and later his son Austen. There was Campbell-Bannerman, Brodrick, Birrell, Morley, Grey, Asquith, Chaplin (who was called 'The Squire'), and there were men of the new group like John Burns.

333

Debates were long and regarded as very important. Speeches were long, and Mr. Chaplin represented the old school of prolixity who would say, "I tell the Right Honourable Gentleman opposite that I assert, I aver, I go so far as to say that I asseverate"—and people thought it was fine. There were colourful characters like Sir Frederick Banbury, possessed of such skill that he could stand on his feet and speak for hours when a Bill had to be talked out. The Irish Members still occupied a position of power and often held the balance of it in the British Parliament. Joseph Chamberlain started something new.

A new menace was arising in Europe. It showed itself more clearly as soon as the old Queen was dead. This was a challenge from the young Power, the German Empire, made into a choate whole from an inchoate mass when Germany had thrashed France in the war of 1870. Germany had become powerful, but was not yet ready to challenge Great Britain to a trial of strength. She was, however, doing so commercially. She was using every means to push those goods all over the world which the British despised because they were 'Made in Germany', and therefore cheap and nasty. They were, however, beginning to be bought in increasing numbers. Over-production in teeming Germany led to dumping of surplus goods on the English market at such ridiculous prices that people just had to buy them.

British labour and British merchants, both slow and conservative at heart, did not compete against the menace. Chamberlain used a new word of power. He wanted a Tariff. Most Middle Class people, when this word suddenly blazed across their Press, blinked their eyes. Chamberlain demanded Tariff Reform. They thought a tariff was a price list in a restaurant—something stuck on a wall where it did not run to menus. It appeared that Joe meant much more. It meant making the foreign prices rise so that ours could be kept up. That was how they understood it.

To many it seemed a good idea. To many it must be right because Joe and the Conservative Party (Unionist, if you like) proposed it. It was aimed against the foreigner, which was good. And there was no denying that there was something in this talk of Unemployment one heard on all sides. "Make the Foreigner Pay" was apparently popular.

The Conservatives had ridden into power on an easy rein on a Khaki election. They had persuaded the country that the Union Jack and the safety of Britain was their especial property. The Liberals had been caught short of cordite—a war material—and some of their leaders had been pro-Boer. Shocking! But they rallied to this new fight. They stood, they said, for a Free Breakfast Table under Free Trade. They declared that the new Tariff Reform would increase the price of food. That was a good card. They also gave more than a hint that it would increase the price of beer.

That was a much better card. Beer was beer then and sincerely believed in and as sincerely consumed.

There was also another issue raised, that of Chinese slavery. Yellow labour had been imported at very cheap rates to work in the newly acquired goldmines on the Rand. Howls of righteous indignation went up from certain quarters that these poor slaves were kept in compounds and paid only a shilling a day. It was not mentioned very clearly that the shilling was the daily pay of the British soldier—who had to take his chance of getting killed on it and that it was subject to many deductions, which reduced it to about ninepence.

Unemployment was an issue. One side drew direful pictures of starving, workless men, which the other side described as unemployables. The theatre was far more political then than now—the radio seems to have superseded it in this respect—and the Gaiety summed up the position in *The Orchid*, when Edmund Payne and George Grossmith Junr. sang their inevitable duet. This time they were 'unemployed':

> We're two British working men, honest and free,
>   But alas we are both unemployed.
> Whenever we start out to look for some work,
>   The coppers always get annoyed.
> They shove us in jail, without a kind word,
>   And I'm sure that there's no luck about,
> For as soon as we both of us get settled down,
>   I'm blowed if they don't let us out.
>
> When will justice be done to England?
>   When will they allow us to earn our own bread?
> It ain't much enjoyment to ask for employment,
>   And only get work instead.

That was applauded nightly, especially by the secure and happy Middle Class. But the political fight came to a clash in 1906. It was Tariff Reform versus Free Trade, the new thought against the old. There were the side issues of Chinese Slavery, the Free Breakfast Table and Beer, and the Unemployed. The Unionists plumped for Tariff Reform, the Liberals proved themselves conservative by sticking to Free Trade, under which, they said, the country had grown prosperous. The Conservative Middle Class supported the Liberal idea and in went the Liberals and Free Trade with an amazing majority. The Unionists were almost wiped out. Balfour was beaten in the first round of the fight and he was the leader. Bonar Law, another promising Conservative youngster—later to be Prime Minister—was beaten too. Manchester led the way of the veritable landslide and only Birmingham stood fast for Chamberlain—his own town. The Liberals were in and stayed in.

But there were happenings abroad. If King Edward officially had no politics he proved a most able Royal Foreign Secretary. He had his eye on that Kaiser, his own nephew. He did not trust him. He did not like him. Despite the necessity for a show of diplomatic friendship and exchanges of visits, he made no secret of his dislike and distrust. He had said, and it was common knowledge, that German William was 'no gentleman'. Nothing was more deadly at that time. There had been trouble abroad in the East. The Kaiser set himself up as the Champion of Europe against what he described as the Yellow Peril. He was not far wrong, except he thought that peril was China instead of Japan. There had been a rebellion in China by what were called the Boxers—and troops of all the European Powers combined to put it down. It was the fault of the Dowager Empress of China, who was much more concerned with keeping the affairs of her own country in her own hands than in menacing anyone.

Japan, whom Britain had taken up on its emergence from medieval life at a very late hour, went to war with China and thrashed the pig-tailed warriors, whose leaders were entirely corrupt. Japan had tasted blood. To the amazement of most people she fell foul of Russia, that truly great Power, whom Great Britain regarded as a secret enemy, despite the fact that the Tsar was a relative of Victoria's too (as indeed who was not?), and was quite certain had designs on India. Also Russia was the last Continental Power whom Britain had fought. The giant of the West went for the pigmy of the East, the Bear reached out at the Rising Sun.

Most people imagined Japan would be overwhelmed. But it seemed this Russian giant had feet of clay. Its fleet sailed to exterminate the saucy Japs. That fleet got an early attack of nerves and opened fire upon some harmless English fishing-boats in the North Sea, sinking one and killing some of the crew. A roar of indignation went up. It was the trawler *Crane*, of Hull, which suffered most. The Russian admiral had the difficult name of Rozhdestvensky, which added to the popular indignation. The British Home, Channel and Mediterranean Fleets rushed to take action. The Home and the Channel Fleets shepherded this unreliable Armada right up to the Straits of Gibraltar, and the Mediterranean Fleet kept it in view thereafter and saw it off the premises as a suspected criminal.

The Tsar had apologized, but it was very nearly war. It is a wonder that Admiral Lord Charles Beresford did not 'have a go'. Nothing would have pleased him better. But the safe hands of Edward the Peacemaker guided the more important ship of State. The Japanese Fleet, British

336

trained, did not wait for the Russian Fleet. It sailed to meet it and sent it to the bottom off the Philippines. Japan won the war but it was almost stalemate. As soon as it was over Britain astonished the world by making an alliance with Japan.

The mention of the Channel Fleet shows very clearly who was, till then, regarded as Britain's chief enemy—her ancient foe of France. The amazing King Edward was to alter all that. He knew that France hated Germany. So, in spite of his ancestry, did he. Or maybe he just hated the Kaiser. It was just as good in the end. King Edward moved about Europe. He went everywhere, he was seen, liked and cheered by all nations. He went to Greece when the Olympic Games were started—or perhaps restarted after centuries of abeyance—and walked in a procession of Royalty wearing a naval cap, an Admiral's dress frock-coat and white trousers—and still remained every inch a King. He had the Queen of Greece on his arm. Queen Alexandra placed her dainty hand within the arm of the King of Greece, the other nations were nowhere.

Bad blood existed in France. Fashoda was not forgotten and the French took a poor view of our policy and action in the Boer War. But France hated Germany and King Edward the Peacemaker played his cards. He made not a treaty, not an alliance—nothing so dogmatic and aggressive as that—with our Gallic neighbours. No, he made an *Entente*—which was called *L'Entente Cordiale*.

At once everything French was perfect. The two nations fell on each other's necks. The King went to Paris and became the most popular man it had ever acclaimed. Streets and hotels were named after him. President Loubet returned the call. The English—especially the Middle Classes—sniggered at his formal evening dress—the perfidious English still—but every Englishman loved Paris and the *chic* French women, and every English woman loved the dresses of Paris even if she disapproved of their native wearers. So that was all right. The British and the French Fleet fraternized, all thought of Trafalgar forgotten. *Vive L'Entente Cordiale* was a Middle Class toast, and the feeling about it was much sounder than the accent.

France had alliances with Italy and Russia. King Edward had his nephew nicely encircled, who had only the weak, sprawling and tottering Austrian-Hungarian Empire to fall back upon—the Empire which had been our only friend in the Boer War. There was no need for that Channel Fleet. It became the North Sea Fleet, sailing the German Ocean.

But all the while life grew gayer and more carefree. The Middle Classes were shocked at the doings of the Smart Set, but began to live in flats. The Home was weakening, the young were straying a little and getting far more independent. The churches and chapels missed regular faces as

people—Middle Class people—indulged in week-ends. The birth-rate
started to fall, people wanted to have a good time. They could have a good
time and they did have a good time because of that golden sovereign,
which was still bright, secure and powerful and worth its twenty shillings
anywhere in the realm, and more outside of it.

Edward the Peacemaker kept the Peace and his sovereignty kept up
the sovereign.

CHAPTER XXII

Pastimes and the Press

FOR THE MIDDLE CLASSES, LIFE DID NOT CHANGE UNDER THE NEW
Sovereign as it did for the Upper and Leisured Classes. The golden
sovereign still reigned for them and gave them happy, sheltered lives.
Life was a much narrower affair; there were no such things as pleasure
cruises. The bulk of the Middle Classes, except men who went on business,
had never been abroad. Some went from Folkestone to Boulogne for
the day, a few took a week in Paris, and a few ventured on Cook's
Tours, remaining together, huddled for safety. You could not trust these
foreigners! Only a sprinkling had ever been to America. And when they
did venture overseas they were always glad to get back again. They
believed the English way was the best, and it certainly took a bit of beating
in those days of prosperity.

They got their fun all the same, for there was plenty to do. They did
not spend their time complaining of boredom induced by satiation of
amusement, and rushing about the countryside in search of cocktails.
They did not drink cocktails anyway—women most certainly did not.
A man would have a mixed vermouth, a gin and It, a sherry and bitters,
peach bitters, or a thing called a 'Cherry Mixture', which tasted very like
hairoil and cost fourpence. Palates were not attuned to snacks; they
wanted joints, steaks, chops, steak-and-kidney pudding, poultry, soles,
salmon and such-like fare, and lots of good beer or spirits. Women
found plenty to do at home, and so did the children.

Boys had a grand time during the Boer War collecting cigarette-cards,
and invented a new form of gambling with them. You stood in a line and
flicked the cards. The flicker who flicked farthest won the kitty. They took
the numbers of steam engines, as they do today, and when cars came on
the road they collected registration numbers, and were very knowing
about the initial letter and the county it represented. To see a car in London
with, say, the Durham registration mark was a great excitement.

Girls did not collect like boys, who went in for stamps, birds' eggs,
butterflies, cigarette-cards, pets (although girls had pets too), and there
were even some connoisseurs who collected matchbox fronts. Girls had
a passion for old bits of ribbon and trifles of a sentimental nature. When
older, they treasured dance programmes.

The picture-postcard craze lasted for years and the postcards were kept
in albums made especially for the purpose. Everyone sent hundreds of

picture postcards to their friends when they went away and expected the same in return. They all went into the albums, but not as a rule into the album which contained the theatrical celebrities. Those were kept apart, as befitted a race apart. Most children, and some adults, kept scrapbooks. Sheets of 'scraps', highly coloured, and glazed cut-out figures, were joined by little white slips which were cut through, and the scraps affixed with a good deal of paste (usually too much) in the scrap-book. The consequence was that the pages usually stuck together. The adults put 'treasures' in theirs, pictures cut out of the papers, fashion plates, recipes, all sorts of things, and an old scrap-book is a good piece of contemporary history and personality.

There were some very odd crazes which went the rounds of the Middle Classes. Such a one was the fashion for making 'rubbish plates'! A tin plate was purchased for a few pence and lined with putty. In this putty were stuck odds and ends of real rubbish, old keys, broken bits of watches, nails, old buttonhooks, bootbuttons, acorns, any litter, and then it was all painted completely over with gold paint. Some people covered the putty with odds and ends of old lace, to be gilded. Others covered it with bits of broken china and glass. The results were regarded as artistic triumphs and hung on the walls. They always looked exactly what they were—rubbish plates.

The Middle Classes read a great deal. There was a 'library' in nearly every house. It was, it must be remembered, a conversational age which the telephone had not spoiled, so one had to be *au fait* with the latest literature. There were books in every house; people bought them and kept them. They did not only rely on the libraries. Outside the free ones and Mudie's, there were not so many libraries as now. *The Times* Book Club made a sensation with a kind of hire-purchase system, but many people were shy of it. If you heard of a book you ought to read, you bought it. You lent it to your friends, who in turn lent you one that they had bought.

Some stationers ran libraries too, but of small scope. The books you wanted were always 'out'. So it was best to purchase, and you got a first-class novel for 4s. 6d., beautifully bound with gilt or olivine edges. There were plenty of cheap editions, as cheap as sixpence, and the market was flooded with attractive editions of the Classics. There were certain restrictions on reading. Young people were not allowed access to 'daring' books, but usually achieved them surreptitiously, and failed to understand most of it. The daring books of those days would be in Sunday-school libraries now—if there are such things. It was an age of greater decency, less frankness and less vulgarity. French novels and 'yellowbacks' were taboo in most Middle Class houses.

People read Conan Doyle—and his 'Sherlock Holmes' series in the

340

Strand Magazine were looked forward to with trembling eagerness; W. W. Jacobs and his real British humour; Anthony Hope (whose *Prisoner of Zenda* put the word 'Ruritania' into the language, even if the sequel was not quite as good); Stanley Weyman, the master of cloak and sword; Charles Garvice (whose sentimental stories had the most phenomenal sales). H. G. Wells?—a bit advanced even then, although his Martian and Moon Stories were terrific—and *Kipps* was acclaimed a classic at once, following his first success with *Mr. Hoopdriver*. People did not pay much attention to the Socialism preached in the books, they read them as stories. They had not realized that they were reading the works of a prophet—indeed, how should they?

Marie Corelli was perhaps the most discussed authoress and she took herself very seriously too. She went to live at Stratford-on-Avon and possibly believed her works were for all time. She is almost forgotten today. 'Ouida' was still read, and still considered a little shocking by mammas, but the younger and better informed people never believed in the hero who leapt lightly into the racing skiff—they knew he would have gone right through it.

But *Under Two Flags* held the stage for years, in dramatic form, and with a very good actress (still very active and very much alive in the theatre) named Ida Molesworth as 'Cigarette'. There was F. Marion Crawford, E. F. and A. C. Benson, Owen Wister, Rolf Boldrewood (American and Australian respectively), Rosa Nouchette Cary, Edith Wharton, Rhoda Broughton, Gertrude Atherton, 'Frank Danby' (a woman writer of daring books), Cutcliffe Hyne, who created 'Captain Kettle', the fearless, pugnacious little red-bearded captain of the Mercantile Marine; Max Pemberton, whose *Iron Pirate* was a best-seller; Bertram Mitford, who, like Rider Haggard, specialized in African stories, but without the true magic Haggard brought to Umslopogaas, Good, Sir Henry, Allan Quatermain in *King Solomon's Mines* and the excitement of *She*; Olive Schreiner, who told stories of the Veldt with mysticism and a religious slant; G. B. Burgin, Quiller-Couch, E. W. Hornung (the creator of 'Raffles'), W. Clark Russell (whose sea stories were a bit old-fashioned in the days of steam), James Payn, Barry Pain (a great humorist), Baring-Gould (does anyone read *Mehalah* or *The Broom Squire* today?), Joseph and Silas Hocking (for serious-minded people), Lucas Malet, Gilbert Parker, Mrs. W. K. Clifford, Mrs. Oliphant, Robert Barr, F. Marriott Watson, Edna Lyall, Maarten Maartens (a foreigner, but liked), Charlotte M. Yonge, Charles Kingsley (amongst the Classics), J. K. Shorthouse, John Trevena (an author who wrote books about Dartmoor and terrified people by his frankness, but who made a big success), Pett Ridge, the true teller of Cockney tales; and scores more.

341

Perhaps the Middle Class adored most the works of Henry Seton Merriman. Here was an author of great narrative skill, who maybe invented the 'strong, silent Englishman'. His heroes were such gentlemanly fellows that female readers took a poor view of their own menfolk, and the menfolk themselves, on reading the stories, felt a bit ashamed of their own shortcomings. There was always a villain in his novels—a real villain too—and, as a set-off to the more volatile hero, a sturdy character of few words but terrific deeds, sometimes a major in the Army, of simple mind, upright soul, pink cheeks and terrific biceps. His heroines were the true Middle Class ideal of Society maidens. There was, as a rule, a couple of elderly people who had loved in their youth but whom force of circumstances, usually to do with finance, had prevented from getting married. Now in their later years, he a diplomat of distinction, she a dowager of high rank, their love still endured, pure, platonic and impersonal, but none the less sincere. Although both widow and widower (or sometimes he had remained single, although the lady had usually married wealth and title), they never thought of getting wed and settling down together. With old-world courtesy he would stand beside her, and with gloved fingers break a lump of sugar into the exact size he remembered she liked as a girl, whilst she wore the colour in her bonnet or on her silk gown which he had praised one summer's evening long ago in the orchard or on the river.

It was all very touching and rather sweet and their politeness was breathtaking. But for all that, Merriman could sweep the reader away with the excitement of his tale, and *With Edged Tools* and *Barlasch of the Guard* are classics of their kind. They appealed to the Middle Classes—and all classes—under the sovereign. Hardy—Thomas Hardy—was being accepted as a great writer. The Middle Class had got over the shocks of *Tess* and some rather crude details in other books, and now believed that Thomas Hardy was of the true soil, as he was and remains.

Alice and Egerton Castle's delightful and fragrant tales—with titles scented to match, of Bath in the days of Nash and 18th-century romance—pleased the Middle Classes. They could not have enough. *Mistress Kitty Bellairs* was very much to their taste—and good judges too—and so was *Young April*, a very charming story which has been very lucky in escaping the doom of being filmed.

Kipling, of course, was a classic already, both in prose and in verse. When he wrote *If* all Middle Class readers learnt it by heart. They adored Jerome K. Jerome—*Three Men in a Boat* was already a classic of home humour and still provides one of the best examples of Victorian Middle Class life. J. M. Barrie caused laughter and tears. That supreme master of narrative, A. E. W. Mason, was always a best-seller with them. They read Meredith because they thought they ought to, but few really understood him. They liked Conrad and Robert Louis Stevenson. *Treasure Island* was a *Boy's Own Paper* serial.

But all of a sudden Romance came into their lives. It came through the work of a handsome, distinguished Civil Servant who wrote a book of great beauty which knocked the Middle Class John and Mary Bull sideways. *The Forest Lovers* took away their breath. And well it might, for here was an illuminated missal and a stained-glass window come to life and action, and a beautiful style in the telling. Hewlett did much other magnificent work, but that was the book for their money. Many romantic mothers christened their baby girls 'Isoult'.

Baby nomenclature was much affected then by outside causes. Many an elderly lady who did not want to appear old cursed the Battle of Alma, which dated her. There was a tremendous crop of Victorias too. And the Boer War left its mark on children and on localities. Speculative builders ran up Mafeking Avenues, Ladysmith Crescents, Kimberley Roads, all over what had been green pastures, and children got saddled with names which shouted their birth period for ever. The music-halls got on to it. Not content with the patriotic songs and the statement that:

> They came to fight from Canada,
> Australia and India,
> They proved themselves in Africa
> A patriotic pattern to the world,

they poked fun at the awful names poor children were getting thrust upon them. There was a very popular song which said:

> The War, the War, the blooming War,
> Has turned my wife insane.
> From Kruger to Majuba, she's
> The Transvaal on the brain.
> So when to christen our first child
> Last Sunday week we tried,
> The parson said, "What's this child's name?"
> And my old girl replied:

> "The baby's name is Kitchener, Carrington,
> Methuen, Kekewich, White,
> Cronje, Plumer, Powell, Majuba,
> Gatacre, Warren, Colenso, Kruger,
> Capetown, Mafeking, French,
> Kimberley, Ladysmith, Bobs,
> Union Jack and Fighting Mac,
> Lyddite Pretoria Blobbs."

343

The song continued to tell of the parson's unavailing protest and the wife's dealing with him in true warlike fashion—'She kicked his mounted infantry, 'Till his Bloemfontein was sore'—and so on. It was a very popular song and just another aspect of the view taken of the Boer War and its effect upon life.

But amongst the later giants of the period towered John Galsworthy, Hugh Walpole, Horace Annesley Vachell, Warwick Deeping (in medieval or modern romance), and Compton Mackenzie—whose *Sinister Street* caused much excitement and is another classic of the period in style, genius and lifelike narrative. *Carnival* is of the period, perfect too.

There was no excuse for not knowing the Classics, which were printed to suit all pockets.

If it was light literature in magazine form that was wanted there was a positive wealth of it, all well printed, well produced and with eminent authors writing it. And those magazines, at 6*d.* and 4½*d.*, were distinctive and gave real value for the money—they were marvellously cheap.

The *Strand*, in its blue cover with the picture of the Victorian Strand, was known to all. It was the leading magazine, fat and thick, with an adroit mixture of informative articles, biographies, long interviews with the famous, and the best fiction. It had given the Middle Classes Conan Doyle and W. W. Jacobs. *Pearson's* had an ornate shiny cover, a blend of red and yellow, and very good contents. The *Pall Mall* was white with Grecian figures on it; the *Windsor* was yellowy green and bore a sketch of Windsor Castle; the *Idler* was a pinky cover, if memory serves, and the *Wide World* was salmon pink, with a female figure with outstretched arms, as if bidding you welcome. The *Wide World Magazine*, of course, is still very widely read, although it differs slightly in form.

In those days this magazine featured true stories of most remarkable excitement. Its slogan was 'Truth is stranger than fiction'. It ran a series of adventures by a man called Louis de Rougemont, who claimed to have been cast away on the unexplored territory of Northern Australia, a vast tract of waterless desert. For a while it was a great success and people marvelled. They began to marvel a bit more when the intrepid castaway-explorer-traveller spoke of wombats flying in the air, for even the Middle Class people knew the wombat was a four-legged animal.

They opened their eyes wider when he rode turtles across fast-flowing, deep, roaring torrents in this waterless territory, found nuggets of gold as big as rocks, and performed other wonders. But when he found two beautiful white women also cast away in the land amongst the aborigines they began to revolt.

Even the magazine took a hand. The editor printed a special note, referring to his slogan, that 'although truth was stranger than fiction, Louis de Rougemont was stranger than both'. No whit abashed, the writer continued to the end of his story and safe return. He could not produce the flying wombats, the rocks of gold, or even the beauteous damsels, but he did succeed in steering a reluctant, large and possibly indignant turtle across the flooded circus ring of the London Hippodrome, after many complete failures, and that one trip, he claimed, justified all he had said. He certainly looked the part. He was gaunt, hardbitten, lean, and deeply tanned, with a face like an Easter Island idol with a pointed white beard. Like the gentleman in *Punch* who saw a unicorn in Woolcombe Wood, nobody believed him.

There was the *Grand Magazine*, all fiction, and scores of others. They all sold. There were quarterlies, many of which still exist, and the *Cornhill*, *Chambers's Journal*, *Blackwoods* (all still going) and the *Review of Reviews*, a magnificent periodical edited by W. T. Stead, one of the truly great men of the period, who suffered imprisonment to prove his word and his cause. There were, on a smaller and cheaper scale, the *Penny Pictorial*, the *Golden Penny*, the *Penny Magazine*—large magazines at a small cost. There were none of the pocket-sized periodicals which exist today; they were all big like their time.

There was, in different style, the *Smart Set*, very well produced, with a picture of a perfectly dressed and modern Adonis in full evening dress (faultless, of course) bowing to a wondrous fair and magnificently gowned lady on a pale grey cover. The editor, Thorold, was the double of George Alexander, and appeared with him once in a play called *John Chilcote, M.P.*

There was a delightful publication on art paper which did much to popularize the famous Gibson Girls in this country, for Charles Dana Gibson, the American artist who created these wondrous creatures— surely George du Maurier was their grandfather—drew regularly for this magazine. And you met the fluffier, more piquant, but no less charming feminine creations of Penrhyn Stanlaws in it too. There were the *Field*, the *Badminton, Town and Country, Horse and Hound* and many more on the purely sporting and country side, and the *Quiver* and *Cassell's Family Magazine*. Many of these and other publications have lasted over.

Amongst the glossy weeklies, then sixpence, now 2s. mostly, there remain the *Tatler*, the *Sketch*, the *Illustrated London News*, the *Sphere*, although the *Illustrated Sporting and Dramatic* has shed its dramatic interest and the *Bystander* is incorporated with the *Tatler*. Both flourished under the Golden Sovereign. So did the *Graphic* and *Black and White*, and for a short time the *Spear*. The *Lady*, the *Queen*, the *Ladies' Pictorial* and the *Ladies' Journal* must be included, all very flourishing concerns then as now. Many others made brief appearances. There was for a time the *Gentleman's Magazine*. It vanished. Perhaps there were no more gentlemen to buy it, or perhaps they did not recognize the title.

Very widely read by women was a pink-coloured little journal called *Modern Society*. Nothing of the lives, doings or relationships of European royalty or the Society of the world was hidden from the editor. Apparently his sleuthlike reporters were everywhere. But women devoured every word—and believed every word too.

Of the lighter masculine papers, some still carry on in different form, and many, alas, have died. They were of their time, they could not long survive the death of the sovereign or the internationalization of this land, for they were very English. The *Pink 'Un*, a weekly paper devoted to sport and the lighter forms of drama, was very famous. On its front page it retailed all the spicy stories of the day. To be seen reading it labelled a man as a gay dog. It was the essence of naughtiness. One might speak of the 'pink of propriety', but the pinkness of the *Pink 'Un* was not that sort of pink—indeed, today it would be called 'blue'. No man ever took it home to the family circle. Yet today its stories are told in the lounge which has succeeded the drawing-room—and worse stories too.

It is, by the way, very significant that the drawing-room has been succeeded by the Lounge. It is a most typical sign of the times. Under the sovereign one did not 'lounge' in public. A 'lounger' was very bad form and a term of reproach. The *Pink 'Un* might go into a lounge (of a pub), but never into a drawing-room, or even a dining-room or parlour.

Pick Me Up was also a very popular paper. It was very well written and very well illustrated, but it was regarded as 'fast'. A rather Gallic young lady in a kind of Phrygian cap, a very tight-fitting, striped bodice revealing a lot of bust, a curious kind of garment of fluff and flounces around her middle, and very pretty legs in long black stockings right to the top of the thigh, like tights, invited your attention to the contents. Sometimes she wore very abbreviated skirts—but she was always delightfully feminine. *Pick Me Up* had a green cover. It got suppressed over something, and the world was the duller for its going.

The *Winning Post*, run by Robert Sievier, took much of the wind out of the *Pink' Un's* sails. This buff-coloured weekly paper was never so amusing as its Pink rival, and did not appear until the *Pink 'Un* had almost run its course. It hovered perpetually on the brink of libel actions —and sometimes slipped over the edge.

London Opinion, now in another form, was a twopenny weekly which started a great craze. It ran a competition for 'Limericks'. You had to supply the last line to the Limerick, of which the first four were printed.

A sixpenny postal order had to accompany that last line and the prize was run on a kind of sweepstake method. The prizes got to fabulous dimensions before the thing died out.

The Limerick craze was started by a music-hall song of George Lashwood, called 'Fol-de-Rol-Lol' and contained such gems as

> In a bootmaker's shop down at Luton
> A lady was trying a boot on.
> When she slipped on the floor
> And the bootmaker saw
> That the girl had a bicycling suit on.

The *London Opinion* Limericks, however, were not on the vulgar side and salacious-minded people did not gain the prizes.

Later there was the *London Mail*, which ran a column called 'Things We Want to Know', which troubled many people whose names appeared therein, either directly or by implication. Those great perennials, *Answers* and *Tit-Bits*, also flourished. For those who liked spice in their pictures as well as in letterpress there were papers like *Sketchy Bits* and *Photo Bits*, which concentrated on the female form in various states of clothing, and were bought by the adolescents. They also were never taken home. And there was a most sensational paper devoted to Crime called the *Police Gazette*. This always had a picture of a murder on the front page with no detail of gore omitted.

There was the *World, Land and Water*, and *Vanity Fair*, which included a coloured cartoon of a celebrity by 'Spy', whose name was Leslie Ward. A *Vanity Fair* cartoon was the hall-mark of fame. Ward was succeeded by Pellegrini, whose *nom-de-plume* was 'Ape'. Many of these cartoons are still framed in clubs all over the world. You find them in legal offices and all sorts of places. They make a picture gallery of contemporary history. They also show how transient is fame.

In 1920 or 1921 there was an exhibition of 'Spy's' cartoons in Bond Street. Hannen Swaffer, the great journalist, went to it. Leaning against the wall, unframed, he saw stacks of 'Spy' cartoons. "Why aren't these framed and on the walls?" he asked. "We don't know the names of one of them," was the surprising answer. Famous enough in their day to be drawn by the leading cartoonist, they were already forgotten. Hannen Swaffer took them back to the offices of the *Daily Graphic* and reproduced a page of them day after day to find out who were the originals, asking the public to identify them. Sometimes twenty different names were sent in for one cartoon.

The thin array of the daily and evening papers of the Paper Age makes

347

a poor show numerically against the serried masses of the journals of the days of the golden sovereign. It is chiefly noticeable in the case of the evening papers. Then you had a wonderful choice of penny or halfpenny evening reading. You were not limited just to three. You had your pick, according to your taste or your politics. Today you can buy the *Star*, the *Evening News*, or the *Evening Standard*.

During the Golden Age, for the greater portion of the time, there were never less than six, and frequently many more. There was the *Sun*, which was for years edited by Horatio Bottomley. It was printed on pale red, it gloried in the stunts of its astute editor, whom Justice had not overtaken at that time. Bottomley used to get celebrities to act as the editor for one day—ranging from Dan Leno, the great comedian, to Dr. Parker, the great Nonconformist preacher.

You could buy the *Echo*, which had been founded by a philanthropic gentleman who succeeded in making £100,000 out of it all the same. Printed on very pale yellow paper, it was at one time edited by Pethick Lawrence. It had a leader writer named Ramsay MacDonald. He had also been an addresser of envelopes, and he became Prime Minister.

There was the *St. James's Gazette*, which outlived the sovereign days and then merged into the *Evening Standard*, but then was a separate penny paper. In its later years Gordon Selfridge had a daily column advertisement on its front page.

The *Pall Mall Gazette* is another paper which is merged and dead. Its most famous editor was W. T. Stead. He printed a series of articles called 'Modern Babylon', alleging that such was the vice of the times that young girls could be purchased, for immoral purposes, from their parents. When challenged on this, he himself 'procured' a girl and handed her over to the Salvation Army right away. He had proved his case. He printed it in the *Pall Mall* and was promptly arrested on the technical offence. Found guilty, he was given a term of imprisonment. He edited the paper from prison, and he was so justly proud of his conviction, and the good it had brought about, that on the day of his release from jail he went down to the offices of his *Review of Reviews* and sat in his office editing in his prison clothes. W. T. Stead, a very great reformer, went to his death on the *Titanic*.

J. L. Garvin was another forthright editor of the *Pall Mall Gazette*.

It was, like the *St. James's Gazette*, printed on white paper. The *Westminster Gazette* was a pale-green paper devoted to the Liberal interests. Its leading articles, written by J. A. Spender, were often supposed to direct Liberal policy. Its great feature was the political cartoons of F. Carruthers Gould ("F.C.G."), which were often based on Tenniel's illustrations to *Alice*, with a topical political twist. You might see Lord

348

Rosebery featured as 'The Walrus' or 'The Carpenter', with A. J. Balfour as an oyster. The *Westminster Gazette's* last attempt at life was as a morning paper—after the sovereign days—but did not prosper in that form. Perhaps one day it will try again and may succeed once more. It would be pleasant, too, to see other publications revived which flourished in those days and it may happen, for no doubt copyright is being kept alive in some cases.

There was, for a few months before the First World War, an *Evening Chronicle*—published by the *Daily Chronicle*—but it did not last long.

An evening newspaper of character was the *Globe*. This was pink. It had a column of short articles on the front page, technically known as 'turnovers' because they finished on the first column of page 2. The *Globe* was in trouble during the First World War for printing, on a Saturday, a story that Kitchener had been sacked from the War Office. Other evening newspapers made short sharp appearances and there were also the three which survive today. Men stood in long ranks in the gutter selling them, or ran about shouting catchpenny headlines. The *Evening News* caused a sensation by dressing its regular vendors in uniform, a grey overcoat and peaked cap.

Amongst the daily papers, many survive: *The Times*, the *Daily Telegraph*, the *Daily Mirror*—which started as the *Ladies' Mirror* and failed but was reborn from the idea of Hannen Swaffer as a halfpenny daily illustrated paper—the *Daily Mail* and the *Daily Express*. The *Daily Sketch* now bears the title of the *Daily Graphic*, which in the Golden Age was a penny illustrated morning paper. This was a most popular publication, and for years the illustrations were in black-and-white until the photographic process came along. Its weather forecasts were illustrated by classical figures behaving in a manner appropriate to the expected weather—which appeared for a short time in the present *Daily Graphic* when it changed its name from the *Daily Sketch*. The old *Daily Graphic* was killed by the *Daily Mirror*.

The *Morning Post* (now swallowed by the *Daily Telegraph*) was the aristocratic newspaper. It had the Social and Court news, its readers were the Upper Classes, and such members of the Middle Classes as were interested in the upper crust. It was the best advertising medium for domestic staff, housemaids, ladies' maids, valets, butlers and the like appendages of the wealthy home. The present *News Chronicle* is a fusion of the older *Daily News* and *Daily Chronicle*, two Liberal papers of the period. Spencer Leigh Hughes was a great journalist of the period with a column called 'Sub Rosa' in the *Morning Leader*, also Liberal, and in the *Daily Chronicle*, the organ of advanced Liberalism, Massingham started the idea of Liberal Imperialism invented by Lord Rosebery and Sir Robert Perks.

The *Standard* was the chief organ of the Conservative Party. Before its end it was taken over by C. Arthur Pearson, who was Lord Northcliffe's most serious rival in journalism.

A morning paper in the Liberal interest had a short life. It was called the *Tribune* and was started about 1907 by a Mr. Tomlinson, son of a wealthy North-country manufacturer, who left a large sum for this purpose. It started with a blaze of trumpets and a most elaborate set-up, but it soon died. Sir Philip Gibbs tells its story in his *The Street of Adventure*. Desperate efforts were made to save it, and its star reporter, Randall Charlton, spent most of his time going round to get money to keep it alive. Thomas Burke was on its staff.

There was for a time the *London Budget*, owned in its later days by William Randolph Hearst. Its main features were articles signed by peers but often written by a sound journalist. Some peers perhaps wrote their own, but it was frequently done by a "ghost". The *Morning Leader*, which was published from the offices of the *Star*, then in Stonecutter Street, was probably the first halfpenny morning paper, though there was a paper called the *Morning* which may have claimed this title but lived for a short time only.

The *Daily Mercury*, founded by Sir George Newnes, ran for a short while, and the *Majority* existed for one week only. The *Daily Paper*, a journal founded by W. T. Stead, never made up its mind if it were a morning or evening paper. It came out about noon. Its main feature was a reprint of the other newspapers' leading articles. It lasted only a few weeks; Stead was taken ill just before its publication or it might have had a different story.

The Times was then, as now, the perfect newspaper. At one time it was bought by Lord Northcliffe, who reduced its price to one penny. It survived even that shock. The *Daily Telegraph* in the sovereign days was a very heavy, if sound, newspaper which clung to the old style of small print, many columns and no headlines in big capitals. But it was always a success and exercised great influence, as it still does today

The daily paper wielding the widest influence was the *Daily Mail*. This had been created and built up by the astounding journalistic genius of Lord Northcliffe. The price was one halfpenny. It let fresh life into Fleet Street, it started things, it screamed rather than spoke. People laughed at it, made fun of it, but they read it. Its circulation reached heights previously undreamt of. Its front page was the finest advertising medium in the kingdom. It wielded terrific influence because of the greatness of its moving spirit. It was always up to something. It championed causes, it made causes to champion. It ran competitions, it brought about a *Daily Mail* Rose, a *Daily Mail* apple, it even tried, but failed, to popularize a

The Taxi-cab arrives—some early types

The Motor Bus in its youth—a challenge to real horse-power

The Middle Classes indulge in the Bicycling Boom

London's buses in the days of the horse

Daily Mail hat, but that was after the golden sovereign time. It gave a prize of £10,000 for the first flight by aeroplane from London to Manchester, which was won by the Frenchman Paulhan, who stole a march on his Engilsh rival, Claude Graham-White, whilst the latter was resting.

France won all the plums of the air. It was Blériot who first flew the Channel. People marvelled, but nobody saw any menace. Blériot landed wearing a straw hat and smoking a cigarette. What was sinister about a straw hat, what evil intent was there in a cigarette? But the *Daily Mail* saw it and it headlined 'England No Longer an Island'. It was right, and it keeps that reputation today.

The *Daily Express*—a younger paper—was the *Daily Mail's* most serious rival, but then it had not the circulation or power it has now attained.

There were the Sunday papers. The *Observer*, the *Sunday Times*, the *People*, the *News of the World* and *Reynolds* we have today, and many others. In the days of the sovereign there was *Lloyd's News*, edited by Thomas Catley, which had the biggest circulation in the world. There were the *Sunday News*, the *Sunday Sun*, and for a very short while there was a Sunday edition of the *Daily Mail* and the *Daily Telegraph*. Sabbatarians went to battle about this, claiming that these were now seven-days-a-week newspapers. Northcliffe argued that they were separate newspapers, separately run. But his opponents threatened a boycott of the numberless magazines which poured out of Fleetway House, his magazine factory, and they won. The *Daily Telegraph* also withdrew the Sunday edition. Northcliffe already had a Sunday newspaper in the *Weekly Dispatch*, now called the *Sunday Dispatch*. Robert Blatchford wrote for this.

One of the most distinctive Sunday newspapers was the *Referee*, edited by 'Pendragon', whose name was Richard Butler. This specialized in sport, the drama, and very well written special articles of national and international matters and interests, called 'Our Handbook'. All the contributors adopted as a *nom-de-plume* the name of one of the knights of the Round Table. A prominent writer of the 'Handbooks', signed 'Vanoc', was Arnold White.

The drama was dealt with by H. Chance Newton, under the name of 'Carados'. 'Chance', as everyone called him, had himself been an actor and had played with Phelps at Sadler's Wells, as he never tired of announcing. He was author and adaptor of numerous plays and burlesques. He knew all about the Theatre and his knowledge was encyclopaedic. Nobody has ever taken his place. His critical faculty was first-class but kindly. He did more to help the Theatre and its people than any journalist before or after his time. Yet when he died and was buried only one journalist, Hannen Swaffer, and only one man of the Theatre—the author of this book—went to his graveside.

'Chance' wrote many books about the Theatre and the music-halls, but he spoke so much better than he wrote and much of his magic is lost. It was practically impossible in those days to launch a new theatrical production without Chance Newton interviewing the actor-manager or the proprietor and running anything from three-quarters to a column in the *Referee*. It was tradition.

The *Referee* had a very good feature on Parisian life, written by John N. Raphael, who signed himself 'Percival' and called his column 'Gossip from the Gay City'. It had also an 'Answers to Correspondents' column, which was amazingly well done. No query, however difficult or abstruse, was ever unanswered—and answered in a most informative manner as well.

But perhaps the backbone of the *Referee* was George R. Sims. He was the outstanding figure in Sunday journalism of his day. A man of tremendous energy and interests, he was playwright, critic, gossip-writer, novelist, poet and social reformer. He brought about many reforms. He wrote that much-parodied ode 'Christmas Day in the Workhouse' which, before the vandals got to work, drew many tears. 'Ballads of Babylon' and 'Dagonet Ballads' poured from his busy pen. 'Dagonet' was his *Referee* name—Dagonet had been King Arthur's jester. Sims could jest but he could be serious too. His book *How the Poor Live* smote London like a bombshell in 1883 and redressed many shameful things.

Sims's page in the *Referee* was called 'Mustard and Cress', and was one of the most widely read features of the time. He could make a restaurant, a resort, a commodity with a paragraph in 'Mustard and Cress', and he did. Usually he ran a little slogan through the page such as 'Don't drink milk —sip it.' He was always well dressed and frock-coated; he was dark and dapper, if stout, and wore a moustache and beard, always very well trimmed. A hair tonic called 'Tatcho' owed its existence to him. He lived facing Regent's Park, and his address in consequence (which was known all over the world) was 'Opposite-the-Ducks'. There is no paper today which has the curious individuality or attraction possessed by the old *Referee* of the sovereign days.

Periodicals like *M.A.P.* (Mainly About People), the *Bookman*, *T.P.'s Weekly*, the *World*, *Great Thoughts* and the *Family Herald Supplement* all flourished and were read by the Middle Classes. So did the *British Weekly*, still as widely read as ever.

There was no lack of paper. Periodicals and newspapers were many times their present size. Journalists were not so well paid and worked much harder. But they had to get their stories themselves and they did.

Telephones were rare and unreliable. Martin Cobbett, a sporting journalist on the *Referee*, swam across a river in his clothes to get to a telegraph office before the others. There was a legend that all reporters drank. Maybe they did. The cult of the teashop was not in being. But those reporters got their story and they got it right. Papers were factual then. A mistake was fatal. A reporter making a mistake got the sack.

News was not 'fictionized'. Yet—or perhaps because of this—people were much more afraid of the Press. They were very careful what they said. They watched their step. People read the news, they did not just scan the headlines and look at the pictures. There were, indeed, none of the 'banner' headlines to scan. Newspapers were British. They had not become Americanized. They were reliable and solid like the times they served. They thundered, they did not scream. It was their job to give the news—and they did it.

There were few combines, especially in the provinces. The papers were free and independent like the people they served.

CHAPTER XXIII

Pleasures, Palaces and Pops

IF THE MIDDLE CLASS PEOPLE OF THE SOVEREIGN AGE DID NOT WANT TO stop at home and did not want to go to the theatre or music-hall, there were plenty of other ways of passing the time.

Two great pleasure palaces flanked London, one on the South and one on the North, gazing at each other across the metropolis like gigantic rivals competing for the city's pleasure. That on the South was the Crystal Palace, that on the North the Alexandra Palace.

When the Victorian Age had passed away from practically the entire kingdom one corner of it remained, unable and unwilling to change, in the Crystal Palace, Paxton's giant glasshouse on the hills of Sydenham. That had been the Great Exhibition of 1851, when all the world had gone to Hyde Park to gaze in wonder. The idea had been that of Albert the Good, the Prince Consort, the spirit that of Queen Victoria. And that spirit had a home there until fire destroyed the crystal monster only a few years ago. Then all that was truly left of the spirit of the Victorian Age was the Albert Hall and the Memorial of the same name.

But Victorian or not, the Crystal Palace was a place of strange enchantment. It had been saved for the nation, along with its grounds, after its removal from Hyde Park, and the Corporation of the City of London were its trustees. With the business and commercial spirit of Victorian times, they never made it a free show; it cost 1s. to go in. It took you quite a long time to go in too, if you landed at the Low Level Railway Station. Yet that was the right approach. If you entered at the top of the hill, you just stepped inside and never had time to create and capture the true atmosphere. But from the Low Level you climbed up an incline of seemingly endless corridors, and trellissed as to walls, with plaster statues of doubtful whiteness in corners and at turns. It was like nothing you met with anywhere else and prepared you for what was to come, for suddenly you were in the Palace itself, under an enormous canopy of glass, like a gargantuan greenhouse. Your feet echoed on the bare boards, everywhere there was a sound of lisping footsteps.

The thing to do was to avoid a Bank Holiday or similar occasion and go to the Crystal Palace when there were only a few people about. You were in a new world, a world apparently of giants, for everything was on a titanic plane. The vast sweep of the roof, the enormous arch of the central transept, the monster organ on the orchestra which seemed like

354

a flight of steps to the stratosphere, the gigantic iron girders and steel trusses, nothing was on a human scale. The sun shone through on groups of statuary which proved to you that, at one time, there were indeed giants in the land. Great palms filled corners like miniature forests, and the stalls which sold mementos, boot polish and novelties seemed just the play-things of pigmies. You yourself began to realize the feelings of a Lilli-putian in a Gulliverian home.

It was impossible to be dull at the Cystal Palace despite its silent, some-what shabby vastness. You could look at an apartment in Pompeii as it might have appeared before Vesuvius overwhelmed it. You could gaze at a Moorish Court right out of the Alhambra—not the one in Leicester Square, but the Granadan variety. You could see a portrait gallery of Victoria Cross heroes in one of the galleries, caught by the artist in the very act which won the coveted 'ninepenn'orth of bronze'. Judged as works of art, these were negligible. But to small boys these were occasions of vast excitement.

In another part was an exhibition of stuffed animals, with whom moth had played havoc. A peculiarly revolting group of some kind of deer, with extremely swollen noses, is pictured in the mind's eye. It was never discovered what breed they were nor did any natural history book show their picture.

Greatly intriguing, on the ground floor, were representations of savages, in the act of being so. They were in large groups and were up to all sorts of tricks. They lived amongst their native jungles, their trees, their huts, all a bit faded and discoloured. But a very frightening-looking savage was spearing a fish, his spear ever poised over his shoulder for the plunge that never came, beside a glass pool of translucent greenness, wherein small eyes could see the actual fish at which he aimed. That he was a good fisherman was proved by a small pile of fish by his side. Men aimed bows and arrows, men fought each other, women ground corn, carried bundles, nursed their ill-favoured babies, and one fearsome savage had a blowpipe in his mouth, in the very act of launching a poisoned dart at an unseen enemy. He had a particular fascination for Middle Class boys, who plied their elders with questions concerning this evil weapon and its deadly poison, to which they never got satisfactory answers. All of which increased the fear and mystery.

There were hundreds of other things to see. There was a theatre in the building as well, where real professional companies performed. There were great choral and orchestralconcerts in that central transept, where Handel was specially honoured. There were brass-band contests, there were demonstrations, there were enormous prize-givings.

At Christmas time the transept became a circus, Wullf's Circus, a splendid affair of much more imagination than most circuses boast, for the last item was quite a spectacular production. A circular transparency of gauze was lowered between spectators and the ring. You could see through the piece immediately before you with uninterrupted view, but the other side of the ring, the lights being in front, was hidden from you and you gazed at a forest or a cavalcade of knights in armour and Queens of Beauty in a great stand, according to what the pageant was about. For it might be a wild boar hunt, or it might be a real chivalric tournament with actual jousting by knights in full panoply bestriding destriers, which a little time before had been just rosin-backs with agile ladies standing on them. It is a wonderful thing that this excellent device has never been reproduced.

You could find ample refreshment in the Palace at any time you liked. Nothing was rationed. The plates of cold ham were as huge as the Palace itself, they even defeated the voracious small Middle Class boys. The buns seemed larger, too, than elsewhere, as did the cups, saucers, tea-pots —everything. It may have been just reflected glory, but it is remembered very clearly.

Out in the very charming grounds bands played, there were flowers and shrubs, and you went down terraces to a very big circular building where, for a small charge, you were allowed in and witnessed a panorama of the siege of Paris. There are no panoramas now, the cinema has killed them. But they could, for comprehensiveness, give points to any film. And you could look as long as you liked and take it all in. Two vast towers flanked the main building and gave extensive views to those who gained the summit.

Down more terraces and the lake was reached. To most children, except the extremely nervous, this was the best of the lot. For here lingered not the Victorian Age but the antediluvian age itself. Here was, in stone and painted like life, the Dinosaurus, the Pterodactyl, the Brontosaurus, all that amazing fauna which Noah, very rightly, did not accommodate in the Ark. Here they were, strolling about, entering the water to bathe or drink, reaching up stone mouths to the boughs of the trees. You came upon them—not altogether, but suddenly—round corners with breathtaking results. It was a rare experience which never palled. It may be remembered that Wells's Kipps took his bride to see them, and found one of them very like the ineffable Coote.

For more mundane-minded folk there was all the fun of the fair: roundabouts, swings, shooting galleries—what you will. But they were not really in keeping with the Crystal Palace and its devotees spent little time there. There was a sports ground, where the F.A. Cup Finals took place in those days, and where in the summer could be seen the G.O.M.

of Cricket, Dr. W. G. Grace himself, leading his own team, the London County Cricket Club. From a boy's point of view it was difficult to say which was the greater, the Doctor or the Palace.

Sometimes there were military displays on this ground as well. That same Middle Class boy who has strayed into these pages before was taken to one of these. The reason for it or the participant troops are faded and dim, but one incident stands out with startling clearness, as well it might.

Shortly before his Palace visit the boy had been to the United Services Museum in Whitehall. He liked museums and was showing early signs of the determination to record history which assailed him later in life. At the museum there was something modern on show—a Maxim gun. So interested was the boy that the attendant showed him the mechanism of the gun, how it loaded, how it worked and how it fired. He drank it all in. In his mind he was master of this new death-dealing weapon. The attendant was the richer by a tip from an aunt.

One of the first things that greeted the boy's sight at the Palace on the occasion of the visit to see the Military Tournament of sorts was a stand of Maxim guns. He told his elders he knew all about them. They said "Really, dear," as elders do. But the boy, proud of his knowledge, was insistent he should show them. No attendant was about, so he got on the stand and demonstrated. That boy was never any good with mechanism, even today the slightest mechanical device is his complete master. And so it proved then. Practice was different from theory. This gun seemed different from the one on which he thought he had been taught. He put up a show, he pulled levers, he pushed bolts, things clicked out but would not go in; however, he made quite a demonstration of it and impressed the elders of the party.

He left the thing at last with an uneasy feeling that he had not left it as he found it, but the fear soon faded in the joys of the Palace and the exhilaration of watching the Tournament—or Assault-at-Arms—when the time came. Troops drilled, cavalry galloped to music, strong men hacked a piece of lead in half with one swoop and then, with a turn of their wrists, the sabre they wielded severed the carcase of a sheep. The lemons were cut by galloping men as they swung from a string, or they were missed as the case might be; tent pegs were lifted from the ground on the points of lances as cavalrymen dashed by, men beat each other with singlesticks, on foot and on horseback, men wearing great masks and also a species of sporran prodded at each other with wooden-knobbed bayonets, all the similar feats of arms were performed which pertained to the Soldiers of the Queen, the peaceful parade of the deeds which had given the British the right to sing

357

> And when we say that England's master,
> Remember who has made her so,

in the very modest unboastful method of the Golden Age, which did not go in for understatement and was consequently taken at face value by foreign Powers.

But at last the climax came. This was the representation of a battle. Some wild tribe had risen in folly against the might of England. It assaulted and captured a peaceful farmhouse, but not before the settlers therein had put up a desperate defence and caused heavy casualties, one shot usually killing two savages. The triumphant natives, no specified race, did not kill the settlers out of hand but bore them off, men and women, with frightful antics and bloodthirsty yells—apparently to subject them to terrible tortures, fortunately out of sight. But help was at hand. A party of mounted men trotted in, possibly scouts. They saw the farmhouse. They knocked—no reply.

Then the open door made them suspicious and they decided there had been dirty work. They gazed in all directions, shading their eyes with their hands from the torrid Afric sun of Sydenham. One of them apparently found a clue. He showed it to the others. They wheeled about and amidst applause galloped off to fetch help. Then from a corner arose a savage, cunningly left behind to watch events and overlooked by the trustful British scouts. He sped away to warn his horde that the white men were coming.

The white men came, quite a lot of them, in squadrons, a very handsome and military sight which got volleys of applause. They dismounted and prepared to encamp for the night. It was apparently not possible to go any further without incurring overtime. All the routine of a military encampment was gone through, eagerly watched by the crowds who had never been soldiers themselves and never expected to be soldiers either, so it was all very novel. A flag was hoisted to show who they were, sentries were posted, camp-fires were lit, there was a sing-song, suppers were eaten, the officers went the rounds, and then the bugles blew and the men turned in at the late and dark hour of about 4 p.m.

But what was this? Sly, stealthy forms came crouching along the ground. The enemy were going to spring a surprise. Like the dirty niggers they were, they were going to rush the camp and slaughter the peacefully sleeping soldiers in a most unsportsmanlike manner. But the sentries were alert. The savages were seen and rifles cracked. At once the camp sprang to life. Bugles blew, men rushed about, fell in, whilst the sentries fired on. The natives, apparently nonplussed by the failure of their surprise, were caught on one foot. They hesitated and they were lost.

They gave the British time to form. Few in number they might be, very much at a disadvantage, still they were British and Soldiers of the Queen. And they had rifles against spears, which seemed to be in their favour.

The fight began, and the boy was beside himself with excitement. The small but gallant band of British put up a stiff resistance, but the savages were being constantly reinforced, and although the rifles did heavy execution, numbers began to tell. Were the savages going to win? Was the Union Jack, fluttering so nobly above the battle in the breeze, going to be captured? No, perish the thought! There was a blaze of bugles and into the arena galloped a machine-gun battery of one Maxim! Where this had been, how it had got so far behind its regular force did not transpire. There must be a little poetic licence in these affairs. The gunners leapt down, unlimbered the gun and got into position. Straddling its seat, the gunner prepared to fire.

The natives charged and one expected to see them mown down in swathes by the priceless gifts of civilization. So it should have been. But that Maxim refused to fire. Men worked at it feverishly but not a pop-pop would it give. The savages were again caught on one foot. This was not in the rules. What were they to do? Their rehearsed job was to die in scores, but it is difficult to get killed by a gun which remains obstinately silent. Nothing the gunners could do would make that gun do its duty. So some of the savages died apparently from sheer fright or because they had not been otherwise rehearsed, whilst others, with more ready wits, either took to flight or threw down their shields and spears and surrendered.

The audience cheered and rocked with laughter at the same time. The settlers came running in, having been obviously left unguarded by the need for reinforcements and there was another great and glorious British victory of the pre-Boer War days with a triumphant march past and final exit. A very worried-looking Maxim gun-crew made the circuit of the arena amidst ribald cheers and rude questions. There was, however, no doubt in the mind of one small spectator, that Middle Class boy. He knew why the gun had jammed. He it was who had wrecked the show and nearly brought mimic disaster on British arms. He kept his own counsel and his guilt was never discovered. But he hugs that secret yet in his heart and only discloses it at a gap of half a century.

On a summer's night the great sight at the Crystal Palace was Brock's Benefit, a truly marvellous firework display. To see this properly one dined in the enormous rooms on the South Front, where sparrows assisted at the meal and put the tables and the rooms to uses never intended. Probably they were the descendants of the same sparrows which had endangered the very opening of the Palace when it stood in Hyde Park, and whose extremely vulgar and insanitary ways had caused the Prince Consort much heart-searching and Queen Victoria a considerable dismay (when she was told as delicately as possible), and which made her send for the Duke of Wellington. He had saved England before. He should do so again. He did so. He used sparrow-hawks and the sparrows gave it up. But probably their descendants had migrated to Sydenham and carried on the family tradition.

The firework display was unforgettable. Every pyrotechnic device came into play. Rockets ascended in droves, to long 'Oo-oo-oos' from the crowd, and burst into constellations of coloured balls; some joined up and floated in chains, others whistled like a gale. Fountains played and changed colours, silver Niagaras descended in incandescent spray, a firework gymnast turned and turned over a horizontal bar, not desisting when his legs burnt out and his head disappeared. Still a glowing partial form went round and round. Enormous set pieces spluttered, smoked and burst into brilliance, displaying naval vessels shelling each other and exploding—the British winning, of course. And finally, with further splutter, hiss and smoke, the features of her Most Gracious Majesty appeared in fire whilst the band played the National Anthem and everyone went home joyfully. Those were nights of brightness which rivalled the sovereign itself.

Across London, on the heights of Muswell Hill and Wood Green, the rival palace was a very different affair. In 1859 a group of gentlemen, actuated partly by a desire to spread culture and partly by a desire to make a little out of it, decided to open a rival palace to the Crystal one. They were a long time about it, they had many debates and arguments, and at first their idea of a name for it was 'The Palace of the People'. They bought the land and they got the grounds open (which included a trotting track, afterwards to be the racecourse) some years before they achieved the building itself, into which they put much of the material which had been used in the Exhibition of 1862, now entirely forgotten.

Some of it may still be seen, with its rose, shamrock and thistle design, in the ironwork of the racecourse grand stand. But before they got the building open they found a better name. The Prince of Wales had married Alexandra of Denmark, who had become one of the most popular figures in the country. So they called it the Alexandra Palace. Whether they had her permission or not is not known. Whether some offence was given to the lady who was to become such a beloved Queen-Consort is forgotten today, but certain it is that Alexandra, either as Queen or Princess, never set foot in the Palace named after her, or even its grounds.

It is possible she may have glanced at it from the train on a journey North, but even that is problematic.

They opened the Alexandra Palace with a big flourish of trumpets on 27th May, 1873, after fourteen years of labour. On 9th June of the same year, fifteen days later, it was burned to the ground. Little water was available, or pumps of sufficient strength to use what little there was. Nobody was killed, but a couple of days later two women who had come to gaze on the ruins were killed by a falling wall.

The Palace went up again in 1875. It still stands. It has had a very chequered career. Despite beautiful grounds, theatres, firework displays, great concerts and a truly magnificent organ, one of the finest in the world, it never paid. The proprietors kept staving off disaster by selling strips of the grounds for building land. In 1888 it had a brief burst of popularity because of Baldwin and his parachute descents. This was a great novelty and crowds went to see the intrepid aeronaut go up in his balloon and descend in his parachute. Most of them hoped to see him dash himself to pieces. He never obliged; indeed, the only accident he ever had was when he sprained his ankle by a fall over a rope before even getting into his balloon.

The people who benefited most were the pickpockets, who reaped a fine harvest whilst all heads and eyes were turned skywards. *The Times* and other newspapers attacked the display, on the grounds of the sadism of the populace and the concentration of crooks. But it lasted a whole season. Admission was 1s. all in. There was no more to pay save for special shows and refreshments.

On the island in the lake, at the turn of the century, a spectacle was staged which was well worth seeing. It was a terrific representation of 'The Last Days of Pompeii', a mixture of drama, ballet, opera and fireworks, remarkably well done. Vesuvius erupted and lava laid Pompeii low. And later still, when Pain's had their great firework displays on the South Front, a tight-rope walker named Hardy, a Canadian, rivalled every feat of the great Blondin and would walk the wire in the dark, whilst the rockets whizzed by and the set pieces blazed below him. So successful was he that when the summer season was over he was re-engaged to do his act in the Central Hall.

The authorities took a hand in the interest of public safety. As he was walking indoors and people would be in the hall, he must have a net stretched below him. Hardy had never had a net, he did not want one. He had never had an accident either. But the authorities were adamant. The net was duly stretched. Hardy went up, did his amazing display and at the end leapt lightly into the net. That net gave way and threw him amongst the chairs on the great Orchestra around the organ. He broke his

361

leg, his collarbone and his arm. That was his only accident, caused by a safety net.

But the Palace declined. At last it closed altogether and came into the market as building land. Two public-spirited local gentlemen did not want this valuable lung lost to the public. Working at great speed and with only a few days at their disposal they persuaded the Middlesex County Council and other local bodies of the district to buy it. It was bought. It was incorporated by Act of Parliament into a Public Trust and a public place forever. But nothing had been left over for upkeep and admission had to be free. Another short Bill was rushed through whereby a charge for admission could be made on Bank Holidays and certain other days in the year—fourteen in all—so as to have a chance of earning its bread and upkeep. And so it stands today. There is little value in a place that is free. A charge for admission glorifies it.

There was not much to see in the Alexandra Palace when it reopened as a Public Trust under a body of well-meaning but inexperienced trustees. King Edward was crowned and some of the Colonial troops over for the occasion were encamped at the Palace. The trustees decided to cash in. They called in Mackenzie Rogan and organized a Military Tattoo with a torchlight procession. The troops were to do this and also line the route. There were to be bands converging on a central point and a great military display by torchlight. Tens of thousands paid to go in to see it.

But this good idea ended in disaster. The Palace had a professional manager. Carried away by enthusiasm, he went to a theatrical costumiers, hired a Field Marshal's uniform and paraded the grounds on horseback. The officer commanding the troops took the deepest of umbrage, withdrew his men and would not let them either take part in the display or line the route. The public got out of hand, the bands could not get through, the torches were carried by anyone who could snatch one and get it alight, and confusion reigned supreme. To make things just a little worse, one of the wheels came off the old four-wheeled cab used to collect the money from the gates and thousands of shillings rolled all over the place, eagerly scrambled for by the populace. The Palace did not live that down until 1922—when it staged something better but made no mistakes.

It did, however, become a nursery for aviation. Cody experimented there with his man-lifting kites, the airship which sailed round St. Paul's to the amazement of everyone was housed there, and there was actually the first aeronautical exhibition in this country at the 'Ally Pally'. But inside it was pretty desolate. There were picture galleries with a lot of indifferent pictures, mostly loaned by people who wanted to be rid of them; there were great paintings of the mural variety, mostly biblical scenes, showing apostles of gigantic stature standing in tiny wickerwork cockleshells of craft not much bigger than shopping-baskets and not upsetting them—a miracle, no doubt; there were excellent choral festivals; there was the organ and recitals thereon which never paid because it cost too much to blow the organ. Things languished and got very dull, and there was much dilapidation.

When John Burns was at the Office of Works he was besought to give the place an Unemployment Grant so that unemployed labourers who were numerous at the time might do something to make it waterproof and more presentable. He appointed a day to meet the authorities. He did not come. What did come was a telegram from him saying, "Came down and had private inspection of Palace. Damn' dismal place." . . .

On early closing nights and Saturdays on a small bandstand at the end of the Central Hall a band would endeavour to add gaiety to life. But it soon got dejected. The gaslight was never equal to the task, and around the bandstand was just a flicker in encircling gloom. Entertainers battled nobly, but were defeated by the tomblike air. The only thing which sparkled was the drinks being poured out at the long bars flanking the so-called entertainment. Those bars and their beer-engines worked whether *The Geisha* was being rendered as a selection or the choir was rendering the Mass in B Minor.

One feature of the Alexandra Palace, however, was of considerable interest. Right along the centre aisle of the Great Hall, a vast place indeed, stood the Kings and Queens of England, in plaster. They stretched in royal array from William the Conqueror to Victoria. They were (so far as could be judged) good likenesses, and they were well painted and often quite full of character. Many a small boy got his idea of what our Sovereigns looked like from contemplation of those effigies. And when the names of the bygone monarchs are mentioned, that is how countless middle-aged men today think of them, from their youthful gazing at those plaster figures.

They stand today as they stood then, not quite so bright, maybe, but still there. Two wars have not destroyed them; they are as enduring as the Royal House itself. But a great plaster figure of Victoria the Good which stood at one end, the replica of a statue sent abroad, was smashed to pieces by German prisoners during the First World War. Today the Alexandra Palace's fame is world wide as the home of television, but otherwise it has changed little, save for gradual decay. And the men of the Paper Age still back their fancy on the Ally Pally racecourse as did the men in the days of the sovereign. It is not so far to walk home. . . .

Londoners of the Sovereign Age would go down to Richmond, often by hansom, and on summer nights dine on the terrace of the Star and Garter. They would make the trip to Hampton Court Palace, then quite a long way out. This could be done by the adventurous by means of a boating expedition. Two large pleasure-steamers, the *Cardinal Wolsey* and the *Queen Elizabeth*, made the trip. It was not easy to forecast one's time of arrival because they often ran aground when the river was low.

It was much safer to go by train from Waterloo to East Molesey Station (Hampton Court), where for small boys there was an additional attraction in the sight of a very able and affable stationmaster who wore a very ill-fitting and improbable red wig. One could have one's tea on Tagg's Island, and there was the Palace, its grounds and Bushey Park. And on Chestnut Sunday thousands of Londoners went to that Royal Park to see the wonderful avenue in full bloom and the sun glinting on Diana's Fountain half-way along it. There was Epping Forest, reached by train from Liverpool Street, with a drive in a hired fly or a public charabanc up to the Royal Forest Hotel or on to High Beech. The forest was really wild, no cars thronged the roads, no crowds penetrated the glades, and glimpses were frequently caught of the deer which roamed there.

For other seasons there was Hengler's Circus, with its second half as a water-show, a wooden building which stood where the London Palladium stands today. There were the Moore and Burgess Minstrels at the St. James's Hall (its site now submerged beneath the Piccadilly Hotel). The Moore and Burgess engulfed the Mohawks from Islington and gave wonderful shows, much appreciated in those simpler days. The nigger minstrel show was a Victorian institution which died in Edwardian days, but was much beloved in its time. And near the St. James's Hall was the Egyptian Hall, in Piccadilly, now gone for ever, with an arcade on its old ground. Here reigned, in the days of the sovereign, Maskelyne and Cook, who would most assuredly have been burnt as wizards a century or so before.

Children went to the Egyptian Hall with delightful anticipation. They were often scared to death and taken out screaming; but mostly they stuck it out, got used to it and then howled with dismay when the show was over. Incredible feats of magic were performed, music played very loudly indeed without any visible agency—or reason, if it came to that. The supreme moment was the Cabinet Trick, presented in a little play, with both Messrs. Maskelyne and Cook, as actors, playing many parts such as butchers, watchmen of the old school, witches, and even full-sized monkeys. It was most enthralling, and children not cursed with nerves revelled in it. They demanded of their elders how it was done, and their elders were shamed and humbled by not being able to tell them. No use trying to fob off the children with such statements as, "Oh, it's done by mirrors." The devastating following question of "How?" always cost those adults much loss of prestige. Many a reputation for infallibility was sacrificed in the Egyptian Hall.

It was small and dark and rather dingy, but it had an atmosphere of its very own such as has never existed elsewhere. It was truly a Home of Magic. You felt it as you went in. And it was not only the children who were scared. When animated pictures (i.e. the cinema) first came to town, of course they showed them at the Egyptian Hall. And many an adult prepared for flight with blanched face and a missed heartbeat when a steam-engine at speed came dashing right at him. It was altogether one of the most fascinating places in London and it took many sovereigns in its time.

There was Earl's Court, with its exhibitions, its sideshows and its Great Wheel, one of London's landmarks, direct in descent from the pleasure gardens which had decked London for centuries and are now no more. Here, for half a sovereign, a Londoner could get a season ticket and get twenty shillings' worth of enjoyment for that ten shillings every night by the mere sight of the myriad little coloured lamps and the varied, gay, laughing throng parading around the bandstands. Earl's Court bowed its head in defeat to another vaster pleasure garden which was brought about by King Edward's *Entente Cordiale*.

At Shepherd's Bush was built the White City, as London itself christened it. It opened with the Franco-British Exhibition and it closed Earl's Court. This was a novelty; it was vast and it was beautiful. It was near at hand, the Central London (the old Tuppenny Tube) took you right to its gates. White buildings shone in the sun and glittered at night with outlines and clusters of electric lights. It was for Londoners a place of romance and great joy. But it never had the intimacy, the softness, nor the homeliness of the smaller Earl's Court. Its lights were bright and dazzling, but those of Earl's Court were soft, and like little jewels in the dusky summer eves.

The spirit of Paris Gardens, Ranelagh, Cremorne and Vauxhall, to say nothing of Mulberry Gardens and Marylebone Gardens, breathed its last in Earl's Court and the White City—and the White City went with the sovereign, when the guns of 1914 blew that coin to bits. Today it means 'the dogs'. But then it meant delight.

In its stadium were held the Olympic Games, and the British shuddered at the frequency with which foreign standards took the air to proclaim alien victories in the field of athletics. But everyone cheered little Dorando, the Italian, when he won the much-boosted marathon from Windsor to the White City, and upheld him when disqualification threw its shadow across him because some busybody helped him to his feet when he fell. 'The White City' as a scene even invaded the Gaiety Theatre itself in *Our Miss Gibbs*. But at either of these two lovely places the men and women of the Sovereign Age would spend half a day of pleasure and do themselves well, and then have change out of a golden half-sovereign, let alone a sovereign, even after a hansom home.

Earl's Court Exhibition had been conceived through an indoor exhibition held at Olympia. There was staged a really remarkable representation of 'Venice in London', with canals and all. Real gondolas took you for rides or rows (whichever you liked) along those canals. Gondolas had been imported for the purpose and driven through the streets on flat lorries, to the amazement of the populace and much accruing publicity.

Few Londoners had ever been to Venice, although they knew that hansom cabs were called the gondolas of London, but this was the real thing. Actually gondolas had to be specially built in Italy to negotiate the narrow canals which pervaded Olympia like a network of veins. But the thing was an immense success and an immense undertaking. It was carried through by Harold Hartley, really a mineral-water merchant, but a showman and organizer of consummate genius, and Imrie Kiralfy. It really was Venice in London—canals, *pallazos*, *gondolieri*, atmosphere and all.

They followed it with 'Constantinople in London', which, although good, was not so fine as Venice. But Mr. Hartley got the idea for Earl's Court and gave Londoners many summers of joy in those spacious days of the golden sovereign. And out of that success sprang that never-ending series of tea-shops and restaurants which are still the most popular feeding-places of those who like their food quickly, well served and cheap. Olympia gave London Earl's Court and Lyons too.

There were other things at Olympia, such as roller-skating, and Sousa's Band played there when it came to town to show London something of the vitality of America and what marches meant on a military band under a bearded *pince-nezed* showman, for bands were very popular under the sovereign. Not the bands which are popular today, and not the sort of music either. That hearty race of people who spent the twenty shillings which made the sovereign did not want negroid music and muted brass and wailing saxophones. They wanted brass with no mutes at all, and the full lung-power of a brass band. They liked the players not in evening dress, white shirt-fronts, foreign features and complexions and shiny heads, but in military uniform to suit what they played. A band called The Kilties, which was composed of Canadian Highlanders, rivalled even Sousa himself and his men in full blast. It was a day of robustness and not of half-tones. People who dealt with a golden sovereign liked their music from instruments which gleamed with golden hue as well.

There was one other sight which must not be overlooked. There were, of course, other customs, and exhibitions, like Madame Tussaud's, which have survived the loss of the sovereign, and indeed the Fun of the Fair on Hampstead Heath still endures on Bank Holidays.

But it is not the same. The feeling may be the same, but it is differently expressed. The terrific high spirits and the true air of carnival vanished when the sovereign chinked its last and paper rustled in its place. But Hampstead Heath on a Bank Holiday under the golden sovereign was something to see and remember. It was purely English. It was the Carnival of the Cockney, and he was pure Cockney then. He is pure Cockney now in breed, but he dresses differently, he thinks differently, and he behaves differently.

Then there were swings, roundabouts, shooters, and all the fun of the fair as there is today. But then the roundabouts blared forth the tunes of this country as popularized on the music-halls. True they were often a few years old, but what mattered that? Everyone knew them and everyone sang them. The pubs were open all day and everyone took the fullest possible advantage of this. The beer was cheap and strong. Half a crown would give you a marvellous day and night, it was difficult to spend five shillings. The coconut-shies yielded real coconuts—all milky—to the throwers of a straight ball at the rate of three shies a penny, roll, bowl, or pitch. There were ticklers, there were squirts, there were penny canes, there were winkles, cockles, stewed eels and sarsaparilla. There were meat pies of immense size and equal staying power at a penny each. There was noise, dust and glory, and there was fun. Lots of fun. Rough and ready, maybe, but none the less true holiday fun for all that.

The Cockney did not get many holidays then, and when he did he celebrated. He got drunk too, for it was by no means a sober age. The police were busy with lost children, lost property, lost dogs and drunks. They never had desperate gang-fights or armed bandits with which to contend. They might break up a fight or two between two rival 'Arrys or even two rival 'Arriets. But beyond black eyes, bloody noses or scratched faces there was little harm and less ill feeling. Of course, it was no place for the respectable Middle Class ladies and gentlemen, but all young Middle Class men had been there to see the fun, often more than once.

From the outer skirts of the Heath by the Vale of Health the fair stretched, right up the hill to the Spaniards Road along the summit.

On the other side there was no fair, but it was sacred to the love-affairs of London holidaymakers, and Middle Class people with sense avoided it or kept their eyes straight before them. Indeed, the Middle Class denizens of respectable Hampstead deplored their Heath's desecration on Bank Holidays. Much the Cockney crowd cared; it was their Heath too, wasn't it? On Bank Holidays, and especially Easter Monday, it most certainly was.

Here was a parade of colour and best clothes, as best clothes were understood in the land of the Cockney. There you could see in droves those two typical Londoners, 'Arry and 'Arriet, now of honoured memory. They were most picturesque and most individual, although they were nearly all the same.

It was individuality of class rather than person. The men wore their pearly suits, mostly grey, with myriads of pearl buttons wherever they would go. They went in cascades down the seams of the trousers, to the bell-bottomed ends thereof. They smothered the coat and the waistcoat, often a fancy one, or black velvet and sometimes moleskin. Their caps, worn at a cheeky angle, gleamed with mother-of-pearl, every suit had thousands of them. No 'Arry wore a collar—he despised that embellishment. Collars were for 'toffs', they were 'lah-di-dah'. He wore a neck handker-chief, often if not mostly of silk, red, yellow or spotted, but always very bright.

Gaudy as he was, 'Arriet outshone him. She had her best dress, often violet or mauve and frequently of silk or satin. She wore a coat over it of velvet, and there were pearl buttons on this too. Sometimes she wore a highly coloured shawl, and on occasions, if she wanted to make a real display, she wore a shawl as well as a coat. She wore coloured stockings in an age which wore plain stockings, and often these stockings were striped with circular stripes. She also wore boots. But the crowning glory was her mass of hair—which had been freed from curlers and was frizzed like any barbed-wire fence, but became untidy under the amorous attentions of 'Arry—and on top of her mass of hair she wore her hat. This was the hallmark of the real 'Arriet, for it was immense and it carried on it as many huge ostrich feathers as she could afford or the hat carry. As a rule she topped up with an ornate apron. She never remained tidy for long, for the lovemaking of 'Arry and 'Arriet was rough—the lady expected to be 'shoved abaht'.

But despite all the Fun of the Fair, it was the dancing that mattered. In long lines they faced each other, women one side, men the other, young and old alike; the lines advanced upon each other, prancing and with heads down. When collision seemed inevitable they retreated, heads back, chests extended and knees working high in the air, the age-old dance of the true Londoner. And the climax came when the 'Arrys and 'Arriets exchanged headgear. That was really the apex of the Carnival, the final expression of unconfined and unrestrained joy. For they enjoyed themselves, even if the Middle Class disapproved. They enjoyed themselves in an age that was carefree, when war was far away, when the Army or Navy gathered only those who enlisted, and when not only a sovereign was a sovereign, but a bob was a bob—and worth its twelve pence or two tanners. Even their silver made a golden holiday for them.

CHAPTER XXIV

'May I Have the Pleasure?'

ONE THING SHOWS VERY CLEARLY THE DIFFERENCE IN THE SPIRIT OF enjoyment of the people who lived under the sovereign and those who exist under the pound note. Dancing is perhaps the most spontaneous method any human being has of showing the joy of life and his or her pleasure therein.

The foreign belief that the English take their pleasures sadly might well seem true by a glimpse at a dance of today, although dancing is so widely indulged in. But it was manifestly untrue at the glimpse of a dance in the Golden Age, even though that dance took place in a small suburban hall over a shop and not in a chromium-fitted jazz-decorated *Palais de Danse*.

Like everything else, dancing then was done with zest. It was done with speed, it was done with energy. Also, with all these things, it was done with grace. For the people who danced had been taught to dance, they had not picked up the steps as they went along. And dancing then had a multitude of steps which had to be performed. It was not just a home-made version, as it is all too frequently today; a matter of hugging, slow movement and sudden spasmodic, painful-looking jerks. There is, of course, that supreme example of modern grace and abandon called 'jitterbugging'. Any man or woman—one could not think of ladies and gentlemen in the same breath—who had attempted such a thing as that at a dance, private or public, would have been thrown out, probably locked up for indecency, and could never have held up their heads again.

So have things changed, so has civilization and progress made strides. So has dancing, as the Middle Class once understood it, ceased to be dancing. You could not hop about like that even at a 'hop'. And there were 'hops' in those days, shilling hops, sixpenny hops and even three-penny hops. The Middle Class never went to threepenny hops, of course, and seldom to sixpenny ones. But the music-hall, that argus-eyed institution, was aware of them and contributed a popular song about them, ending something as follows:

> When you start a-dancing you never know when to stop.
> It's Hi, hi, clear the way, at our Threepenny 'Op.

It was 'when' they began that they did not know when to stop, nor

370

'where'. They were fully aware of that. Even though the 'H' might be missing, their manners were not. The music-halls did so much to picture life and to enrich it, even to the popular catch phrases of each succeeding year, which were bandied from mouth to mouth and were often quite apposite. If they meant little they meant no harm, those shouted statements like "What Ho, She Bumps", "There's 'Air" (with its answer, "Like Wire"), "Get Your Hair Cut", "Ginger, You're Balmy", "A Little of What You Fancy Does You Good", "Whoa, Emma!", "Now We Shan't Be Long", etc. They are rare now, although the Second World War contributed "Get Up Them Stairs". The First World War demanded "Are We Downhearted?", with a roaring, "No!" as the reply.

Dancing in the Golden Age was a thing of dignity, deportment, courtesy, as well as light-hearted fun. There were all sorts of dances, but there were very few public dance-halls which existed solely for that purpose. The 'hops' were public dances, but of extreme respectability, and none the worse for that. They were given either in halls hired for the purpose by 'Professors of Dancing', who presided over them and had a large sprinkling of their own pupils in the attendance, or at the 'Academies' of these said Professors and Madame the wife, which were very often either the basements of old Victorian houses in slightly decaying neighbourhoods, or decayed corners of still good neighbourhoods, or it might be in the converted stables and coach-houses of these same mansions. It might even be in a specially built shed with corrugated-iron roof.

Dignity and decorum reigned. Evening dress was not worn except by the Professor in charge, who was in full rig, except that his waistcoat was black and his collar might be low. But he had silk socks, dancing-pumps, a gold watch-chain, and he wore an array of medals to show his many victories over the intricacies of Terpsichore.

He was an imposing, not to say awe-inspiring, figure, with his moustache often waxed and his deportment equal to a Turveydrop. It was impossible to think of indecorous deportment under his eagle eye, or that of his wife, in her black silk but *décolleté* dress and her maybe rubicund but still dignified face and demeanour. The Professor always wore gloves, either white or lavender, kid or silk—no male ever danced unless his hands were covered. It was the lower strata of the Middle Classes who used these hops, the shop assistants, the lower ranks of clerkdom, the decent, law-abiding, hard-working people of that kind; and, despite the general respectability of the proceedings, they thoroughly enjoyed themselves. That is because they were interested primarily in dancing and wanted to be good dancers.

In those days people liked to do things well and not just be able to get through them. They did not mind taking pains, they did not want to do so much at such a lightning speed. Many of the couples might be engaged couples and danced together, but that evening their dancing was a more important thing than their love-making, although as they waltzed they were in an ecstasy of joy. They were not in evening dress but in their 'best' clothes.

At a shilling hop there was a small band, six, seven or eight in number, but they played well, and strings predominated. The floor would be excellent and the dancing of a very high quality indeed. There was no nonsense, no unorthodox movements—the Professor would have stopped them, but he never had any cause, and there was extremely good behaviour. If it was not a very carefree and gay sight, at any rate it was a sight of young people enjoying themselves and doing their best to dance very well indeed.

The Waltz was the favourite dance, but they danced all sorts of dances, from Cotillon to Lancers, where there was a certain amount of romping, very carefully watched by the Professor as he called the movements.

There were refreshments, but nothing alcoholic. And ninety-nine per cent of the people were young. There were very few middle-aged folk about—the middle-aged in those days were pleased to look on, or at private dances to dance together once or twice and recapture their youth. Forward young misses who enticed old men to dance for gold-digging were in a very, very infinitesimal minority and not to be met with at shilling hops, or indeed at the Middle Class functions.

The dancing was not so far removed from the grace and dignity of the Minuet and the stately Gavotte. That spirit still hovered. The men bowed, the women inclined their heads or made a little curtsey. It was all very well bred and well behaved. As the century advanced around 1904 or 1906, some Professors of Dancing, desirous of being thought go-ahead and modern, introduced the 'Cake Walk', the latest thing from America. Few could dance it, few wanted to dance it. The Professor would maybe lead the way and just a handful capered with him, but the rest looked on in amazement and British superiority at some alien half-savage exhibition. The Barn Dance and the Lancers had abandon enough for them. This was not English.

England then was an exporting as well as an importing country and did not surrender at once to anything which crossed the Atlantic. Crooning was unknown, our own variety did it at public-house doors and were given more curses than halfpence, and the intimate embrace of modern dancing was unthought of and would not have been either desired or allowed.

Dancing was dancing, not a mixture of walking about and unrestrained acrobatics. Yet those shilling hops were largely attended, eagerly looked forward to, and were the bright spots of many young lives.

Most Middle Class dances were either social functions given by invitation or dances held in halls by teachers of dancing a little above the mere Professors who held public shilling hops. These teachers were often Middle-Class ladies themselves who had suffered financial reverses and had taken to the teaching of dancing—referred to jocosely as 'the light fantastic', although anything fantastic would have suffered immediate suppression. These ladies were of terrific gentility if of limited means. They did their job well, they ruled gently but firmly, they saw to it that the conventions were strictly enforced. And they had not a hard job in this, for there were very few outlaws who would have tried to outrage good behaviour at a Middle Class dance.

As the procedure, either at a private dance or a superior dancing-teacher's ticket of admission function was the same, it is better to describe the latter.

The dance would be held in a small local hall known to everyone in the suburb as the local rendezvous for such affairs. The ticket of admission cost either 2s. or 2s. 6d., and this included refreshments, which consisted of sandwiches (ham, beef, tongue, egg-and-cress or just cress). You knew which was which because a small banner was impaled on top of the pile giving the necessary information. This got lost after a while, and there would be speculation and perhaps the delicate lifting of a thin layer of bread by a gloved fingertip. There were very minute fancy pastries, and coffee to drink. That coffee got weaker and weaker as the evening proceeded, but nobody minded that, for everyone enjoyed themselves without the need of cocktails or constant visits to the bar. These people made their own enjoyment, they lit up the affair without needing to be lit up themselves.

They were eagerly looked forward to, these functions, by the local young Middle Class ladies. The young men were keen too, but perhaps not so keen as the girls. However, for many of them it meant that 'he' or 'she' might be there, and that was excitement. For they did not 'make dates', go dancing in public until the small hours, dash about in cars or on motor-bikes to country clubs and road-houses and behave with the casual, offhand familiarity of today. Not a bit of it. Things were formal, young people had reputations to keep and a good name was valuable. Courtship was not haphazard, it was serious, with nearly always 'a view to matrimony', and the parents kept a watchful eye. So a dance where the couple might meet and waltz together was something to look forward to.

373

Those girls made the most of themselves. They wore their best evening frocks, which had been bought or made because they suited them and were not just something which was in 'their colour' and the prevailing style. They were not something to be slipped on, but something to be assumed and to be 'worn'. They carried fans, which were tied around their wrists by a pretty ribbon bow, and swung as they danced. These bows had the additional value of drawing attention to a pretty wrist, hand or arm.

They did not, unless quite well-to-do, have special evening cloaks, but they wore their 'winter coats' with a 'fascinator' over their heads to protect the coiffure. They had their little shoe-bags in which they carried their dancing-shoes, into which they changed in the privacy of the ladies'-room in the hall. Their stockings were never the universal 'beige' colour so all-pervading today. Not that they would have known what 'beige' was, the word never got into use until 1912 or so. If they had not stockings to match their dress they wore their precious black silk ones, or otherwise white ones. But it must be borne in mind that you seldom saw their legs.

But they made the prettiest possible picture of feminine charm and excitement in their becoming chosen fashions of real womanhood, their foam of frilly lacy petticoats a-swirl around their ankles, their faces alight and eager—for they were not sated with entertainment, long hours, tobacco smoke and much alcohol, they were not *blasé* or bored, they were fresh, young and alert, and they were out for a good time as they understood it. They had not come expecting to be bored, expecting to find the band indifferent, the floor poor, or the place 'lousy'. They knew not the word and would not have uttered it if they had.

It may sound very simple today, it may sound even stupid and what is now called 'corney', but it had its points, and good points too. In their feminine dresses, with their feminine manners and their long gloves, they got far more kick out of it than does the modern miss in the modern dance-hall, despite the restrictions they knew and she knows not. Yet they had heartbreaks too.

It was the convention of those days, when conventions were very strong indeed (maybe that is why they seem so far off) that if a girl had not the supper-dance booked she went without food. It was not etiquette to get your own refreshment. A girl so situated, if she had no brother or escort to look after her, had a thin time.

And the supper-dance being booked meant just what it said. For every dancer had a programme. It was printed in black, gold or silver on coloured card, white, pink, green, blue or yellow. There were little pencils attached, with silk cords fluffed out at the end into a little tassel.

374

The pencils seldom wrote very clearly, but they sufficed. The dance-programme held romance, it held memories. Girls treasured them, they kept them in a drawer; they took them out, pored over them, recalled moments of triumph, of pleasure, of defeat and sorrow. Those dances printed thereon, the initials scribbled on the ruled lines against them, what stories they had to tell! It was often the beginning of a lifelong story, it was often the beginning of the first real sorrow. Women kept them even in old age. It was a sentimental time, but none the worse for that.

The little lady of the Golden Age who was to dance would secure her programme on arrival, and she would chat with her friends before entering the room. Perhaps she had come with a friend, perhaps with a middle-aged relative, perhaps with her family. Perhaps a whole party of girls and young men had arrived together in a private bus or wagonette. It depended on means and how far away one lived from that hall where the dance was to be held.

And the hall itself? Sometimes it rejoiced in the name of 'The Assembly Rooms', recalling the patches and powder of Bath and the Georges. Perhaps it was a church or even a chapel hall, earning its mite by such lettings towards the diminishing of the inevitable church or chapel debt. Or maybe it was a hall belonging to an enterprising tradesman and over his main place of business, and even bearing his name. Such halls were good for trade and brought custom. It might be upstairs over a furniture shop. In that case you would enter a door which led not through the shop but to a staircase, upon which stood the commodities the shop supplied and which were not taken away, dance or no dance. There would be articles of furniture, rolls of oilcloth and that smell of wood, wax, polish and varnish undetachable from such merchandise. But that made no difference. This was only the ante-room to pleasure, to romance. It was a mere passing through mundane things to a state nearer heart's desire—everyone read Omar Khayyám in those days, and many knew Fitzgerald's word-painting by heart.

Up the stairs was a landing, brightly lit, decked with screens, palms and ferns to hide the rolls of oilcloth, and with a chair or two from stock for 'sitting out'.

The hall itself was gay also, flags and bunting fluttered, the lights were all on, the little platform at the end was draped with red baize, or festooned in red, white and blue, with a row of ferns in pots along the edge, the pots swathed in coloured *crêpe* paper. On the platform was the little band and the pianist. Round the edge of the room were rout seats. That hall played a pretty big part in the life of the young Middle Class people of the neighbourhood. They danced there. The amateur actors performed there, when the platform became a stage with a green curtain—'tabs' which seldom worked properly but never made much difference to the show, working or not. It was to this hall that parents might take you to political or other meetings, to lectures to improve your mind, to wedding breakfasts, coming-of-age parties, to bazaars, for it was the hub of the social life of the suburb. But tonight it was a ballroom, and to the Middle Class girl, who saw it through eyes which drew their own picture, it was a most delightful place.

The gentlemen were there. Sometimes they were called 'the fellows', but that was not very good form. They were there, gallant and ready. They were wearing evening dress. Tails and white ties, sometimes white waistcoats as well. Their shirt-fronts gleamed, their collars were high and glossy. Hardly a man there wore a dinner-jacket. They had not become very popular, and to most men evening dress meant tails. Few possessed both tails and a dinner-jacket. And, indeed, dinner-jackets were not worn when ladies were present. They were informal attire, and this, although it was a dance, was a formal occasion. The men wore pumps and some even had silk socks, with either clocks up the ankles or little spots of colour all over the foot. They brought their pumps in their overcoat pockets, and they wore a white silk muffler to keep their shirt-fronts clean. There were special gadgets for this too. One could obtain a kind of black chest-protector which fastened across the chest and protected that starched plastron from dirt, being lined with white silk.

No man ever dreamed of wearing a soft dress shirt. Indeed, no shirt-maker had ever dreamed of making one. It would have been the worst of bad taste. It simply could not be done. All the men would be wearing gloves: white kid, white silk, or white cotton. Some might even sport gloves of pale lavender. No man ever danced with bare hands, it was not correct to touch the ladies' flesh with your rough, masculine hand. It was ungentlemanly—worse, it was indelicate. Nervous men sometimes split their gloves putting them on, and suffered agonies of embarrassment in consequence.

If a young man took a girl to a dance he always bought her flowers to wear. That was part of the ordinary male courtesy to the female sex. Strange as it seems today, men then always walked on the outside in the street, or if there were two ladies, he walked between them. He would always carry the parcels. If he met a female acquaintance so burdened he promptly assumed the load. "Allow me," he would say. The lady might protest, but he insisted. "It is a pleasure," he assured her.

And no man ever allowed the lady to pay for anything. To pay was the male prerogative, his pride and privilege. The expense might cripple him for weeks, but it made no difference. It was impossible for the lady to pay for anything. He would have died at the thought. He took pleasure in finding out her taste in flowers, in books, in scent, in sweets, in music. He took pleasure in sending little gifts. There was no thought of the equality of the sexes then. The woman had no rights and was dreadfully downtrodden. She was even given a seat in a crowded vehicle by a man who raised his hat as he offered it. If she were young and attractive, there would be a rush of offers. But any woman, of any age and any appearance, always got a seat.

The same courtesy prevailed at the dances. Girls seldom went accompanied by a male partner. This was permissible if they were engaged. To go to a dance with a young man was to set tongues wagging and to invite the question as to why the engagement had not been announced. But hardly a girl monopolized one man the whole evening. That was not good form either. It was 'fast', unless it was obvious that an engagement was pending. The social mill ground in full sight.

Girls did not need a chaperone at these dances, but they never went alone; always at least two of them together, or in parties.

The room would fill up, and conversation buzzed all round. Then the band struck a chord and the Master of Ceremonies announced the first dance. The gentleman would approach his lady and bow. You were very formal in your invitation to the waltz. "May I have the pleasure?" he would enquire, and the girl, if not already booked, would hand him her little programme on which he put his initials or his name. But most dances were booked beforehand. The men went round the room finding their friends and entering up the cards.

Popular girls soon had their cards filled, and were happy as soon as that supper-dance was booked by the right man. It was a bit awkward sometimes if he had not arrived and another man solicited the honour. She had to use tact—or put her favoured one's initials on the card herself. There were always more women than men, and consequently there were 'wallflowers'—plain, unobtrusive or unpopular girls with sparsely filled programmes. The M.C. would do his best for them, round up men, introduce them, and stand over them until at least one dance was booked. The girl would smile with embarrassed pleasure when asked if she had a dance vacant, and surrender her programme with an eagerness she did her best to conceal. Some, however, got few dances, and brothers of more fortunate girls were made by their sisters to give the unlucky ones a dance.

But the poor wallflowers would sit fanning themselves with a fixed smile, pretending to enjoy every moment, but with bitterness in their hearts. A man sought out the partner whose name appeared on his programme. He bowed before her. "Our dance, I believe?" he murmured. The girl then rose and they joined in the dance. When it was over, the man returned his partner to a seat and sat chatting with her until her next partner arrived to claim her. Then he went in search of his. Sometimes the sought-for young lady might be 'sitting out' with her favoured young man and took a little finding. She would be a little reluctant to come when claimed, but she had to do it, and finally went with a fixed smile and a backward glance at the man she was leaving.

But when the dancing began, then the dancers enjoyed every moment of it. They really waltzed, they did not just walk round—and they 'reversed'. The Waltz was the chief and the most popular dance. There were Polkas, the Barn Dance, Paul Jones, the Waltz Cotillon, and early in the period the Quadrilles and the Schottische, and—later—the Valeta. When it came to the Lancers, they really let themselves go. The Lancers were the highspot. Danced as a rule to a specially arranged selection from a popular musical comedy, it was the real joy of the Golden Age period. And there were nearly always two sets of Lancers during the evening. There were shouts of delight and excited feminine screams as brawny young men whirled the graceful girls, their skirts and petticoats flying, right off their feet.

It was really exhilarating to dance the Lancers and give high spirits a chance. There was none of the hugging, cheek-to-cheek lounging of the moderns, but dancing by people who had been taught to dance and who loved every movement of it. Men's collars sagged, they got hot; the girls got a bit tousled, but they had no make-up to worry about, so they just enjoyed themselves.

Supper was a time of laughter and chatter. There were no intoxicants, but the Golden Age dancers did not worry about food—or drink either, for that matter. They wanted to dance. Sometimes there were ices—an extra. "May I get you an ice?" asked the young man and, if consent was given, he would struggle in the crowd around the buffet and finally return with a little glass dish and a small spoon. He would hand it to the lady with a bow, sit by her and indulge in chit-chat whilst she ate it, and when she had finished, "Allow me," he would say, and take the little dish away again. The lady was not expected to do anything for herself. It was man's privilege to serve.

Then, supper done—on with the dance. Couples met, danced and parted, even engaged couples seldom danced every dance together—dancing was communal, it was to be enjoyed by all. There were no streamers, balloons, spotlight, spot prizes, or suchlike—but there was dancing, and that was all these people wanted. They were all Cinderellas and Prince Charmings in the ballroom, and when midnight struck it was over. The girls went home dreamy-eyed, the young men, pumps in greatcoat pockets, would go home perhaps a bit thoughtfully—if Eros had chanced to be an extra partner.

Many a Middle Class home owed its inception to a dance. There were sometimes disagreements as well, if a girl had, according to her young man, bestowed too many dances on another man—obviously a cad and bad form, according to him; and sometimes a non-dancing *fiancé*, arriving to escort her home, would have a serious and heart-to-heart talk, with clenched fists and angry eyes, to another youth whom he had found 'paying too much attention', as he called it, to his chosen one. But these were the exceptions. It was all happy, it was gay. It was decorous and it was wholly delightful.

Men sometimes chose a dance at which to 'propose'. Contrary to belief, the young man of the Golden Age did not fall on his knees before his adored one, offering his hand, his heart and his three or four sovereigns a week. Nor did the young lady blush and exclaim, "This is so sudden!" She was a woman and never taken by surprise in such matters. Besides, she would have had all the usual warnings of the period. He would, according to her, her friends, and even her mother, have been 'paying her marked attention' for some time. He would have sent little floral offerings to her. He would have haunted the places where he might meet her, and run across her at all sorts of functions and at odd times. He would have found a chance of joining her after church in the little pre-lunch—only they probably called it dinner—parade. He had probably called round, dressed in his best, a bit nervous but determined, and had a cup of tea. He would have been inspected by the family, if he were not known to them, but he probably belonged to the same cricket club as her brothers, the same tennis club as she did, or the same church or chapel. As like as not, his family knew her family, which made it easier. Then he would become a more regular caller, and after a while the young lady would see him alone, the family (if his suit was favoured) retiring tactfully and leaving the young couple alone.

The length of the wooing depended very largely upon the confidence of the young man or the art of allure and encouragement of the young lady. Only if it were too drawn-out would the lady's father have a word with him and ask 'his intentions'. That very seldom happened, despite the novelists' and story-tellers' belief. The climax was reached soon enough. And he probably made his offer at a dance, when 'sitting out', with the strings throbbing a romantic waltz and the whisk of dancing feet as accompaniment. Having put his fate to the touch and conquered, the couple would re-enter the ballroom with such an air about them that everyone knew. Eager eyes had been watching, intimate girl friends 'in the know' could tell at a glance. Romance filled the air around.

The young man would, in due course, interview his loved one's father and state his prospects. He would get the family blessing and the ring would be bought. Another Middle Class home was in process of formation. But even though engaged, the couple never stopped out too late. That was not done. Parents sometimes grumbled at the length of time the drawing-room was occupied and the additional cost of the gas bill (though that was probably infinitesimal). The couple kept the rules. As for going away together for a holiday—that was unthinkable, and scandalous. The solid Middle Class conventions were observed until the day of white dress, bridesmaids, orange blossom, male frock-coats and buttonholes, broughams with white favours—and the report in the local paper, with most of the names spelt wrongly—of 'Pretty Wedding at St. John's'. They were all pretty weddings according to the 'local'. And they nearly all were just that.

There were other dances: lawn-tennis club dances, 'flannel dances' in the summer evenings, when the men wore whites and the girls their summer frocks, and there were heavier, much more pompous affairs given by the local political associations, at which 'the Member' might be present. These were treated almost like State balls, and girls went to them in a state of full chaperonage.

There were whist drives, which were enormously popular, but more amongst the middle-aged than the young. Ladies who had passed their first youth took their whist extremely seriously, and woe betide the partner who made the slightest mistake.

Men went to smoking concerts, from which ladies were excluded. They sat at small tables, they drank and they smoked. The artistes were of the more bohemian kind, and the comics could be as blue as they liked—though they were never so blue as today. It was a full-blooded male affair, a smoking concert, and a good excuse for a drink. There were what were known as 'heads' the morning after, and a disinclination for breakfast in any shape or form, save a strong cup of tea or black coffee and an early resort to 'a hair of the dog that bit me'.

There was, however, another dance during certain months of the year to which the young men—and the old men too—could go if they knew their way about and had a sovereign or two to spend. They did not take their womenfolk, they went alone if they were engaged, or if single they either went alone or took a lady whom they would not have taken to the ordinary Middle Class dance. But if they went alone, they seldom remained lonely for long, for the ladies they would meet were all extremely 'matey' and all extremely 'bohemian'. You needed no introduction. You spoke to whom you liked and you danced with whom you liked, for it was the field in which you could scatter some of your wild oats, it was part of the Kingdom of Bohemia even if it were actually inside the walls of the Royal Opera House, Covent Garden.

There is nothing like the Covent Garden Ball of the Golden Age to be found in London today. It was High Carnival, it was Saturnalia, it was perhaps pagan, but many people found it a pagan paradise. It was the last glimpse of the 'masquerade', the ridotto, which had flourished in the 18th century. It had held sway at Ranelagh, at the Pantheon, at Vauxhall, it had languished, it had turned up again at Covent Garden.

Unlike the gay Lothario played by George Grossmith in *The Spring Chicken* at the Gaiety, who declared that

> When the autumn leaves are falling
> I can hear my conscience calling.
> Duty waits for me,

that was the very time when the youth of London heard the call of Covent Garden. From October to April was the time of the Covent Garden Ball, though sometimes they ran right through the spring and early summer as well. The mists of October, the dark evenings, the golden glow of the lights were the heralds of these joyous London nights, when cares were thrown over the shoulder and Misrule reigned. They were pure Topsy-Turveydom, a night stolen from Pantomime Land.

They did not start until most Middle Class people were in bed and fast asleep, for all the ladies of the ballet at the Empire and the Alhambra received a ticket and it was not much use going until they were there.

They were not cheap affairs, as cheapness went then. Your ticket cost a guinea, which allowed you to dance. If you simply wanted to be a spectator, you could go into one of the great circles at the Opera House and look on for a few shillings. But that was not much good. You had to participate in the fun if you wanted the full flavour. You were expected to go in fancy dress and masked. You could, however, hire a domino and a mask on the premises to cover your evening dress, and that saved a lot of trouble.

All the 'ladies' wore masks during the early part of the ball, which did not start until midnight, although they shed them later. Sometimes, however, a couple would arrive and both wear masks all the time. You drew your own conclusions from this, and perhaps you might, without knowing it, one day read the sequel in a report of a sensational divorce case in the evening papers.

Many people wore complete fancy dress and very elaborate ones. There would be a competition later and prizes for the best ones—valuable prizes too. Covent Garden did nothing by halves. This gave the girls a chance. Some of the daring ones wore very short skirts and showed a lot of shapely, silk-stockinged leg. Some of the most daring ones had discarded skirts altogether and had appeared in male attire—so far as their legs went. There were always quite a lot of 'coons'. These were girls wearing what the music-hall imagined was the usual attire of the cotton-fields of Alabama, 'Ole Virginy' and that unknown region (to Britons, anyway) watered by the Swanee River.

This cotton-growing was evidently a very picturesque business, and could not have been very hard work, for the young ladies who joined the ranks for that evening wore large floppy circular straw hats, a white silk blouse with quite a deep V opening, a sash round their waists tied on one hip, striped silk breeches, one turned up above the knee, the other coming below it, black silk stockings and the daintiest high-heeled shoes. If they did not get much cotton, they got a fine crop of partners. And they did themselves well.

There was plenty to eat and drink, long bars abounded with attendants behind them dressed in red, white and blue. There were supper-tables galore, mostly to seat two, and champagne popped all over the place.

You looked around and selected your partners, hoping you would find them when you wanted them. If you did not, there were plenty more. And when the very excellent band struck up—it was often that of Dan Godfrey—the perfect floor was a kaleidoscope of colour and movement. Here was none of the genteel subdued chatter and the ladylike laughter of the Middle Class dance. Here there was no restraint. People shouted, people yelled with laughter, feminine shrieks and squeals rent the air, as partners were enjoined to "Give over now, do." It was Carnival all right and a golden glow over all.

The boxes could be hired and supper served in them. The first and last balls of the season saw them packed. At other times there were excellent sitting-out places where a chaperone would have been embarrassed to complete collapse. For the *demi-monde* went to Covent Garden and the lads in search of an evening's fun without licence of clergy. It was not at all respectable. It was an oasis of disrepute in a world of convention—but nobody was any the worse. Everyone knew what to expect, and everyone knew why they went.

Midway in the proceedings there was a lull in the dancing as the costumes were judged. The dancers crowded on to the floor leaving an alley down the middle along which the contestants walked to the judges, who were on the bandstand. Those contestants ran a gauntlet of chaff, badinage, criticism and applause long before they came under the judges' eyes, but they held their own and gave as good as they got. The judging done, the winners applauded, the dancing went on and things reached their height.

It was riotous now, and all pretence of reserve had gone. It was a huge romp, with the highest spirit and the very least respectability. Couples showed what they could do in the way of high stepping, girls did solo dances and acrobatic feats, cartwheels were turned with great applause, and there was a display of lace, limbs and lingerie such as could be seen nowhere else. The champagne was in every vein, and lit every eye, and the last waltz, just before five o'clock, was more akin to the Lancers than anything else. But no jitterbugging. Then five struck and the band played 'God Save the King'.

Out amongst the vegetables and the sharp-tongued but kindly porters went the revellers, looking a little pinched as the keen morning air struck them, but still warm with the memory, good food and good wine of the lovely night's entertainment, a Covent Garden Night's Entertainment in the modern Baghdad. The 'all-night' pubs of the Garden served some queerly dressed customers with eggs and bacon, kidney and bacon, hot rolls and plenty of coffee. They were used to it, it did not seem at all strange to them. The understanding and fatherly policemen from adjacent Bow Street Station took paternal care of young men who had let the wine go to their heads as well as the women and the dancing. They found out their names and addresses with much patience, tucked them into a cab and told the grinning driver 'where to'—and morning began again in grey workaday London, whose nights were made so wonderful by the glow of the golden sovereign.

Of course, the respectable Middle Class husbands did not go there— oh no! But you saw some unexpected faces when the masks came off about 4 a.m. Middle Class ladies certainly never went to the Covent Garden balls, and their menfolk, if these affairs were mentioned, would tell them they were not at all nice. On being questioned how they knew, it would appear that a bachelor friend of theirs had once been taken to one and had suffered considerably. He had sworn he would never go again. Details were never gone into—ladies were not supposed to know about such things, let alone talk of them. And the proportion of women who had any curiosity on the subject was very small.

For it was the home which occupied her, and her family. She led a very sheltered life, she was kept as far as possible from the seamy side. She was on a pedestal to the extent that few girls of today could understand, and if they did, they would laugh.

But was it so bad, was it so foolish, were women so much the worse off? In that masculine age, when men were the breadwinners, a woman had no freedom. She could not stop out late at night, go to a public function—or very few—alone. She could not walk about the streets at night. She was not allowed to smoke in public, and if she drank much in public or went into a public-house her reputation was gone. She was not allowed to fight her way on to a bus or a tram and hang on a strap; she was not allowed to pay for her dinner, her fares, her tea or her refreshments. She was not allowed to pay for anything if a gentleman was of the party. She was not allowed to carry her own parcels, or to be pushed into the gutter. She was not allowed the freedom of being shooed out of her turn in a crowded place. She knew nothing of queueing except for the pit or gallery of a theatre. She was not taken seriously if she argued about politics, and she had no say in who should represent her in Parliament. She was not allowed to be insulted in shops, to haul home baskets of food far too heavy for her, or to have the joy and freedom of doing her own boots, her own washing, of cleaning her own windows or lighting her own fires.

That wicked, possessive male with sovereigns in his pocket paid everything for her, saw to it that she was served, saw to it that she got a seat and was taken care of, saw to it that she ran her home as she wanted it done. He did not expect her to do heavy work—he would have died if he had seen her in trousers unloading carts, pushing great barrows, carrying other people's luggage on stations, or throwing herself headlong at motor-cars containing very ordinary men with American accents and a certain easiness on a screen of shadows.

As for joining the fighting forces, manning guns or dashing with dispatches on swift motor-bikes, breeched, goggled and uniformed—well, the might and power of the golden sovereign, so strong and so invulnerable, kept even the Middle Class man from doing that himself. Policemen walked the beat to prevent the Middle Class woman being assaulted in the road, bashed on the head as she opened her front door, or being tied up and gagged in her own bedroom. The old-fashioned 'copper' with his big flat feet might have been a good joke, but he had a habit of 'getting his man', and crime was very restricted. Nor were the criminal classes so large or so well equipped.

The Middle Class woman of the Golden Age had not the freedom of the woman of the Paper Age. She did not want it. She did not do the rough things of life. They were done for her by the Working Classes.

Now there is no difference. Freedom has come to all. The Middle Class is no more. The barrier of the golden sovereign is down, and the paper of the pound admits of no class distinction. It may be better, it may be a happier state of things. Posterity will judge. But the Middle Class woman is off her pedestal, out of her secure home, well in the rough and tumble.

She is one of the Working Classes again and maybe she likes it. Maybe she does not. Maybe some of the middle-aged women who were once Middle Class girls would like to hear a gentleman say once more, "May I have the pleasure?" or "Allow me," instead of "Come on, sister," or "How yer doin', Toots?" You never know.

CHAPTER XXV

The Lights Go Out

THAT NEW FACE ON THE SOVEREIGN, THE FACE OF KING EDWARD, HAD set a brisker pace. Life grew into a trot instead of a stately dignified walk. Nobody minded that. It was a new century under a new King, and a good King too. A King of whom the music-halls sang:

> Peace with Honner
> Is 'is motter,
> So—Gawd Save the King.

But that increase of pace perhaps obscured from the Middle Classes the immense changes which were taking place around them. Their emergence from Victorian discipline to Edwardian ease made them take so much for granted. When change is general, individual changes do not make such a great impression. The sovereign still shone, it was still worth twenty shillings, and life was still secure and good. Yet life was becoming different. Money entered into it more. Wealth was replacing birth, there was a new aristocracy of the sovereign. There was a new freedom, a loosening of restriction, a less strong regard for morality, and a lesser regard for the Sabbath. There was so much change that one or two more or less did not matter. At least, that was how it seemed to the younger Middle Class people.

Political strife was rampant if warlike strife was stilled. Changes were coming in our old and tried constitution. The House of Lords was challenged as to its hereditary right to baulk the desires of the people as expressed by their representatives in Parliament assembled. Now the Middle Classes, in common with a great part of the other classes, dearly loved a lord. Yet the case against them was very well put and seemed cogent.

The Lords, it seemed, were old-fashioned and were standing in the way of Progress. Had not W. S. Gilbert told the truth about them in *Iolanthe*? Had he not said that England and her golden days endured so long as the House of Peers withheld its legislative hand and noble statesmen refrained from interfering in matters beyond their comprehension? Well, it did not seem to matter very much if the Lords had their wings clipped. And clipped they were. It did not make much difference either. But it seemed also that the other end of the social scale was not being fairly created. It seemed that Progress considered that such things as workhouses were out of date and that old people, tired and worn with labour, should receive a pension from the State. It seemed also that as they could not afford decent doctors they should be given medical help and that their employers should assist in payment for it. Lloyd George made a phrase ring through the land. "Ninepence for fourpence" he promised, and it did not seem such long odds, except that his opponents foretold that the country would become a nation of stamp-lickers.

This same fiery Welshman, who had been described by Middle Class fathers to their sons in horror-stricken voices as a 'Radical', also said that it was not right that the land should be owned by the few whereas it really belonged to the many. He made a bit of a mistake in one of his orations and drew a pitiful picture of farmers being ruined because of the partiality of the carefully preserved pheasants, playthings of the rich, for mangel-wurzels, which were apparently the staple crop of the agriculturist. This was seized upon avidly by cartoonists of Unionist newspapers, because it so happens that the pampered pheasant not only never ate a mangel-wurzel but held it in contempt.

But Lloyd George was determined to tax land and eventually to free land. The Conservative section of the Middle Classes shook their heads. "What would become of the stately homes of England?" they wanted to know. They need not have worried. Those stately homes were safe so long as the sovereign was safe. When it went, they went with it, Lloyd George or no Lloyd George.

That pioneer Keir Hardie, in his deerstalker cap, had now quite a numerous company with him at Westminster, some of them, it is true, describing themselves as 'Lib-Lab'. The Liberal Party, strongly in power and seeming eternal, did not see the danger that little hyphen was to bring them.

Mr. Asquith, as Prime Minister, caused a good deal of amusement by his advice to an opponent to 'wait and see', a phrase which stuck to him and did him little good. Parliament also made history by the description of a lie as a 'terminological inexactitude'.

A. J. Balfour aroused amusement too, when he said that he would write the policy of the Conservative Party on a half-sheet of notepaper and nail it to the mast. They were simpler days, even politically. It would puzzle a government today to get a policy on any piece of paper, let alone nail it to a mast.

But perhaps it was the irrepressible Winston Churchill, when Home Secretary, who made the most considerable impression of that period, for that impression was made by action and not words. The whole of the country had been shocked by armed criminals. A policeman had been

387

shot in the execution of his duty. That was unheard of. The criminals were traced to Stepney, to a little house in Sidney Street. One of them bore the picturesque name, straight out of a 'penny dreadful', of 'Peter the Painter'. There Peter, perhaps by himself, perhaps with others, nobody ever knew, held the police at bay and bullets sprayed the road. That was unprecedented in London. Mr. Churchill, the Home Secretary, went down in person to see for himself. He wore his tall hat and his frock-coat on that London battlefield. He called out the troops and even artillery from the Tower. They burned the house finally and the criminals with it.

All Britain was aghast at such a thing as shooting by criminals in the open thoroughfare. Nowadays it would only get a few lines in the papers. But crime was quickly dealt with and people walked secure in the days of the sovereign.

But Parliament was still the finest club in the world, and it still required money to attain, for members were still unpaid. The Labour men, of course, got a stipend from the vast millions which were known by the Middle Classes to be locked in the Trade Union chests!

The Middle Classes did not realize that there was no time 'to wait and see', they did not realize that they were indeed living through a revolution, social and scientific, which was taking place, as revolutions in this country (save one only) have always taken place without bloodshed, undue excitement or undue haste. You don't know there has been a revolution until it is over.

As time went on the horse was driven steadily from the road. The internal combustion engine was all-conquering. It conquered transport, it conquered the land and it set about the Air. Flying was now being indulged in. Two American gentlemen, the Wrights, had got off the ground in America, and now men were getting off the ground all over the world. Speed was beginning to matter, the old leisurely days were drawing to a close.

But Sport went on, Society went on, everything went on, without really radical change, even if the telephones grew more and more numerous and even if Signor Marconi had found out how to send messages without the aid of telegraph or even telephone wires at all. It had something to do with the Ether, the Middle Class said. Ether to them meant some kind of thing which doctors or dentists monkeyed about with.

The tremendous commercial zeal and concentration of the Victorian Age was relaxed too. The country was so rich, so powerful, that it could take a breather, surely! That contempt for foreigners which was so true a part of British mental outlook prevented them from studying what was going on abroad. But the heir to the Throne had been round the world. He went, on his return, to the Guildhall, and there, as guest of the City

Fathers, he blew a trumpet. He blew a fanfare, a call to arms. His note of warning was 'Wake Up, England!'

It did a little good—some of the people opened their eyes. But it was no dismal prospect which they viewed. Britannia still ruled the waves, life still went on, the sovereign still jingled, the Empire was firm, and South Africa, so recently the scene of war, was made into a Union under the British Crown and Flag. It was a fine bit of statesmanship, this giving back the Boers their freedom of choice in the government of their own affairs. General Botha came out strongly for the Union, and he and General Smuts became British citizens, of which Britain has every reason to be proud.

Things did not seem so bad at all. Sir Thomas Lipton was still failing to win the America Cup with his yachts, all named *Shamrock*.

Yet there were undercurrents. There was growing labour unrest and growing dissatisfaction in Ireland. There was unemployment and it could not be blinked at. This seemed strange to the Middle Class people, that there should not be work for all in so rich a country. But the fact remained. The dissatisfaction in Ireland was not dispelled by a Royal Visit from Edward and his Queen.

But if there was progress at home—and there was lots of it—there was also progress abroad, and that was the real root of the trouble. That grandson of Queen Victoria, that German Emperor Wilhelm, who had sent that wire to Kruger, was doing a bit of progress on his own account.

If not he, then his people. But he was their Emperor, a despot, an Absolute Monarch—or so the Middle Classes believed—and he was demanding 'A Place in the Sun'. It appeared to him that Britain had all the plums and the Germans had nothing. It appeared that we basked in the sunshine whilst they moped in the shade. There were certainly a great number of them, whilst in Britain the birth-rate was falling.

German merchants vending the once despised German-made goods were invading all markets, underselling and undercutting. They took the mean and unsportsmanlike advantage of talking the same language as their customers, which they were at pains to learn, of carrying on correspondence in that language and even quoting prices in the ridiculous coinage of those realms and in their own silly weights and measures.

The Middle Classes, when they became faintly aware of this, decided that King Edward was right when he had said that Kaiser Bill—Middle Class for the All-Highest—was no gentleman. He was no sportsman, either, but the two things were synonymous. Wasn't the English language the finest in the world? Did not the British own a fifth of that world? Very well, then, it was up to the foreigner, if he wanted to buy the best goods—our goods, that is—to learn English.

389

But it appeared the foreigner had also gone in for progress as well, and it had led him to believe that there was money to be made by buying in the cheapest market, even if the goods were not the best. Then this German Emperor, or Kaiser, or whatever you like to call him, committed a sin which immediately damned him in all Middle Class eyes, if not indeed in all British eyes. He began to build a large Navy. Now what did he want that for? He had an immense Army. It had proved its quality by simply walking over the French only a few years before. It was regarded as the finest army in the world. The British did not think so. They believed in 'The Soldiers of the King'. They believed in quality, not quantity, and it was their fixed conviction that one Briton was equal to any six foreigners.

Then there was King Edward's cleverness in bringing about the *Entente* so that we had the French Army on our side. That was a large one—a conscript army like the German war machine. It had been beaten by the Germans, it is true, but there was a lot of talk about '*Revanche*', and anyway, if it ever came to war again, which was unthinkable, it would have the stiffening and assistance of that little British Army which went such a long way. Tommy Atkins, despite the Boer War, and his red-trousered friend the *poilu*, could more than account for any jack-booted, goose-stepping Prussian.

But besides all that, there was the British Navy, the Navy which had won Trafalgar just as Wellington had won Waterloo. It was an accepted fact that the British Navy was invincible. There was no Nelson nowadays, it is true, but his spirit and his genius lived on in Charlie Beresford and Jacky Fisher, as the two great admirals were familiarly described.

Yet here was the Kaiser building ships! He had little seaboard, or Colonies. What did he mean? The Middle Classes, in common with the other classes, decided that he meant 'US'.

Now, even if England had not woken up when the Prince of Wales sounded the alarm clock, one section of it never slept, and that section was its most trusted and most beloved service: His Majesty's Royal Navy. It had observed the German activity in ships and it had produced in answer to it the most powerful floating fighting machine the world had ever seen in H.M.S. *Dreadnought*. It was hailed as the last word. That would stop the poor benighted Germans, said the Middle Classes, said all England. But it did not. The Germans went on building, and it was discovered that their shipbuilding capacity was much greater than had been imagined.

The British public, which included the Middle Classes, were now, like Joe Bagstock, wide awake and staring. This must be stopped. This German upstart must learn once and for all that the Trident was held by

Britannia by Divine Charter and that Germania, that big blowsy female, must keep off the High Seas.

A tremendous Dreadnought crusade arose. "We want eight and we won't wait," the people chanted. And they had their way. There was a thing called the submarine to be reckoned with too. But it was so frequently coming to disaster and brave lives were so often lost that people did not believe in it. Battleships were the things. Dreadnoughts—that name had the true British ring.

So Peace seemed to be maintained safely. The Dreadnoughts would see to that. But still social reform went on and still Ireland was dissatisfied. The Middle Classes did not worry about that. Ireland had always been dissatisfied, she always would be. One-fifth of the world was satisfied, so Ireland, that minute minority, must be wrong.

The Middle Classes went on with their sports, their games, their dancing, their holidays, their 'At Home' days, their marrying and giving in marriage, and fewer of them than ever enlisted in that Territorial Army which had replaced the old Volunteers. They still had Edward the Peacemaker on the throne, and 'Teddy' 'would stand no nonsense', the country said. It had great faith in its sovereigns, human and metal.

King Edward went abroad. There was nothing in that, he was always going abroad. He went to Biarritz. He did all the things he did as a rule. But he caught a cold. He spent some days in his room. Well, it was reported that the weather was bad, so he was quite right. He must not take any risks, said the loyal Middle Class. He was out again when the sun shone and reported quite well. He went to Pau in April. It was noticed that his doctor was with him, but why not? A very wise precaution. He came home on 27th April, and seemed in excellent health and spirits. He gave audiences, including one to Lord Kitchener, who had just finished his job as Commander-in-Chief in India, and the King handed him his Field Marshal's baton. He went to the opera and saw *Rigoletto*. He went to Sandringham. He looked well.

He came back to London on 2nd May, 1910. It was a dull, depressing day, an example of a bad English spring. He went to Buckingham Palace and he stayed there. He did not go about, he did not visit the theatre. As it was the beginning of the Season, this was noticed. He was not at Victoria to meet the Queen, who had been abroad. And then rumours began to spread and confirmation followed them. The King was ill. The nation read with dismay:

"His Majesty the King is suffering from a severe bronchial attack and has been confined to his room for the last two days."

The papers rushed out special editions, as they did in those days—'Serious Illness of the King'. Despite the wind, the rain, the chill cold, crowds began to gather at Buckingham Palace. And at 8 p.m. they read another bulletin:

"The King is suffering from an attack of bronchitis and has been confined to his room for two days. His Majesty's condition causes some anxiety."
(Signed) F. H. Laking, M.D., James Reid, M.D., R. Douglas Powell, M.D."

The nation was still not without hope. A great many of them, including the Middle Class, had had bronchitis and got over it without such skill and care as the King must have around him. They did not know of the family weakness which made this a dangerous complaint.

At 11 a.m. on Friday, 10th May, a bulletin struck them dumb:

"The King has passed a comparatively quiet night, but his symptoms have not improved and His Majesty's condition gives rise to grave anxiety."

It was now signed by five doctors, the names of Bertram Dawson and St. Clair Thompson being added. The waiting crowds outside the Palace increased. There was no radio to give them the news, to bring them almost to the bedside of a dying King as a quiet English voice repeated at intervals, "The King's life is drawing peacefully towards its close." That British crowd, and mostly a Middle Class crowd, waited patiently outside the Monarch's house, to be as near to him as possible. At half past six on the same evening they read with sorrow:

"The King's symptoms have become worse during the day and His Majesty's condition is now critical."

The crowd had watched the Royal Family gather. It knew the worst, but it still clung to hope. The weather was dreadful, yet they hung on, and more joined them as the theatres emptied. Not very many, for the news of the Royal illness had half emptied the theatres in advance. A Court official assured the crowd there would be no more bulletins that night. The crowd faded away, all but a few who determined they would not leave their post at the nearest point they could reach to the bedside of the King they trusted.

At half past twelve (midnight) a closed carriage drove out of the Palace. They glimpsed the man they knew as the Prince of Wales. In reality they saw their new King, George V—for King Edward the Peacemaker was dead.

392

A member of the Household came to the gates and told them, in just that phrase. "The King is dead," he said. The official statement followed.

In the morning the nation knew, and the nation mourned. No portion mourned more deeply than the Middle Class, for he had always seemed one of themselves. Royal he was in every sense, but his outlook had been that of an ordinary man, one of the men with whom he mixed so freely on the racecourse and elsewhere. There had never been the aloofness of Royalty about him. He had been one of themselves, a man as they were men and women; he had been, to all of them, 'Teddy'. Now he had gone.

There was national mourning, the theatres closed, there was gloom and despondency. That Middle Class boy, who had seen so many great events, saw the new King on the first day of his accession, as he drove down the Mall. By his side was seated the Home Secretary, a determined-looking man who was to do so much for his country and who was, and still is, Mr. Winston Churchill. That Middle Class boy, now a young man, with the girl who is now his wife beside him, stood there bareheaded as his new King passed.

The nation wondered and the Middle Classes wondered. They did not know this new King as they had known the old. He had always been over-shadowed by his father's greatness. Some said openly they wished the Duke of Connaught was to be King. But so many more remembered that call to England to 'Wake Up'.

King Edward was laid to rest in Regal state and pomp, but it had not the heart-throb ot the old Queen's funeral, loved and mourned though he was.

The new King was crowned with general rejoicings and good wishes. They were to come to know him and his words soon enough. Few men who sat on the throne of England had such a stormy passage as he, and few handled the ship of State so well. He was a Sailor King, and that was much in his favour. Some of the older of the Middle Classes remembered that his Queen—now so generally beloved and respected—had been formerly engaged to his brother. But that did not matter.

There was a new face on the sovereign again and it was still worth twenty shillings in the pound. But it seemed that the storm which had marked the passing of King Edward, the bad weather which had sur-rounded the death of a King, still lingered and gathered in force. The seasons might be fine, but the air was charged with thunder. It rumbled and it grumbled in the distance. Labour troubles grew, great strikes took place, surpassing all other trade disputes of many years. And still Germany built the ships and still this country built against her. The new King was not having an easy time.

393

In 1911 a stormcloud showed over the horizon. That wind was gathering force, that gale was growing. The Kaiser had been over here and had helped his cousin King George unveil the Memorial to their grandmother, Victoria, which stands outside Buckingham Palace. There had been State Banquets, State Balls, a Gala Performance at Drury Lane. Royal protestations of friendship between the two countries were exchanged. But the people remained aloof. Especially the Middle Classes. They did not trust this Kaiser. He was 'up to something'. It did not need much foresight to know that, but still they saw it.

It must be borne in mind that this chronicle attempts to put down in print the outlook of the average Middle Class mind of the time—minds which had for generations been lulled by peace and world power and the power of the sovereign. That outlook was far more insular—war, the films and the radio had not brought internationalization. But it did not seem right to them. The world indeed seemed out of joint. This German business was serious. Someone wanted a lesson.

Germany made a covert challenge. She sent a gunboat to Agadir in direct breach of international law. Europe was up in arms. France saw war ahead. She prepared for mobilization. Germany wanted to test the strength of the *Entente Cordiale*. She soon knew. England spoke with the voice of the Rt. Hon. David Lloyd George, who had been the despised Radical, the robber of hen-roosts, the man with the pheasant and the mangel-wurzel, the opponent of the Lords, the destroyer of landed estate. And was now the voice which said that Britain stood behind France.

That Middle Class young man was in Paris when the news broke. He had a little Union Jack in his buttonhole. His drinks cost him nothing that night. His arm was nearly broken with handshaking, and he just escaped being carried shoulder high round a café. That was how the French responded to Britain. Germany climbed down. She had found out what she wanted to know. The Kaiser bit his nails and decided to wait. Germany was not yet quite ready.

But the winds of discord still roared around the world and the kingdom rocked on a stormy political sea. The word 'Socialism' was now freely uttered, it was seriously discussed. Liberals and Conservatives were being challenged by Labour, and to most Middle Class eyes Labour meant Socialism, which they did not understand at all. Had that class then either made the Labour Party its own, as it could have done, or thrown in its lot wholeheartedly with one of the other parties, history since might have been different. But the backbone of the nation was so firmly set that it could not change. It has not changed yet, though conditions are wiping it out. It will go down as it lived, the Middle Class, the nut between the crackers.

The fateful year of 1914 was reached. The nation was still on an even keel and Middle Class life was in the same position because of the ballast of the golden sovereign. But otherwise the nation was torn by internal strife.

Outside, the German menace, now very thinly veiled, grew and grew. Inside, there was another menace. There was the menace of Civil War. Ireland was determined to get Home Rule. Ulster was determined to stand by the old order and by the Crown. Ireland was prepared to fight for Home Rule. Ulster was determined to fight to stay inside Britain. It looked as though a clash was quite inevitable. The South of Ireland armed and drilled. Ulster armed and drilled. The newspapers were full of news and pictures. English politicians actually joined the Ulster forces. Galloper Smith and Galloper Churchill got into the news. Galloper Smith became Lord Birkenhead and Lord Chancellor of Britain. Winston Churchill became Prime Minister at a time when he was most needed. Then they were younger but always belligerent. Lord Northcliffe threw his vast weight on the side of Ulster. His newspapers clamoured about the iniquity of it all.

King George V did his gallant best to bring about and keep the Peace which his father had bestowed upon his country. But Civil War seemed absolutely certain.

Then away in a small town, in a small country hardly any Middle Class person had ever heard of, a shot rang out. That shot killed the Archduke of Austria, heir to the Middle European Empire of Austria-Hungary. That shot also killed the British golden sovereign. The name Sarajevo leapt into the news. It did not mean much to the Middle Class at first, these foreigners were always assassinating people, especially in the Balkans. The Servian King had been assassinated, the King of Italy had been assassinated, so had the King of Portugal. They had thrown a bomb at King Alfonso of Spain and his English bride during the wedding procession. A rotten lot, these foreigners. They shrugged their shoulders and turned to the cricket news, for it was summer time and cricket was important. As regards the warring factions in Ireland, the Middle Classes were inclined to say, with Mercutio, 'A plague o' both the houses.' What had Middlesex scored? How was the County Championship?

But it seemed this shooting really did matter. Austria had sent an ultimatum to Servia which amounted to annihilation. The German Kaiser indulged in a prolonged session of his favourite game of sabre-rattling. Austria the mighty invaded Servia the tiny. It was war. England roared when little Servia gave the Austrians a good thrashing. But now Germany and its Kaiser acted. He came out plump on the side of his 'brother' of Austria. Servia appealed to its natural guardian, the Tsar of

Russia, linked to this country by blood and by his alliance with France. He was, indeed, the double in appearance, though not by any means in character, of our own George V.

Germany threatened Russia. France sided with its ally, Italy sat on the fence. Russia mobilized, Germany mobilized, France began mobilization.

The Middle Classes stood astounded. Was it here, the thing they had never believed could happen? Was England at last going to war again, and to fight a mighty European foe—they could not admit a rival even then—and not a race of savages in some remote part? Great efforts were made for peace. But there were vacancies in many Government offices, in many commercial offices, in many banks, insurance companies and institutions. Naval reservists had got their papers. The British Fleet, nominally commanded by Prince Louis of Battenberg, had vanished into some mysterious corner of the North Sea (or German Ocean). The Middle Class did not like the sound of the name of the British Commander. He had done much for the Navy and he was a true son of this country, but they did not like the name.

They read that the Royal Navy was to be commanded by Admiral Jellicoe. They had never heard of him before. His face appeared in the papers, a rather wistful, scholarly face, not a bit like Beresford or the older type of sea-dog. Still, they thought he looked all right. Patriotism flared up. The war in Ireland was dropped like a red-hot coal by both would-be participants.

Great Britain had one great interest in this affair, besides her *Entente* with France. She was a guarantor of the neutrality of Belgium. So was Germany. Britain asked Germany that in the event of a clash would she respect the neutrality of Belgium? Germany would give no such undertaking. Indeed, she referred to the treaty as a scrap of paper.

That was just what the British people needed and just what the Middle Class needed to set the war fever alight. That Britain should go to war to respect her word and a scrap of paper was Cricket. So it was right.

The last days of July and the dawn of August saw turmoil. Germany edged towards the Belgian frontier. France massed to meet her. Russia began to take a hand. Russian stock went up; she became known as 'The Steam Roller'. She did not live up to her name, working mostly in reverse. The *Daily Express* broke into banner headlines and called the Kaiser 'The Mad Dog of Europe'. The Middle Class discussed his punishment, either hanging or the good old British prison of St. Helena. Most inclined to the gallows.

There was a howl of indignation that Lord Kitchener, the country's military idol, was being allowed to go back to India. He was stopped at Dover and took over the War Office. England breathed again.

Glances went up to the skies. The Germans had Zeppelins. These giant airships were expected to deal death and destruction on the civilian population, though a large portion of the Middle Classes did not believe that any nation would war with women and children. Meanwhile they were seeing strange sights.

They saw the rush of their own kind to enlist. For the first time this was, they saw, to be a Middle Class war. Some had participated in the Boer War, but only a fragment of the mass. This was different. This was Germany. They might try invasion. Well, said the Middle Class, they would find England a tough proposition. Every hedgerow would be a fortress bristling with riflemen. They still put their trust in rifles, and conceived a war like the Boer War, the only one most of them knew.

Soldiers and sailors in uniform were allowed to ride free on public vehicles and given free admission to theatres. War fever ran high. It would soon be over. Germany stood no chance against England, let alone the fact that she would have France and Russia against her as well. And still Italy sat on the fence.

Bands of young Frenchmen, called to the Colours, marched through the London streets singing the 'Marseillaise' and cheering. The usually phlegmatic English, even the Middle Class, cheered back.

Travellers in trains saw a young Frenchman and a young German, both going home to fight, sitting bolt upright opposite each other, and staring at each other in silence. When they got out they bowed curtly and went off in opposite directions. The Middle Classes approved such behaviour. For England was not at war yet, although she was mobilized and her Fleet, unseen but ready, was at battle stations. Actually, it was said to have had the German High Seas Fleet in its power but had not struck because it was not actually at war. That was Cricket, you see.

August Bank Holiday came. Tension was at its height. Britain had tried every power of persuasion and diplomacy she had to avert war. She had done everything a self-respecting Great World Power could do. But it was of no avail. Germany was determined. It was the hour. It was *Der Tag* to which the young German Navy had drunk a daily toast. She was going to get her place in the sun.

There was something of financial chaos. People—many Middle Class people of small means—drew their money out of the banks. They drew it out in sovereigns. That was safe, the sovereign was solid and could not alter—so long as you had golden sovereigns you were all right. But generally speaking there was no panic. A nation so unused to war as this was might have gone mad. It might have done all sorts of things. But it believed in itself, it believed in its own invincibility, it believed in the soldiers of the King, and the boys of the bulldog breed who'd made old England's name. It also believed in its own sovereigns and its own personal Sovereign.

The general Middle Class view was that if war was averted at the last moment, very good, but they really felt it would be best to teach the upstart Germans their lesson now, give France back Alsace and Lorraine, help themselves to the German Colonies and take back Heligoland —they began to doubt that Queen Victoria had done the right thing in letting it go—and to hang the Kaiser out of hand. That was how one dealt with mad dogs.

Recruiting offices were so overwhelmed with applicants that they had to send them home, to await calling up. The Middle Class was going to enlist, war or no war. It was going to do its bit. It was going to show the foreigner.

And still Germany refused to say anything about Belgium and her neutrality. Then came the news that German troops had actually violated the Belgian frontier at Visé. The fat was in the fire.

The British Government sent an ultimatum to the German Government that unless they cleared out by midnight on 4th August, 1914, a state of war would exist between the two countries.

The hours wore on. Catchpenny newspapermen came running round corners shouting fictitious news. "Great Naval Battle off Margate" one howled as he sped down St. Martin's Lane. "Why Margate?" asked a Middle Class girl of her Middle Class boy. "Why do they want to fight off Margate? Why, that's where we go for our holidays." Her escort bought a paper. Of course, there was no such news.

The West End was thronged. Nobody could settle down. The hours went slowly by. There was no reply. But there was no fear. Cheering crowds converged on Buckingham Palace. They, the people of the Sovereign Age, were going to show their Sovereign that they were loyal and steadfast. They were going to cheer him. They expected he wanted cheering up. "My dear boy," said one well-dressed man to another, "it cannot possibly last long. Finance will govern it all. No nation can stand a long war. The expense will kill them. Of course, we can stand it best of all. We are rich. Our sovereign will resist the shock, but the German mark will be lost for ever."

And even as he spoke, the sovereign was dead. That Sarajevo shot had killed it. It might still be in the pockets of that mob which marched down the Mall, but it was dead all right. It would be buried in a very few days.

The hours went by, one by one, marked by Big Ben's chiming. Each stroke was a passing bell for the sovereign, each one a passing bell for the power that sovereign had wielded for so long, the security it had meant, the sure shield it had proved. The Sovereign King George V was to give that title to the Royal Navy and give it justly. The Navy remained a shield when the golden sovereign had gone.

Outside Buckingham Palace stood a massed throng, cheering and singing. At Westminster, taut-faced statesmen waited the answer which never came. The Middle Classes all over the country and in that crowd were entering their final phase and did not know it. Never again would gold coins in their pockets be paid into their banks, be their safeguard in life. Never again would they need those sovereign purses which so many of them carried that day. Strangers spoke to each other. Men met other men they had not seen for years. "What are you going to do?" asked one young man of an old schoolfellow met in that crowd by chance after many years. "I've put my name down for the Westminster Dragoons," said the other. "I'm trying to get there now, but I'm stuck in this mob. How about you?" "I don't know yet," said the other. "The Navy, if they'll have me." They shook hands and wished each other luck. The crowd pushed them apart. They never met again. There were many little things like that in London on that night when the world changed and the golden sovereign died.

Night time brought no change. The crowds grew thicker. At home the older Middle Class people sat and wondered. "Would the Zeppelins come at once?" many women asked their husbands. The husbands scoffed in the true Middle Class way. "Great gasbags," they replied. "Let them try. Why, the Navy'll do for them. And then there's this Army Flying Corps. They know their job. Besides, a man who knows someone in the War Office told me . . ." and there would be a long tale of a secret weapon. Those weapons were so secret that not even our authorities knew about them.

If ever a great nation was unprepared for war—with the exception of its Navy—that nation was Great Britain in 1914. It was as officially unprepared as its people were mentally unprepared. But that nation, which had never known defeat, believed in itself, in Kitchener, its Navy and its King—and it believed implicitly in its golden sovereign.

It cheered, it sang, and it waited and it wondered.

If that great crowd of Middle Class—and others—outside the Palace had known! If those millions of Middle Class people who waited the midnight hour all over the Kingdom had known! They were not only waiting for a declaration of war, they were waiting for a world to change. They were waiting to see all that they had loved taken from them, for their methods of life to alter, their values to fade away and for their security,

2C

their safety, their stability, their happy freedom of life to pass from them.

Never again would they, their children or their children's children know that England which had been theirs so long. Those who did not know this land before 1914 never knew it at all. Those who did not live before then ever saw this country at its greatest, its height, its Imperial might, its wonderful security and its wonderful peace. That peace was ticking away as Big Ben's hands crept nearer and nearer to midnight, but they never knew. That green, lovely England, of peaceful roads and lanes, of hedgerows and farmsteads, of quiet, peace-loving people, of ancient ways and traditions, of pride and security and the highest standard of living in the world, all based on the cherished golden coin—its supreme knowledge that it was worth what it stood for, no fake but a solid reality —like the British people themselves and like its great solid backbone, the Middle Classes, was drawing towards its last breath.

Big Ben struck. The midnight hour boomed forth. It was all over. England was at war, and everything must go into the whirlpool. The Sovereign and his wife came out to greet the people. But that other sovereign, the one of gold, died, and Big Ben's boom was its passing bell forever.

A great statesman, Sir Edward Grey, the Foreign Secretary, who had worked so hard for peace, spoke its epitaph. "The lights are going out all over the world," said he . . . and amongst those lights went out what was perhaps the greatest of them all, the Golden Sovereign, whose last gleam of gold faded away for ever . . . and the whole world changed.

AFTERTHOUGHT TO A GOLDEN AGE

TO THE YOUNG MODERN OF TODAY, THE LIVES OF THE PEOPLE OF THE Middle Class of yesterday must have seemed very circumscribed. Just imagine it, they had to walk quite a lot, and if they wanted to go a little distance away it was necessary to take a train, and go through all the tedium of waiting for it to start—and even arranging one's day so as to catch it, going or returning. No getting into a car and leaving or coming home just when one liked. No dashing along at sixty miles an hour so that the surrounding countryside—when reached at long last—is almost invisible. No watching the road for fear of accidents, no great traffic jams on arterial roads put there for the very purpose of preventing them, no joy of penetrating country lanes never meant for such forms of traffic and causing trouble all round. In those spacious times the country was near at hand, so far as distance went, yet far enough away to give it remoteness, a sense of change and even adventure.

The Sovereign Age people knew the joy of what is now called 'going places' in quite a different way. To them it was real change of surroundings—at a leisurely pace—and with full enjoyment of those surroundings and ample time to see them.

Buses were urban things and seldom ventured outside the suburbs. Trams were purely for townsfolk and their lines finished before the houses ended. So if you were a Middle Class person who wanted a Saturday afternoon in the country you went to your station, you bought a ticket for a very little money, you caught your leisurely train, and you had all the thrill of a real country trip, for a travelled distance of seven, eight or ten miles. England was very near to that English city of London; England which had not changed in centuries lay at your very doors.

You used to get out of the train, which ran on a single line as a shuttle service, at a country station, and cross a highroad through a typical English village. Down another lane, with one or two new villas in it, and you walked with meadows on each side.

There were larks everywhere and greenfinches in the summer's heat churred out their request for 'bree-eeze, bree-eeze'. Cattle grazed and there were sheep in the fields.

Down the lane a vast haywain proceeded slowly, its carter walking beside it, his whip slung by its lash round his neck, and his fine horses, in brass-studded leather harness, shook their heads, so that their metal trappings and bells jingled pleasantly and mingled with the bird song. Over their backs were stretched nets to guard them from the flies. Past an old church, with a smithy still near it and in full use, where a great composer had once been organist and inspired to write a famous piece of music. Over a stile, across fieldpaths, through a noble avenue of elms, with glimpses of a great house—where an Earl had held semi-regal sway and which was still endowed with that peace, tranquillity and eternal solidity which all great Georgian houses—and pre-Georgian houses—possessed, past a pond where swallows hawked and skimmed, and an old barn with a plough or two inside, round which shot swifts and martins—and into a green lane—almost as old as England. The entrance to the lane was through a farmyard—remote and lonely as any Devon farm or Cumbrian holding—and which bore a Saxon name.

That lane led straight uphill. It had never been metalled, it was little more than a cart-track, but it had been there when the Romans came—it had seen Saxon England, Norman, Plantagenet, Tudor, Stuart, Hanoverian, Victorian, and still remained exactly the same in the days of Edward the Peacemaker and the very early days of George V. It had not altered, it was like England itself, green, steady and going on its way to the top of its hill, undeterred by all changes up to now, by all the fate of kings and downfall of less fortunate nations.

Its hedges were ancient and tangled. Birds had built in them since time immemorial, their descendants were there still. Blackbirds flew across, with dipping tails; thrushes shot over the topmost boughs to feed in the meadows; tits chirred and squeaked; jays called; finches twittered. You could see a 'charm' of goldfinches there, and a shrike or two. And at night time—nightingales. . . . Rabbits by the score, a weazel or a stoat, and the sudden laugh of a woodpecker. Perhaps, in early morning or at night, if you passed that way, you would catch the musky, undeniable scent of a fox. . . . And there was no sound of mankind save your own grass-muffled footsteps. The wild flowers grew, the brambles blackened, the seasons came and went—and the lane went on.

It was England, that quiet, peaceful, spacious England of the golden days, when no machines roared about and above it, when science was a thing groping its way amongst test-tubes, when pedestrian pace was good enough for man who, when he wanted to hurry, used the four legs of a horse to help him. The sun shone, cloud shadows crossed the fields, and there was a sense of ageless well-being everywhere.

It was only when you reached the summit of the hill, and rested, that you got a shock. You turned to survey your ascent, and there in a hollow before you lay London. You could see nearly all of it, the sun catching the golden cross on St. Paul's, the spires, the chimneys, the smoke haze, the vastness of a great city. And in the blue distance, something shimmered with light—the glass mass of the Crystal Palace.

It was only then that you realized that Charing Cross was less than twelve miles from you, and that you were still on the outskirts of the greatest city of the world.

About you lay the complete beauty and peace of the English countryside, undisturbed. Not yet had the flood of motor traction, the machine transport, come to crowd the country out of its elbow room, to make its lanes and byways into the maelstrom of city streets. Not yet had great arterial roads cut through the woods, the fields, the meadows and the villages. Not yet had country houses become country clubs, road-houses with swimming pools. Not yet had the quiet little inns blossomed out with cocktail bars, radio and dance-bands.

One could still drink one's beer within those few miles of London, sitting on a bench outside an inn, talking to agricultural labourers who lived on the land and who had its soil in their accents and voices. London, to them, so near by distance, was still a great way off. And you were not covered with the stench of petrol and deafened by the machine-gun effects of motor-bicycles. The scents of the countryside reached you; you heard the breeze hum through the telegraph wires. Trout were still in the streams, not poisoned by the tar from the roads. The roads themselves were macadam, and their dust was good white dust which dimmed the hedges—hedges which only shone the brighter when a shower bathed them and brought forth their perfume and the delicate tints of their wild roses again.

There were a few country houses still holding their state, there were a few mansions which still had stabling and lodges with lodgekeepers, poor serfs who touched their hats, as did the countrymen who passed you by, and gave you a civil good day in their own native tongue. Nobody said, "You're telling me," "Scram," "What do you know about that?" or talked of cuties or of Broadway melodies, or of the eternal blessing of the Hollywood film. They were still English people, living in England, in the year 1914.

It was that English England, sure of itself, proud of itself, contemptuous but tolerant of the less fortunate foreigners who were not living in a land which ruled one-fifth of the globe, and which possessed such power and wealth as is now undreamed of in actuality, although spent in the ledgers of the men who control the world finance. But the sums they write exist on paper only and the sums those people knew were in gold. They did not see much gold, those workers in this peaceful spot, but they lived upon its solidity and its credit, and their silver shillings and their copper pence bought things which would stagger their descendants.

They did not know the time would come when Science would bless them by bringing Death over their heads, to strew its seed on to their land with blasting explosion and searing fire.

They knew only an England at peace, restful, secure, mighty, powerful, with her foundations cemented by a Golden Sovereign . . . and they lived their lives and went to their graves in their own serene churchyard when it pleased God to call them.

Today that green lane has gone, that village is no more. Its little wayside station is in the bowels of the earth, and from it hurtle hordes of workers into the upper air, to scurry to villas which stand where the fields stood, to enter gates bearing fancy names where once bloomed those immemorial hedges. Down the main street grind motor-buses, cars, lorries and all the noisy fleet of modern traffic. The city has burst its bounds, the countryside which graced it has been driven farther—much farther—off. Now you are in a suburb, just like all other suburbs, its individuality gone, featureless, shapeless, only its name remaining.

Where the birds sang now blare American accents and saxophones from countless radios. The beer, if one can get it, is washy, poor stuff, the good, potent spirits are out of spirit with themselves and have gone into hiding. The little country shops are now multiple stores, and the stables have become garages and petrol pumps. The people who live where the fields once spread pay sums in taxation which would have seemed fortunes to their grandparents or even their parents, whose golden sovereigns went so far and who paid so little to enjoy the right to live in their native land.

But the hearts are still the same. For these people who have turned country into town, who never knew the golden sovereign, have in turn seen their poor pound notes devalued as their parents saw their sovereign go. They saw it happen from the same source, and they went and fought that evil which once more menaced them. Those who stayed at home, and their women and children, fought that war too, and lived for six years in constant peril of death.

But that England which lay beneath their houses, beneath their streets, through which their tubes burrowed, and which they had so defaced with gimcrack modernity, sustained them, for they were of it still. It forgave and stood by them. Its virtue was with them, and they won through.

The memories of their middle and old age can never be the same as those of their elders, their whole lives will be blighted as was never the youth of their immediate forbears. They will, one fears, never see the better days their sires had known.

But what lies underneath them is England, and it is a tenacious, determined thing. The land does not alter, nor the spirit of the land,

404

which nobody, the Romans or the Normans, ever conquered. It overcame and absorbed them. So perhaps the children of the present day may know once more a better, happier, merrier England than that in which they live now. But never—if they are of the Middle Class which is now making its bow in the social status of our race before vanishing into the wings of time for a long period—never, despite the prophecies of politicians, will they know the freedom, the beauty, the peace, the security and the wellbeing that their Middle Class ancestors knew in the days when there were really Twenty Shillings in the Pound.

THE END

INDEX

INDEX